Public Administration in Theory and Practice

Hailed for its timelessness and timeliness, *Public Administration in Theory and Practice* examines public administration from a normative perspective and provides students with an understanding of the *practice* of public administration. Combining historical, contextual, and theoretical perspectives, this text gives students a truly comprehensive overview of the discipline and focuses on the practical implications of public administration theory. This substantially revised third edition features:

- Increased emphasis on and expanded coverage of management skills, practices, and approaches, including an all-new "Managerial Toolkit" section comprising several new chapters on important topics like transboundary interactions, cultural competencies, citizen engagement, and leadership and decision-making.
- Expanded part introductions to provide a thematic overview for students, reinforce the multiple conceptual frameworks or lenses through which public administration may be viewed, and provide guidance on the learning outcomes the reader may anticipate.
- Still deeper examination of the connections between historic theoretical perspectives and current practices, to help students think through practical and realistic solutions to problems that acknowledge historic precedence and theory, yet also leave room for creative new ways of thinking. This expanded analysis also offers a forum for comparative perspectives, particularly how these practices have emerged in other countries.
- PowerPoint slides, Discussion Questions (with a focus on practice), Learning Outcomes, and "Things to Ponder" at the end of each chapter that may be used as lecture topics or essay examination questions.

Public Administration in Theory and Practice, third edition is an ideal introduction to the art and science of public administration for American MPA students, and serves as essential secondary reading for upper-level undergraduate students seeking a fair and balanced understanding of public management.

Raymond W. Cox III is Professor Emeritus in the Department of Public Administration and Urban Studies at the University of Akron.

Public Administration in Theory and Practice

Third Edition

RAYMOND W. COX III

Routledge
Taylor & Francis Group
NEW YORK AND LONDON

First published 2020
by Routledge
52 Vanderbilt Avenue, New York, NY 10017

and by Routledge
2 Park Square, Milton Park, Abingdon, Oxon, OX14 4RN

Routledge is an imprint of the Taylor & Francis Group, an informa business

© 2020 Taylor & Francis

The right of Raymond W. Cox III to be identified as author of this work has been asserted by him in accordance with sections 77 and 78 of the Copyright, Designs and Patents Act 1988.

All rights reserved. No part of this book may be reprinted or reproduced or utilised in any form or by any electronic, mechanical, or other means, now known or hereafter invented, including photocopying and recording, or in any information storage or retrieval system, without permission in writing from the publishers.

Trademark notice: Product or corporate names may be trademarks or registered trademarks, and are used only for identification and explanation without intent to infringe.

Library of Congress Cataloging-in-Publication Data
Names: Cox, Raymond W., author.
Title: Public administration in theory and practice / Raymond W. Cox III.
Description: Third edition. | New York, NY : Routledge, 2019. |
    Includes bibliographical references and index.
Identifiers: LCCN 2019003567 (print) | LCCN 2019006568 (ebook) |
    ISBN 9781351003940 (E-book) | ISBN 9781138544383
    (hardback : alk. paper) | ISBN 9781138544390 (pbk. : alk. paper) |
    ISBN 9781351003940 (ebk)
Subjects: LCSH: Public administration. | Public administration—United States.
Classification: LCC JF1351 (ebook) | LCC JF1351 .C66 2019 (print) |
    DDC 351—dc23
LC record available at https://lccn.loc.gov/2019003567

ISBN: 978-1-138-54438-3 (hbk)
ISBN: 978-1-138-54439-0 (pbk)
ISBN: 978-1-351-00394-0 (ebk)

Typeset in Sabon
by Apex CoVantage, LLC

Printed and bound by CPI Group (UK) Ltd, Croydon, CR0 4YY

CONTENTS

Preface to Third Edition   vii

Introduction and Overview   1

PART I   Theoretical Foundations   7

CHAPTER 1

Normative Foundations of Public Administration   9

CHAPTER 2

Ethical Foundations   28

PART II   Organizational Functions and Competencies   49

CHAPTER 3

Personnel Practices   53

CHAPTER 4

Budgeting Practices   97

CHAPTER 5

Administrative Law   124

CHAPTER 6

Policy Analysis   139

CHAPTER 7

Program Evaluation   154

CHAPTER 8

Organizational Dynamics and Change   174

PART III   The Managerial Toolkit   200

CHAPTER 9

Transboundary Interactions   203

CHAPTER 10

Cultural Competence   216

CHAPTER 11

Citizen Engagement   234

CHAPTER 12

Strategic Management   245

CHAPTER 13

Leadership and Decision-Making   261

PART IV   Outside Looking In   277

CHAPTER 14

Bureaucracy, the Rule of Law, and Representative Democracy   279

CHAPTER 15

Administration in a Global Perspective   294

CHAPTER 16

Concluding Thoughts   321

Suggested Readings   334
Index   343

PREFACE TO THIRD EDITION

In 1989 I began writing a textbook on public administration. It was an attempt to set the boundaries of a field and discipline that was somewhat in disarray. The Reagan administration had barred federal employees from seeking training funds to pay the tuition for an MPA, even as they could get funding for virtually any other degree. The number of students enrolled in MPA programs would drop by nearly half in the 1980s, and, parenthetically the number of MBA students would grow seemingly exponentially. By the middle of the 1990s it was as likely that well-educated professionals in civil service and personnel departments would hold an MBA, not an MPA; similarly, the preferred degree for hospital administration shifted from the MPA to the MBA. The theoretical foundations of the field were changing from organizational and political theory to economics and public choice theory. Seemingly, the solution to every government problem was privatization, or the kindred public-private partnership (PPP). The public was never quite sure what the problems were, but they were confident that turning to the private sector and allowing the "market" to work its magic was better than allowing incompetent public administrators and corrupt politicians to continue to waste money. To most citizens in the US and around the world, public administration, which had built its foundation upon ideas of economy, efficiency, and effectiveness, had proven a failure at the first two and seemingly had forgotten the third. Business methods in the office and market-driven practices in public policy were the answers.

Not much has changed. Economic theory and anti-government rhetoric still abound. For twenty years governments around the world introduced and implemented changes based upon the New Public Management (NPM). The academy followed. MPP programs replaced MPA programs and those MPA programs that remained created emphases in nonprofit management. Yet, those challenges are not necessarily a bad thing. Professional managers at every level of government and across the globe proved resilient in protecting and preserving the core values of public service and effective performance. The discipline of Public Administration has hung in, refining the trade and offering students who are still interested in the public service the tools to be competent, professional, and ethical public managers. Challenges and threats abound, but professionally trained and ethically competent public service employees and managers continue to work through the competing demands and impossible expectations of the public.

Even as our approach to the study of public administration has not changed, this book, as an attempt to capture public administration today has been transformed in other ways. Most critically, this new effort benefits from the insights gained from many more years of experience in presenting and explaining public administration and policy. The enigma of the enduring questions that Dwight

Waldo asked in *The Administrative State* remain, but we have more tools and resources for pondering those questions. The questions are at some level "unanswerable," yet that does not mean that we cannot continue to discuss the possibility of answering them. We hope this book gives students (whether undergraduate, graduate, or even doctoral) insights that permit them to be part of the discourse on what it means to be part of the public service. Toward that end there are four basic refinements to this iteration of that dialogue begun those years ago. First, we have more self-consciously segmented the book by offering introductions to the parts of the book. We did this to provide a thematic overview for the students and also to reinforce the multiple conceptual frameworks or lenses through which we see public administration. Second, we have updated the chapters to reflect the course of events. In this we found ourselves returning repeatedly to a topic that was only just emerging in the 1980s—performance measures. Third, we have probed a little deeper into the connection between historic theoretical perspectives and current practices. Our goal is to help students think through to practical and realistic solutions that acknowledge historic precedence and theory, yet also leave room for moving beyond old ways of thinking. Toward that end several chapters offer commentary on the practical implications of the ideas presented and/or present current examples of forms, reports, and professional perspectives that illustrate how governments *administer* the topics and themes in each section of the book. Fourth, in an acknowledgment that technology has moved light years from a time when having a "computer" doing "word processing" was the cutting edge for most faculty and students, we now offer both a traditional text and an e-education version suitable for web-based instruction.

This new text is a testament to those who still believe that the practice of good governance is possible through the application theories that promote competence in the processes, and skill in the tools, by which complex public organizations are organized and managed. What has changed is that we have learned much in the last years since the first book about organizational complexity and the skills to navigate that complexity. The basic framework for this book is still the same; we begin with the historical, theoretical foundations of public administration, but the management toolkit has grown well beyond the earlier discussion of organization change and organizational dynamics. Secondly, many of the issues in the text are issues that face most governments. While the historical frame of reference remains the evolution of American Public Administration, the remainder of the text is more intentionally global in outlook.

Most importantly, I would be remiss if I did not acknowledge the considerable contributions of Susan Buck and Betty Morgan, who made the earlier versions of this work a success.

RAYMOND W. COX III
AKRON, OHIO

Introduction and Overview

Nearly four decades ago, colleagues and I began a dialogue to explain public administration by offering a perspective on public administration and policy that reflected the approaches and philosophy of the then relatively new doctoral program in public administration and policy at Virginia Tech. Given the volume of work produced by the original faculty and the graduates since that program began, this book now seems more like gilding the lily than setting a new course. Much has changed in government and in our collective understanding of governance since 1991, yet at a fundamental level the history of the last three plus decades has played out much as we might have anticipated. The historical, contextual, and theoretical perspectives outlined in earlier works have been affirmed and reinforced. Therefore, there is much in this new edition that was captured in the earlier versions; fundamentally this is still an examination of public administration from a normative perspective, but for understanding practice. That perspective is the driving force in shaping the book. What has changed is a greater emphasis on practice—the everyday work of the public service manager.

This book incorporates the historical/political/legal framework outlined above into the text while focusing on such issues as how our understanding of public administration is shaped by our changing values concerning the scope of government, the meaning of democracy, and the meaning of management and organization. Even in presenting four distinct perspectives on public administration, this work does not comprehensively "explain" it. The perspectives presented include normative foundations, public administration as management support systems, and public administration as organization theory, public administration as planned change, and, finally, public administration as politics. As such, each perspective is presented as separate yet interconnected. Thus, the groundwork laid in normative foundations forms the theoretical basis for the subsequent sections. Similarly, the other perspectives are connected to redefine and understand the same basic issue, that is, governance, albeit from different orientations and value structures.

In the early 1950s, one of public administration's eminent scholars, Dwight Waldo, observed that the actions and decisions of bureaucrats obtrusively and unobtrusively touch our lives in countless ways. In a later work, he elaborated on this theme when he commented on the long tradition of bureaucratic involvement with virtually all aspects of society or, as he would suggest, with civilization itself. He comments:

> Historically, public administration has had a role in every important field of endeavor: agriculture, mining and metallurgy, commerce and manufacturing, medicine, transportation, engineering, education. From the beginnings of physical science and mathematics, government has been a support for them and a spur to them; this is because control of rivers, production of crops, constructing public works, and creating and sustaining a military needed the tools, measurements and predictions they could supply. Even art has, historically, a close association with public administration, something likely to be overlooked in a time in which so much art is not only "private" but more or less anti-Establishment.
>
> (Waldo, 1981, p. 25)

The increased involvement of public administrators in the actions and activities of organized society has continued over time. This involvement inevitably brings public administration more and more into the realm of what is thought of traditionally as "politics." Governmental decision-making is the product of the interaction of both administrators (civil servants) and politicians (both elected and appointed). Finding the proper balance of political and administrative participation is the central problem of governance in a modern representative democracy. Again, Waldo (1981) offers a cogent and useful summary of the interrelationship:

> In the United States, if one chooses to do so, nearly all contemporary public problems can be framed in terms of relating the political and the administrative: thus, randomly, the amount of autonomy the Federal Reserve Board should enjoy, the growth of Congressional research staffs, the propriety or impropriety of "whistle blowing," tax reduction through popular initiatives, the development of synthetic fuels. Within self-aware Public Administration the relationship of the political and the administrative is germane to questions of inquiry: What kinds of knowledge are needed? Is the needed knowledge I principle obtainable? How can it be obtained? The relationship of the political and the administrative is relevant also to nearly all aspects of education for public administration: What meaning and emphasis should be given to *public*? Why is it necessary that administrative technology be reconciled with Constitutional-democratic norms? *How* can it be reconciled? To which political impulses is it proper for the public administrator to respond; to which improper?
>
> (pp. 65–66)

The reality of modern governance is that public administration can be understood only by placing it within an historical/political/legal frame of reference. Therefore, public administration cannot be understood outside the same historical, political, and constitutional context that has shaped the evolution and development of the other institutions of government. As this, or any nation, has developed and grown, the role of the bureaucracy in governance has grown. No student of public administration can appreciate the constraints upon and opportunities of public-sector management without an understanding of the challenges of the bureaucratic role in governance. This is not to imply that the bureaucracy bears the full weight of the burden of governance: The three constitutional institutions carry a lion's share of that chore. Yet it cannot be denied that the policy-making and decision-making role of the bureaucracy has steadily grown. The interaction between the constitutionally mandated institutions and the bureaucracy is the key to understanding modern American government. The tug-of-war between the legislature and the agencies, the chief executive and the agencies, the courts and the agencies, and even the states and the agencies are outward manifestations of the process of defining and redefining of roles in determining a formula for governance. While clearly the core responsibility and challenge for all those working in the public sector is that of governance, our contextual placement emphasizes that the contemporary task of governance in the United States and across the globe is a responsibility shared by *four* branches of government.

The framework for this text is unapologetically normative and unabashedly theoretical. We felt that exploring how we should act establishes a better starting point for understanding public administration than does a "snap-shot" description of some particular point in history. Understandings and relationships among and between governmental actors are seldom static. Thus, we adopted a normative stance to provide students with a theoretical background and an historical perspective so that the "relativism" of normative theory can be appreciated. Further, the text emphasizes the concept of "praxis" (the interrelatedness of theory and practice) as the final arbiter of normative statements. This perspective on theory and practice is critical in a discipline such as public administration where theory is incorrectly deemed irrelevant unless it relates to day-to-day practice.

This work incorporates the historical/political/legal framework outlined above into the text while focusing on such issues as how our understanding of public administration is shaped by our changing values concerning the scope of government, the meaning of democracy, and the meaning of management and organization Thus, the groundwork laid in normative foundations forms the theoretical basis for the subsequent sections. Similarly, the other perspectives are connected to redefine and understand the same basic issue, that is, governance, albeit from different orientations and value structures.

The text is organized so that the interplay of theory and practice is addressed throughout. In addition, the text is divided into four parts that offer a particular vantage point from which to understand the theories and practices that shape public administration. Each vantage point offers a different way to frame public administration in both theory and practice. For example, Parts II and III both address elements of management and administrative practice. Part II examines the practices that we often associate with staff functions. These are the activities and practices typically conducted by staff experts (and in larger organizations by distinct departments). As such these are activities that are prior to decisions and actions. Part III examines practices which are done by managers as part of their management responsibility. As such these are activities of decision-making and implementation.

Both are important tasks of *managing* a public organization, but by whom, when, and possibly even how they are practices is quite different.

Part I develops the core framework by which we define the discipline of public administration. The first chapter focuses on the issues that academics have presumed to be central to our understanding of public administration. It examines the evolution of the discipline; from its political roots in the progressive era even as the academic and political basis for advocating for an expert-driven, professional (incorruptible?) public service as a solution to the problems of the period, perversely by advocating a division of government into two spheres, one political and one non-partisan, to a field that is caught between the need to be professional, yet operating within and in close partnership with the political arms of government. The second chapter is both an extension of and an explanation for professional administration. Public-sector ethics is a complex topic, but the importance in the examination of the topic is not its difficulty but rather the fact that with an ethical public service, there is no professional public service and ultimately no democratic governance.

Part II approaches the idea of public administration as a cluster of organizational competencies and processes. As with the other sections of this text, there is no attempt to be "descriptive" in the accepted sense of the word; rather the chapters focus on the distinct organizational management tasks: budgeting, personnel, administrative law, policy analysis, program evaluation. Each chapter is a historically based discussion of the changing or evolving understanding of what each of these concepts has meant. Critically these chapters discuss the processes that impact the ability of a public service manager to manage. These are practices that managers must understand in how they impact their management. Process experts bear the responsibility for developing these processes; the public service manager must understand the organizational implications for practice. A simple example is that the quality of the recruitment process (done by the experts) influences the hiring choices available. The better a manager understands the recruitment, advertising, and preliminary assessment of applicants, the better the manager can anticipate (and influence) the quality of the final applicant pool. After all it is the manager, not the personnel expert who must live with the outcome. These competencies and processes greatly influence the performance of the manager, but they are processes over which the manager rarely (the major exception being city managers) has much control.

Part III takes a quite different approach, by picking up from the outcomes of the expert-driven actions. This part describes the manager's toolkit. How does one manage people and processes? The success or failure of most government endeavors is in the quality of the management practices applied in the job. This part is most distinctly practical in focus. It offers discussions about things managers "do." In some instances they are linked to some of the competencies presented in Part II. For example, there are elements of policy analysis and formal program evaluation in the work of a manager, and certainly the skills that are part of cultural competence are related to ideas of basic humanity found in personnel management. Also, cultural competence is introduced in Part II as a training program for a personnel department, but addressed in the context of management practice in Part III. Another aspect of this is an issue that is embedded in virtually all the skills in the toolbox—being an ethical manager. In contrast to Part II, Part III is very much about the work of the manager as an individual. These are the skills that are part and parcel of managerial success.

Finally, Part IV continues the theme of politics and administration with a fuller discussion of the theoretical and practical implications of the interaction of political and administrative activities of bureaucrats. This is done first in the context of comparative administration and then returns to the broader topic of the theoretical and practical understandings of the role of bureaucracy in the policy process.

The objective of this book is to re-examine, expand, and build upon the theoretical and historical foundations that define the study of public administration. While our questions about the work of public officials in modern government are enduring ones, we believe that our understanding can be enhanced by carefully examining the character of specific governments, the roles that appointed officials play in them, and how those relationships have evolved over history. Context is important. Why and how things are done are only partially historic artifacts. The present and the future are also important. To better appreciate the present and prepare for possible future paths each chapter will conclude with discussion questions.

As Francis Rourke (1992) has observed, political responsiveness and administrative professionalism will always remain highly ranked values in a democratic bureaucracy. The American public has consistently had a strong, well-recognized interest in preserving the responsiveness of its bureaucracy to political control. The ultimate quandary may be, however, that in an era of divided government, when directives from the Congress and the White House conflict, career administrators take on an increased importance as professionals who can reconcile and integrate conflicting directives into effective national policies. We hope that this work will provide a springboard for those attempting to understand and accomplish this task.

BIBLIOGRAPHY

Rourke, Francis. "Responsiveness and Neutral Competence in American Bureaucracy", *Public Administration Review*, 52 (6), pp. 539–546. 1992.

Waldo, Dwight. *The Enterprise of Public Administration.* Novato, CA: Chandler and Sharp Publishers, Inc. 1981.

PART

I

Theoretical Foundations

What is the basis of government by bureaucracy? Upon what theoretical and practical foundations rest the work of civil servants in government? These are necessarily enduring questions that can be addressed only by a close examination of the character of a specific government and the role that appointed officials play in that government. The next two chapters, therefore, are about American bureaucracy, not from any sense of superiority about that form of government, but from the need to connect political theory to administrative theory. This would be an easy task if the political theory upon which this nation's government was founded included an examination of the role of the "civil servant" in the affairs of state. Unfortunately, American political theory directs little attention to this question beyond a few somewhat vague admonitions of the need for good administration. In *Federalist 68*, Alexander Hamilton pronounced that the "true test of a good government is its aptitude and tendency to produce good administration" (Hamilton, Madison, and Jay, 1961, p. 414). Two points are obvious: (1) the political and constitutional responsibility of elected officials is more clearly documented than that of appointed officials, and (2) the responsibilities of elected and appointed officials are intertwined. The difficulty is that the first point has produced a tradition that contradicts the second point. As Carl Friedrich commented, "It is characteristic of our age that legislation is looked upon as policy-deciding. Hence, policy-making in the broadest sense is not supposed to be part of administration" (Friedrich, 1941, p. 168). If, as Friedrich went on to point out, policy making is "continuous," then fixing the political and constitutional responsibility of the appointed official is a necessary corollary to understanding how government does and should run.

The issue of responsibility of public officials, while closely connected to ethics, is not the same. Administrative ethics is concerned with the behavior of officials in the performance of their regular duties, while administrative responsibility looks at their relationship to their government and its underlying political philosophy.

A normative foundation for public administration is necessary to fit together the disparate political and administrative pieces of public policy making. These linkages can be established only through an examination of the concept of administrative responsibility. There is no simple answer to this task, and any conclusions we may draw might well be as much a matter of perspective as of fact.

In the first chapter of Part I it is argued that despite public perception to the contrary, American public administration does fulfill a constitutional role. In attempting to make that case, we must begin by discussing the impact of the Roman administrative apparatus on continental law, contrasting this with the post-feudal development of the English civil government. This will show how the early bureaucratic structure of American government was patterned on the English system. The concluding sections demonstrate how, in response to the industrial revolution and subsequently the welfare state, the national government began to rely upon the functions of the bureaucracy to implement policy. The final sections return to the question of administrative responsibility and, ultimately to a statement of the legitimate foundations of bureaucrat decision-making in government.

The second chapter of Part I explores the issues of ethics management and ethical management. It is asserted that ethical behavior (my European colleagues would call this integrity) is the means by which the normative foundations discussed in the first chapter are manifest in practice. The norms and values that are associated with more bureaucracies in representative democracies are the values that underlie ethical behavior and ethical judgment.

Learning Outcomes
At the conclusion of Part I a student should be able to:

- Define public administration as a academic discipline, with an emphasis on the unique aspects of public administration practice
- Explain why many academics define public administration as an unofficial fourth branch of American government
- How theoretical perspectives influence current practice and how current practice influences theory development
- Distinguish between ethics and integrity as both organization constructs and as differing approaches to public decision-making
- Explore how the ethics is first and foremost about decision-making practices
- Define the concept of administrative responsibility and how it is manifest in practice
- Provide examples of behaviors which are exemplars of competent and professional administration
- Define professional public administration

BIBLIOGRAPHY

Hamilton, Alexander, James Madison, and John Jay.
 The Federalist Papers. New York: The New American Library. 1961.

CHAPTER
1

Normative Foundations of Public Administration

ANCIENT HISTORY

Even in ancient times, bureaucratic organizations were part of the institutional design of government (for an extended discussion see Heady, 2005). By 1500 B.C., the Chinese Shang dynasty had a bureaucratic government with ministries. This type of hierarchical and ministerial government continued through many dynastic changes. Even today China retains many of the essential characteristics of the ancient bureaucracy. The Fertile Crescent, Egypt, and Mediterranean civilizations were also governed by bureaucratic systems. The first formal legal code, the Code of Hammurabi, dates to the eighteenth century B.C. Egypt also had a long history of successful administration as an integral part of the Pharaohs' rule:

> [c]learly one of the reasons for Egyptian institutional longevity was the high level of administrative services achieved, ranking the Egyptians with the Chinese as creators of the most impressive bureaucracies in the ancient world.
> (Heady, 1984, pp. 150–151)

Of course, the Roman Empire and the Roman Catholic Church are the "dominant" historical influences on development of Western political and administrative institutions (Heady, 2005). Weber would not have found anything amiss with the institutions of Roman government. The Roman pattern based on control by citizens, hierarchy, and division of labor was familiar to Western rulers coping with the demands of a post-feudal age. Those nations with a history of Roman conquest, such as France and Spain, retained the hierarchical and functionally separated forms of government and designed their legal systems to reflect the Roman codified law. It was otherwise in England, which had never been completely controlled by Rome and, indeed, was abandoned by Rome in A.D. 407.

As its language reflects, Britain was not greatly influenced by its interactions with Rome. Roman place names and ruins still dot the countryside, but the political history of England is molded by Saxon invasions and Celtic disagreements.

Only in legend does Arthur unify the nation, and in fact, after the withdrawal of the Roman legions, Britain divided into small kingdoms controlled by warring and short-lived lords.

Each titled landowner controlled his various manors absolutely, and manorial courts decided disputes based on their own individualized customs and politics. Some continuity was provided by the church, which despite its abuses, remained a training ground for clerks and scholars and the repository of learning. Often the church itself was a landlord; the larger abbeys and their abbots were as rich and powerful as any hereditary lord.

As the barons yielded power to the king, the king's various courts and administrative offices became regularized (Feilden, 1895). The treasury developed accounting devices and routinized records, while the courts began to reconcile local court decisions with each other. This is the beginning of English common law, a system that, unlike the Roman system of codified law, developed piecemeal from judicial efforts to accommodate varying and often conflicting legal decisions. However, the royal power still rested with the person of the sovereign, and the legal system often bent to his personal desires and policies. When the feudal system in Britain began to decline, the organizational structure of the royal administration was riddled with nepotism, corruption, and incompetence.

As the absolute power of the kings waned and the middle class grew, a professional cadre of clerks and accountants developed to assist England's mercantile empire. The notion of professional administration was familiar to the government ministers.

In the reigns of George I (1714–1727) and George II (1727–1760), the ministers became increasingly important because these Hanoverian kings were incapable of governing. The ministers were forced to govern because the kings could not; during this time, the king's ministers began to meet without the king being present. Thrown on their own resources during a period of imperialism, the civil service became an elite governing force with strong professional standards. Staffed by the younger sons of the aristocracy (who could not inherit land and thus chose the army, the Church, or the government as careers), the British civil service evolved into a prestigious and essential arm of the British government, renowned for its impartiality, discretion, and professionalism. Reformed after the Northcote-Trevelyn Report of 1854 to include merit hiring and the abolition of patronage, the British model was the basis for the modern American civil service.

BUREAUCRACY IN THE FOUNDING PERIOD

Just as we search the Constitution in vain for references to political parties, judicial review, or executive orders, we also cannot find mention of bureaucracy. In fact, the words *administration* and *bureaucracy* are not found in the original Constitution; the closest we come is the admonition that the Executive "shall take care that the laws be faithfully executed" (Article II Section 3) and Article II Section 2, the President "may require the opinion, in writing, of the principal officer in each of the executive departments upon any subject relating to the duties of their respective offices," which surely implies administrative departments. In *Federalist 72*, Hamilton defined what he meant by *administration*:

> The actual conduct of foreign negotiations, the preparatory plans of finance, the application and disbursement of the public moneys in conformity to the general appropriations of the legislature, the arrangement of the army and navy, the direction of the operations of war—these, and other matters of a like nature, constitute what seems to be most properly understood by the administration of government.
>
> (Hamilton, Madison, and Jay, 1961, pp. 435–436)

It is unlikely that Hamilton or, indeed, any of the framers envisioned the size and complexity of today's bureaucracy. In 1791, the year the Bill of Rights was ratified, the federal government employed 4,479 people; by 2018 it employed nearly two million and contracted for the services of three times that number. Only four cabinet-level positions were created in the early years of the republic: State, War (changed in 1947 to *Defense*), Justice, and Treasury, all of which were established in 1789. Sixty years passed before the fifth department, Interior, was established. By 2005, there were fifteen cabinet agencies; two agencies with "cabinet" status, and another dozen departments working directly for the president. How can this large structure, which is not even mentioned in the Constitution, be reconciled with the normative foundations of American political theory? More specifically, does it *need* to be reconciled?

INFORMAL CONSTITUTIONAL AMENDMENT

Over the past several centuries, the Constitution has been formally amended only twenty-seven times (and ten of those amendments were the Bill of Rights, a condition for ratification of the Constitution), although thousands of amendments have been proposed. However, informal changes—fundamental rearranging of our political institutions—have occurred more frequently and with arguably greater impact. Among these informal changes are the power of the federal courts to review and to shape legislation, the virtual monopoly of political parties on elected offices, the greatly expanded power of the president and the phenomenal growth of the federal bureaucracy. While the impacts of these changes often raise controversial issues, for example, when court decisions overturn long-standing cultural norms, rarely is their legitimacy questioned, in part because the changes were accomplished in the early years of the republic. However, the controversy over more recent changes, especially those connected with the New Deal and the rise of the welfare state, revolves around their legitimacy as well as their impacts.

The increase of both the size and role of the administrative state is regularly criticized by the media and the electorate. Because each person's daily life is affected by some government agency, the bureaucracy is a constant individual irritant. While court decisions or party activities may provide headlines, unless a citizen is directly affected, these issues soon fade from memory. Not so the bureaucracy. We must inspect the car, vaccinate our dogs, pay taxes, sign wills, fly on airplanes, watch (or not watch) cable television. The homeless beg from us on the streets, and at the grocery store we watch people use food stamps. Bureaucracy is resented because, for most citizens, it represents only a negative force. The protective activities we rarely see. And because we believe that government is *for* the people, we deeply resent government activities that interfere with our own freedom to act. Resenting the bureaucracy reduces its legitimacy.

In *The Case for Bureaucracy*, Goodsell identifies "dangerous manipulation of political power" as one of the central criticisms of bureaucracy (1985, p. 6). Among the basis of this criticism are two themes with important ramifications for our understanding of the connection between bureaucratic theory and representative democracy.

First is the Weberian concern for the preservation of parliamentary democracy. Weber sees bureaucracy as an indestructible instrument of power. Using this power converts the bureaucrat from a dedicated servant of the elected politician to the master. Viewers of the BBC program, *Yes, Minister*, will understand Weber's concern. The bureaucrat, who has technical expertise, experience, and longevity, can at least partially subvert any political agenda his or her elected superior presents. The only protection from this behavior is the sense of responsibility developed by or forced upon the bureaucrat. The second theme accuses bureaucracy of an inherently elitist bias that protects the status quo:

> Bureaucrats engage covertly in the formation and manipulation of policy, despite an official ideology that separates politics from administration. They are seen as taking bold initiatives, abusing discretion, forming alliances, and co-opting other centers of power in order to steer the ship of state in the desired conservative directions. In short, *representative government is sabotaged, and democracy becomes overwhelmed by bureaucracy.*
> (Goodsell, 1985, p. 8, [emphasis added])

According to this perspective, bureaucrats have a vested interest in protecting their own agencies and jobs; organization theory leads us to predict more expansion and growth of bureaucracy as a way to increase each civil servant's own prestige.

Rosenbloom (1989) proposes a third critical theme, the conflict between the bureaucratic ideals of uniformity and the constitutional ideal of diversity. He writes:

> In the United States, the conflict between bureaucratic power and democratic constitutionalism is highly pronounced. In part, this is because whereas bureaucracy and public administrative theory generally stress dehumanization or impersonality in the quest for uniformity among individuals, the Constitution and much of the theory behind it seek to promote diversity among the citizenry.
> (p. 20)

In other words, the Weberian imperative for uniformly applied procedures runs headlong into the pluralist theories of Madison's *Federalist 10*.

Regardless of the truth of these accusations, much of the public would agree with them. Even bureaucrats themselves agree with the general public when asked to comment on the place of administration in the American system (although they naturally tend to defend their own bureaus). The question of administrative responsibility has become bound up in the question of the conflict between the role of the politician and that of the bureaucrat. To get past this problem, it is necessary to refocus our attention on the legitimate role of the bureaucracy as part of public decision-making.

LEGITIMATING ADMINISTRATION

Legitimation is interconnected with administrative responsibility, the topic of our final section. While administrators may be responsible without necessarily being legitimate, they cannot be legitimate if they behave irresponsibly, especially given the tenuous acceptance already accorded bureaucrats in our culture.

We may all agree that the administrative state is necessary, but we must also justify its existence and legitimacy. If public administration as it currently exists is *not* legitimate, then calls for reform must be taken very seriously. Rohr (1986) writes:

> It is degrading for administrators to govern and for citizens to be governed by institutions that are deemed illegitimate. . . . If the administrative state is both inevitable and illegitimate, our dignity as citizens of a constitutional republic is in jeopardy.
>
> (p. 81)

As he notes, the Supreme Court has consistently upheld the constitutionality of the administrative state, but judicial fiat is not sufficient to establish legitimacy.

The spirit of the Constitution is representation and diversity. The people and the states each were accorded some influence, and the actual governmental structure was designed to give to each some measure of autonomy and control over the other political actors. Thus, in the Connecticut Compromise, the small population states were satisfied by the Senate representing each equally, and the large population states welcomed the House of Representatives being determined on the basis of population. Only the House was popularly elected. The Senators were chosen by their state legislatures until the Constitution was amended in 1913 to allow popular election of the senators. Even the president is not chosen directly by the people, but rather indirectly by electors. Within the government each branch oversees the other. The Senate confirms presidential appointments while the president is allowed the option to veto legislation. The judiciary is virtually independent once confirmed, but they are chosen by the president and confirmed by the Senate. When we speak of the separation of powers we tend to think—incorrectly—of total separation, but in fact it is only the institutions that are separated while the powers are shared.

Events have conspired to increase the power of the federal bureaucracy (and indeed of the federal government in general) at the expense of the states. Although the Constitution was drafted to protect, at least in part, the independence of the states, by 1819 when the Supreme Court decided *McCulloch v. Maryland*, the "necessary and proper" clause of Article I Section 8 was construed to allow the members of Congress to enact any legislation they could justify as necessary to perform their constitutionally assigned functions (Rohr, 1986, p. 171). Since the Constitution also makes the federal Constitution supreme in any conflict with the states, the necessary and proper clause soon allowed dramatic increases in federal power. Even the Bill of Rights, initially designed to protect citizens from the illicit activities of the federal government, was eventually applied to the states through the post-Civil War Fourteenth Amendment.

The traditional functions of the three branches of our government are legislative, executive, and judicial. Public administration combines all three but does not fully utilize any; it is quasi-legislative, quasi-executive, and quasi-judicial. For example, the quasi-legislative function enables agencies to promulgate rules that have the force and effect of law, a process often called *secondary legislation*. However, the agencies must still operate within the constraints of whatever guidelines the elected legislature has given. Similarly, the quasi-judicial function is constrained by legislative rules and judicial oversight. It may be helpful to think of the agency functions as auxiliary to the functions of the traditional branches of government laid out in the Constitution:

> American bureaucracy may not harmonize perfectly with the forms of our Constitution, but it is compatible with its spirit. . . .
>
> American bureaucracy is an independent force, and from its independence it draws much of its strength and prestige. It is a powerful and viable branch of government, not properly subject to complete control by Congress, the President, or the judiciary. But its independence does not mean that it possesses total discretion. It functions within a checks-and-balances system in much the same way as the original three branches of government. Its boundaries of action are set by Congress, and these must not exceed constitutional limits as determined by the courts. The President plays a varied role in relation to the agencies but is unable and unwilling to supervise all of their myriad activities.
>
> (Woll, 1965, p. 248)

Rohr presents a different view, one that is focused on constitutional tradition. His argument is based on three points. First, the assumption of legislative, judicial, and executive powers by the bureaucracy does not violate the standard of separation of powers. Secondly, the administrative state has come to fulfill the advisory role intended for the Senate. Third, the career civil service, being drawn from a diverse population, reflects more closely the characteristics and interests of the people than do the elected representatives and thus the bureaucracy "heals the defect of inadequate representation in the Constitution." While subordinate to all three branches of government, the public administration's role is "to fulfill the object of the oath of office: to uphold the Constitution of the United States" (Rohr, 1986, p. 171).

Stillman (1991, 1999) offers yet another perspective; one that is both historical and theoretical. He argues that *American* Public Administration is different because of the unique way in which political institutions were evolved during the eighteenth century. He notes that the American conception of government was different than that emerging in Europe. The continental model involved an increasingly sophisticated governmental apparatus that offered to citizens the services and programs deemed appropriate. Weber's concern about "dilettantes" is a product of the recognition that government was both a professional activity and the ultimate reflection of society. The American experience was decidedly different. The American experiment in governance was based upon the assumption that a "professional" governmental apparatus was not necessary. Thus, Stillman notes that this "stateless" government was based upon the principles of:

- Dominant faith in "republicanism"
- Good citizens doing their duty
- Faith in electorate and elected officials

He does note that this arrangement was not without contradictions. For example, the effectiveness of government was predicated upon the good works of a virtuous citizenry, yet we also "checked" that citizenry through layers of overlapping jurisdictions and complex decision processes to ensure that the capacity to act was constrained. The role of government was to resolve these contradictions. Thus, we became advocates of majority rule even as we were advocates of individual rights. We advocated a system based upon co-equal branches, yet our history is one of dominance by a single branch (legislature first, executive later). Most critically, we saw the fundamental threat to citizens is government.

With such a background, how was a *professional* public service to develop? Stillman describes the emergence of professional government as a "chinking in" process characterized by

- Slow evolution of professional administration
- Regulatory agencies as fourth branch
- Private (corporate) threats, not public
- Half-way answers

What kind of state does this leave us? Stillman sees four models still competing for dominance. Those models are:

- No State (public choice minimalism without knowledge of why government exists)
- Bold State (activist, government employees are competent!)
- Pre-State (mid-ground, keep doing what we are doing)
- Pro-State (welcome to the global village)

While each of these models may be in their own way "legitimate," they represent quite different governments in terms of the relationship of the public servant to citizens, the relationship of the public service to the political branches, and the role of the public service in shaping public policy. The controversy over legitimation is one of conflict among the political and institutional practices and processes implied by the models. With the possible exception of the "no-state" model, the legitimacy of the public service is no longer challenged, though even in these models the bureaucracy remains the appendage that must prove and re-prove itself.

We cannot hope adequately to present here the arguments of these and other scholars who have argued that public administration is a legitimate part of the American constitutional system. We accept their conclusions; we hope students will be inspired to do further reading and to accept them as well. Our position is that we work within and study about a discipline that is fully compatible with both the letter and the spirit of our constitutional tradition. Given that, we must accept a double imperative for administrative responsibility: As honorable people, we are bound to responsible behavior, but we are additionally bound by the normative demands of our social contract and constitutional heritage.

ADMINISTRATIVE RESPONSIBILITY

Herbert Spiro (1969) wrote that "[c]onstitutional democracy is based upon the political responsibility of individual citizens" (p. 4). This is the first imperative for a responsible bureaucracy. As citizens, bureaucrats must behave responsibly; as bureaucrats, they bear additional responsibilities. Government employment is not an excuse to avoid responsible behavior.

Spiro distinguishes three commonly used connotations for *responsibility*: accountability, causality, and obligation. Accountability means being required to answer to external institutions for one's behavior; we may say, "I am responsible for my parents' house while they are on vacation." The second form, causality, requires a direct correlation between someone's actions and the observed outcome of those actions: "I ran the red light and am responsible for the accident."

Obligation, the third connotation for responsibility, combines accountability and causality. It requires a balance of the two. No one should be accountable for a situation over which he or she has no control; conversely, no one should have significant control without accountability. Obligation implies a positive duty to act— to exercise causality—balanced by being held accountable for errors of judgment, misuse of resources, or support of illicit outcomes. Responsibility in this sense is a value judgment.

No one argues about whether or not bureaucrats should be responsible. Instead, the main concern is how best to ensure responsibility and accountability. Friedrich (1940) and Finer (1941), exemplify the two approaches used most often. Finer favors external constraints; for him, responsibility is an "arrangement of correction and punishment even up to dismissal of both politicians and officials" (Finer, p. 248). He is concerned with bureaucratic sins of both omission and commission as well as with the tendency to do too much. This external check protects the citizen not only from deliberate impropriety but also from the well-meaning but overzealous official. Finer quotes Montesquieu: "virtue itself hath need of limits." Friedrich rejects external constraints and instead advocates internal checks such as proper recruitment, training, and professional socialization. Finer would minimize administrative discretion while Friedrich feels such discretion is inevitable and must therefore be controlled.

Whether we tend to agree with Finer or Friedrich, in actuality the bureaucrat is often left to make policy decisions. These decisions may be required at the very initial stages of the policy process; indeed, occasionally the delegation of legislative authority is so complete that an entire policy originates at the bureaucratic level. At other times, civil servants may be so constrained by bureaucratic rules, legislative directions, and judicial oversight that they have virtually no autonomy at all. The civil servant's problem, as Spiro pointed out, is that he or she is still inevitably held responsible. Even in a poor "situation of responsibility" (the balance between accountability and causality), the bureaucrat is held responsible. Weber (1946) also addressed this issue in his classic essay, "Politics as Vocation."

In reviewing "Politics as Vocation," we should not be too surprised that the Weber writing in mid-career and the older, postwar Weber teaching in Munich (from which the essay, "Politics as Vocation," is derived) might see even the bureaucracy in a new or at least different light. Many of Weber's discourses begin with a detailed historical analysis with particular reference to the values and ideals that support and reflect that history, and then proceed to analyze the consequences for society *now and in the future* as a result of that history. History emerges as both a set of events and a set of ideas. This is true of his analysis of bureaucracy, his examination of the Protestant "work ethic," and it is true of his companion analyses of politics and science (Weber, 1946). We should not be surprised that the consequences of actions are of great importance. Peter Berger (1963) notes that "one of the major themes in Weber's sociology is that of the unintended, unforeseen consequences of human actions in society" (p. 38). Weber's method, while taking the present as a given, uniquely and specifically examines the historic antecedents of the present in order to anticipate *the future*. His concern is about the future, not the present. Weber would heartily concur with Gale and Hummel (2003) that "as context changes, their meaning changes" (p. 409).

Politics as Vocation

In March 1919 Weber was invited to present a lecture at the University of Munich. The lecture covers such diverse topics as the sources and character of political power, pacifism, and the likely consequences of the peace process. Weber (1946) himself suggests that the lecture would "raise certain questions concerning the significance of political action in the whole way of life" (p. 77). The message to the audience was that the path out of political turmoil and chaos was in following those with the vocation for politics.

Why vocation? This is a discussion about a profound commitment to an idea or ideal. It is based upon an inner drive that transcends experience and education. We associate the term vocation with religious positions. We often hear that someone has been *called* to the vocation of ministry. Few attribute this term to politics. Yet this is the context within which Weber wishes us to understand politics. This choice of terminology is critical to the perspective Weber offers.

Three points are important to state at the outset. First, Weber's notion of ethics will require a "transcendent" perspective that has much in common with the views of Hegel and Kant. Second, Weber expresses disapproval in describing bureaucratic ethics. Third, this is a study in *practical* ethics. It is about the realities of decision-making in the state. Or, as Weber (1946) describes it: the single "human community that (successfully) claims the *monopoly of the legitimate use of physical force* within a given territory" (emphasis in original, p. 78).

To Weber, ethical decision-making requires courage, firmness of principles, and concern for consequences of actions/choices, or as he states, passion.

> This means passion in the sense of *matter-of-factness*, of passionate devotion to a "cause," to the god or demon who is its overlord. . . . And for this, a sense of proportion is needed. This is the decisive psychological quality of the politician: his ability to let realities work upon him with inner concentration and calmness. Hence his *distance* to things and men. "Lack of distance" *per se* is one of the deadly sins of every politician.
>
> (Weber, 1946, emphasis in original, p. 115)

To make sense of the passionate politician who distances himself from "things and men," Weber asks us to look to the historic antecedents of the *political* situation in Germany. He introduces the discussion by asking, "What do we *understand* by politics?" (Weber, 1946, emphasis added, p. 77). As he notes " 'politics' for us means striving to share power or striving to influence the distribution of power, either among states or among groups within a state" (pp. 77–78). The whole of political history is the result of the changing circumstances through which persons come to seek and share power. It is important to note that the universe of those who participate actively and frequently in politics is not all those for whom politics is more than an avocation. This is the basis of the distinction that Weber draws in defining his ethic. For many in politics, the concern is for what he refers to as the "material rewards" of politics—a position in government. Much of what passes for politics is little more than the pursuit of material reward. The pursuit of such reward is not a question of ethics. Rather, it is precisely the lack of an ethical referent that is the issue. In contrast to those for whom politics is about material benefit, the "genuine official" must be willing to stand up to superiors for his or her principles (Weber, 1946, see especially pp. 83–87 and pp. 99–103). Importantly, standing up for principles means taking responsibility for the actions that result from decisions. As Weber (1946) remarks:

> To take a stand, to be passionate—*ira et stadium*—is the politician's element, and above all the element of the political *leader*. His conduct is subject to quite a different, indeed, exactly the opposite, principle of responsibility from that of the civil servant. . . . The honor of the political leader, of the leading statesman, however, lies precisely in an exclusive *personal* responsibility for what he does, a responsibility he cannot and must not reject or transfer.
>
> (italics in original, p. 95)

The Ethic of Responsibility

What is unique about political ethics is that it must be approached differently than that of religion, or even of administration. It is here that Weber introduces two ethical perspectives: the ethic of responsibility and the ethic of ultimate (or absolute) ends.

Those for whom politics is a vocation must confront the realities of the power that they share. A career in politics grants a feeling of power.

The knowledge of influencing men, of participating in power over them, and above all, the feeling of holding in one's hands a nerve fiber of historically important events can elevate the professional politician above everyday routine even when he is placed in formally modest positions.

(Weber, 1946, p. 115)

The three qualities vital for the politician are passion, a feeling of responsibility, and a sense of proportion (Weber, 1946, p. 115). It is upon these pre-eminent qualities that the leader who has the vocation for politics is evident. At first blush these are not qualities that people necessarily would see as linked, nor for that matter would everyone agree that they are virtues. The connections are more apparent when this "ethic" is contrasted with the ethic of absolute ends.

Stated most simply the ethic of absolute ends is the ethic of a saint. Only a saint could possibly consistently and continually *act* on the basis of such a standard. Weber's shift in terminology to that of the ethic of ultimate ends reflects his judgment that the ethic of absolute ends is unrealistic. It is an ethic adhered to by those of faith. But it is also the ethic of the few. Yet even the ethic of ultimate ends fails as the appropriate ethical perspective for politics. The difficulties are two-fold, first in the resistance to the mediating influence of the social consequences of our actions and second in that the "believer in an ethic of ultimate ends feels 'responsible' only for seeing to it that the flame of pure intentions is not squelched" (Weber, 1946, p. 121). The "believer" is irresponsible in the sense that the practicality, or even possibility, of reaching the goal is never considered. It is not that the believer is unwilling to acknowledge "popular opinion," but rather the believer cannot recognize that the results of actions, and in particular the actions of organized society through government, have consequences for individuals and groups that are anything but beneficial. For Weber, to ignore those consequences is not the solution, *precisely because some of the consequences are negative*. By the very nature of its existence, the state is an organization which *must* apply force. While the ethic of ultimate ends may represent an acceptable personal ethic, it cannot apply to the "public" ethic of responsibility, which necessarily acknowledges the reality of the possibility of the use of force by the state.

How then to summarize the ethic of person with the vocation for politics—the ethic of responsibility? As we noted above Weber describes the critical attributes of such a person as having passion, responsibility, and a sense of proportion. The key to this perspective is its emphasis on the *consequences of actions*, not merely its purpose. This is, as Weber describes it, the ethic of the *mature man*. The ethic, which Weber advocates, is an ethic that is fully conscious of the consequences of actions yet remains grounded (soberly and intentionally) in principle. *Perspective* is both at the heart and head of this matter. His conclusion to this work is both profound and apt in its depiction of the ethical individual.

Politics is a strong and slow boring of hard boards. It takes both passion and perspective. Certainly, all historical experience confirms the truth—that man would not have attained the possible unless time and again he reached out for the impossible. But to do that a man must be a leader, and not only a leader but a hero as well, in a very sober sense of the word. And even those who are neither leaders nor heroes must arm themselves with that steadfastness of heart, which can brave even the crumbling of all hopes. This is necessary right now; or else men will not be able to attain even that which is possible today. Only he who has the calling of politics who is sure that he shall not crumble when the world from his point of view is too stupid or too base for what he wants to offer. Only he who in the face of all this can say "In spite of all!" has the calling for politics.

(Weber, 1946, p. 128)

In addressing the values or "ethic" of the politician Weber argues the need to consider and even anticipate those unintended and unforeseen consequences as the basis for public policy. In fact, the ideal typical methodology was developed as a heuristic device to analyze and anticipate the "unintended and unforeseen." The goal is seemingly quite pedestrian—that which is possible—yet it requires heroes, those with passion and perspective, to be achieved.

Presciently, it is Kant (1983) who notes that the basis for peace is not in agreeing to end war, but in constructing a mechanism for ensuring peace. There is no means to prevent the lawless from engaging in a renewed war, especially if the terms of peace are seen as unjust. In this regard Kant shows himself to be something of a realist about human nature, even as he constructs a theoretical doctrine of law and duty that transcends that nature. He offers this "*transcendental formula* of public right: . . . . 'All actions that affect the rights of other men are wrong if their maxim is not consistent with publicity' " (Kant, 1983, emphasis in original, p. 135).

Both Kant and Weber would agree that the central point about ethics is how it affects *society*. Each judges behavior from the standpoint of society (politics) rather than from some inward-looking perspective. Furthermore, the emphasis on principle is found in both. The difference between the two is not in the importance of "principle," but rather in their disagreement over the behavior implied by that principle. Kant sees but one possible behavior emanating from principle, whereas Weber sees history changing our understanding of certain values (principles) and, thus, altering behavior.

Certainly, Weber did not expect remarkable or heroic bureaucrats to emerge. But he did hope that a few passionate politicians would populate the government to move it forward. These mature individuals of passion can make a difference precisely because they will tolerate the dispassion and rule-following behaviors of the majority. They seek that which is best for the broader society, not because they can, but often because they cannot. Kant's vision of a "peaceful" world similarly rests on the need for such maturity of judgment and commitment to principle. Ultimately, the need for maturity is demonstrated in the capacity to have passion at a distance. It is a passion for ideas and *results*, not behaviors.

ON A PRACTICAL NOTE: THE PROFESSION OF PUBLIC MANAGEMENT

Are their "heroes" in the public service? Are there those who have the maturity to understand the concept of passion at a distance—a passion for ideas and *results*? We believe that they do exist. Without labeling it as such we have been describing the public service as a "profession." But what exactly do we mean by "profession"? According to any basic text in sociology, professions are distinguished by three characteristics:

- Norms or values
- Perspectives
- Practices

Professions evolve as a specific set of practices and shared norms that are first taught (often in what are characterized as "professional schools") and then emerge as "proper" or accepted behavior (practice). Shared credentials and ultimately a shared "language" separate those who are capable of "understanding" from those who cannot understand. A profession, then, is an explicit career that usually requires a college degree, often at the master's level. Additional features of a profession are client recognition, professional identity, professional culture, a code of ethics, a formal measure of professional competence, and sufficient discretion to perform at a professional level (Fitzpatrick, 1990, p. 32).

The emergence of the profession of local government management is instructive. Therefore, we will look at that cohort of public managers—the city manager—as an exemplar of the mature, professional public manager.

City Manager as Exemplar

The profession of city management (and much of the public service as we know it today) is the quintessential twentieth-century profession. Not only was it born in the century, but also, the precepts and notions of governance and management that emerge around the turn of that century to this day heavily influence it. Furthermore, it can be argued that it is the first *self-conscious* profession in that it represents the first effort to shape a job to notions of professionalism. Most of the professions of the day were based in old and even ancient practices. The emergence of "professions" was the result of long years of debate and disagreement over who could claim the job title (i.e. who could be a lawyer, or a doctor, or even a military officer). Often this was a process marked by shedding old images and old practices and the pursuit of prestige. Many closely related practices and occupations were divided through this process. As practices evolved some elements took on distinct characteristics that resulted in a division of occupations. The root of most early professions was in occupations and practices, which today we might not necessarily define as "professions" yet maintain some similarity to the now separated professions (mid-wives and doctors; or the distinction between an RN nurse and a nurse's aide, who now performs the tasks that barely fifty years ago were assigned that RN). What distinguished the "professional" is the level of education and depth of skill.

There is no predecessor occupation for the local government manager. In creating the "profession" of local government manager the norms, perspectives, and precepts of the profession were defined and then the practices determined. *In a very real sense city management was a profession before it was an occupation.* To this day the fundamental characteristics, which distinguish the professional local government manager, are not those of occupation, but of credentials, recognition, and experience. Local government managers are professionals in that the norms, values, and perspectives that are necessary to distinguish a profession are carefully laid out (one of the truly critical distinguishing features is the development of and adherence to a code of ethics). Yet the work itself, the day-to-day practices of the profession have changed.

Most professions redefine themselves in relation to changing perceptions and values (think of the "patient's rights" movement and its impact on the medical profession). The local government manager changes practices to keep true to values and norms of the profession, some of which go back to the "founding" of the profession. This historic continuity of purpose and values is both the greatest strength and greatest weakness of the profession.

As we noted earlier in this chapter, public management emerges from two related, but separate intellectual movements of the late nineteenth century: the urban reform movement and scientific management. This odd coupling of a political movement with an organizational and structural perspective remains relevant to the profession to this day. The attributes of the new profession included a zealous commitment to transforming the very structures of government coupled with the introduction of new theories of management (the modern notion of the "manager" comes from the twentieth century). The new profession required transformation of governmental structures to be able to "practice" its vision of the new urban society. The vision begins with the separation of political activities from administrative functions so that governments would be to a large extent operated as though they were "apolitical."

What were and are the implications of this melding of government form (the embodiment of the dichotomy) and professional practice? The experience and evolution of city management is instructive, because they so well reflect the tension and conflicts in our expectations of how things "should" be:

- For decades the profession meant "City" management linked to a particular form of government (council-manager)
- Never a single "occupation"
- Practices more varied and idiosyncratic than other professions
- As governments have changed and evolved since the 1950s the profession had to become even more diverse
- Norms of behavior critical (thus early introduction of code of ethics)

A unitary, executive centered, style of government was a central feature of the ideal of the council manager form of government. While the policy issues were to be the responsibility of the council, the execution of policy and the *administrative* details of government were to be the responsibility of the manager. The manager and the council worked as one, seamlessly shifting from policy to practice. This type of government worked as long as the structure reflected the intended relationship. It also worked as long as the "administration" was left to the CEO, the manager (Svara, 1989). The professional *city* manager was the ultimate apolitical administrator, separated from politics (policy making), but with the skill and acumen to ensure that the city "worked." The fit between politics and administration was to be an arm's-length relationship.

Most professions reflect a single "occupation" with a fairly narrow range of duties and responsibilities, which demark the occupation. While sub-specialization occurs, the basic work responsibilities remain. City management, much less government management, was never an "occupation" in this sense. The work environment has always been too varied. The duties and responsibilities of the manager were defined and constrained not only through the ethics code and membership requirements, but also by the economic, social, and cultural differences among cities. Day-to-day practices of managers varied quite widely. Certain technical skills were more critical (finance or public works), depending on the community. Furthermore, over time, the needs of communities meant that certain skills were paramount for a period (i.e. public works in the early years, but public finance in the Depression and growth management in the 1980s). From the very beginning the professional local government manager was not a single occupation, which mandated a specific background, but was potentially many different occupations with different skill sets.

Professionals are general thought of as specialists. The government manager was and is a professional "generalist." As the range and types of "local government" administration occupations became linked with the "profession" of city management (including those who may wish to be department heads, rather than the CEO of a city or county), this generalist rather than specialist notion became more and more to be one of the defining features of this profession.

In part because the manager is a professional generalist, many of the standard methods for judging performance and practice are missing. To understand performance and practice of such a profession required a stricter adherence to norms of behavior than is typical of most professions. The creation of an ethics code, an act that helps delineate most professions, was in fact a more necessary step for this profession because it represents the primary basis for judging performance and practice. The "integrity" of the manager was and is a more important part of the understanding of the occupation than in most professions. The *enforcement* of a code of ethics is more important. Few professions take their code of ethics as seriously as that of local government management. There is less latitude and the need to enforce the code is more critical. Without the code there is no profession.

New Political Context

The nature and character of government has changed radically since the beginning of the last century. The level of professional and technical skill needed to be a competent "manager" is quite different than in 1920 or 1960. There is a need for new approaches. Those changes have come only slowly. There is a general recognition that the core values of the profession are expressed through ethical practices and professional development, not form of government. There has always been an interest in and commitment to professional education. However, there remains a considerable "hangover" of older views. Suspicion of politics and the resulting comfort level with the least political form of government, the council-manager form, has meant that the espoused views of managers belie their own behavior.

The Revolution of the 1980s and 1990s

The period of the 1960s and 1970s had been a time of a rising insistence that government do more, especially for those with the least political clout. Praise for the street-level bureaucrat as the advocate and voice of the disadvantaged was frequent. Those "closest to the people" were held in high esteem, at least by academics and political activists (Marini, 1971). Those at the top were suspect. They were "part of the problem." By the 1980s this discontent had broadened. The very concept of the "public service" was viewed with considerable disdain. Politicians at every level of government and across a broad ideological spectrum found that the best way to get elected was to run against the government and especially the careerists in government. The label "bureaucrat" was virtually an expletive. Being a professional "bureaucrat" was as bad as being a professional "politician." Oddly, this was a battle that would be waged on the turf of the politician—in elections and in the halls and corridors of government buildings.

New Politicians

Research by Svara (1999) and others has also noted that the make-up and character of those who serve on councils (and in state legislatures) is changing. The most commonly cited examples are the single-issue candidates that have emerged at all levels. The presumed problem is that such candidates when elected have little regard or concern for most of the policy issues and practical service-delivery problems of local government; unless, of course, the issue or problem relates to their singular concern. While such persons can be troublesome, the problem is the lack of input on policy matters, not their single-mindedness. The more critical problem is that what most often concerns those who seek local office are issues that would have in other times been thought of as issues of implementation. This is further exacerbated by the "relegation" of council members to a less important status than the mayor. When they seek refuge in their "legislative" functions, it is often the narrow constituent service aspect of the legislative function, not the broad policy-making responsibility that attracts the councils' attention. In fact, it is often "constituent service" issues that are the core of the campaign for election, or re-election. The assertion of administrative control becomes a political issue. The outlook of many council members is shaped by three interrelated perspectives:

- Intent to challenge management practices
- "Private sector knows best"
- Privatization of public enterprises

While at some point the desires and goals of managers and councils inevitably collide (this is the one profession where being fired is a badge of honor), the above phenomenon has put the manager much more in the spotlight. In some cases, the management practices of the manager are a topic of political debate. Whether the disagreement is primarily ideological (public service vs. private enterprise) or merely a matter of experience, the council assumes that careful scrutiny of the managerial and administrative decisions of the manager is its primary task. Judgments are made on very narrow grounds, or over specific decisions, not on "performance" in a broader sense. The relationship between the council and the manager that is at the very core of the council-manager form has been altered by the presence of "mayors" and by the antagonism between council and manager that are presumed to be healthy and appropriate, rather than an aberration.

Where has this left the manager (any public manager)? While the role at the local level has broadened just as Richard Child predicted in 1918, the outlook is quite different than the one Child would have anticipated. The "professional" knowledge and understanding about responsibility for executing the policy directives of the council is replaced by the need for survival skills based upon juggling the *competing* demands of mayor and council. In an odd sense the changing nature of municipal and county government has meant that the local government manager is less the technical *administrator* of the early twentieth century and more a *manager* of diverse interests and perspectives. Many of the expectations and practices, which were the hallmark of the profession, were disappearing. Managers are much more deeply engaged in *policy making*, rather than mere *policy implementation* than has been acknowledged. Many council members seem more comfortable "judging" the management style and practices of a local government manager than they are wading through the complexities and idiosyncrasies of public-sector regulations, rules, and mandates. Success as a manager now depends upon skills and relationships unlike those envisioned two decades ago. Having moved from technical-professional "administrator" to professional manager, the "new" manager needs the skills of leadership to be successful. The skills and competencies implied by the distinction between administration, management, and leadership are certainly not mutually exclusive (just the opposite), but the emphasis and application have changed. The city management profession at this junction is distinguished by:

- An inverting of the old policy-administration relationship
- The recognition that "leadership" skills are broader and more critical than "administrative or managerial" skills
- Positions are more precarious and more subject to influences beyond the control of the manager (now more than ever elections threaten longevity), and
- The need to emphasize core values . . . standards of practice and ethical behavior

What are those core values? As an exercise in a graduate class in public administration in Ghana, I asked these early- to mid-career students what they would include in a list of core values. The list is worthy of close examination.

BUREAUCRATIC VALUES

- Service
- Competence/Professionalism

- Participation/Engagement
- Transparency
- Accountability
- Responsibility
- Integrity/Ethics
- Leadership

CONCLUSION

Helping an organization follow an unknown path of change and innovation is not an easy task. It takes a manager of insight and courage. The attractiveness and resulting persistence of old notions of control and direction as key attributes of management practice is because it is a safer course. Especially if the final goals are so far into the future that those who set the goals will not be around to be judged by the outcome, a more controlling style seems a wise course. That may be the path of the manager, but in a book simply titled, *Leadership* (Burns, 1978), an alternative approach was clearly articulated. The key tenets of transformational leadership are:

- Importance of active leadership
- Change organizational performance by changing its culture
- Future orientation

The normative foundations of public administration are found in the quest to acknowledge the importance of democratic values, in having the courage and passion to act on those values and the knowledge and skill to lead and manage.

DISCUSSION QUESTIONS

- Is history (or perceptions of history) important in shaping values?
- How might one reconcile democratic values with bureaucratic values?
- How much of a role in policy making should bureaucratic expertise and public managers have?
- What does it mean to be a professional administrator?
- What are the key differences between public and private sector administration?
- How are the concepts of administrative responsibility and the rule of law related?
- Are clashes between bureaucracy and the legislative branch inevitable? Does it depend on the type of government structure?
- How do bureaucrats actively participate in governance?

BIBLIOGRAPHY

Berger, Peter. *An Introduction to Sociology: A Humanistic Perspective*. New York: Anchor Press. 1963

Burns, James McGregor. *Leadership*. New York: Harper Collins. 1978.

Davis, Kenneth C. *Discretionary Justice*. Baton Rouge: Louisiana State University Press. 1969.

Feilden, H. St. Clair. *A Short Constitutional History of England*. Boston: Ginn and Co. 1895.

Finer, Herbert. "Administrative Responsibility in Democratic Government", *Public Administration Review*, Summer, pp. 335–350. 1941.

Fitzpatrick, Daniel W. "City Management: Profession or Guild", *Public Management* (January-February), p. 32. 1990.

Friedrich, Carl J. "Public Policy and the Nature of Administration", in Freidrich (ed.) *Public Policy*. Cambridge, MA: Harvard University Press. 1940.

Friedrich, Carl J. "Public Policy and the Nature of Administration", in Francis E. Rourke (ed.) *Bureaucratic Power in National Politics*. Boston: Little, Brown and Co. 1965.

Gale, Scott A., and Ralph P. Hummel. "A Debt Unpaid—Reinterpreting Max Weber on Bureaucracy", *Administrative Theory and Praxis*, 25 (3), pp. 409–418. 2003.

Goodsell, Charles. *A Case for Bureaucracy, 2nd ed.* Chatham, NJ: Chatham House. 1985.

Goodsell, Charles. *A Case for Bureaucracy, 4th ed.* Washington, DC: CQ Press. 2003.

Hamilton, Alexander, James Madison, and John Jay. *The Federalist Papers*. New York: The New American Library. 1961.

Heady, Ferrel. *Public Administration: A Comparative Perspective, 3rd ed.* New York: Marcel Dekker. 1984.

Heady, Ferrel. *Public Administration: A Comparative Perspective, 6th ed.* New York: Marcel Dekker. 2005.

Kant, Immanuel. *Perpetual Peace and Other Essays*. (T. Humphrey, Trans.). Indianapolis: Hackett Publishing. 1983.

Lowi, Theodore. *The End of Liberalism, 2nd ed.* New York: W. W. Norton and Company. 1969.

Marini, Frank, ed. *Toward the New Public Administration*. Scranton: Chandler Publishing Co. 1971.

Miewald, R. D. "The Origins of Wilson's Thought: The German Tradition and the Organic State", in Beryl Rabin and James Bowman (eds.) *Politics and Administration: Woodrow Wilson and American Public Administration*. New York: Marcel Dekker, pp. 17–30. 1983.

Nalbandian, John. *Professionalism in Local Government: Transformations in the Roles, Responsibilities, and Values of City Managers*. San Francisco: Jossey-Bass. 1991.

Rohr, John A. *To Run A Constitution*. Lawrence, KS: University of Kansas Press. 1986.

Rosenbloom, David. *Public Administration*. New York: Random House. 1989.

Spiro, Herbert J. *Responsibility in Government*. New York: Van Norstrand Reinhold. 1969.

Stillman II, Richard J. *Preface to Public Administration*. New York: St. Martin's Press. 1991.

Stillman II, Richard J. *Preface to Public Administration, 2nd ed.* Chatelaine Press. 1999.

Svara, James H. "Dichotomy and Duality: Reconceptualizing the Relationship Between Policy and Administration in Council-Manager Governments", *Public Administration Review*, 47 (1), pp. 221–232. January–February 1989.

Svara, James H. "Complementarity of Politics and Administration as a Legitimate Alternative to the Dichotomy Model", *Administration and Society*, 30 (6), pp. 676–705. 1999.

Waldo, Dwight. *The Administrative State, 2nd ed.* New York: Holmes and Meier. 1985.

Weber, Max. "Politics as Vocation", in Gerth and Mills (trans.) *From Max Weber*. New York: Oxford University Press. pp. 77–128. 1946.

Woll, Peter. *Public Administration and Policy*. New York: Harper Collins. 1965.

CHAPTER

2

Ethical Foundations

In the discipline of public administration, we have spent decades laying to rest the idea of separation of administration and politics. We must also abandon the idea of moral neutrality. Administrative actions are of ethical as well as political concern.

This chapter is not an exploration of the illegal byways of bureaucratic life. Embezzlement, burglary, bribery, abuse of position—these are all illegal activities and are not the focus of our concern. There can be no justification of or debate about the propriety, even "just this once," of these activities. We are concerned with the ethical dilemmas of bureaucracy. Should a union supervisor try to protect the job of an admitted sexual offender who has harassed a coworker on the job? Should an Environmental Protection Agency employee compromise environmental standards enforcement to save a company that is the lifeblood of a small community? Often, we do not have answers to these questions. What does seem clear is that it is not enough merely to behave ethically, however that may be defined. One must also know why the behavior is ethical. We believe that government bureaucrats, by the simple fact that they are employed in government, have an obligation that differs from the ethical obligation of almost any other citizen. What we hope to accomplish is to direct students to the philosophical and logical tools to make their own choices in accordance with their consciences and their special obligations.

ADMINISTRATIVE THEORY AND ETHICS

Trust in government and in government employees is not high. Surveys on the morality of various professions routinely rank political officeholders below lawyers and barely above car salespeople, hardly an inspiring position. Ethics as a formal topic public administration education is relatively new: the shock engendered by Eisenhower's lie about the U-2, the numerous deceptions of the Vietnam War, the Watergate scandal, the Iran-Contra debacle, the threatened impeachment of a second president within a quarter century, the controversy over the war in Iraq, and the scandals of the fiscal crises of 2008 and 2009 have continued to erode the public's trust in government.

Practitioners have tried to ignore the moral aspects of their jobs by invoking the ethic of neutrality, which holds that administrators "are to give effect to whatever principles are reflected in the orders and policies they are charged with implementing" (Thompson, 1985, p. 556). Classical understandings of bureaucratic structure and organization theory have provided little in the way of an ethical basis for administrative activity. Weber's bureaucratic model was one source of the "ethic of neutrality." Widely misunderstood as advocating a model behavior, Weberian bureaucracy become the archetype of an alienating organization. Individual morality had no role to play in the popular conception of a bureaucracy. The morality of policy decisions was a problem for the politicians, not the administrators. A chilling example of neutrality is Adolph Eichmann's defense of the Nazi slaughter of the Jews: He was only following orders and thus was free of moral responsibility for the deaths. Despite numerous pleas in the literature of public administration to abandon the dichotomy between politics and administration, administrators still find shelter beneath the umbrella of neutrality. This approach has been reinforced by the organization theory developed in the century, starting with Taylor's scientific management.

Scientific management stressed technical efficiency as the vehicle for successful management. Good management was not concerned with the humanistic and ethical components of organization behavior: the satisfaction of the employees and the impact of the organizational output on society was not the concern of administration. One clear example was in public personnel reform, which borrowed heavily from the scientific management ideas of efficiency and "one best way." The personnel performers visited England, studying the civil service that had a long-standing tradition of neutral competency, of following the mandates of ministers regardless of the personal ideological inclinations of the administrator. The reformers failed to see that political culture of the American system was so different from the English that many of the ideas could not be transplanted to the New World. They used the idea of neutral competence, coupled with the scientific management ethos, to reinforce the ethically neutral focus of public personnel reform. Moral issues were viewed as irrelevant to the new civil service: Administrators simply should do as their political superiors desired. No one really believed that this had been accomplished, but the polite fiction that it had been done provided legitimacy for the new civil service.

Organization theory soon came to realize that it was missing an important dimension of worker concerns in the workplace, but it persisted in ignoring the moral dimensions. This is partially because the initial work in organization theory revolved around the private sector, where assembly-line technology and profit-driven management styles were dominant. Developments in the human relations school of organization theory focused on worker productivity: The incentive for better treatment of workers was increased productivity. The utilitarian value of ethics persists in the private sector. Ethics, writes one consultant, "can motivate people to transcend organizational circumstances and continue to be productive contributors" (Wheatley, 1988, p. 142) in a time of financial cutbacks. While the corporate and financial scandals of the first decade of the twenty-first century has engendered some rethinking (see Ciulla, 2004), private-sector discussions of ethics are usually focused on the role of the employee vis-à-vis his or her manager or company; rarely do they discuss the ethical impact of the employee's actions on a larger audience.

Public policy analysis also tried to separate itself from the ethical dimensions of policy. Policy analysts, trying to gain acceptance for their work by paralleling the scientific and statistical methodologies of the natural sciences, for the most part consciously divorce their work from moral considerations. Since, even in the social sciences, nature abhors a vacuum, applied or situational ethics, which lack a theoretical basis and rely instead on codified rules and narrow legal analysis, seeped in to replace more rigorous considerations.

Public choice, the economics-based approach to administrative theory, in its most extreme form rejects all notions of the public interest or even of altruistic behavior. All decisions, whether personal or organizational, rest on a calculus of maximizing gain and minimizing loss. Advocates of economic analysis as the basis for political decision-making use the neutral calculus to endorse policy decisions that have harsh consequences. For example, although deliberate species extinction is debatable ethical behavior, an economically rational fisherman would deplete a profitable fishery to extinction to free his capital for other investments. In a market, some participants must lose so that others may win. The market model leaves no room to discuss whether some people deserve gain without sinning in the market, or if perhaps—an even worse heresy—some winners should relinquish gain on ethical grounds. This is, of course, oversimplifying an extremely complex economic and political theory.

Moral arguments are no longer the primary basis for public policy debates. For example, our increased national sensitivity to the rights of minorities does not rely on the moral imperatives that should underlie such debate. Instead, groups seeking redress for their civil wrongs cite the constitutional protections of procedural due process for the remedy. Segregation in public schools was banned not because it was immoral but because it had adverse psychological impacts on black children. In part, the American political system is not designed to take the high ground on such issues; the interest groups have learned to use the system to advance their causes rather than relying on moral suasion. However, the lack of moral debate means in part that as a nation, we have not resolved the underlying causes of much of our civil unrest.

Many Americans would agree that individuals may take any ethical position they choose, from advocating white supremacy to condemning laboratory research on animals. These same Americans would also support acting on those positions as long as no other citizen is harmed. Thus, we allow KKK parades and nonviolent demonstrations against medical supply companies. The rule seems to be "do no harm" or, as a variation, "do not violate constitutional freedoms." But we no longer address the fundamental political theories that underlie a moral debate. How can we make sense of the stew of moral relativism that feeds our national culture? To begin, it is helpful to separate *kinds* of moral responsibility facing today's public administrators.

TYPES OF PUBLIC MORALITY

York Wilbern (1984) developed a classification scheme for analyzing the types and levels of public morality. Wilbern's system provides a concise framework that will be employed here to examine the range of ethical orientations and dilemmas public officials may confront. His system offers the following categories:

1. Basic honesty and conformity to law
2. Conflicts of interest
3. Service orientation and procedural fairness
4. The ethic of democratic responsibility
5. The ethic of public policy determination
6. The ethic of compromise and social integration

(Wilbern, pp. 102–103)

Basic Honesty and Conformity to Law

At the first level of basic honesty and conformity to the law, public servants do not differ significantly from any other citizen. Public opinion may be more outraged by a public servant's breach of the law—a teacher using drugs for example—and this may lead to stiffer penalties, but the offense is no different for public or private citizens. The ensuing outcry and punishment is political rather than legal. Indeed, we excuse some public officials from the normal exercise of honesty: spies, undercover police officers, and space launch technicians must all be prepared to lie—or worse—in the performance of their public duties.

Conflicts of Interest

Conflict of interest, while still concerned with the private behavior of public officials, is more easily separated from private activities. Public officials often have access to information with great potential for profit. They must be sensitive to even the *appearance* of impropriety. Codes of conduct (Chart 2–1) and financial disclosure regulations are often seen as remedies for conflicts of interest (see also the discussion on ethics commissions below). One problem with codes of ethics is that they cannot cover all circumstances. They of necessity have legalistic loopholes and yet also are inflexible because they do not have mechanisms built in to accommodate change. Administrative discretion is not recognized. The codification approach leads to discussions on ethics that are based on situations and personalities. A survey distributed to a group of North Carolina administrators asked how each would react in the following situation. A newly elected city councilman chairs the committee that decides the plumbing contract for the city. His best friend (his college roommate and best man at his wedding) has treated him to an elaborate dinner on his birthday for the past thirty years. This friend also is the major supplier for plumbing supplies for the city. Should the councilman go to a birthday dinner with the plumber this year? Yes or no?

While this sort of question may provoke lively discussion, it does not generate any lasting principles to help officials decide future cases. One of the surveyed North Carolina officials said, "the public be damned. I'm not missing a good dinner." Another murmured about Caesar's wife and politely declined the invitation. With no laws or uniform philosophical principles upon which to base an answer, both officials must be allowed their views. This does not help the novice administrator who is trying to formulate his or her own personalized code of conduct.

CHART 2–1

Codes of Ethics in Operation

In the American Society for Public Administration (ASPA) code, the position statement "Serve in such a way that we do not realize undue personal gain from the performance of our official duties" is followed by:

> The only gains you should seek from the public employment are salaries, fringe benefits, respect and recognition for your work. . . . No elected or appointed public servant should borrow or accept gifts from staff of any corporation which buys services from, or sells to, or is regulated by, his or her governmental agency. If your work brings you in frequent contact with contractors supplying the government, be sure you pay for your own expenses. . . . Make it clear by your own actions that you will not tolerate any use of public funds to benefit yourself, your family, or your friends.

The International City Management Association (ICMA) may sanction members who violate its Code:

> One manager and two council members took advantage of confidential information to invest in real estate just outside the city limits. A short time later, the land was annexed to the city. The land went up in value, the public took notice, and the manager expelled from ICMA.
>
> (Balanoff, 1990, p. 14)

One hundred years ago, George Plunkitt would have called this "honest graft" and been offended at any hint of impropriety.

Service Orientation and Procedural Fairness

The third type of public morality, service orientation and procedural fairness, reflects our society's individualistic approach to equality: equality before the law and equality of opportunity. Our legal tradition asserts that uniform procedures lead to equitable results. In an administrative hearing, citizens each are given the same notice and opportunity to present evidence. In theory wealth and position do not influence the outcome of a legal proceeding. Administrators are obligated to ensure that procedures are applied evenly. Differences in legal process are tied to the policy rather than the claimant. In the George Bernard Shaw play *Pygmalion*, Henry Higgins is accused by Eliza Doolittle of treating her like a flower girl, and not like a lady; his response is that he treats *everyone* like a flower girl. While we would prefer that bureaucrats treat all persons like ladies (and lords), procedural fairness demands only that we treat everyone alike.

This is one of the strengths of Weber's bureaucratic model, for Weber also stresses bureaucratic regularity. The difficulty with the service orientation and procedural fairness approach is that it complicates the proper exercise of bureaucratic discretion. Scholars of administrative law have often discussed the impact of discretion on policy, and case law abounds with decisions that silhouette the boundaries of the proper use of administrative discretion. However, *ethical* boundaries and legal boundaries area not necessarily congruent, and so case law on discretion is sometimes of limited usefulness (see discussion on discretion below).

The Ethic of Democratic Responsibility

The ethic of democratic responsibility focuses our concern on the result of official action. Some writers assert that the popular will is the only arbiter of public policy:

> In a democracy we are not so much concerned with how (fundamental) decisions are made as by whom they are made. The ideal of democracy is that the desires of the people, no matter how they are arrived at or how unwise they may be, should control the actions of the government.
>
> (Lewis, 1987, p. 217)

Others are more inclined, especially in technical matters, to defer to administrative expertise. Wilbern writes:

> Democracy may be interpreted not as government by the people, but as government with the consent of the people, with professionals . . . making most decision on the basis of standards and values derived from sources other than a Gallup poll, and submitting to only an infrequent exercise of electoral judgment as to general direction of policy. . . . They try to give the people, and the political officials representing them, what they would want if they had full information, meaning of course, the information available to the person conducting the activity.
>
> (p. 106)

The Ethic of Public Policy Determination

The fifth level, the ethic of public policy determination, is complex. Virtually all policy decisions are made within the constraints of limited resources, so that even superficially simple decisions become conflicts between value systems. Budgeting is especially problematic because its financial nature encourages analysis based on economic utility while criticizing political inputs. V.O. Key (1940) stressed the philosophical problems of budgetary theory:

> Further examination from the viewpoints of economic theory and political philosophy could produce valuable results . . . the most advantageous utilization of public funds resolves itself into a matter of value preferences between ends lacing a common denominator. As such, the question is a problem in political philosophy; keen analyses in these terms would be of the utmost importance in creating an awareness of the problems of the budgetary implementation of programs of political action of whatever shade.
>
> (pp. 1143–1144)

Economic considerations are inescapable in making policy choices. At the federal level, the president has mandated that all promulgated federal regulations be preceded by economic analysis. Thus, the economic utility of a policy becomes the primary consideration for executive adoption.

Additional complications with this fifth level come from the design of our legislative system. The federal government and state governments are designed to be slow in formulating policies and in responding to interest group pressures. This leads to policy decisions that favor the loud and the powerful and effectively disenfranchise the poor and the meek. A social culture that often equates democracy with capitalism and the free market accepts the political impotency of the ineffective citizens as both self-induced and deserved. To a large segment of the American public, the proper penalty for failure in the marketplace is failure in the polity as well.

The Ethic of Compromise and Social Integration

The ethic of compromise and social integration is the final level of public morality. Given the diversity of national interests, how are bureaucrats to achieve any hope of ethical policy and acceptable bureaucratic behavior? If our political culture is designed to allow diversity of religious and moral opinion—and indeed, not only to allow it but in some instances to encourage it—how can a bureaucrat structure and evaluate his or her own behavior? Is there any ethical foundation for our governmental behavior, or must we fall back on Lewis's ultimate will of the sovereign people?

CONSTITUTIONAL VALUES

John Rohr in *Ethics for Bureaucrats* (1978) argues that the oath of office taken by virtually every public administrator provides a constitutional foundation for ethical decision-making. Once the Constitution is chosen as the basis for public ethics, certain values become especially important in public discourse. While recognition of public values does not provide a blueprint for ethical decisions or behavior, it does provide a standard against which to measure actions. Examining situations in light of these values clarifies the motivations and possible outcomes. While the results may vary, discussing public values while making public decisions provides some confidence that normative issues were explicitly considered, even if the moral arguments for or against a policy were ultimately rejected.

We begin by examining what obligations a bureaucrat has to constitutional values in his or her work for the public sector.

Loyalty Oaths

Emphasizing loyalty oaths fell into disrepute in the McCarthy era, and Joseph Heller's *Catch-22* made any discussion of them difficult to initiate with a straight face. Nonetheless, we wish to begin our exploration of public-sector ethics with loyalty oaths. Most public officials are required to take a formal oath of loyalty to the regime, and in these oaths, the officials swear to uphold the Constitution of the United States (Chart 2–2). What obligations does an official assume when he or she takes an oath?

CHART 2-2

Oath of Office

I,_____, do solemnly swear (or affirm) I will support the constitution of the United States and the Constitution and laws of the State of Arizona; that I will bear true faith and allegiance to the same, and defend them against all enemies, foreign and domestic, and that I will faithfully and impartially discharge the duties of the office of (name of office) according to the best of my ability, so help me god (or so I do affirm).

Oath of Office City of Flagstaff, Arizona

Some illumination of this question is provided by examining the approaches taken by two prominent public officials whose jobs required them to implement policies that conflicted with their own deeply held religious beliefs. Governor Mario Cuomo of New York and former Secretary of Health, Education and Welfare (HEW) Joseph Califano, both staunch Roman Catholics, publicly grappled with the problems of implementing abortion policies. Both find in the Constitution a way to reconcile their public responsibilities to their private consciences.

The source of this obligation is the official's oath to uphold the Constitution. To what has an official agreed when he swears to his oath? Rohr (1978) suggests that at a minimum the official has agreed to uphold the values of American society. These values, he asserts, may be found in public law, more precisely in the law announced in Supreme Court decisions (pp. 77–84).

Regime Values

Some values expressed in the Constitution are quintessentially American; were these values to change, the United States itself would be changed. Rohr discusses three: equality, which includes issues of race and gender; freedom, encompassing the First Amendment freedoms of religion, press, and speech; and property, both "old" property in the sense of possessions and the "new" property, which is vested in certain entitlements. Rohr (1978) calls these values regime values: "the values of that political entity that was brought into being by the ratification of the Constitution that created the present American republic" (p. 68). While these are not the *only* American values, they are among the most important in the American legal tradition. These values were, in part, the codification of the values established in the two hundred years of largely English settlement in the Americas prior to the Revolution. They are the values that make persons peculiarly American. Regime values may also conflict with long-established customs. The custom may, in an earlier age, fit the notion of proper "American" behavior, but as the law changes, the customs must follow. An example of this sort of conflict is given in Chart 2–3 in the discussion of the abolition of part of the patronage hiring system in Cook County, Illinois.

Privacy was added as a fourth value when first enunciated as a constitutional right by Justice Douglas in *Griswold v. Connecticut* (381 U.S. 479 [1965]). This is a deduced value; a right that Douglas claimed was necessary for the enjoyment

CHAPTER 2 Ethical Foundations

> **CHART 2–3**
>
> *Elrod v. Burns* (427 U.S. 347 [1976])
>
> In 1976, several employees of the Cook County, Illinois Sheriff's office brought a class action suit to halt the dismissal and threatened dismissal of employees who were not of the same political party as the newly elected Democratic sheriff. The Cook County Sheriff's department had traditionally operated under a patronage system.
>
> Justice Brennan, writing the majority opinion and joined by White and Marshall, found that the patronage system inhibited freedom of association and was therefore contrary to the Constitution. Justice Stewart concurred, based on *Perry v. Sinderman* (408 U.S. 593 [1972]), writing that a satisfactory employee cannot be dismissed purely because of political beliefs. Justices Powell, Burger, and Rehnquist dissented on the grounds that the state interest overrode the extent of infringement of First Amendment rights and that government employees who had profited from the patronage system could not object to others profiting likewise. In addition, patronage has a long history of acceptance in Cook County. Finally, Justice Burger objected to the Court ruling in a matter he perceived as completely within the authority of the state of Illinois.
>
> Because *Elrod* was argued on First Amendment grounds and not on due process, the appropriate regime value is that of freedom: freedom of speech and press and assembly. In this case, the exercise of those values is inhibited by the threat of dismissal from government employment. Had the case been argued on property (due process) grounds, an affirmation of *Board of Regents v. Roth* (408 U.S. 564 [1972]) might have decided against vested rights in patronage jobs. An argument based on equality (professionally the weakest of the three) might have gone either way, either renouncing patronage in favor of equality or affirming the dismissals based on previous actions.

of people's other rights such as free speech and freedom of religion. The idea has proven useful in many spheres of policy. For example, environmentalists attempting to establish a right to a clean environment have used Justice Douglas's argument: How can citizens enjoy any of the explicit constitutional rights if they are enervated by unbreathable air or undrinkable water? The concept of the right to privacy has been generally accepted by American society. Most people believe it is an explicit constitutional right and are amazed to find it a relatively recent legal invention.

Careful and thoughtful analysis of these values is a productive way to isolate the ethical dimensions of policy discussions. Rohr's approach, which requires familiarity with legal scholarship and constitutional law to be truly efficacious, is the most useful we have found.

> If the public administration curriculum is to maintain its professional focus, certain valuable intellectual investigations must be sacrificed. . . . But I do not think we can prudently demand extensive philosophical investigations from the public administration students after they have started their professional studies. To settle for a smattering of political philosophy as part of a course in ethics would not fair either to the students or to philosophy itself. For this reason, we must look elsewhere for the foundation for a course in ethics
>
> (Rohr, pp. 65–66).

The discovery of constitutional principles has several advantages as the foundation for work in ethics. First, it is *American*. Political philosophy ranges over continents and centuries: our concern is with the public bureaucrat in Washington, DC, or Atlanta, Georgia, or Waco, Texas, who must choose *today* policies that affect the lives of others. Second, it is accessible. While some training in constitutional law is necessary, the dialectic and flow of legal argument is not difficult to grasp. Third, it records the changes in our national values. A student with basic knowledge of American history can readily see the development of values. This gives him or her the invaluable sense that, within limits, no values are static or absolute. Values change—and they should change. Public bureaucrats are in a unique position both to note change and to affect it.

DISCRETIONARY JUDGMENT

For many scholars the attitude towards the exercise of discretion must be described as ambiguous and even ambivalent. While the necessity of the exercise of discretion is not disputed, there is little agreement on the normative foundation for those decisions. Nor for that matter are the necessary individual and organizational elements by which to study the exercise of discretion fully explored. Yet without a frame of reference for these elements, there is a little basis upon which to judge the exercise of discretion.

Put most simply, discretion represents the judgment as to what activities in an agency are to receive priority. The exercise of discretion *presumes* both the need for and the capacity to exercise judgment which is not about simply implementing the "routine." The situation and circumstances drive the decision to exercise discretion. The fundamental question is how to ensure that the discretionary decision-making by bureaucrats is done "rightly." What will be argued here is that the capacity to exercise discretion well is not merely the result of thinking or wanting to do things well. The exercise of discretion is the result of *judging* events and circumstances at a moment in time and then acting on that judgment (Cox, 2004). A central concern before us is to examine the components of those a priori judgments. It will be asserted that those judgments are informed by an *understanding* that emerges from the application of specific individual and organizational tacit knowledge. By understanding we mean that capacity to "judge particulars" and then act upon that judgment (Arendt, 2003).

This topic will be addressed in more detail in chapter 13. For now, suffice it to note that the exercise of discretion is preceded by three interrelated and intertwined *pre-requisite* activities: experiencing or sense making, (which involves thinking and knowing), judging and acting. In other words, understanding (whether organizational or individual) is the result of the three activities. First, we make sense of a situation by thinking about it in the abstract and then knowing the situation by defining the current situation. Second, we judge (and, therefore, decide) based upon our understanding, all in order to take the third and most critical step—action.

As stated earlier, situation and circumstances drive the decision to exercise discretion, and it is important that the discretionary decision-making by bureaucrats is done "rightly." An important aspect of discretion is derived from the desire to behave ethically. To use the old saying: Ethics is about doing what is right, not merely doing it the right way (Burke, 1989, Cooper, 1994). The ideal of ethical decision-making as an element of policy implementation (Bowman, 1991; Frederickson, 1982) may produce some unexpected results, when combined with other values, such as democracy and representative government. The difficult or hard choice (the most critical time for the exercise of discretion) by any public servant is not whether to help someone, but rather the limits of that help. There are inevitably more who seek help than can be served. The difficult choice is to determine, ethically, when to end assistance. One must remember that the longer an official spends on the special case (the non-routine case) the lengthier the waiting list of those as yet not helped. Worse, this is precisely the situation for which neither bureaucratic routines, nor policies, nor court rulings can provide professional guidance.

How does an ethical perspective help people in organizations make "hard choices"? Hard choices imply not only a complicated situation, but also a desire to act ethically, a focus on the outcome of the decision, and a willingness to accept public scrutiny both during the decision and after the outcome is known (Bok, 1999; French, 1983). Therefore, every time one exercises discretion s/he is shifting from the realm of post ethical framework or known rules to creating a new rule based on prior ethical framework or tacit knowledge.

Aristotle noted more than two millennia ago that ethics is not a skill taught but is something that is observed and experienced. Ethics relates to tacit knowledge in that both should begin from a definition of "good" and then attempt to act. The concern here is with the need for discretionary judgment because the situation is outside the routine. Under such circumstances we need either new rules or amended rules. This requires "creativity" that comes from maturity (post conventional wisdom), i.e. tacit knowledge.

The challenge for organizational leaders is to find a way of synthesizing tacit and explicit knowledge in a manner which fosters sound judgment at all levels of the organization. One method of accomplishing this is through the use of "informal organizations" which initiates mentoring and peer evaluations within the organization. These attributes of informal organization are instrumental in passing tacit knowledge from senior employees down to inexperienced junior level employees (and back up from junior levels to isolated senior levels). Mentoring teams used in conjunction with peer evaluation can eliminate factors such as the lack of knowledge or inexperience at the junior level while at the same time reduce the effects of burn-out on senior employees by involving them in the continued development of the organization. Additionally, mentoring and peer review place an inner check on organizational corruption. Finally, the use of mentoring teams and peer review place the emphasis on the collective or organization-wide aspects of decision-making and create conditions whereby both individual responsibility and collective accountability may be achieved.

We began this analysis by seeking a framework within which to understand discretionary judgment. For all intents and purposes, we are suggesting that those who *should* exercise discretion are those with tacit knowledge. The capacity for judgment, i.e. the skill to *fully* understand and decide before acting, is embedded in the ability to internalize and socialize knowledge. More importantly, from this ability comes the *informally assigned* authority to judge. This is the reality of organizations—most are driven by and succeed through the informal network, not the formal organization. Discretionary judgment is not an assignment or position. It is not the product of explicit knowledge. It cannot be delegated based upon explicit criteria. But it will emerge from the practices and activities of tacitly defined informal networks. As noted earlier, the "problem" of the exercise of discretion is embedded in this dilemma—we need those with the capacity for judging, not those with the capacity for thinking, to exercise discretion. It is the "authority" of place in the informal organization and the demonstrable capacity for judgment that is labeled "maturity" or "instinct" or "skill" that is the realm of those who should exercise discretion.

ON A PRACTICAL NOTE: ENFORCEMENT OF ETHICS RULES

Ethics Commissions in the United States

In August 2005, Ohio Governor Bob Taft pled "no contest" to charges that he violated §102.031 of the State Ethics Law, thus becoming the first Ohio Governor to be convicted of a crime (washingtonpost.com, August 19, 2005: A06). Taft was charged with failing to disclose fifty-two gifts worth approximately $5,700 over a four-year period (toledoblade.com, August 19, 2005). After pleading no contest, he was convicted of four misdemeanor counts for his failure to disclose gifts received from Republican fundraiser Tom Noe (cincinow.com, September 19, 2005). Mr. Noe was subsequently indicted by federal authorities for illegal campaign contributions to President George W. Bush's re-election campaign (Seewer, 2005, p. A1).

At first glance, the speed and efficiency with which the *Ohio Ethics Commission* dealt with Governor Taft's ethics violations would seem to indicate that the State of Ohio, as well as the United States in general, has been relatively successful at implementing ethics laws and developing commissions to deal with the dilemmas faced by public employees across the globe. Admittedly, state commissions have moved toward ensuring compliance with ethics law. For example, the *Fair Political Practices Commission* (in the State of California) "dismissed" nearly one-third of its caseload because it did not have sufficient staff to review and research all of the allegations and charges made during the election process (latimes.com, October 18, 2005). The Ohio Ethics Commission announced its decision on a case involving charges and counter-charges of unethical campaign advertising in a judicial race nearly three years after the race ended. New Mexico's State Treasurer, Robert Vigil, came under federal investigation and faced possible impeachment for participating in an alleged kickback scheme involving investment firms working with the State's Investments Committee (Terrell, October 18, 2005). In Florida, Republican Governor Jeb Bush accused four fellow Republican state legislators of a "faux fundraising" trip with representatives of the State's gambling interest. These four went to a gambling resort with the lobbyists. They did not pay for the trip. The cost of the trip was reported by both the legislators and the lobbyist as a "campaign contribution." The governor called for a new law to prevent such trips from being labeled as fundraisers to avoid fundraising reporting laws (Bousquet,

October 18, 2005). In a press release dated December 31, 2004, Connecticut Governor, M. Jodi Rell, herself governor because of the indictment and conviction of her predecessor William Rowland, called for legislation to "transform the ethics commission into a new agency that will more effectively administer and enforce state ethics laws" (CT. Gov, December 31, 2004).

Despite the existence of ethics commissions and laws in virtually all of the fifty states and in many of the major cities and counties in the United States, we seem anything but "scandal proof" (Mackenzie, 2002). As Michael notes, the "spiraling rise of accountability" (2005, p. 96) is not a guarantor of changed behaviors among those we seek to hold "accountable." In state after state, an examination of the record of those charged with managing and enforcing ethics code violations demonstrates that the California experience—characterized by too little staff and too few indictments—is all too common (Smith, 2003).

Unfortunately, the reality of public employment is that mandated ethics law, and the presence of ethics commissions, will not prevent those who "intend" to break the law from doing so (Mackenzie, 2002). It may be even more critical to note that much of what passes for ethics law in the United States is merely the reporting of requirements that depict "past" events. It seems ethics law is focused on a system that seeks to make past indiscretions right rather than on creating a system in which public employees consciously choose not to engage in a particular activity simply because such an act would be unethical. Consequently, such laws are based upon the "low-road" approach posited and found wanting by Rohr nearly three decades ago. Ethics violations may often be considered the "gotcha" aspect of public employment. It is the mistake of omission, rather than the illicit act of co-mission, that is regularly uncovered. While the "adherence to formal rules is critical, it is not the best basis upon which to train and educate public officials. Accordingly, ethics commissions may be of more value for their political symbolism than for their capacity to thwart corrupt practices" (Smith, 2003).

Legal Structure

Most states have adopted some formal legalized forum for dealing with ethical dilemmas. Often these states formed ethics commissions in order to create a framework under which public employees are expected to function in order to ensure the public is appropriately safeguarded from self-interested officials (two states have limited their commissions' authority to elections issues). These commissions mandate public employees to submit yearly financial disclosure and/or conflict-of-interest forms. Simply, employees may be required to report any potential interest that violates ethics laws. For example, many states have laws requiring that officials report any gifts they receive that could be perceived to influence that official's professional decisions.

To ensure public employees are reporting financial interests, as well as any conflicts of interest, most ethics commissions have been given the authority to fine public employees for a failure to file timely reports. These commissions have also been given the power to investigate allegations of misdeeds and to subpoena witnesses. Generally, the results of commission investigations, in instances in which a violation has occurred, are given to the local prosecutor for legal action. Violations carry financial costs (up to $10,000) and may also include jail time (up to five years). These formalized legal processes are focused almost entirely on creating a system that ensures compliance from public employees.

Institutional Structure

Since its founding, the United States has witnessed numerous "ethical lapses" that led to the creation of the ethics commissions. These commissions are intended to address, limit, and combat the ethical issues associated with public employment. There is a distinct pattern in the structure and organization of ethics commissions in the American states. Critically in the American system is that typically the organization that addresses the problem of ethics is an independent regulatory commission. The intent of this organizational design is to isolate the commissioners and investigators from political influence. The problems experienced by federal inspectors generally suggest that such isolation may be more symbolic than real, nevertheless, such a buffer is critical to the credibility of these bodies. Changes to laws in both Wisconsin and Connecticut focus on new organizational arrangements to enhance the capacity for independent judgment.

The role of the commissions is a combination of "watchdog" and "advocacy" that is similar to the regulatory agencies created at the state and federal levels at the beginning of the twentieth century. On the one hand these agencies are responsible for reviewing conflict of interests and financial disclosure information, as well as investigating reports of unethical (more likely illegal) behaviors by public officials. On the other, most have a mandate to provide "advisory opinions" and produce training manuals and provide training focused on ethical conduct. Thus, the same agency is required to serve as the advisor and counselor on how to behave and to investigate and punish those who do not heed the lessons of that training. By the time of the creation of most of these commissions in the last quarter of the twentieth century, such dual roles were deemed a problem. The division of the US Civil Service System into the Office of Personnel Management and Merit Systems Protection Board, mandated by the Civil Service Reform Act of 1978, was based upon a presumption that the role of advocate and enforcer were incompatible within a single organization.

The dual roles described above are apparent in the persons employed by such commissions. There seems to be a division among commissions between those that hire "investigators" and those who hire "attorneys." The distinction here is often between an emphasis on investigating reports of unethical conduct and an emphasis on the examination of documents to determine compliance. Critically, few commissions hire trainers. The priority in who is hired by these commissions is instructive in understanding the work environment and organizational culture of these commissions (see the section on cultural dimension below).

Training for Ethical Conduct

Maesschalck (2005) calls for an integration of both the compliance (low road) and integrity (high road) perspectives of ethics frameworks as the best foundation upon which to establish and maintain a system of ethical management. Yet, an analysis of the ethics training provided to public employees suggests that we are a long way from being able to integrate the two ethical perspectives envisioned by Maesschalck. While public-sector ethics "courses," especially in graduate programs such as public administration, would readily incorporate the goals set by Maesschalck, an examination of the "training" offered to those already employed in the public sector paints a different picture.

With few exceptions (i.e. the training conducted by the International City/ County Management Association providing the best example), ethics training is often simply a rehash of the rules and prohibitions associated with state conflict of interest laws. Such measures, which may appropriately be referred to as the "thou shalt not" method of training, place a particular emphasis on the prohibited behaviors that those involved with the public sector should not engage in over the course of their employment. Moreover, even non-jurisdiction specific training, such as that available within police academies, is often brief and focused on what not to do (Johnson and Cox, 2004–5).

It is important to note that one should not consider the enforcement perspective an inappropriate base upon which to begin building a system of ethics. Nevertheless, this perspective is certainly problematic when it serves as the sole focus of public-sector ethics training. Under systems centered solely on an enforcement perspective, a fair summary of ethics training for public employees in the United States can be best characterized as too brief, too infrequent, and too focused on compliance. In fact, with the very notable exception of the Ethics Commission created in 1999 in Miami-Dade County (Florida), where training was mandatory for "all" County employees, training is not a major (or even minor) responsibility of most state ethics commissions.

Cultural Dimension

The "cultural" dimension of state ethics laws and commissions can be examined from two distinct perspectives. First, it can be viewed in terms of the application of the rule enforcement (low road) approach to the problem of corruption. Second, it can be analyzed through the political culture which helped create the commission and/or encouraged the development of expanded powers for its functions. Nevertheless, most state ethics laws share several common threads. First, they tend to prohibit public officials (sometimes all officials, sometimes only elected officials) from accepting gifts over a certain value (the threshold is as low as zero and as high as $250). Second, these laws also create a self-report system whereby public employees annually provide information on gifts received and/or their families' financial interests. It is also common for elected officials to be required to report the amount of monies received in the form of campaign contributions. Both of these mandatory self-reports constitute the "evidence" used by commissions to determine when a violation of an ethics law has occurred. Often, it does not matter whether the mistake is one of omission or co-mission. Nor is the "direction" of the transgression at issue. Evidence of a violation is can be the result of differences in reporting between the "contributor" and the elected/public official (although, as was the case with Ohio's Governor, "gift providers" and public officials may both fail to report contributions). The centrality of the self-reports in the process means that in those states where all gifts of any value are barred, and, therefore, there are no reporting requirements, the only way an investigation can begin is through an allegation from a "witness." Outside of some discrepancy brought to light through a political crisis (such as that experienced in Ohio), witnesses are also necessary in instances in which public employees and contributors both fail to report gift exchanges.

Consequently, it is arguable that "compliance" approaches represent the dominate method employed within state ethics systems. This choice of approaches reflects a bias toward a formalized and highly legalistic understanding of ethics practices. That some commissions use attorneys instead of investigators further indicates that the organizational culture of most commissions is grounded in legalisms and rule enforcement. Unfortunately, fixation on the legal aspect of ethics leaves little room for the pursuit of a high road, which would focus on incorporating integrity into the system, largely because there is no place within a narrow, legal framework for describing integrity, much less applying it.

The ability to integrate integrity into the current ethics system is further complicated by the fact that ethics enforcement is infused with politic processes. In fact, the simple observation that the impetus for the enactment of ethics laws tends to be linked to a political scandal provides the clearest example of the importance of politics in the creation of ethics laws and in the focus on compliance-based approaches. Furthermore, as Mackenzie (2002) noted, one of the primary motivations for changes in the rules controlling work and even post-employment activities of senior federal officials is the desire of each new administration to be seen as "tougher" on corruption than predecessors. At the state level, the proposal for a new ethics commission introduced by Connecticut Governor Rell and the explanation for the introduction of legislation in Wisconsin (Marley, 2005) are both justified because of scandals and the promise of stricter enforcement of ethics statues. In fact, the need to be "perceived" as being tough on corruption often trumps the need to change the law, which after all may well have been the reason for the scandals in the first place.

The dilemma associated with examining the role and purpose of ethics commissions is largely linked to the notion that ethics tends to be perceived by public officials, as well as the public itself, as an after-the-fact judgment. Reporting past activities creates an atmosphere in which mistakes of omission are more likely to be caught than mistakes of co-mission. The "high road" ethics are lost, not only because of the emphasis on post hoc reporting of activities, but also because the tougher ethical problems are not the failure to conform to law, but true ethical dilemmas that emerge from the need to exercise discretionary judgment.

At least in the context of the United States, ethics commissions may be valued as symbols rather than as enforcement mechanisms. As long as these commissions are focused almost solely on achieving compliance through purely legal mechanisms, the role of public employees with respect to ethics law will be defined almost entirely in a legalistic manner. Such compliance is certainly an integral component of ethics systems, particularly insofar as some employees may willfully violate ethics standards. However, it creates a fundamental dilemma for these officials who might otherwise be trained to follow ethics notions. These employees are likely to perceive ethics law as little more than a legal requirement. Moreover, commissions who approach ethics law as if little more than a mechanism by which employees may be held accountable for their actions fail to address ethics comprehensively. The focus on compliance ignores the development of a deeper understanding of the value and point of systems of ethics. Is it possible that the pursuit of ethics compliances has led to a system in which we have too much of a good thing? Or, is it simply that Rohr's lesson that we not forget to educate public officials about the "high road" has in fact been forgotten?

ETHICS AND PUBLIC POLICY

On the same day a couple of months before the start of the war in Iraq (March 2003) two commentaries on that situation noted the conflict between the ethicists and the followers of *Realpolitik*. The latter were described as pragmatic and realistic, the former as naïve. The advocates of realism (or more properly neo-realism), and its rational assessment of political relationships, is accepted by most people as "hard-headed," rational and decisive. Ethical politics is therefore the opposite; it is naïve, vacillating, and "unworldly." The troubling implication is that to be ethical is to be too soft to be effective in international relations. It seems it takes a cynical and devious mind to be successful in politics. In an unfortunate parody of Machiavelli, it is all too easy to say, "they lie and cheat, so I must." Another implication of the charge of being soft is that the ethical person will shrink from "hard" decisions (i.e., war), and only the hard edge of cynicism can face the "reality" of war and politics.

Is ethical judgment fuzzy and naïve? Are ethical leaders weak? Are politics and political decision-making so corrupting and "dirty" (Walzer, 1973) that ethics disappears, or can ethical perspectives impel a concern for the consequences for people and thus create some level of "justice" (Niebuhr, 1932; Weber, 1946; Rawls, 1999)? We must explore these ethical questions. We must also confront how the realist view has succeeded in claiming the pragmatic "high ground" of necessity. We will examine these questions through the lens of the decisions made leading up to the war in Iraq. The contrasting and polarized views on the war in Iraq follows less the traditional partisan political divisions and more the disagreement over the fundamental nature of politics as expressed by advocates of a neo-realist approach and the advocates of an ethical perspective.

Despite the "problem of dirty hands" and political skepticism, there is another tradition—that of the public service. It is perspective found in the analysis of Aristotle and Weber, both of whom found the "ethics" of politics superior to that of the ethical perspectives of society or "bureaucracy." For these and others, it was the concept of responsibility for the consequences of actions that set the "politician" apart. It is not so much that politicians are better than others, but rather that politicians, by choice or by fact of office, must look to the future. These are individuals who must be firm in their convictions that the decisions they make are right and necessary, even if the personal price is quite high.

Many think that the problem is in sorting out those for whom public service is a responsibility, from those who seek self-aggrandizement. How does one know the difference between the "policy decision" that represents a careful weighing of the consequences for others from decisions made to make someone look good?

The lesson of ethics is that *motives* are not the best way to judge decisions. Good things come from self-interested choices and bad things can come from altruistic decisions. Ethics must be judged by the consequences for others, over the long haul.

Those we call "statesmen" are those who have understood that to be ethical is to face hard choices (French, 1983). Great political leaders make hard choices. Ethical decision-making is anything but naïve or unworldly. It takes considerable courage and strength of will to do what one thinks is right, regardless of the personal consequences. But that is the essence of ethical decision-making because the concerns are directed to the consequences for others, not for oneself.

How does an ethical perspective help make "hard choices"? French would argue that the very purpose of an ethical framework is to make those hard choices. If the decision is simple, or straightforward, it is unlikely to rise to the level of an ethical problem. Hard choices imply not only a complicated situation, but also a desire to act ethically, a focus on the outcome, and a willingness to accept public scrutiny both during the decision and after (Cox, 2000). Borrowing liberally from French, Broad, Weber, and Bok, the elements of this framework include:

- Complexity: The circumstances are confused and difficult
- Self-awareness: Honesty toward self and toward what we want as an outcome; a desire to be consciously and methodically ethical in reaching a decision
- Responsible: A concern for others and an acceptance of the consequences to others of the action taken
- Justifiable: Decisions can be justified, but never excused
- Public: Willingness to explain to others how a decision is made
- Factual: Accepting of the world as it is, not as we wish

Such a framework is not for the faint of heart. It requires both a commitment of purpose and the strength to endure failure. Great political leaders make hard choices. Ethical decision-making is anything but naïve, or unworldly. It takes considerable courage and strength of will to do what one thinks is right, regardless of the views of others or of the personal consequences. That is the essence of ethical decision-making, because the concerns are directed to the consequences for others, not for oneself. But it is also more than a lack of concern for person or career. Public decisions have consequences beyond person and "political" interests. Not all actions produce only "benefits." An examination of consequences is an articulation of "what is next." Hiding from consequences does not make them go away, but rather it means we will be caught unaware when they inevitably occur. Hiding from consequences is a way of pretending that actions do not have consequences. Only by confronting the consequence of an act can we decide whether or not we accept that consequence. There are no rosy scenarios in this examination. In all likelihood, every action has "negative" consequences (this fact is the real "dirty hands" of politics). Ignoring consequences, or denying their existence, is to prevent hard choices from being made.

By ignoring or denying the consequences in communications with the public, we are not preventing those actions from taking place. Rather, we are preventing the public from acknowledging those consequences as an element of the decision to act. Only the ethical leader can acknowledge the precarious nature of events. Only the ethical leader will stay focused on the outcomes of action and the consequences for others as a factor in decision-making. Only the ethical leader will act despite the "bad" that will happen along with the good. And, only the ethical leader will accept responsibility (and, possible negative personal consequences) for the decisions made. It is not easy, nor simple, but it is needed.

In terms of ethics education and training, Cox (2011) introduces the following ethical competencies:

- Using an ethical framework as a model for and the logic of decision-making.
- Decisiveness in making hard choices; to acknowledge that no alternative is going to "solve" the problem. It represents an approach to decisions that emphasizes the consequences of actions. It is tempered by considerations of public outlooks and perspectives. It also requires the conviction to act despite the likely negative consequences (for some, if not all) in the decision.
- While a compliance model is certainly an integral component of ethics systems, it nevertheless is only a partial model. The capacity for applying ethical concepts beyond mere rule compliance is needed.
- Defining conceptual foundations for how practical ethical guidelines should be set up. What is required is a dialogue on what the code means in easy-to-define terms, so that it can serve as a guideline for correct actions and becomes the basis for a cultural transformation. Then those practical rules must be made part of the training agenda of academics and departments.
- As long as ethics is taught as a retrospective look at past decisions to decide what to not to do, it will come across as little more than the mental equivalent of an Internal Affairs investigation. Only when ethics is introduced as a way of exercising discretion and making "good decisions, in a timely manner" will students appreciate it as necessary to doing the job.
- Acting in a *public* environment implies the acknowledgement of the critical role of the public in shaping the definition of the problem and creating solutions.

CONSEQUENCES

Ethics is the path to making hard choices. It represents an approach to decisions that emphasizes the consequences of actions. It is tempered by considerations of public outlooks and perspectives. The fact that others lie and cheat is not a justification (Bok, 1999) for doing it ourselves. The hard choice is to continue to be ethical in the face of deceit. The hard choice is to acknowledge that no alternative is going to "solve" the problem. An ethical perspective also acknowledges that there is never a single reason or cause for an action. Motivations are not that important. Without understanding the consequences of actions, decisions which appear sound may prove difficult to justify, especially if such actions are turned upon us. We have set a precedent without acknowledging the consequences of such a precedent for ourselves or others.

DISCUSSION QUESTIONS

- Have you ever thought about the relevance of an oath of office?
- What does it mean to be "loyal"? To whom do you owe loyalty? Why?

- What are the differences between the European idea of integrity and the American ideal of ethics?
- Is it sufficient to not be unethical?
- Do state and local ethics commissions have a meaningful purpose? If so, what is that purpose?
- What do we seem to see ethics violations as minor, or at least less important that other forms of illegality?
- If you could start from scratch, how would you approach the writing of an ethics code (or wouldn't you bother)?

BIBLIOGRAPHY

Arendt, Hannah. *Responsibility and Judgment*. New York: Schocken Press. 2003.

Argyris, Chris. *Knowledge for Action: A Guide to Overcoming Barriers to Organizational Change*. San Francisco: Jossey-Bass. 1993.

Argyris, Chris. *Organizational Learning, 2nd ed*. Malden, MA: Blackwell. 1999.

Ball, Howard. *Justice Downwind: America's Atomic Testing Program in the 1950s*. New York: Oxford University Press. 1986.

Balanoff, Howard, ed. *Public Administration Annual*. Guilford, CT: Duskin Publishing. 1990.

Balz, D. "Taft Admits Ethics Violations: Ohio Governor Apologizes for Lapses that Could Hurt GOP", *Washington Post*, (Retrieved August 19, 2005, from www.washingtonpost.com).

Baumard, Phillipe. *Tacit Knowledge in Organizations*. Thousand Oaks, CA: Sage. 1999.

Bennet, Robert H. III. "The Importance of Tacit Knowledge in Strategic Deliberations and Decisions", *Management Decision*, 36 (9), pp. 589–597. 1998.

Bok, Sissela. *Lying: Moral Choice in Public and Private Life, 2nd ed*. New York, Vantage Books. 1999.

Bousquet, S. "Governor says 4 Legislators' Trip 'Inappropriate'", *St Petersburg Times*, (Retrieved October 18, 2005, from www.sptimes.com).

Bowman, James S., ed. *Ethical Frontiers in Public Management*. San Francisco: Jossey-Bass. 1991.

Burke, John. "Reconciling Public Administration and Democracy; The Role of the Responsible Administrator", *Public Administration Review*, 49 (2). 1989.

Burns, James McGregor. *Leadership*. New York: Harper Collins. 1978.

Casey, Steven. *Cautious Crusade*. New York: Oxford University Press. 2001.

Choo, Chun Wei. "Sense-Making, Knowledge Creation and Decision Making: Organizational Knowing as Emergent Strategy", in C. W. Choo and N. Bontis (eds.) *The Strategic Management of Intellectual Capital and Organizational Knowledge*. New York: Oxford University Press. 2002.

Ciulla, Joanne B. "Leadership and the Problem of Bogus Empowerment", in Joanne Ciulla (ed.) *Ethics, the Heart of Leadership*. Westport, CT: Praeger, pp. 59–82. 2004.

Cooper, Terry L. *An Ethic of Citizenship for Public Administration*. Englewood Cliffs, NJ: Prentice Hall. 1991.

Cooper, Terry L., ed. *Handbook of Administrative Ethics*. New York: Marcel Dekker. 1994.

Cox III, Raymond W. "Creating a Decision Architecture", *Global Virtue Ethics Review*, 2 (1), pp. 1–31. 2000.

Cox III, Raymond W. "On Being an Effective Local Government Manager", in Newell (ed.) *The Effective Local Government Manager, 3rd ed*. Washington, DC: ICMA, pp. 1–19. 2004.

Day, Carla. "Balancing Organizational Priorities: A Two-Factor Values Model of Integrity and Conformity", *Public Integrity*, 1 (II), pp. 149–166. Spring, 1999.

Eder, S., and James Drew. "Taft Declared Guilty; Judge Scolds Governor, Orders Him to Apologize", *Toledo Blade*, (Retrieved August 19, 2005, from www.toledoblade.com).

"Ethics Training for Citizens and Agencies", *Miamidade.gov.*, (Retrieved October 29, from www.miamidade.gov/ethics/training.asp).

"FFPC Quits 225 Cases", *Los Angeles Times*, (Retrieved October 18, 2005, from www.latimes.com).

Frederickson, H. George. "The Recovery of Civicism in Public Administration", *Public Administration Review*, 42 (6), pp. 501–508. 1982.

Freeman, Samuel, ed. *John Rawls: Collected Papers* Cambridge, MA: Harvard University Press. 1999.

French, Peter. *Ethics in Government*. Englewood Cliffs, NJ: Prentice-Hall. 1983.

Friedman, Thomas. "Breaking a Cycle of Mutual Destruction", *Akron Beacon Journal*, June 17, p. B3. 2003.

Fuller, John G. *The Day We Bombed Utah: America's Most Lethal Secret*. New York: New American Library. 1984.

Gallagher, Carole. *American Ground Zero: The Secret Nuclear War*. New York: Random House. 1994.

"Governor Rell Announces Proposal to Revamp State Ethics Commission", *Press Release*, (Retrieved December 31, 2004, from www.CT.gov).

Gruber, Judith E. *Controlling Bureaucracies*. Berkeley, CA: University of California Press. 1987.

Horowitz, Robert, ed. *Moral Foundations of the American Republic, 3rd ed.* Charlottesville, VA: University of Virginia Press. 1986.

Hummel, Ralph P. "The Triumph of Numbers: Knowledges and the Mismeasure of Management", *Administration & Society*, 38 (1), pp. 58–78. March 2005.

Hummel, Ralph P. *The Bureaucratic Experience, 5th ed.* Armonk, NY: ME Sharpe. 2007.

Johnson, T. A., and Raymond W. Cox III. "Police Ethics: Organizational Implications", *Public Integrity*, 7 (1), pp. 67–79. 2004–5.

Keating, C. "Rell May Veto Contract Reform", *Hartford Courant*, (Retrieved October 26, 2005, from www.courant.com).

Kikoski, Catherine K., and John Kikoski. *The Inquiring Organization*. Westport, CT: Praeger. 2004.

Lewis, Verne B. "Toward a Theory of Budgeting", in Shafritz and Hyde (eds.) *Classics of Public Administration*. Chicago: Dorsey. 1987.

Mackenzie, G. Calvin. *Scandal Proof: Do Ethics Laws Make Government Ethical?* Washington DC: Brookings Institution Press. 2002.

Maesschalck, J. "Approaches to Ethics in the Public Sector", *Public Integrity*, 7 (1), pp. 21–41. 2004–5.

Marley, P. "Panel Votes to Create Agency with Broad Powers to Fight Corruption", *Milwaukee Journal Sentinel*, (Retrieved October 26, 2005, from www.JSOnline.com).

Menzel, D. C. "Research on Ethics and Integrity in Governance", *Public Integrity*, 7 (2), pp. 147–168. 2005.

Michael, B. "Questioning Public Sector Accountability", *Public Integrity*, 7 (2), pp. 95–110. 2005.

Morgan, Gareth. *Images of Organization*. Newbury Park, CA: Sage. 1986.

Niebuhr, Reinhold. *Moral Man and Immoral Society*. New York: Charles Scribner's Sons. 1932.

Petter, J. "Responsible Behavior in Bureaucrats", *Public Integrity*, 7 (3), pp. 197–217. 2005.

Relyea, N. "Ethics Commission Frustrated with Latest Taft Gift Disclosures", *WCPO-TV*, (Retrieved September 19, 2005, from www.cincinow.com).

Rohr, John A. *Ethics for Bureaucrats*. New York: Marcel Dekker. 1978.

Safire, William. "Caution, Not Lies Account for Omissions", *Akron Beacon Journal*, June 3, p. B3. 2003.

Seewer, J. "Republican Donor Indicted", *Akron Beacon Journal*, October 28, p. A1. 2005.

Selznick, Philip. *Leadership in Administration*. Berkeley, CA: University of California Press. 1957.

Smith, R. W. "Enforcement or Ethical Capacity: Considering the Role of State Ethics Commissions at the Millennium", *Public Administration Review*, 63 (3), pp. 283–295. 2003.

Spanier, John. *Games Nations Play, 7th ed.* Washington, DC: CQ Press. 1990.

Stewart, Debra. "The Moral Responsibility of Individuals in Public Sector Organizations", in E. K. Keller (ed.) *Ethical Insight Ethical Action*. Washington, DC: ICMA. 1988.

Terrell, S. "Vigil Refuses to Testify for Panel", *Santa Fe New Mexican*, (Retrieved October 18, 2005, from www.enewmexican.com).

Thompson, Dennis. "The Possibility of Administrative Ethics", *Public Administration Review*, 45 (5). 1985.

Walzer, Michael. "Political Action: The Problem of Dirty Hands", *Philosophy and Public Affairs*, 2 (2), pp. 160–180. 1973.

Weber, Max. *From Max Weber: Essays in Sociology*. (H. H. Gerth and C. Wright Mills, Trans.). New York: Oxford University Press. 1946.

Weick, Karl. *Social Psychology of Organization, 2nd ed.* Reading, Ma: Addison-Wesley Publishing. 1979.

Weick, Karl. *Making Sense of the Organization*. Malden, MA: Blackwell. 2001.

West, J. P., and E. Berman. "Ethics Training in US Cities", *Public Integrity*, 6 (3), pp. 189–206. 2004.

Wheatley, Margaret. "The Motivating Power of Ethics in Times of Corporate Confusion", in Wright (ed.) *Papers on the Ethics of Administration*. Provo, UT: Brigham Young University Press. 1988.

Wilbern, York. "Types and Levels of Public Morality", *Public Administration Review*, 44 (2). 1984.

PART

II

Organizational Functions and Competencies

The environment in which a public manager must work is ever-changing. The manager's ability to make decisions and keep up with the public's demands for services is predicated on several factors, two of which are (1) the ability to gather the necessary resources and information to make decisions and (2) the knowledge of administrative practices and procedures to utilize those resources and information successfully. The chapters of Part II address these factors, focusing on a specific set of administrative practices we are calling the management support system. These processes and programs represent the administrative and support functions that make it possible for a manager to carry out the tasks of governance. The specific practices to be examined here are budgeting, personnel, administrative law, policy analysis, and program evaluation.

This analysis requires further explanation, because it is not a concept commonly used in public administration. The basic assumption here is that the capacity to manage is not only affected by an individual's personal competency as a manager but also by his or her success in making use of the expertise and activity of others. The management support systems, then, are activities undertaken by persons other than the manager, who may or may not be working directly under the manager's direction or supervision. These circumstances reformulate the manager's requisite skill set and require him or her to develop sufficient understanding of these subprocesses to make use of them to accomplish agency objectives. For example, a manager need not be an expert in personnel practices, but a manager must understand the timing, pace, and legal constraints that define personnel practice in order to obtain personnel and operate within the agency's personnel structure.

Public budgeting plays an interesting role in policy implementation and management. Depending on the rank of the manager, the manager may have little more than a paper submission role in the budgeting process, yet the outcome of the internal deliberations within the executive agencies may well have more influence over the amount of money available for program operations than the much more public budget enactment of councils and legislatures. Understanding how the budget process "works" more than its legal requirements are vital for the manager. The chapter will explore that evolution of the budget process and particularly in the dynamic relationship between revenues and expenditures. Lastly it is the context of intergovernmental relations that the budget that is available for operations is best understood.

Similarly, administrative law encompasses the specialized functions of independent regulatory agencies, the practices and procedures for rendering decisions in an agency, and certain procedures with regard to the handling of documents. Failure to grasp the implications of the role of the regulatory and administrative processes can lead to failure as a manager, since the decision processes in public organizations often are defined and specified in an administrative procedures act. The root issues here are procedural fairness or "due process" and the manager's understanding of the public nature of agency decision-making processes. Administrative procedures are not intended to negate administrative discretion but to establish the context within which that discretion is exercised. The manager who fails to conform to these procedures is challenging a fundamental aspect of the "publicness" of public administration.

The manager's relationship to policy analysis has a more traditional supervisory tone, yet it is specialized activity that the manager must understand and utilize, even when the manager never acquires the skill to be an expert. Two factors are most pertinent to the manager's effective use of policy analysis. First is the ability to define with sufficient specifically the task of analysis so that the context of the analysis results can be shown. Second, it is the ability to understand the nature of the analysis itself, particularly with regard to the meaning of the data manipulations that are part of the analytic process. Understanding the limits of the analytic process is critical to the manager, who must appreciate both the potential and the limitations of policy analysis as a tool for decision-making.

Another system practice that is closely related to policy analysis is program evaluation. While considered standard practice today, much like policy analysis it was only in the late 1960s that the need for program evaluation was codified, first in federal practice in the requirement to include an evaluation component of federal grant applications. Since then evaluation has become an expected practice in program reviews at all levels. Program evaluation methods have much in common with policy analysis and as such suffers similar limitations, but it is in the differences between analysis to decide what to do (policy analysis) and analysis to determine if things are being done "right" (program evaluation) that affect the utility of evaluation.

The support system for management subprocesses represents a way to understand a set of primarily technical activities that support the management function. Every public manager must be conscious of these activities, although they are performed by others who may have no direct link to the manager. The manager's success is predicated on the ability to make use of these systems. This is not to downplay the interpersonal and leadership skills that are the stock-in-trade of a skilled manager, in fact Part III is devoted to those skills, but understanding the support system provides the opportunity, information, and resources needed to "manage."

Two points in the effective use of these support systems are:

1. The goal of the manager is to know how such processes aid and/or constrain the task of management, and
2. Recognition of the difference between the technical proficiency of the subprocess expert and the understanding needed to properly apply the knowledge acquired from those technically competent individuals

Learning Outcomes

At the conclusion of Part II a student should be able to:

1. Explain what is meant by a management support system.
2. Explain the differences between policy analysis and program evaluation both as functions and as activities.
3. Understand how budget outcomes are influenced by the form of the budget.
4. Define administrative procedures.
5. Explain the difference between formal and informal rulemaking and how those procedures affect management practices.
6. Be able to debate whether policy analysis is art or science.
7. Understand how decades old processes and practices continue to influence practice today, including how it affects the potential for change.
8. Explain the overlapping roles of public sector unions and civil service systems, as well as where those arrangements differ.
9. Understand how to effectively utilize the recruitment and hiring systems to identify the best candidates for a position.

Personnel Practices

The nature of public administration, with its special set of expectations and rewards accruing to public employees, does contribute to making public-sector personnel practice fundamentally different from private-sector personnel management. Most texts in personnel management, both in business and public administration, look at personnel processes as very mechanistic operations. Employees are recruited from a pool of applicants meeting pre-established guidelines. The hiring process is circumscribed by restrictions on information; employment applications as well as interview questions are carefully screened to avoid illegal questioning but to be certain that any bona fide occupational qualification questions are included. The fundamental tenants of personnel practice from this perspective are simplistic. Absenteeism should be reduced; employee turnover is deplored. Hiring is to occur based summarily upon the applicant's "fit" with the requisite knowledge, skills, and abilities (KSAs) as defined in the position classification guidelines. Promotion is to be based on merit. While in most cases, a personnel manager could organize his or her office using this "by-the-book" and somewhat robotic approach, the manager learns nothing of why the employees behave as they do. This approach to personnel management ignores the context in which people work—a critical element to any understanding of public-sector personnel practice.

An alternative view begins its examination of personnel practices from the perspective of how to utilize the contributions of government personnel to achieve the objectives of governance. This more dynamic view of personnel practice places personnel management at the very center of governmental activity. The "government" does not exist independent of its employees. The people who work in government determine, in large part, the kind of government we have. Conversely, government works the way it does because of its personnel systems. This leads to two important ideas. First, our government has changed in the two hundred years since its inception. We can understand these changes more clearly by examining the changes in personnel practice. Secondly, by learning how the personnel system and the government interact, we can both predict and, to some extent, make suggestions that may facilitate more effective governance in the near future.

Public personnel is more than a series of steps or organizational constructs. It is more than recruitment, hiring, retention, job analysis, evaluation, and promotion. It is a cluster of activities that are changing and evolving, with some activities changing more rapidly than others. For example, affirmative action, although a relatively recent development in personnel decision-making, is once again in transition after a series of conservative court decisions from the 1980s through the 2000s. These latest changes reflect both the history of the civil service system as well as a reinvigoration of the notion of representative bureaucracy for the 1990s. Since the beginning of this century the role of personnel administrators in improving and altering organizational performance has become a central feature of personnel departments (since the 1980s governments have mimicked the private sector by changing the name of personnel departments to that of human resource management departments).

Throughout this book we emphasize the importance of understanding history as a prologue to understanding the future. This is no less important in understanding personnel practices. The goal of this chapter is to help you recognize not only what government personnel practice is but also what it is becoming. The necessary first step, then, is to understand where it came from.

PERSONNEL PRACTICE IN THE FOUNDING PERIOD

Our image of the American government of the late eighteenth century as a very small, close-knit club is, in a limited way, correct. The size of the government was small, though it was soon to grow quite significantly. This imagery is deceiving in that it makes it too easy to assume that the tasks of government were so very simple that they could be performed by dilettantes. The core administrative activities of government were conducted by a group of highly educated men (education was more pertinent than wealth) who much like the silversmith or merchant learned the job of government clerk through experience and practice. The clerk moved from apprentice to journeyman to master as in any other craft.

The feature which most distinguished the government official of the period was his commitment to *service* in the government. The institutional arrangements ushered in by the Constitution of 1787 presented the appointed official with the same choices available to those seeking elective office—whether to seek state or national office. (The key to this decision was often a political assessment made by the prospective civil servant as to which level of government he determined was to become most important!) Further, loyalty to the idea of the new American experiment in government was proven by prior service in the Revolutionary War. Politics as ideology rather than as a partisan activity dominated the selection of government officials.

What most distinguished the early government official was the predominance of Revolutionary War veterans. Service in the Revolutionary War was the litmus test of loyalty to the new government (although certainly many who supported the war effort opposed the new Constitution). More to the point was that the loyalty was to the government as a whole, not to any particular individual. It was the great new experiment in governance that bonded the official to government, not merely loyalty to political figures. Thus, even as political parties could develop during the 1790s, loyalty was focused on the government more broadly, not on a person or party (while the term had not yet come into vogue, this may have represented the first understanding of neutral competence).

The nature of the work performed during this period could be summed up as technical and experiential. The government official learned his craft. That these men were highly educated (often with a college degree) was indicative of the kind of work performed. But also, as a craft, the work was more idiosyncratic than routinized.

The personal moral character of the individuals seeking public employment was considered along with any educational, experiential, or ideological qualifications the applicant might present. This work was considered a *calling* (Chart 3–1). In making the choice to serve as a public official, it was likely that the governmental employee would continue to work with persons whom he knew. The cadre of college-trained men was small at that time, and it would not have been unusual to work with a college classmate throughout a career even if some sought elective office and others appointive office. Government was virtually a closed shop in that few had the requisite combination of education, experience, ideological commitment, and desire to commit to a career in public service.

The government officials of the founding period were men set quite apart by experience and training from the general public. Their identification as an aristocratic elite would be somewhat of an overstatement, however. By tradition and experience they were republicans, not democrats, and would have heartily agreed with the Burkean conception of representation as a trusteeship.

By 1800, however, the strong counter-strain in American political thought, which was initially pro-state sovereignty and anti-constitutional, came to prominence during the presidency of Thomas Jefferson. Gradually this viewpoint became more democratic and anti-national government (as opposed to anti-constitutional). With the victory of Andrew Jackson in 1828, this political viewpoint fully displaced the republican perspective. With this fundamental political change came a new perspective on public employment.

CHART 3–1

CHARACTERISTICS OF FEDERAL EMPLOYEES OF 1790S

- Education important for work
- Elite group connected by educational ties
- Fought in Revolutionary War
- Supported new Constitution
- Loyalty to government, not an individual
- Guild approach to work
- Work highly individualized
- Public service as a calling

THE SPOILS SYSTEM

Contemporary American moralism condemns the spoils system of political appointment by the victorious in popular elections. We are so imbued with contemporary ideals of merit that we find the notion of patronage offensive. Indeed, in common parlance, to be "patronized" is considered an insult. Despite the fact that patronage—or the spoils system—is enthusiastically supported in some areas of this country and abroad, our twentieth-century perspective condemns the practice as abhorrent. In the early nineteenth century, however, the spoils system was regarded with great respect. During the federalist period, the personnel system had been based upon personal rather than political connections and was looked upon as vaguely undemocratic. The argument advanced by proponents of political patronage was that the political will of the people had been demonstrated by their electoral preference for one party over another. Political will was thwarted when officeholders of the *losing* party were retained in office.[1] In fact, the spoils system of patronage appointments dominated state-level politics long before the Jackson presidency. While the spoils system would be ultimately exploited by unscrupulous politicians who manipulated growing democratic sentiments in the states, its inception mirrored popular opinion. Just as democracy meant an expanded franchise, political patronage came to mean an expanded opportunity to participate in governance as a public servant. Despite the insistences of later reformers, the spoils system was considered, at the time, as appropriate in a government becoming less republican and more democratic. Thus, the patronage system or "rotation in office" was itself a *reform* measure when introduced by Andrew Jackson.

Jackson justified his position by arguing three main points. First, his policies would give ordinary citizens a greater chance to serve in public office by rotating employees as political fortunes changed. Second, the spoils system permitted Jackson to remove superannuated personnel. These older government employees remained in office far past their useful working careers, protected by family ties and convention. To say the least, their presence reduced effectiveness and limited opportunities for younger personnel to assume positions of responsibility. Finally, the spoils system eliminated the abuses of nepotism (Rohr, 1978, p. 16). William Dickson, writing in 1882, supported Jackson's viewpoint, observing that

> With a reasonable rotation, every citizen of political aspirations and experience . . . may hope to crown his family with the reflected honor which office confers. . . . This is the peerage which the republic offers.
>
> (White, 1958, p. 292)

Jackson also felt that by rotating offices through political appointments the officials would be forced to be more responsive to public interests. If the jobs depended upon the political party and the continuance of the party in office depended upon a satisfied electorate, then the bureaucrats would be forced to accommodate voters' wishes. Jackson also felt that tenure in office was unnecessary because "the duties of all public officers are so plain and simple that men of intelligence may readily qualify themselves for their performances" (White, 1954, p. 30).

The Four-Year Tenure of Office Act, passed in 1820 over the objections of Jefferson and Madison, formed the legal basis for Jackson's rotation in office theory. The action was originally intended to

> educate as many of the people as possible in the business of political life, and to protect them from the usurpations of men habituated in office. It did not apply to the appointive offices of the civil service. By association of ideas, however, rotation in office came to be regarded as an end in itself, and to be regarded as applicable to all offices.
>
> (Fish, 1963, p. 83)

This concept of rotation in office coupled with the use of offices as rewards for party loyalty comprised the spoils system. Rotation in office was not intrinsically evil; it was the abuse of the system that led to the evils of spoils.

While Jackson did not remove more officials than Jefferson or Madison, congressional opposition developed quickly. Jackson's lack of concern for his appointees' fitness for the duties of office led to appointment excesses. This conflict quickly became a partisan battle. An anti-Jackson Congress resisted confirming many of Jackson's appointments.[2] Jackson's poor judgment in his political appointments often got him in trouble. Samuel Swartwout, whose accounts were $210,000 short during his first term as Collector of the Port of New York, was nonetheless renominated by Jackson. After his reappointment he absconded to Europe with over a million dollars of government money (US Civil Service Commission, 1941, p. 22).

The image of political spoils was quickly set in the public mind as corrupt, yet the practice was to persist for decades. After twelve years of Democratic administration, over thirty thousand office seekers deluged Washington during President Harrison's inauguration in 1841. Paradoxically, while Harrison planned a large-scale removal of officials for political reasons, he prohibited political activity by federal employees. The spoils system remained firmly entrenched during the administrations of Tyler, Polk, and Taylor. While Polk removed 13,500 of the nation's 16,000 postmasters, Taylor, in his one year of office, removed over half of the presidential officers and one-third of the total government employees (Hoogenboom, 1968, p. 6).

In 1851, during Millard Fillmore's administration, Congress passed a resolution attempting to remedy some civil service problems by requesting cabinet officers to devise a system for "examination, classification, graded pay, and systematic promotion" (Hoogenboom, 1968, p. 6) for their subordinates. In 1853, Congress passed yet another largely ineffectual measure that did include provisions for examinations. While the examinations were often meaningless, the precedent for civil service examinations was set by the 1853 legislation.

The nadir of the spoils system came with the election of James Buchanan. Buchanan succeeded Pierce, a fellow Democrat, to the Presidency in 1857; yet he ruthlessly removed the Democrats who had supported Pierce for renomination, leading William Marcy to observe plaintively that he never intended to pillage his own camp (Fish, p. 83).

When Lincoln became president in 1861, he was besieged by office seekers. Many claimants were successful; Lincoln made 1,459 of the 1,639 removals within his power (Fish, p. 170). His justification was that to preserve the Union he must preserve the Republican party which in turn could be preserved only by application of the spoils system (Van Riper, 1958, p. 43). However, upon his re-election, Lincoln refused to review his previous appointments, and several prominent historians mark this as the apogee of the spoils system (Fish, p. 172; Van Riper, p. 44).

Some initial steps toward reform were made during Lincoln's administration. In 1863, John Bigelow wrote an evaluation of the French customs service; the report included recommendations for competitive examinations. In 1864, Senator Sumner introduced a civil service reform bill calling for examinations and for promotions based on seniority and merit, but the bill was tabled (Fish, p. 210).

Also, in 1864, Congressman Thomas Jenckes introduced the first of his many bills dealing with civil service reform. This was defeated as were his bills in 1865, 1867, and 1868. The 1868 bill was accompanied by an extensive report on several foreign civil service systems, and it furnished much information to the civil service reform movement (Van Riper, pp. 65–66). In 1871, the first modern civil service legislation was passed as a rider to a civil appropriation bill. It read

> Sec. 9 That the President of the United States be, and he is hereby, authorized to prescribe such rules and regulations for the admission of persons into the civil service of the United States as will best promote the efficiency hereof, and ascertain the fitness of each candidate in respect to age, health, character, knowledge, and ability for the branch of service into which he seeks to enter; and for this purpose the President is authorized to employ suitable persons to conduct said inquiries, to prescribe their duties, and to establish regulations for the conduct of persons who may receive appointments in the civil service.
> (Van Riper, p. 68)

Much to congressional surprise, President Grant acted on the legislation, appointing a seven-man commission with George Curtis, a leading reformer, as chairman. The legislation, which is still in force, is remarkable for three reasons. First, it gives the president an authority over federal personnel management that the president had not had before. Second, it provides a central personnel agency to the government. Third, it provides the president with the first instance of advice and assistance that typifies modern line and staff relationships. The commission finally failed when Congress refused to renew its funding in 1873 and 1874 (Van Riper, pp. 69–71).

Outside the political structure, the reform movement was organizing. In May 1877, the New York Civil Service Reform Association was founded; in 1881, the National Civil Service Reform League was organized. They were both prodigious propagandists; in 1880, 1881, and 1882, the New York Association circulated over half a million documents on reform. They wrote articles, held essay contests, and published magazines (Van Riper, p. 78).

Although President Hayes made some inroads on reform, he personally utilized the patronage system to its fullest. The reformers therefore supported the candidacy of James Garfield. Garfield was assassinated in 1881 by a disappointed office seeker, and Chester Arthur, the deposed collector of the New York Custom House, became president.

The reform organizations immediately publicized the connection between the murder of Garfield and the spoils system. Dorman Eaton declared, "the source and

CHART 3–2

MERIT SYSTEM: PRO AND CON

Senator Hawley said the following during the debate:

> I will not have the responsibility of putting any live, active, good, steady, moral young American into the Government offices in Washington until the service shall stand on a better foundation.
>
> (14 Congressional Record 245 [1882], quoted in Robert Vaughn, *Conflict-of-Interest Regulation in the Federal Executive Branch*, Lexington, Massachusetts: D. C. Heath and Company, 1979, p. 3)

George Washington Plunkett, Tammany district leader, disagreed:

> (Who ran up against civil service examinations?) Isn't it enough to make a man sour on his country when he wants to serve it and won't be allowed unless he answers a lot of fool questions.
>
> (William Riordan, *Plunkett of Tammany Hall*, New York: E.P. Dutton, 1963, pp. 11–12

significance of Guiteau's acts have been found in our spoils system of administration" (Eaton, 1881, p. 148). The reformers at long last had a powerful image and the attention of the public. When coupled with the scandals of Grant's administration and the conviction in 1882 of General Curtis for levying political assessments, the power of the reform movement became the principal issue in the 1882 congressional elections. The Republicans suffered severe reversals in the election. Fear of reprisals if a Democrat became the next president spurred members of Congress to consider a bill already before them. Senator George Pendleton, aided by the New York Civil Service Reform Association, placed a reform bill before the Senate in January 1881.

The proposed civil service examinations came under fire from legislators as well as party bosses on the grounds that examinations are not only elitist but also unrelated to requisite job skills. Civil service reformers successfully rebutted these arguments (Chart 3–2). The House passed the bill without debate, and on January 16, 1883, President Arthur signed the Pendleton Act into law (Van Riper, p. 94). The reformers were equally successful with the states, as Massachusetts and New York quickly followed with state laws creating civil service commissions.

INTRODUCTION OF MERIT SYSTEMS

The Pendleton Act is based largely on the British civil service model. The central concept is appointment by competitive examination, with political neutrality of appointment as a vital corollary. Its provisions for practical tests and for entrance at any level of office are uniquely American. In 1900–1901, fewer than 200 of the 1,477 civil service appointments required more than a secondary school education (White, p. 349). Theodore Roosevelt, a civil service commissioner, tried—and failed—to require cattle inspectors to pass a test on branding, reading, shooting, riding mean horses, and roping and throwing steers (White, p. 350). To guarantee congressional support, Washington offices were awarded to citizens of various states in proportion to the states' population. No more than two members of the same family could hold public office (Van Riper, pp. 98–101).

The Act established a Commission comprised of three full-time members. At first these commissioners were to serve indefinite terms, but in 1956 a system of staggered, renewable six-year terms of office was established. The chief examiner was to administer the system. Minor administrative details were established: A six-month probation for all appointees was put in place, no drunkards could be hired, only references as to character and residence were to be accepted from Senators and Representatives, appointments were to be made from those receiving the highest grades (thus allowing some discretion by the employer), and criminal sanctions were established for corrupt administration of the exam (Van Riper, pp. 103–104).

State laws followed the federal pattern by using a board of commissioners and by emphasizing testing for job entry. In fact, the state laws were often much broader in scope. For example, the new Massachusetts law applied prospectively to all state officials. Thus, within a relatively short period most employees were covered. It required a specific exemption in statute for employees to be left out of the civil service system. In contrast, only about 10 percent of the federal positions were placed in the classified civil service; the remainder was left to be brought under the Act at the president's discretion, and even then, laborers and those whose appointments were subject to congressional approval were exempt. The Pendleton Act is permissive in that immediate and total compliance is not required. The Act does not compel the president either to implement or to enforce it. The proposition was made that perhaps the Act was unnecessary because it did not compel presidential compliance and because the president already had the authority to implement reform under the 1871 Act. The accepted response was that the president could not act effectively without the encouragement of Congress, and in addition, the executive branch lacked the authority to impose criminal sanctions for violation (Van Riper, pp. 104–106).

Because the implementation of the Pendleton Act was at presidential discretion, only later presidents returned some formerly classified civil service positions to the unclassified service and, hence, to spoils politics or classified positions to lock-in political appointees. President Arthur gave his support partly because the Act aided him in the long-standing battle between the presidency and the Congress for control of appointments. In 1884, when Grover Cleveland was elected, Republican Arthur classified approximately 1,200 jobs to save their Republican holders (Van Riper, p. 118).

As the first Democratic president in twenty-four years, Cleveland was hard-pressed by his party for offices. He left the classified service alone; however, he changed half of the jobs in the unclassified system. Cleveland is probably deserving of some sympathy; he confided to a friend, "I am trying to do what is right. I have a hungry party behind me, and they say I am not grateful" (McElroy, 1923, p. 8). Cleveland's actions during his two terms strongly supported the reform issue.

He forced repeal of the Tenure of Office Act of 1867, and when he lost his bid for re-election, he followed Arthur's example and extended the classified system to protect more than five thousand positions. Benjamin Harrison, a Republican, served as president from 1888 to 1892, and his reversions to a spoils system contributed greatly to his loss in 1892 to Cleveland (Van Riper, p. 98–101).

Cleveland's second term of office was marred by his manipulation of the patronage system to gain political advantage on the silver question. However, he included during his administration over thirty-seven thousand positions in the merit system. "By 1896, the bulk of the offices, which it was then either legal or politically and administratively practical to place under the merit system were included, and in many of the rest the spoils system was on the defensive" (Van Riper, p. 130). During the 1896 presidential campaign, civil service reform was no longer a major issue. While the need for reform was not completely obliterated, civil service was an established reality.

The Civil Service Reform Act of 1883 (Pendleton Act) may be seen as the convergence of two major political conflicts: the controversy between the spoils system and the merit system, and the battle between the presidency and the Congress for control of political appointments. The Pendleton Act marked the beginning of today's massive Civil Service Commission, a bureaucracy that is still, almost a hundred years later, refining and defining its ethical and moral responsibilities.

The Civil Service System in the Twentieth Century

The emphasis in the early years of the Civil Service Commission was that of policing the system. In effect, the primary effort was in attempting to force "good" practice. Two key activities of the Commission were attempting to depoliticize the government service and creating and administering selection instruments to promote "merit." The image more than the reality of practice of the "watchdog" Civil Service was to endure into the 1970s. However, the focus of the Civil Service Commission would shift relatively quickly. It is in these changing emphases that the Commission repeatedly ran into political difficulty.

Civil Service and Scientific Management

Shortly after the turn of the century, the Civil Service Commission began an effort to improve management practice. The most important aspect of this change was the pairing of the emerging concepts of the Scientific Management Movement with the processes of hiring, selection, and recruitment already underway at the Commission. From Scientific Management, the Commission borrowed concepts such as chain of command, efficiency, planning, and the "one-best-way" concept of job performance. These ideas fit well with the emerging concern for structuring and classifying positions as a means of ensuring compliance with merit principles. Thus, the Commission came to see its role as threefold:

1. Development of standards of performance
2. A focus on positions not people
3. A classification scheme to control jobs, performance, and pay

Control of the personnel processes of government was ostensibly possible by adherence to a classification scheme that dictated how and what tasks would be performed in an agency. From the perspective of the Civil Service Commission, the success of an agency was achieved through the proper application of the principles of scientific management and the resulting "best-way" performance standards that emerged as part of the classification process (Charts 3–3 and 3–4).

CHART 3–3

Principles of Position Classification

Job analysis determines the key activities and tasks that constitute a job.

Job descriptions outline the skills, competencies, and knowledge necessary to perform the key activities and tasks that result from job analysis.

Position analysis seeks to categorize positions by type of work output, level of responsibility, skill and education required, and complexity of tasks.

Position classification defines the work outputs and activities of the multiple jobs that constitute a position. Classifications are tied together by clusters of related positions.

Pyramid of positions which, taken together, represent the responsibility of an agency.

Salary-based levels set by position classification process. Salary levels are limited, and, therefore, many different types of jobs are assigned the same salary class.

CHART 3–4

Sample Job Description

Audit/Budget Technician I

General Duties: Performs supervisory and above average paraprofessional audit/budget work.

Supervision Received: Works under general guidance and direction of an administrative superior.

Supervision Exercised: Exercises supervision over personnel as assigned.

Examples of Duties

Audit

Examines accounting records, claims, or accounting ledgers to determine accuracy; verifies arithmetic computations, coding entries, funding sources, and legality of entries; makes or initiates procedure to change errors; brings major discrepancies to supervisor's attention; may make reports on audits; may contact individuals to audit or correct audits; may train assigned personnel; may travel and do routine field audits; performs work as required.

Budget

Supervises and assists in the preparation of budget requests submitted by the University to various state agencies; supervises and assists in the preparation of budget forms and other interpretive materials to aid in the preparation of the University budget; supervises and assists in analyzing and monitoring approved budgets and expenditures to maintain budget control; works with accountants in preparing monthly and periodic fiscal reports for specific funds and activities; performs a variety of accounting and auditing tasks of unusual difficulty and other related duties as required; supervises and prepares material for data processing; may operate CRT equipment; makes recommendations for improving methods and procedure for service; carries out details involved in setting up various types of meetings; supervises departmental filing and visitor reception; performs related work as required.

Minimum Qualifications

> *Knowledge*: Working knowledge of accounting and auditing applications, laws, rules, and regulations affecting the related work; accounting principles, office practices, and procedures.
>
> *Skills*: Skill in the use of typewriter, adding machine, and desk calculator.
>
> *Abilities*: Ability to compute arithmetic calculations accurately; interpret and apply laws, rules, and regulations to audits; establish and maintain effective working relationships with associates; communicate with others; keep accurate, complex records.
>
> *Education*: Two (2) year associate degree or equivalent with strong emphasis on courses in accounting and finance.
>
> *Experience*: Six (6) years of progressively more responsible clerical auditing or accounting/bookkeeping experience.
>
> or
>
> Any equivalent combination of education and experience.

From this early emphasis on management, the Commission broadened its control through regulations that defined still more aspects of the work environment. Thus, by the 1930s, the Commission had available an array of regulations to control not only the classification scheme but also training, working conditions, health and safety, and retirement and transfer. The narrow, physical activities focus of scientific management coupled with the control mechanisms put in place by the Commission meant that by the mid-1930s, the federal government's personnel system was rigid, highly structured, and rule-bound.

The Decline of Centralized Control

The civil service system just described was under considerable fire by the late 1930s with three primary concerns dominating the debate. The first was that the watchdog role, now filtered through the scientific management approach, was too limiting for agencies. The second was that the system was insufficiently responsive to the needs of the president.

The President's Committee on Administrative Management (1937), commonly known as the Brownlow Commission, was particularly vigorous in criticizing the Civil Service Commission. In fact, the Brownlow Commission went so far as to suggest replacing the independent Civil Service Commission with a Civil Service Administration whose chief would be appointed by and serve at the pleasure of the president. While this particular notion was not approved by the Congress, controls were shifted from the Civil Service to agencies. Following the recommendations of the Brownlow Commission, Roosevelt issued an executive order mandating personnel offices in all federal agencies.

The slow decline of the Civil Service Commission was to proceed for another thirty years. In 1947, President Truman issued an executive order, which stated in part:

> authority for the conduct of personnel matters within each agency shall be delegated to the extent compatible with provisions of law and economical and efficient administration to those officials responsible for planning, directing and supervising the work of others.

A year later Wallace Sayre (1948) wrote an article for *Public Administration Review* whose title aptly summarized the views of many practitioners and academics: "The Triumph of Technique over Purpose."

The most critical blows were struck by Congress following state legislative practice dating from the 1930s. As new government agencies were created in the 1950s and 1960s, Congress exempted some agencies from the civil service system. In effect each was free to establish its own personnel process and regulatory scheme. In the creation of agencies such as the National Science Foundation, the National Institutes of Health, and the National Cancer Institute, the argument was made that the Civil Service Commission was too slow and too unsophisticated to assist in the hiring of persons with highly technical backgrounds.[3]

The Civil Service Reform Act of 1978

While the duties of the Civil Service Commission were both varied and important, by the late 1970s the political assessment seemed to be that the Commission was an agency with too many jobs; few, if any, of which were being done well. It was in this atmosphere in 1977 that President Carter introduced a set of sweeping changes in the way personnel would be managed in the federal government.

These changes, which were incorporated into the Civil Service Reform Act (CSRA) of 1978, were presented to the public in the context of much anti-bureaucrat rhetoric and the telling of horror stories of a failed system which was touted as slow, inefficient, and contrary to good management practice. The actual content of the new law was an amalgam of virtually every reform proposal proffered for the preceding forty years. There was something for everyone, drawing as it did from the Brownlow Commission, the second Hoover Commission (1955), state practice, and even proposals emerging from the new concerns raised by Watergate.

The law was correctly cited as the most significant change in the civil service system since the Pendleton Act itself. The very scope of the changes was a clear indicator of the decades-long discontent with the old system.

While much of the early attention focused on the obvious structural changes in the law, that is, the abolition of the Civil Service Commission itself, the new law put forth major changes in at least seven areas.

1. The law abolished the Civil Service Commission, reassigning some of its functions to the *Office of Personnel Management* (OPM). The Director of OPM

serves at the pleasure of the president. This change is directly taken from the Brownlow Commission Report.

2. To hear grievances and otherwise ensure the efficiency of the merit system, a *Merit Systems Protection Board* was created. Because this board would be responsible for the watchdog, anti-corruption, anti-politics aspects of the civil service system, it was created as an independent agency with its three members serving staggered seven-year terms.

3. A *Federal Labor Relations Council* was created to perform on behalf of federal employees some of the functions of the National Labor Relations Board.

4. To respond to the problem of the interface between the career bureaucrats and the political appointees at the head of agencies, the law created the *Senior Executive Service* (SES). This group of some nine thousand executives, formerly in the general schedule grades 16, 17, and 18, were to form a cadre of management generalists. In exchange for reduced civil service protection, these individuals could be assigned to work in an agency because their expertise was in management.[4] These individuals were placed in a separate pay plan and expected to compete for bonus monies (up to $10,000 for 3 years) based on performance. The idea of the SES originally was proposed by the Second Hoover Commission and had been in operation in the State of California since the mid-1960s.

4. A second, but much larger, group of bureaucrats were also created. Those mid-level managers (GS13–15), who were also supervisory personnel, were assigned to a new performance appraisal and pay schedule. The intent was that future salaries were to be based on performance of management assignments and tasks. Interestingly, although this system was somewhat similar in intent to the pay-for-performance system for SES, the method of evaluation and potential salary changes were completely different.

5. In response to the post-Watergate concern for higher standards of conduct in government, a provision was included in the law to *protect whistleblowers*. This was to encourage this activity and to ensure that the practice of firing or demoting whistleblowers (as had happened to Ernest Fitzgerald at the Department of Defense) would not continue. Prior to the law, the only recourse for the whistleblower was to take the time, effort, and expense of suing the government in court to get his or her job back. The underlying assumption was that, assured of job protection, far more employees would "blow the whistle" on illegal or unethical behavior by colleagues.

6. The least publicized but possibly most significant long-term change achieved by the law was the incorporation into law of definition of "*merit principles.*" The problem that is likely to be encountered with this codification is precisely the problem that existed prior to the law. While most agree with all aspects of the definition of merit when viewed separately, the reality is that in practice some aspects of the definition are incomparable and even contradictory. This is the result of the "pure" nature of the definition without regard to the fact that the American-style merit system has never been a pure system but has always been a blend of purist goals and practice built around exceptions. This was a true in the 1890s when only 10 or 15 percent of federal employees were included in the merit system—but veterans were given preference—as it is today when problems of racial and gender discrimination (among others)

CHAPTER 3 Personnel Practices

require hiring techniques that may discourage the hiring of the most "advantaged." The system has always been a blend of social policy and meritocracy. The codification of merits principles includes these contradictions rather than confronting them.

The significance of the CSRA may well be in the process of changes that result from the definition of merit rather than in the structural changes it introduced. The burden for reconciling the process with other laws and even the Constitution rests with the US Supreme Court. In its delineation of the rights and duties of public employees, the Court has played an increasingly significant role for four decades or more. That task is not complete; numerous questions, particularly those that are raised by the codification of merit, will not be settled until late in this century (Chart 3–5).

PERSONNEL PRACTICE

To this point, this chapter has looked to the past; focusing on the dominant ideas that have shaped personnel policy. Now we turn to an examination of current personnel practice, taking particular note of the interplay of past policies that help shape contemporary practice. The specific practices that are to be examined are job analysis, recruitment and selection, performance appraisal, training, and pay.

Job Analysis

How do we know what kinds of persons to hire? This apparently straightforward question is not particularly easy to answer. We hire people to do a "job." But how

---

CHART 3–5

Merit Principles as Defined by CSRA of 1978

Recruitment from all segments of society

Selection and advancement based on ability, knowledge, and skills, under fair and open competition

Fair and equitable treatment without regard to politics, race, color, religion, sex, handicap, marital status, and so on

Equal pay for work of equal value

High standards of integrity and conduct

Efficiency and effectiveness

Retention of employees who perform well, correction of performance of those who do not, termination for those who cannot meet standards

Improve performance through training and education

Protection from arbitrary action, favoritism, or political coercion

Protection for whistleblowers

did the job get created? That job was created because someone (or more likely some group) analyzed and examined the tasks assigned to an organization, then broke down those tasks into discrete activities. When the analysis has reduced the task into manageable clusters of similar activities, those activities are designated as a job.

This particularistic description is only the first step in actual practice. Job analysis extends beyond the behaviors and activities associated with the performance of a particular job to include the skills, knowledge, and responsibilities needed to be successful in that job (Bureau of Intergovernmental Personnel Programs, 1973). The information gathered about the work activities that constitute a job and the skills associated with those activities put job analyses at the core of personnel practice (Chart 3–6). The job analysis serves as the foundation of a position classification and pay scheme by relating and grouping jobs. Additionally, the job analysis is the organizing structure of all recruitment, selection, and training activities (US Office of Personnel Management, 1979).

CHART 3–6

How Job Analysis Contributes to Personnel Practice

1. *Preparation of Job Descriptions*: A complete description contains a job summary, the job duties and responsibilities, and some indication of the working conditions.
2. *Writing Job Specifications*: The job specification describes the individual traits and characteristics required to perform the job well.
3. *Recruitment*: Job analysis information is useful when searching for the right person to fill the job. It helps recruiters find and seek the type of people that will contribute to and be comfortable with the organization.
4. *Selection*: The final selection of the most qualified people requires information on what job duties and responsibilities need to be performed. This type of information is provided in the job description.
5. *Performance Evaluation*: The evaluation of performance involves comparison of actual versus planned output. Job analysis is used to acquire an idea of acceptable levels of performance for a job.
6. *Training and Development*: Job analysis information is used to design and implement training and development programs. The job description provides information on what skills and competencies are required to perform the job. Training and development work is then conducted to satisfy these skill and competency requirements.
7. *Career Planning and Development*: The movement of individuals into and out of positions, jobs, and occupations is a common procedure in organizations. Job analysis provides clear and detailed information to those considering such a career movement.
8. *Compensation*: The total job is the basis for estimating its worth. Compensation is usually tied to a job's required skill, competencies, working conditions, safety hazards, and so on. Job analysis is used to compare and properly compensate jobs.
9. *Safety*: The safety on a job depends upon proper layout, standards, equipment, and other physical conditions. What a job entails, and the type of people needed also contribute information to establish safe procedures. Of course, this information is provided by job analysis.
10. *Job Design*: Job analysis information is used to structure and modify the elements, duties, and tasks of specific jobs.

CHAPTER 3 Personnel Practices

CHART 3–7

Position Audit Questionnaire: Name_____

Department _____

Job Title_____

Position Classification_____

There are four elements of any job that are crucial to understanding the nature and complexity of that job. Those elements are:

- Knowledge required
- Skills employed
- Abilities demonstrated
- The setting/environment in which work is performed

The questions that follow are designed to establish the relationship of this job to the other jobs in your department and to comparable jobs in other departments. The more information you provide the more accurate the analysis.

1. What is the level of education required to perform this job?

    GED/High School diploma   _____
    Certifications   _____
    Associates degree   _____
    Bachelors degree   _____
    Graduate degree   _____

2. Other specialized coursework or degrees needed to perform the job?

    _____

    _____

3. How would you classify this job in terms of experience required? (NOT how much you have, but how much you needed to get the job originally)

    Entry Level   _____
    Early Career (1–4 years)   _____
    Mid-Career (5–10 years)   _____
    Senior (10+ years)   _____

4. What words best describe the level of skill and competence required to perform this job?

    Limited Skills/Apprentice   _____
    Certified/Journeyman   _____
    Specialized/Master   _____
    Professional   _____
    Interdisciplinary   _____

5. What are the central elements (practices, activities, responsibilities) of this job?

    _____

    _____

    _____

_____

_____

6. What specific skills or competences must you have to perform this job?

_____

_____

_____

_____

_____

7. What are the key tasks that you perform on this job?

_____

_____

_____

_____

8. What level of responsibility do you have in your job?

Non-supervisory	_____
Supervisory	_____
Managerial	_____
Policy	_____

9. What are the unique features of this job, which require the greater exercise of responsibility than may be apparent?

_____

_____

_____

_____

_____

10. Which work arrangement best represents your relationship to your co-workers (check only one)?

Dependent	_____
Interdependent	_____
Independent	_____
Autonomous	_____

11. Which of the following terms best describes your work relationship with your supervisor (select no more than two)?

Directs	_____
Controls	_____
Coaches	_____
Mentors	____
Supports	_____
Delegates	_____

70 | CHAPTER 3 Personnel Practices

12. With whom and how frequently do you have interaction with others in the day-to-day in order to perform your assigned work?

    Co-workers   Almost never ___ Infrequently ___ Often ___ Constantly ___

    Citizens   Almost never ___ Infrequently ___ Often ___ Constantly ___

    Mid-level managers Almost never __ Infrequently __ Often ___ Constantly ___

    Senior managers Almost never ___ Infrequently ___ Often ___ Constantly ___

    Elected officials Almost never ___ Infrequently ___ Often ___ Constantly ___

13. Are there other features of your job that make it different or unique?

    _____

    _____

    _____

    _____

    I certify that the above descriptions and statements are accurate.

    _____

    Signature   Date

SUPERVISOR'S Review:

Name of employee   _____

Department   _____

Job Title   _____

Position Classification   _____

1. What is the level of education required to perform this job?

   GED/High School diploma   ____

   Certifications   ____

   Associates degree   ____

   Bachelors degree   ____

   Graduate degree   ____

2. Other specialized coursework or degrees needed to perform the job?

   _____

   _____

3. How would you classify this job in terms of experience required?

   Entry Level   ____

   Early Career (1–4 years)   ____

   Mid-Career (5–10 years)   ____

   Senior (10+ years)   ____

4. What words best describe the level of skill and competence required to perform this job?

   Limited Skills/Apprentice   ____

   Certified/Journeyman   ____

Specialized/Master   _____
Professional   _____
Interdisciplinary   _____

5. What specific skills or competences must an employee have to perform successfully in this job?

_____

_____

_____

_____

_____

6. What level of responsibility do you have in your job?
Non-supervisory   _____
Supervisory   _____
Managerial   _____
Policy   _____

7. What are the unique features of this job, which require the greater exercise of responsibility that may not be apparent?

_____

_____

_____

_____

8. Which work arrangement best represents the relationship of this employee to co-workers?
Dependent   _____
Interdependent   _____
Independent   _____
Autonomous   _____

9. Which of the following terms best describes your work relationship with the employee (select no more than two)?
Directs work   _____
Controls priorities   _____
Teacher/Coach   _____
Mentor   _____
Assigns, then delegates   _____

10. With whom and how frequently does this employee interact with others in the day-to-day in order to perform your assigned work?
Co-workers   Almost never ___ Infrequently ___ Often ___ Constantly ___
Yourself   Almost never ___ Infrequently ___ Often ___ Constantly ___
Citizens   Almost never ___ Infrequently ___ Often ___ Constantly ___
Mid-level managers   Almost never __ Infrequently __ Often __ Constantly __

Senior managers Almost never ___ Infrequently ___ Often ___ Constantly ___
Elected officials Almost never ___ Infrequently ___ Often ___ Constantly ___

11. Are there other features of the job that make it different or unique?

_____

_____

_____

_____

I certify that the above description of the job is accurate

_____

Signature   Date

None of the above activities in Chart 3–7 would be possible in the modern context without the information generated by a job analysis. In the effort to define jobs in a manner that is unrelated to the person in the job (what are the activities and skills needed for the job, not what does the person in the job do), job analysis is the key to any attempt at achieving "neutral competence." The position classification scheme is based almost completely in the job analysis process. Closely related to position classification and, therefore, job analysis is job evaluation. This process is an attempt to distinguish among jobs (or more likely job classes) for the purposes of pay. The controversy over comparable worth is the result of a challenge to the way job evaluations are performed (i.e., that there is bias in the grouping of jobs for pay purposes). Those governments that have sought to confront this problem often have been required to reconstruct the job analysis to ensure that principles of neutrality (no bias) exist in the categorization of the jobs and classes of jobs.

The link between job analysis and recruitment, selection, and training are still more obvious. The description of the skills and competencies necessary to perform a task that is one end result of the job analysis can easily be converted into a job description. The job description in turn serves as the basis for determining who should get a job (recruitment and selection) or what specialized skills are necessary before the job is undertaken (training).

Recruitment and Selection

We have discussed the process of defining and creating jobs so that the government may get on with the task of serving the public. The next step is to find the person with the necessary skills and competencies to perform those jobs. The recruitment and selection of government employees has long been the most controversial and political personnel endeavor. Not surprisingly, most of the reform efforts of the past have focused on the hiring process. Who the government hires is a very clear statement of political and social policy. Whether the choice is a Federalist or Anti-Federalist in 1790, a "party man" in 1840, or a minority in 2010, the process of hiring creates a workforce that reflects society in its political, economic, and social character. The type of person sought dominated the recruitment and selection processes throughout the nineteenth century. Performance appraisal can be restated as a series of questions: What qualities are we now recognizing, rewarding, and developing in employees? What messages are we conveying to individuals about their behaviors, skills, and attitudes? What ideal qualities do we wish to see developed and enhanced in our employees, for historically, the jobs performed in government could be made relatively simple through division of labor (remember Jackson's dictum that no government job should be beyond the capability of any American). Certainly, by the progressive era (although arguably by the Civil War period), many government tasks were too complex for persons without specific skills and education. Second is the product of performance in the job. The concern was not willingness to serve but capacity to serve. Whereas the nineteenth-century concern was to find people to fill government jobs (i.e., recruitment), the twentieth-century concern was to match the skills of the recruit to the demands of the job (i.e., selection).

The shift to emphasis on selection has caused other problems in the hiring process. Our modern understanding of objective, merit-based selection is based on assumptions of the neutral objectivity of the selection process (including the job analysis and position classification scheme). But what happens if that objectivity is lacking, or if this pursuit of objectivity produces results that are politically or socially undesirable? These questions are the core of the problem in political controversies over equal employment, affirmative action, and comparable worth (issues to be discussed later).

How does bias, or lack of objectivity, slip into the selection process? Such bias occurs in two ways. First, bias may be the product of the conscious or unconscious beliefs of those in decision-making positions (discrimination). The difficulties of minorities in getting hired into government have been attributed to such bias. The other problem of bias is in the nature of the selection process itself.

This latent form of bias is often the product of human nature. We are limited in our knowledge of how to connect selection processes such as examinations and interviews to successful performance in the job. This problem is one of validity: "The key dimension to validity is job relatedness. Job relatedness means essentially that the criteria being measured in the test [selection instrument] are relevant and significant factors in the jobs for which selection decisions are to be made" (Shafritz, Hyde, and Rosenbloom, 1986, pp. 428–429). Also, we are limited by the idiosyncrasies of the selection process. Thus, for example, interviews during the selection process can be biased by factors such as the timing of the interview, the character of the other interviews, or the bias of interviewers based on appearance or background. In some instances, these forms of bias are conscious, although more typically they are unconscious. This difficulty is exacerbated because such unconscious forms of bias cannot be eliminated. The only way to deal with such a difficulty is to multiply the numbers of selection processes to counteract such biases. Thus, for example, if interviews are part of the process of selection, the appropriate practice is to have more than one person conduct interviews to eliminate whatever bias (unconscious) may exist with each individual who serves as an interviewer (Chart 3–8).

CHART 3–8

Selection Instruments

Application forms
Letters of recommendation
Interviews
Intelligence tests
Psychological tests
Physical tests
Simulations

Performance Appraisal

The purpose and goal of performance appraisal is periodically to evaluate the performance of the individual. Such evaluations can be used to determine training needs, pay, or promotion. Performance appraisals are intended as a major input in determining career directions and opportunities for employees. Yet such efforts are beset by numerous problems.

Few problems have been as vexing to personnel administrators as that of performance appraisal. Certainly, it is the most maligned area of personnel and in many cases seems to be tolerated only because no one can think of any realistic, better alternatives. At stake is a process that should control the development and growth of the organization itself. Performance appraisal can be restated as a series of questions: What qualities are we now recognizing, rewarding, and developing in employees? What messages are we conveying to individuals about their behaviors, skills, and attitudes? And what ideal qualities do we wish to see developed and enhanced in our employees for the accomplishment of our future objectives (Ivancivich and Glueck, 1983, p. 244)?

The performance appraisal process is central to a merit-based personnel system. Yet that relationship is keyed on the development of a relevant, unbiased, significant, and practical performance appraisal process. These limitations are as often a product of human nature as deficiencies are in the process. Shafritz, Hyde, and Rosenbloom (1986) assess those defects as follows:

1. Appraisals tend to be subjective, impressionistic, and noncomparable
2. The standards of some raters are much tougher than those of other raters
3. Rating may be more a test of the writing skills of the rater than of the performance of the employee
4. Goals of performance analysis and potential in future positions may conflict
5. Lack of credibility and fairness in ratings

(pp. 434–436)

The two key problems for the future are to improve the training of supervisors and managers so that they use the appraisal process more properly and to improve the managerial system to restore the credibility of ratings.

Personnel Practice **75**

CHART 3–9

The University of Akron

Classification Specification

Job Title:	Administrative Assistant	Job Code:	41311
Job Function:	Staff	Grade:	116
Job Family:	Classified	FLSA:	Non-Exempt
SOC Description:	1000 Administrative Support Division	Date:	1/1/04; 9/14/01; 7/1/99

Job Summary:

Provides assistance to supervisors in the administration of departmental programs or activities. Directs daily office operations pertaining to departmental programs and procedures. Relieves supervisors of routine and some non-routine administrative duties.
Exercises independent judgment in resolving issues or concerns related to departmental policies and procedures.

Essential Functions:

10%–40% Researches, collects, and interprets data for the purpose of providing information to others, developing programs, making recommendations, and preparing materials. Evaluates programs, provides input in the decision-making process, and administers new policies and programs.

10%–25% Maintains highly confidential personnel files and payroll records. Tracks available positions, compiles information for job descriptions, new job openings, and employee searches. Interprets policies/procedures and transmits decisions and directives for the benefit of support staff, faculty, and student assistants.

15%–40% Maintains calendars, organizes meetings, coordinates special events and travel arrangements, and composes correspondence. Updates and manages computer databases and file systems. Utilizes software packages and computer applications to create spreadsheets and documents for the completion of projects.

5%–15% Monitors budgets, establishes start-up accounting procedures, and manages or closes out special accounts for the department. Researches products, vendors, and prices to properly appropriate funds for the purchase of equipment and supplies.

5%–10% Coordinates public relations activities for the purpose of responding to inquiries and complaints, furnishing information to the public, and providing explanations. Acts as a liaison between the department and the university community.

5%–15% Assigns, trains, supervises, and reviews the work of designated clerical support personnel and student assistants.

Education:

Requires 18 months of education or training beyond high school.

Licenses/Certifications/Requirements:

None.

Experience:

Requires a minimum of 4 years experience in office/clerical procedures. Ability to coordinate programs, work in a fast paced environment, and utilize new technology required. Advanced computer skills including word processing, spreadsheet, and database software packages required. Strong interpersonal, problem-solving, and research skills required.

> **Leadership:**
> Functional guidance over nonexempt staff including general scheduling, assigning tasks and monitoring work activities.
>
> **Physical Requirements:**
> Job is physically comfortable; individual is normally seated and has discretion about walking, standing, etc. May occasionally lift very lightweight objects.
>
> **Working Conditions:**
> No major sources of working conditions discomfort, standard working environment with possible minor inconveniences due to occasional noise, crowded working conditions, minor heating/cooling or ventilation problems, and/or up to 40 percent use of PC terminal.
> The intent of this classification specification is to provide a representative summary of the types of duties and responsibilities that will be required of positions given this title and shall not be construed as a declaration of the specific duties and responsibilities of any particular position. Employees may be requested to perform job-related tasks other than those specifically presented in this description. The University requires that all University employees whose assigned duties include some involvement with The University of Akron's intercollegiate athletics program, comply with all relevant NCAA Bylaws in performing their work.
>
> Source: University of Akron 2004

Training

One of the uses of performance appraisal is to determine the training and developmental needs of the employee. Approaches to training have varied widely over the years. Often there has been a tendency to reject training as unnecessary, since the employee should have had the requisite skills to perform the job when hired. This attitude has contributed greatly to the tendency to cut training funds first when fiscal problems emerge.

In the last two decades the role of training has expanded. First was the recognition that if minorities were to have a chance at employment, pre-employment and promotion enhancement training programs were needed. Second, the approach to jobs that suggests that all the skills that will be needed should be acquired before hiring has been replaced by the recognition of the changing character of many jobs. Training has become a career-long need, even for those who remain in a single field for their entire work life. Third, training has emerged as a way to enhance the skills of those in the job to improve the quality as well as productivity of the work performed. Finally, training and development have been promoted as a way to enhance career goals and long-range job prospects.

Innovative ideas in training and career development are symbolized by such efforts as the creation of the Federal Executive Institute to foster better management performance. The effort to create skill- and competency-based management certification programs in such states as Georgia and Arizona reflects a commitment to training as a central feature of a broad-gauged personnel development program. While some still view training as a waste of money and therefore an appropriate starting point for budget cutting, others have recognized that success in attracting and keeping skilled public-sector employees is based in part in responding to the needs of those employees to hone the skills necessary to perform well now and to develop the skills to undertake all future challenges on the job.

Pay

One of the great myths of personnel management is that pay is the key personnel motivator. Public personnel practice has suffered greatly from a schizophrenic tendency to use pay, and then not use pay, as the way to produce better performance. The result has been to create the worst of all possible worlds: Salaries are low, and good performance does not yield higher pay.

The primary concern in creating public employee pay systems has been equity. While equity can be thought of as having both internal and external components, the focus has most often been on internal equity. Linking pay to the position classification scheme, the emphasis on longevity of service, rather than performance, and the effort to ensure stability of income all reflect the concern for internal equity. These efforts at internal equity are not without difficulty, particularly where they are linked to position classification, job analysis, and performance appraisal processes, which themselves may be deficient. Politically controversial problems such as comparable worth emerge because of defects in the job analysis process that are reflected in the pay scheme rather than in the pay scheme itself. Also, the highly questionable validity and fairness of performance appraisal processes lead many to overemphasize longevity in the job for pay raises, and this discourages superior performance.

Concern about external equity similarly creates controversy. External equity refers to the salaries paid to public employees relative to that paid to private-sector employees or other public employees with similar jobs. The central problem is that of the appropriateness of many such comparisons. Should, for example, the salaries of police officers in San Diego, Atlanta, and Indianapolis be the same? Are the jobs of police officers and private security guards the same? Is the job of a middle manager in the Department of Defense handling contracts worth millions comparable to that of a manager in a regional grocery chain? These questions are difficult to answer. At a minimum, an emphasis on comparability results emphasizes average increases and average salary structures. Differences of skills and competencies and differences of circumstances disappear in this process of averaging.

Another concern about compensation concerns the structure of the pay scheme. In personnel systems that are not founded on merit, the pay scheme is based on perception of performance and possible connections. Merit-based systems link salaries to the position classification system. Typically merit systems also rely on a salary matrix that provides for increases within a grade for longevity. Under such a system, each position has a salary range designated for it. The employee progresses through the salary range based on performance and longevity (see Chart 3–1).

The above pay structures make assumptions about pay that are not always accurate. While the public sector generally is better than the private sector, nevertheless, there are concerns about the inequality of pay for men and women. This problem comes in two forms: the refusal to pay a woman the same salary as a

CHART 3–10

Position and Salary Grade Classifications

Grade Position Class Title

1 Administrative Support
2 Operations Support/Project Support
3 Technical Support/Operations Specialist/Research Support
4 Administrative Support Specialist/Technical Support Specialist/Researcher-Investigator
5 Administrative Support Supervisor/Citizen Support Supervisor/Technical Support Supervisor
6 Office Administrator/Technical Administrator/Project Leader/Manager/Policy Analyst
7 Project Administrator/Program Specialist/Policy Specialist
8 Senior Technical Support/Program Manager/Project Manager
9 Services Administrator/Legal Services
10 Administrative Bureau Chief
11 Technology Services Bureau Chief/Deputy Administrator/Legal Specialist
12 Division Director
13 Senior Policy and Management Specialist
14 Department Administrator
15 Executive Department Administrator/Executive Staff Administrator

Source: Summit County, Ohio, 2002

man when they perform the same job and the offering to men of higher salaries for jobs of similar complexity and responsibility. The Equal Pay Act of 1963 specifically outlawed the first form of discrimination, although controversies about the continuation of the practice remain. The second issue—equal pay for similar or comparable work—has become increasingly controversial. The Equal Pay Act did not offer protection from the latter form of discrimination. However, comparable worth challenges have been argued relying on the Civil Rights Act of 1964 and the equal protection clauses of the Fifth and Fourteenth amendments. Also, it can be assumed that the inclusion of a statement on equal pay for work of equal value as part of the statement on merit principles under the CSRA offers adequate protection for federal employees.

The only time the courts have confronted the matter concerned state employees in Washington. That decision, *American Federation of State, County, and Municipal Employees (AFSCME) v. Washington State* (1981), heard in the US District Court for the Western District of Washington, affirmed protection for women paid lower salaries than men for what were essentially similar jobs. The major problem uncovered by this case was the presence of pay discrimination by the creation of job titles that were in practice gender specific and therefore institutionalized the disparity in pay (Chart 3–11).

The problem in Washington State was for all intents and purposes the product of conscious choice. The more difficult and insidious problem is the conscious and unconscious bias in position analysis and evaluation that leads to a consistent undervaluing of jobs predominantly performed by women. Recognizing that a major reason for the existence of pay discrimination was the failure to do proper position evaluations, the state of Minnesota required that all applicable public positions be re-evaluated and re-classified as a necessary step toward ensuring pay equity when it mandated comparable worth.

The final concern about pay is whether or not it is, in reality, a motivator. A number of analysts suggest that pay is, at best, a temporary satisfier. Others also suggest that other factors, such as a sense of accomplishment, may be as important as pay. Finally, it is generally accepted that a broad-based perception among civil servants that public-sector salaries are too low is a source of dissatisfaction. Salaries are inevitably problematic. In an environment where the general public regards civil salaries as too high, but the public-sector employees see themselves as underpaid, controversy is bound to ensue.

CHART 3–11

Who Is Worth More?

The problem of comparable worth is most difficult to root out when it is the result of long-standing bias or "type-casting." Thus, the position analysis that helps set salaries is biased by unwarranted assumptions about the gender of the worker. Thus, a job that is performed by a woman is frequently given low marks on independence and responsibility because of a cultural bias that indicates that women be given orders. Jobs that require no more independence or responsibility, but which are performed by men are rated higher. Ask yourself, who is more responsible—a secretary or a garbage collector? Who must demonstrate more independent thinking and exercise discretion—a nurse or a chauffeur? Despite how you might answer, these jobs are not classified to reflect that answer. This reflects cultural biases that are at least partly unconscious, and *that* is the *problem*. Even re-analysis and re-evaluation will not always resolve this difficulty because few of us even recognize that we are being discriminatory.

Try this exercise:

> Rate on a scale of 1–10 the following skills and competencies for these jobs:
> Garbage collector (non-driver), Secretary-typist (Word processor certified)
> Educational level (no more than 4 GED, 7 for college degree)
> Specialized knowledge
> Specialized skill
> Independence in every day work (no more than 2 if closely supervised, 5 if loosely supervised)
> Discretionary judgment permitted
> Complexity of assignment
> Requirements of working with others
> Physical demands of job:

Which job scored higher? Which job do you think is more highly paid?

CONTINUING ISSUES AND CONCERNS

This section focuses on the concerns of academics and practitioners as we work together to change personnel practice in the future. Although there are a myriad of issues to choose from in summing up the state of current research, three are particularly relevant to this discussion. Those issues are the relationship between the ideal of neutral competence and the reality of the role of the modern government bureaucrat; the problem of affirmative action and the representativeness of the bureaucracy; and performance measurement.

Political Neutrality

Herbert Kaufman suggested that the three cornerstones of public personnel administration are executive leadership, representativeness, and neutral competence. The changing understanding of personnel practice largely is based on the emphasis of one of these three cornerstones. The core concept of the civil service reform movement of the late nineteenth century represented a renewed emphasis on neutral competence and, somewhat, the rejection of executive leadership (at least to the extent it embodied "spoils").

In the last two decades of the twentieth century the centrality of neutral competence has been challenged. First, in the 1970s, the advocates of the "New Public Administration" chose to emphasize representativeness. Thus, the bureaucrat was to be a policy advocate who exercised independent judgment and who struck a pro-client attitude in the management of operations. The ideal was the model of the street-level bureaucrat who knew very well the problems of his "clients" and exercised any available organizational discretion on their behalf. The bureaucrat became the representative of these groups, advocating programs for them before the central administration. The emphasis on the concept of the bureaucracy as the "fourth branch" of government also distanced this group from the philosophical advocacy of executive helped reinforce the importance of the concept of neutral competence. Thus, on the one hand, the advocates of the new public administration sought policy activists who would use the power of government to help the "underclass" and, on the other hand, sought advocates of a view that partisan politics must be held at arms' length. The classic British civil service model of neutrally and unbiasedly implementing the law regardless of personal views was upheld. Government thus was both the problem and the solution to social and economic difficulties.

The late 1970s and the early years of the 1980s brought a reaction to the new public administration. The work of politically conservative think tanks such as the Heritage Foundation sought to re-emphasize executive leadership as the core concept in personnel management. This group linked itself to the concepts of the bureaucracy of the 1930s, when an earlier generation of academics sought to reshape the bureaucracy in support of a president whom they agreed with politically and ideologically. This viewpoint (in contrast to the 1930s efforts) explicitly rejects as an impossibility the concept of neutral competence. The "proper" role of the bureaucrat is to seek the interests of the president, not to execute the laws if a conflict exists between policy and the law. This attitude about law is derived from the effort to distinguish between statutory enactments and regulations. Statutory enactment and regulations must be obeyed, although the president has considerable discretion as to how to implement the statute. Regulations are deemed nothing more than the embodiment of the discretionary choices of prior administrations. For a bureaucrat to continue to enforce regulations created by prior administrations is defiance of the president. The keys to understanding this perspective are, first, to recognize the fundamental assumption that bureaucracy is not a fourth independent branch but merely an extension of the president and his or her policies and, next, to accept the idea that neutral competence is meaningless; and, therefore, only obeisance to executive leadership can serve as the cornerstone of personnel management and practice.

ONGOING AND EMERGING ISSUES

Affirmative Action

Representativeness as a goal for personnel management is most clearly indicated by the efforts to change the racial, ethnic, and gender composition of the workforce. One indicator chosen to indicate the "representativeness" of the workforce is whether the relative percentage of any minority group in the workforce approximates the percentage of that group in the total population. This quantitative approach to defining representativeness has yielded mixed results over the years. Only the federal government has achieved anything close to this hiring pattern. Frequently it has only been decisions of the Supreme Court or regulatory efforts of the Equal Employment Opportunity Commission (EEOC) that have moved the private sector and state and local government to seek such a representative workforce.

The statutory bases for most governmental efforts in employment are the Civil Rights Act of 1964 and the Fair Employment Practices Act. Relying on these laws and their prohibitions against discrimination was a significant step, but it had limited impact on the actual practice of recruitment and selection. The EEOC, therefore, took the step of developing regulations that required public and private employers to make a considerable effort toward redressing the lack of representativeness in the workforce. Thus, a rather significant shift in the government policy occurred. Rather than merely seeking out those who discriminate in hiring, the government was mandating that positive and concrete actions be undertaken to avoid the possibility of discrimination. This policy, known as affirmative action, has succeeded in stopping the most blatant forms of discrimination in hiring and promotion.

Affirmative action has always been controversial because of its emphasis on redressing past practice by altering current decisions. Those who challenge affirmative action point out that many who are hired under such programs have never experienced discrimination. They argue that only individuals who have specifically experienced discrimination should be protected (i.e., through the courts, not regulations). Supporters of affirmative action point out that discrimination occurs because of bias against groups of persons; therefore, redress to protect groups is proper. Further, affirmative action programs, as endorsed by the US Supreme Court, do not deny anyone a job but merely prevent a person from being denied a job for highly inappropriate reasons—the color of the person's skin, the person's age, or the person's gender (Chart 3–12).

Affirmative action has been politically controversial since its introduction in the late 1960s. The issue has become increasingly partisan and ideological. An

82 | **CHAPTER 3** Personnel Practices

CHART 3–12

Key Issues in Employment Discrimination

Affirmative Action. A plan or program to remedy the effects of past discrimination in employment, education, or other activity and to prevent its recurrence. Various federal and state statutes require affirmative action to redress past discrimination against racial or religious minorities, women, and, to some extent, the aged and the handicapped. Affirmative action usually involves a work-force utilization analysis, the establishment of goals, and timetables to increase use of underrepresented classes of persons, explanation of methods to be used to eliminate discrimination and establishment of administrative responsibility to implement the program. Good faith and a positive effort to remedy past discrimination must also be shown. Affirmative action is required by law or regulation for all governmental agencies and for recipients of public funds, such as contractors and universities. Affirmative action is to be distinguished from antidiscrimination or equal opportunity laws, which forbid unequal treatment rather than requiring positive corrective measures. In 1978, the Supreme Court held that affirmative action programs are valid, but that elicit racial quotas are prohibited (*Regents of the University of California v. Bakke*, 438 U.S. 265).

Significance. Affirmative action is supported by those who argue that some form of preferential treatment is essential to break down long-standing patterns of discrimination against minorities and women so that employment patterns will more accurately reflect the pluralistic nature of American society. Such action, it is believed, will strengthen confidence in public and private institutions. Critics of affirmative action claim that it constitutes "reverse discrimination," and whatever the merits of preferential treatment, the result will be to deny equality of opportunity based on merit. A 1984 decision of the Supreme Court, *Firefighters Local Union No. 11783 v. Stotts* (104 S. Ct. 2576) held that in the case of layoffs, affirmative action considerations cannot override valid seniority systems unless the results adversely affect specific victims of discrimination. In general, the courts have not upset established practices unless some discriminatory purpose is found, or the impact of the practice clearly favors one group.

In the early part of this century a movement to extend job protection rights in hiring and promotion for those in the "LGBTQ" community began to gain traction. Some states and numerous large cities extended the definition of protected class under it EEO and Affirmative Action rules. An interesting political dynamic in this effort was the effort to change laws regarding the definition of who could marry. While still controversial a combination of successful court challenges and the enacted of state laws changing the laws on marriage seemed to create a rapid shift in public perception. For some communities (including my own while I was on the Akron City Council), the issues of job protection, but more critically, fringe benefits for city workers came up. In 2009, this was still viewed as quite controversial. By today (2018), it has become accepted practice. . . .

Fair Employment Practices Laws. Laws that forbid private and/or public employers, labor unions, or employment agencies to discriminate in hiring or in other personnel policies on the grounds of race, color, creed, or national origin. More than thirty states have enacted such laws. In the Civil Rights Act of 1964, Congress provided for equal employment opportunities in businesses and labor unions engaged in interstate commerce. Equal treatment for women is also required by the Act. Later legislation forbids discrimination in employment because of age (Age Discrimination Act of 1967) or handicap (Rehabilitation Act of 1973).

Significance. Fair employment laws represent positive governmental action in the field of private rights, in contrast to the traditional concept of civil liberties as a restraint against government. Both the national and state laws stress education and conciliation, although several state laws provide criminal sanctions. The national law encourages state action in this field. For a number of years, presidential executive orders had prohibited racial discrimination in public employment and by government contractors. Increasingly, challenges to racial and sexual discrimination have made their way through administrative agencies and courts. Where discrimination is found, awards of back pay and seniority have been made (*Albermarle Paper Co. v. Moody*, 422 U.S. 405 [1975]; *Franks v. Bowman Transportation Co.*, 424 U.S. 747 [1976])....

Reverse Discrimination. Preferential treatment that favors a previously victimized minority to the disadvantage of the majority. Specifically, reverse discrimination refers to programs designed to redress past discrimination against women, blacks, or other minorities that result in depriving Caucasian men and/or women of benefits or opportunities that they would otherwise obtain. In 1978, the Supreme Court held in *Regents of the University of California v. Bakke* (438 U.S. 265) that affirmative action programs are valid, but that explicit racial quotas are prohibited.

Significance. Proponents of preferential treatment for minorities argue that the attainment of socially desirable goals (e.g., more black doctors, more women lawyers) is more important than the application of criteria which the minority cannot meet because of past discrimination. Opponents fear any classification based on race or sex or the setting of quotas to meet affirmative action goals; such policies or programs, they argue, are tantamount to the racism and sexism that contemporary society seeks to overcome and punishes the present generation for the acts of their forebears.

Source: Jack Plano and Milton Greenberg, the *American Political Dictionary*, 7th ed. (New York: Holt, Rinehart and Winston, 1985, pp. 73, 91)

example is the wide swings in policy interpretation for the extent to which race can be considered a factor in college admissions. During the administration of George W. Bush the Departments of Education and Justice offered advisory information on how best to interpret government affirmative action requirements in admissions. The Bush administration guidance essentially minimized the need to include race as a factor in admissions (though it did not go so far as to say it need not be considered). The Obama administration's Departments of Education and Justice pulled back and re-emphasized the need to at least consider race in admissions. In July 2018 the Justice Department of President Trump (but not the Department of Education) returned to the wording of the guidance under Bush, but public statements strongly suggested that the preference was race be not considered at all.

The Myth of Reverse Discrimination

The mandate of affirmative action as the most effective practical tool for ending discrimination in hiring and promotion produced a legal and political debate about the possibility that the rules as applied caused "reverse discrimination" or instances where more qualified white males were denied jobs they desired because they were most qualified in favor of less qualified minorities. As a legal matter the courts (especially in the parallel issue of college admissions) have slowly eroded affirmative action protections by accepting the argument that qualifications that should be paramount are being diluted in favor of race, gender, and other distinctions. Despite the political popularity of such arguments, these views do not reflect personnel theory or practice. The simple reality was that the basis for biased hiring was that the socio-political culture dominates the process of culling through an applicant pool which dictated that certain persons were prima facie unqualified. There was significant social pressure on "minorities" to not apply, reinforced by the reality that they would rarely if ever reach the stage of an interview. After the changes in civil rights laws in the 1960s, minorities would reach later stages of the hiring process before being rejected.

Getting to be a finalist for a position often proved a pyrrhic victory. The pushback of the reverse discrimination efforts was advanced by the court's misunderstanding of the hiring process. The façade of objectivity and precision in distinguishing among applicants led judges to misinterpret the process of selecting someone to hire. What is left at the end of the applicant review process (the point at which "finalists" are declared) are not necessarily the best applicants but merely the survivors of the review. Search processes are not sufficiently precise to even be sure that the finalists are the "best." Yet the language of the hiring process often declares the survivors the best candidates and often goes so far as to rank order those finalists. The goal of the search process is to yield the very practical and realistic outcome of well-qualified finalists, any of whom can be successful in the job. To believe that the finalists are necessarily the "best available," much less that one is better than the others is well beyond the capability of the tools available in hiring. To, as the courts have done, suggest that the identifiably "best" (i.e. the white male) was passed over in favor of a less qualified women, black, Hispanic, or someone from the LGBTQ community, is false.

Again, the goal is to have a situation where all the finalists can do the job. To be more precise is beyond our capability and leaves a process in which dominate social norms carry extra weight.

Cultural Competence

One of the emerging results of attention to discriminatory hiring practices has been the transformation of the public workplace from one that is predominantly white and male to one that is diverse—reflecting the many facets and experiences of humankind. Regardless whether or not we have yet to extinguish the prejudices and biases that required affirmative action to expand opportunities for employment and promotion in the public sector, that transformation of who can be employed has changed the culture of public organizations. The management of public organizations is changing because the people working there have changed. The first aspect of this new workplace is a personnel issue. A diverse group will introduce new dynamics of interpersonal relations. This will be discussed as an issue of managing in Chapter 10, but it is also a personnel issue. It is the responsibility of personnel offices to prepare the entire workforce for these new dynamics. We must recognize that the differences at the heart of diversity extend beyond race to socialization experiences so that everyone appreciates the distinct contributions of others. Those contributions are based upon those differences. Knowing that people are different is insufficient. It is learning to cooperate and collaborate because we are different that is the task. In a sense the question of race in the workplace was in affirming that, as workers, we are the same. Race distinctions are not relevant to the workplace. Skin-color do not make one better than another. On the other hand, cultural competence is predicated on how we are different. Cultural competence training is learning to value those differences as a tool for organizational decision-making. In undoing the damage of racial prejudice, we free the organization to more fully use the skills and competencies of all people to do the work they have been asked to do (it is about qualifications for a job). On the other hand, the differences of life experiences of people whether because of race, ethnicity, gender, religious affiliation, or sexual orientation (LGBTQ), help organizations solve problems by expanding the vision and understanding of the problems being addressed.

The earliest models for cultural competence training were applied first in health care. Those models now are more widely utilized, particularly in public administration and business administration. The model frameworks undergird a variety of training perspectives as those and other fields of study and practice have adopted and adapted these models.

Campinha-Bacote model: One of the most commonly used models was designed by Josepha Campinha-Bacote. According to Campinha-Bacote (2002), the cultural competence model has five attributes that make up this construct. These attributes interact simultaneously to create the dynamics of cultural competence. These characteristics are cultural awareness, cultural knowledge, cultural encounters, cultural skill, and cultural desires.

1. Cultural awareness—self-examination and in-depth exploration of one's own cultural and professional background, focusing on recognition of personal biases.
2. Cultural knowledge—seeking and obtaining education foundation about diverse and cultural ethnic groups. In doing this, the public servant hones in on beliefs around civil servants, cultural values, and interactions and prevalence.
3. Cultural encounters—this process happens when two people from different ethnic/racial backgrounds engage in cross-cultural interactions with clients from cross-cultural interactions from culturally diverse backgrounds. Cultural encounters modify or refine one's existing beliefs.
4. Cultural skill—ability to collect relevant cultural data regarding the clients' ability to communicate a problem as well as the public servant's performance in completing an accurate needs assessment for the client.
5. Cultural desires—the motivation of the public servant to "want to" rather than "being required to" engage in the process of becoming culturally aware, culturally knowledgeable, culturally skillful, and familiar with cultural encounters.

PROFESSIONAL DEVELOPMENT

Creating a competent and professional civil service is a key goal for all governments. The development of that civil service is strongly influenced by the historical context of national development and the ongoing evolution of the government itself. At the same time there are a set of core values and practices shared across nations that shaped the decision to pursue the creation of a career-based professional development program. In 2003 a team from the Latvian School of Public Administration, the University of Latvia and the University of Akron (Ohio, USA) prepared for the Chancellery of Latvia a proposal for the creation of a career-long professional development program for the civil service of that country. The program was designed to address the training and education needs of civil servants at three distinct stages of their career, entry/early years, early mid-career, and senior-level. It is a useful model for understanding professional development in this earlier part of the twenty-first century. The program focused specifically on a small cohort of young professionals who will be identified for this training and for rapid promotion through the ranks. In addition, the program design offered flexibility to meet the training and education needs of others within the civil service by permitting them to take the same workshops to ensure that all managers have opportunities to enhance their skills, create more effective organizations, and, therefore, better serve the public. The reasoning behind the choice of a competency-based and career-long program and the formal structure of the program offer lessons that may be instructive for a variety of governments and organizations.

The program directed toward developing the core professional competencies of the public administration manager, which were for the purposes of this effort defined as:

- Information Distribution/Intergovernmental Relations
- Orientation and Attitudes
- Personnel Development
- Communications Skills
- Professional/Personal Development

Combining the notion of career-long development with the mandate of the strategic plan yielded the following program goals:

- To enhance the professionalism of public-sector managers by developing a career-long training curriculum to enhance the skills and capabilities of managers
- To identify highly qualified and skilled civil servants early in their career to give them the skills and knowledge needed to contribute to the public welfare
- To facilitate career planning and lifelong learning for all managers
- To integrate and coordinate the training and educational programs of the Latvian School of Public Administration and the University of Latvia (specifically the MPA program) to create a career-long training program that fits the needs of young professionals as well as mid- and senior-level managers, and
- To create an organizational culture that requires significant professional training as a complement to experience as the basis from career advancement

Performance Measures Under Civil Service

An interesting case study of how we conduct performance measurement is in its use as part of employee evaluations and appraisals. Two examples serve to illustrate the point. The first involves the mandate in the Civil Service Reform Act of 1978 to revise the performance appraisal instruments and processes in all federal agencies. The second involves a comprehensive position classification study for a municipality in Florida. Although twenty years separated the two projects, many of the same issues emerged in revising the performance appraisal processes. Two problems emerged; first, the considerable resistance by workers and managers to include team and organizational factors in the evaluation and second, the tendency of managers to use simple, numerically based factors to judge performance. The former problem is partly cultural. Americans are uncomfortable in situations where their individuality is not acknowledged (try to grade students on the basis of a group project and hear the complaints about how much "harder" the student worked than everyone else!). It is not relevant that we recognize that we are dependent upon others to accomplish our work. Hummel (1994) would argue that workers intuitively understand that their work activities are unrelated to organizational goals. To have part of their performance appraisal based upon the accomplishment of organizational goals is to automatically give them a failing performance rating. Since it is the managers who have a major responsibility for goal displacement, evaluating workers on the basis of organizational goals will make known this simple fact. The notion that performance appraisals are "qualitative" was a deeply troubling revelation for many managers. To them a qualitative judgment was biased and "wrong." Only a quantitatively formulated appraisal process, whereby the sum of a set of numbers yielded a result, was appropriate. The managers did not want to be a "judge." They wanted the numbers to be the judge, so that they could not be held "responsible" for the rating. This abdication of responsibility in the name of objectivity is a prime example of goal displacement. Performance appraisals were not a way to improve organizational performance and develop employees; they were simply a "task" to be performed with as little time and thought as possible.

If we are unwilling and unable to develop measures by which to judge the performance of colleagues and peers, how can an organization expect these same persons to develop appropriate measures by which to judge *organizational* performance? The obvious answer is that they cannot. But once performance appraisals of the individual are separated from any relationship to organizational performance, then both activities can be conducted without recognizing the incongruity of the practices.

Public Employee Labor Unions

Public employees in some states and then in the federal government have had the right to bargain over a limited range of topics for up to six decades. The number of states that have granted broad bargaining rights (i.e. including the right to bargain over wages) has not changed in twenty-five years (the last was New Mexico in 1992); nevertheless public employee unions are viewed as a major problem and successful bargaining is often linked to tax increases. While unpopular among some politicians, most of the efforts to change the bargaining laws have not been successful. In non-unionized states, laws dealing with the rules on removal from a position have been changed, but most of the efforts to outlaw the right to bargain collectively (whether a broad right as in Hawaii, Minnesota, and California, or narrow right as with the federal government) have generally been unsuccessful.

The focus of those efforts was not to abolish the entire law but rather to focus on the contracts, practices, and statues that affirmed a provision—that required public employees who did not wish to join a union but benefited from the contract that the union negotiated to pay, colloquially called a "fair share" payment—to defray the costs accrued by the union in bargaining on behalf of persons not in the union. Efforts to abolish the fair share when brought to public referendum have been rejected. However, in July 2018 the United States Supreme Court overturned a long-standing decision (*Abood v. Detroit Board of Education* 431 U.S. 209 1977) and declared all fair share requirements whether in state law or in contracts to be unconstitutional (*Janus v. AFSCME* U.S. 2018). The dissenters on the Court suggested the decision was a back-door way to abolish public employee unions. Given the political climate and prior state efforts to hamstring or abolish unions, the speculation of the dissenters is likely correct.

Ongoing Conflict with Politicians

Studies conducted by Joseph Boateng concerning the push to eliminate civil service protections for public employees found in states where civil service protections and job security had been abolished (Georgia for example) disturbingly low interpersonal trust levels among career public managers. But also, it suggested that such development could have important implications for the contemporary public management paradigm. Particularly in respect to managerial discretion and communication relative to interpersonal trust, it can be argued that the entrepreneurship culture, which is the focus of contemporary public management, remains to be fulfilled. Behn (1995) and Nyhan (2000) have established the role of trust in public organizations, and argued strongly that public management cannot escape the question of trust given the rapidity with which the public-sector environment is changing.

The way forward does not require mere rhetoric and political gimmickry. It calls for concerted and strategic efforts to enhance the capacity of the bureaucratic leadership to dispense its professional responsibilities with vigor, zeal, and adequate authority. To this effect, structural and cultural changes are imperative so that strict hierarchy and paternalistic approaches to decision-making could give way to equal collaboration, active participation, and information sharing. Fundamentally, the focus should be on managerial entrepreneurship facilitated through intra-organizational variables including relaxed procedure, effective communication, and informal interactive engagements (Bozeman and Kingsley, 1998). Flexibility of professional discretion requires accommodation of failure. Therefore, efforts should be directed at developing the environment in which risk-taking and experimentations are tolerated. By so doing, managers will be willing to engage in proactive actions, and will also refrain from adhering to strict routines that tend to undermine trust building. When professional public managers are allowed to think independently and explore diverse and innovative ways in performing their tasks, they develop high morale and build the necessary trust to complement the efforts of the political decision makers (Nyhan, 2000).

Uncertainties, ambiguities, and conflicts in organizations often arise when the communication channels are ineffective. This is more the case when emphasis is placed on single-loop or top-down communication approach (Argyris, 1994). The present study has revealed a similar trend. To address the problem, efforts should be made to promote a double-loop communication which is deemed to be critical for trust building in organizations. This will require less emphasis on hierarchy. In a double-loop communication environment, participants are able to share their concerns and ask pertinent questions about organizational decision-making. Competency rather than partisan loyalty could be explored in making prudent decisions when there is double-loop communication. Moreover, the mutual mistrust between the political and career managers could be eroded since there is openness in explaining why certain actions were countenanced. Thus, the feedback loop has the propensity to ensure goal and mission clarity among organizational members. Such development can build trust by lowering the risk-averse culture among employees and employers as well (Bozeman and Kingsley, 1998).

Barrier to trust building in organization may sometimes be as result of cultural differences. Psychological theorists argue that social categorization as an aspect of the cognitive processes may be a fundamental source of distrust and suspicion regarding the relationship between individuals or groups of different background within an organization (Kramer, 1996). Politicians and bureaucrats have different organizational cultural background, aspirations, competencies, and experience. Therefore, there is the possibility for them to premise their individual perceptions on wrongful assumptions. In this regard it is imperative to encourage and facilitate lateral communication and orientations to decode the cues that undermine trust building (Sproull and Kiesler, 1986). Orientations have been found to be effective tools to limit the deeply held suspicions and apprehensions between the political leadership and the career managers. The Charlottesville workshop example cited by Lorentzen (1985) in which political appointees and career managers came to appreciate the position of each other through perceptual mirror and joint problem-solving could be emulated by the states to improve the relationship between the incoming political managers and the incumbent career bureaucrats. It is also important to revisit and pay deserving attention to the 1984 recommendations made by the various professional associations in public administration in respect of trust-building orientations for political appointees and career managers (see Lorentzen, 1985, p. 412).

Ethical responsibility and accountability remain the primary levers to activate the mechanisms of trust building. Often times, the strict rules, centralization, and adherence to hierarchy are preferred because answers to the questions of ethics and accountability have not been found yet (Cox, Hill, and Pyakuryal, 2008). The continuous manifestation of government scandals such as conflict of interest, corruption, and abuse of office give credence to external controls over the tasks of public officials. Stakeholders will be willing to facilitate the appropriate environment necessary for trust building when reports of the scandalous occurrences are reduced. Therefore, through policies, concerted efforts could be initiated to re-orient public officials on their ethical obligations.

The study underscored the fact that the recent public management reforms sweeping across the states intrigues a lot of varying concerns relative to how such reforms have impacted on the organizational environment and for that matter the level of interpersonal trust and its related antecedent variables. In the overall multiple regression model, a specific approach to reforms played no significant role in predicting interpersonal trust. This observation calls into question the notion that the political or radical business-oriented reforms are the panaceas for trust building and effective collaboration between political and professional actors in government. It is therefore important not to relegate the concerns in the literature regarding the possible long-term ramifications of the contemporary radical reforms on public service values, particularly those aptly mediated by mutual understanding and collaboration between political and bureaucratic leadership. Issues regarding government efficiency, effectiveness, accountability, and responsiveness are explained by several other factors, particularly those that underline public service motivation and retention and attraction of competent energetic personnel. These should be the guiding principles of any form of administrative changes rather than hammering on a particular paradigm.

As suggested above a key aspect of trust is a tolerance for failure. Certainly, the rhetoric and focus of the NPM and management initiatives that erode traditional civil service protections demand less tolerance of failure. At the very time that an entrepreneurial approach is being demanded of senior managers, mid-level managers are threatened with removal from office for exercising the same risk-taking behavior. The message is clear; "risk" is allowed only when successful. Flexibility in the exercise of discretion is a pathway open to few.

A more complex set of relationships emerges as the need for trust as fundamental for effective communications is accepted. The paradox is that distrust is widespread and deeply engrained on both sides. The political rhetoric of the incompetence and risk aversion of the civil servant is just that—rhetoric—not reality. The professional ethos of the civil servant is supposed to be cautious. But caution and risk aversion are not the same. Nor does that mean that the opposite of caution is the correct path. The core of entrepreneurship is in seeing opportunity (in these cases, policy construction opportunity) where others see insurmountable problems. Entrepreneurship is not the absence of caution. Public entrepreneurship can and does exist among civil servants.

Civil service as the very embodiment of the politics-administration dichotomy makes work at the margin between the administrative and political parts of an agency difficult. Ultimately only those who embrace the two worlds of administration and politics are successful at the margin. Introducing political assessments of performance at lower levels of the organization seemingly changes little. Reconciling professional administration and political decision-making is no less difficult if it is encountered sooner in one's career. The skill of working at the margin is as much a habit of mind as it is experience. Civil servants who have difficulty reconciling such "intrusion" will have no better time of it earlier than later.

The choice to politicize the civil service does little. Threatening to remove someone is not the path to encouraging more entrepreneurship in public decisions (or probably in any setting). The core problems of effective communications and fostering trust among those who must collaborate at the margin are not addressed by the structural changes introduced. In a small way the problem is made worse, but the distrust from both sides is engrained. Changes of attitude that leave both political appointees and civil servants open to trust and collaboration require changes in attitude by both civil servants and political appointees. The very thrust of the structural changes implies that the failure rested with distrustful and risk-adverse civil servants. Distrust is mutual, but equally fundamental is that changing the employment status of civil servants does not make them less risk adverse. This seems to be organization reform by stereotype.

What is of essence is that the twenty-first century challenges can only be confronted when political appointees forge effective collaborations with their counterpart career managers. A significant manifestation of interpersonal trust is required to cement the complementary engagements and dialogue between the political and career mangers so that political imperative could optimally be reconciled with administrative values. But as it stands now, particularly given the levels of interpersonal trust, professional discretion, participative management, and communication, there appears to be much room for improvement.

CONCLUSION: THE MANAGEMENT SUPPORT SYSTEM

Personnel practice has changed radically since the founding period. During each period of change the central question remained the effective performance of government activities. Each period focused on a different aspect of personnel management in the search for a more responsive government. Thus, the early period emphasized loyalty to the government and specialized skills derived from education and experience. The middle years of the nineteenth century were a period in which political skills and connections were particularly pertinent. The civil service reform movement emphasized concepts such as professionalism, expertise, and controlling partisan influence. During the middle of the twentieth century, the concept of using personnel practice to aid managers in carrying out the mission of government became more important. Attempts were also made to reassert control by the president over personnel management. In this last quarter of the twentieth century, the concern is more on the relationship of the individual employee and the structures of government. This concern is manifest in two contradictory trends: the granting of "rights" to public employees, which has given them more latitude or discretion in the performance of their jobs, and the effort to again invoke the authority of the president as the leader of all civil servants.

DISCUSSION QUESTIONS

- Define organizational diversity. Why is it considered important?
- What is a career ladder? Why is it important in structuring positions?
- How are the concepts of knowledge, skill, and ability used in developing a comprehensive personnel system?
- Why is performance appraisal such a problem in most organizations?
- Are unions relevant in the public sector? Why or why not?
- Explain the relevance of expanding an applicant pool for effective hiring.
- Why do Americans more than any of the developed democracies prefer more rather than fewer political appointees in senior management?
- Is civil service still relevant and viable?

NOTES

1. This argument is still used today to justify dismissal of career civil servants with a supposed ideological bent different from that of the current administration. Indeed, one of the primary tasks of public administration theories in the 1970s and 1980s has been to reconcile the administrative state with American conceptions of democracy and constitutionalism. See John A. Rohr, *To Run a Constitution: The Legitimacy of the Administrative State*. Lawrence, KS: University Press of Kansas, 1986; and Dwight Waldo, *The Enterprise of Public Administration*. Novato, CA: Chandler and Sharp Publishers, Inc., 1981.
2. During the Senate debate on the nomination of Martin Van Buren as minister to Great Britain, the phrase "to the victor belong the spoils of the enemy" was coined by Senator William Marcy in his defense of Van Buren's spoilsmen policies. U.S. Civil Service Commission, *History of the Federal Civil Service 1789 to the Present* (Washington, DC: U.S. General Printing Office, 1941), p. 20.
3. As noted earlier, the practice of exempting agencies from civil service rules began in many states in the 1930s. The point was that faith in the ability of the Commission to manage the federal personnel system was rapidly disappearing.
4. The reality, unfortunately, has been that many, particularly at the Department of Defense, were assigned SES status but continued to perform technical staff functions.

BIBLIOGRAPHY

Aberbach, J., and B. Rockman. "Mandates or mandarins? Control and Discretion in the Modern Administrative State", *Public Administration Review*, 48 (2), pp. 606–612. 1988.

Adams, G., and D. Balfour. "Abu Ghraib, Administrative Evil, and Moral Inversion: The Value of 'Putting Cruelty First'", *Public Administration Review*, 66 (5), pp. 680–693. 2006.

Albrecht, S., and A. Travaglione. "Trust in Public-sector Senior Management", *The International Journal of Human Resource Management*, 14 (1), pp. 76–92. 2003.

Allen, D., L. Shore, and R. Griffeth. "The Role of Perceived Organizational Support and Supportive Human Resource Practices in the Turnover Process", *Journal of Management*, 29 (1), pp. 99–113. 2003.

Argyris, C. "Good Communication that Blocks Learning", *Harvard Business Review*, 72 (3), pp. 77–86. 1994.

Atkinson, S., and D. Butcher. "Trust in Managerial Relationships", *Journal of Managerial Psychological*, 18 (4), pp. 282–304. 2003.

Balfour, D., and Bart Wechsler. "Organizational Commitment: Attachments and Outcomes in Public Organizations", *Public Productivity and Management Review*, 19 (3), pp. 256–277. 1996.

Barnard, C. *The Functions of the Executive*. Cambridge, MA: Harvard University Press. 1938.

Barrett, K., and R. Greene. "Grading the States '05: A Management Report Card", *Governing*, 18 (5), pp. 24–95. 2005.

Battaglio, P., and S. Condrey. "Reforming Public Management: Analyzing the Impact of Public Service Reform on Organizational and Managerial Trust", *Journal of Public Administration Research and Theory*, 19 (4), pp. 689–707. 2009.

Behn, R. "The Big Questions of Public Management", *Public Administration Review*, 55 (4), pp. 313–324. 1995.

Bennis, W. *An Invented Life: Reflections on Leadership and Change*. Reading, MA: Addison-Wesley. 1993.

Berman, E., and X. Wang. "Performance Measurement in U.S. Counties: Capacity for Reform", *Public Administration Review*, 60 (5), pp. 409–420. 2000.

Bigley, G., and J. Pearce. "Straining for Shared Meaning in Organization Science: Problems of Trust and Distrust", *Academy of Management Review*, 23 (3), pp. 405–421. 1998.

Bok, D. "Government Personnel Policy in Comparative Perspective", In *For the People: Can We*. 2003.

Bowman, J., J. West, and S. Gertz. "Florida's Service First: Radical Reform in the Sunshine State", in J. E. Kellough and L. G. Nigro (eds.), *Civil Service Reform in the States: Personnel Policy and Politics at the Subnational Level*. Albany: State University of New York Press. 2006.

Bozeman, B., and G. Kingsley. "Risk Culture in Public and Private Organizations", *Public Administration Review*, 58 (2), pp. 109–118. 1998.

Brudney, J., T. Hebert, and D. Wright. "Reinventing Government in the American States: Measuring and

Explaining Administrative Reform", *Public Administration Review*, 59 (1), pp. 19–30. 1999.

Bryer, T. "Towards a Relevant Agenda for Responsive Public Administration", *Journal of Public Administration Research and Theory*, 17 (3), pp. 479–500. 2007.

Bureau of Intergovernmental Personnel Programs. *Job Analysis: Developing and Documenting Data.* Washington, DC: US Government Printing Office. 1973.

Campinha-Bacote, J. "The Process of Cultural Competence in the Delivery of Healthcare Services: A Model of Care", *Journal of Transcultural Nursing*, 13 (3), pp. 181–184. 2002.

Campinha-Bacote, J., and M. C. Narayan. "Culturally Competent Health Care in the Home", *Home Care Provider*, 5 (6), pp. 213–219. 2000.

Carboni, N. "Professional Autonomy Versus Political Control: How to Deal with the Dilemma. Some Evidence from the Italian Core Executive", *Public Policy and Administration*, 25 (4), pp. 365–386. 2010.

Carnevale, D. *Trustworthy Government: Leadership and Management Strategies for Building Trust and High Performance.* San Francisco: Jossey-Bass. 1995.

Carnevale, D., and B. Wechsler. "Trust in the Public Sector: Individual and Organizational Determinants", *Administration and Society*, 23 (4), pp. 471–494. 1994.

Carpenter, M., and B. Golden. "Perceived Managerial Discretion: A Study of Cause and Effect", *Strategic Management Journal*, 18 (2), pp. 187–206. 1997.

Choo, C. "The Knowing Organization: How Organizations Use Information to Construct Meaning, Create Knowledge and Make Decisions", *International Journal of Information Management*, 16 (5), pp. 329–340. 1996.

Choudhury, E. "Trust in Administration: An Integrative Approach to Optimal Trust", *Administration and Society*, 40 (6), pp. 586–620. 2008.

Christensen, T., and P. Laegreid. "Trust in Government: The Relative Importance of Service Satisfaction, Political Factors, and Demography", *Public Performance and Management Review*, 28 (4), pp. 487–511. 2005.

Coggburn, J. "The Decentralized and Deregulated Approach to State Human Resources Management in Texas", in J. E. Kellough and L. N. Nigro (eds.) *Civil Service Reform in the States: Personnel Policies and Politics at the Sub-national Level.* New York: State University of New York Press. 2006.

Collins, D., R. Ross, and T. Ross. "Who Wants Participative Management? The Managerial Perspective", *Group and Organizational Studies*, 14 (4), pp. 422–445. 1989.

Condrey, S. "Reinventing State Civil Service Systems: The Georgia Experience", *Review of Public Personnel Administration*, 22 (2), pp. 114–124. 2002.

Condrey, S., and P. Battaglio. "A Return to Spoil? Revisiting Radical Civil Service Reform in the United States", *Public Administration Review*, 67 (3), pp. 425–436. 2007.

Cox, R., S. Buck, and B. Morgan. *Public Administration in Theory and Practice.* New York: Longman. 2011.

Cox, R., M. Hill, and S. Pyakuryal. "Tacit Knowledge and Discretionary Judgment", *Public Integrity*, 10 (2), pp. 151–164. 2008.

Coyle-Shapiro, J., and I. Kessler. "Consequences of the Psychological Contract for the Employment Relationship: A Large Scale Survey", *Journal of Management Studies*, 37 (7), pp. 903–930. 2000.

Crowell, E., and M. Guy. "Florida HR Reforms: Service First, Service Worst, or Something in Between?" *Public Personnel Management*, 39 (1), pp. 15–38. 2010.

Dachler, P., and B. Wilpert. "Conceptual Dimensions and Boundaries of Participation in Organizations: A Critical Evaluation", *Administrative Science Quarterly*, 23 (1), pp. 1–39. 1978.

Dansereau, F., J. Cashman, and G. Green. "Instrumentality Theory and Equity Theory as Complementary Approaches in Predicting the Relationship of Leadership and Turnover among Managers", *Organizational Behavior and Human Performance*, 10 (2), pp. 184–200. 1973.

Dery, D. "'Papereality' and Learning in Bureaucratic Organizations", *Administration and Society*, 29 (6), pp. 677–689. 1998.

Dirks, K., and D. Ferrin. "Trust in Leadership: Meta-analytic Findings and Implications for Research and Practice", *Journal of Applied Psychology*, 87 (4), pp. 611–628. 2002.

Dolan, J. "Influencing Policy at the Top of the Federal Bureaucracy: A Comparison of Career and Political Senior Executives", *Public Administration Review*, 60 (6), pp. 53–81. 2000.

Eaton, Dorman. "Assassination and the Spoils System," *Princeton Review*, VIII (September). 1881.

Fairholm, M., and G. Fairholm. "Leadership Amid the Constraints of Trust", *Leadership and Organization Development Journal*, 21 (2), pp. 102–109. 2000.

Feeney, M., and H. Rainey. "Personnel Flexibility and Red Tape in Public and Nonprofit Organizations: Distinctions Due to Institutional and Political Accountability", *Journal of Public Administration Research and Theory*, 20 (4), pp. 801–826. 2010.

Fish, Carl. *The Civil Service and the Patronage*. New York: Russell and Russell. 1963.

Frazier, L. "Organizational Justice, Trustworthiness, and Trust: A Multifoci Examination", *Group & Organization Management*, 35 (1), pp. 39–76. 2010.

Frey, B., F. Homberg, and M. Osterloh. "Organizational Control and Pay-for—Performance in the Public Service", *Organizational Studies*, 34 (7), pp. 949–972. 2013.

Garnett, J., J. Marlowe, and S. Pandey. "Penetrating the Performance Predicament: Communication as a Mediator or Moderator of Organizational Culture's Impact on Public Organizational Performance", *Public Administration Review*, 68 (2), pp. 266–281. 2008.

Golembiewski, R., and M. McConkie. "The Centrality of Interpersonal Trust in Group Process", in C. L. Cooper (ed.), *Theories of Group Process*. New York: John Wiley & Sons. 1975.

Guy, M. "Productive Work Environments", in Marc Holzer (ed.), *The Public Productivity Handbook*. New York: Marcel Dekker. 1992.

Hass, J., and S. Wright. "Administrative Turn Over in State Government: A Research Note", *Administration and Society*, 21 (2), pp. 265–277. 1989.

Hays, S., and J. Sowa. "A Broader Look at the "Accountability" Movement: Some Grim Realities in State Civil Service Systems", *Review of Public Personnel Administration*, 26 (2), pp. 102–117. 2006.

Heclo, H. *A Government of Strangers: Executive Politics in Washington*. Washington, DC: Brookings Institution Press. 1977.

Ho, A. "Accounting for the Value of Performance Measurement from the Perspective of Midwestern Mayors", *Journal of Public Administration Research and Theory*, 16 (2), pp. 217–238. 2006.

Hoogenboom, Ari. *Outlawing the Spoils*. Chicago: University of Illinois Press. 1968.

Hood, C., and M. Lodge. *Politics of Public Service Bargains*. Oxford: Oxford University Press. 2006.

Huang, X., J. Lun, A. Liu, and Y. Gong. "Does Participative Leadership Enhance Work Performance by Inducing Empowerment or Trust? The Differential Effects on Managerial and Non-managerial Subordinates", *Journal of Organizational Behavior*, 31 (1), pp. 122–143. 2010.

Hummel, Ralph P. *The Bureaucratic Experience, 4th ed.* New York: St. Martin's Press. 1994.

Ingraham, P., and S. Selden. "Human Resource Management and Capacity in the States", *Public Personnel Management: Current Concerns, Future Challenges*, pp. 210–224. 2002.

Ivancivich John, and William Glueck. *Foundations of Personnel, rev. ed.* Plano, TX: Business Publications, Inc. 1983.

Kaufman, H. *Red Tape: Its Origins, Uses, and Abuses*. Washington, DC: Brookings. 1977.

Kearney, R., and S. Hays. "Labor-management Relations and Participative Decision Making: Toward a New Paradigm", *Public Administration Review*, 54 (1), pp. 44–51. 1994.

Kearney, R., and S. Hays. "Reinventing Government, the New Public Management, and Civil Service Systems in International Perspective: The Danger of Throwing the Baby Out with the Bathwater", *Review of Public Personnel Administration*, 18 (4), pp. 38–54. 1998.

Kearney, R., and C. Scavo. "Reinventing Government in Reformed Municipalities: Manager Mayor, and Council Actions", *Urban Affairs Review*, 37 (1), pp. 43–66. 2001.

Kellough, E., and L. Nigro. *Civil Service Reform in the States: Personnel Policy and Politics at the Subnational Level*. Albany: State University of New York Press. 2006.

Kellough, E., and L. Nigro. "Civil Service Reform in the United States: Patterns and Trends", in S. E. Condrey (ed.), *Handbook of Human Resource Management in Government*. San Francisco: Jossey-Bass. 2010.

Kellough, E., and C. Selden. "The Reinventing of Public Personnel Administration: An Analysis of the Diffusion of Personnel Management Reforms in the States", *Public Administration Review*, 63 (2), pp. 165–176. 2003.

Kettl, D. *The Politics of the Administrative Process*. Washington, DC: CQ Press. 2012.

Kramer, R. "Divergent Realities and Convergent Disappointments in the Hierarchic Relation: Trust and the Intuitive Auditor at Work", in R. M. Kramer and T. R. Tyler (eds.), *Trust in Organizations: Frontiers of Theory and Research*. Thousand Oaks, CA: Sage. 1996.

Lam, A. "Tacit Knowledge, Organizational Learning and Societal Institutions: An Integrated Framework", *Organization Studies*, 21 (3), pp. 487–513. 2000.

Lee, S., and D. Olshfski. "An Examination of Variations in the Nature of Employee Commitment",

International Review of Public Administration, 7, pp. 29–38. 2002.

Lorentzen, P. "Stress in Political-Career Executive Relations", *Public Administration Review*, 45 (3), pp. 411–414. 1985.

Lynn, D. "Personnel Deregulation and the High Performance Workforce: State Government Outcomes from the Winter Commission", *Review of Public Personnel Administration*, 20 (4), pp. 55–69. 2000.

Maesschalck, J. "The Impact of New Public Management Reforms on Public Servants' Ethics: Towards a Theory", *Public Administration*, 82 (2), pp. 465–489. 2004.

Mayer, R., J. Davis, and D. Schoorman. "An Integrative Model of Organizational Trust", *Academy of Management Review*, 20 (3), pp. 709–734. 1995.

McHugh, M., and H. Bennett. "Introducing Teamworking within a Bureaucratic Maze", *Leadership & Organization Development Journal*, 20 (2), pp. 81–93. 1999.

Meyer, J., and N. Allen. *Commitment in the Workplace: Theory, Research, and Application.* Newbury Park, CA: Sage. 1997.

Mouritzen, P., and J. Svara. *Leadership at the Apex: Politicians and Administrators in Western Local Governments.* Pittsburgh, PA: University of Pittsburgh Press. 2001.

Moynihan, D. "Managing for Result in State Government: Evaluating a Decade of Reform", *Public Administration Review*, 66 (1), pp. 77–89. 2006.

Nachmias, D. "Determinants of Trust with the Federal Bureaucracy", in D. H. Rosenbloom (ed.), *Public Personnel Policy: The Politics of Public Service.* Port Washington, NY: Associated Faculty. 1985.

Nanoka, I., and H. Takeuchi. *The Knowledge-creating Company: How Japanese Companies Create the Dynamics of Information.* New York: Oxford University Press. 1995.

Nigro, L., and E. Kellough. "Personnel Reform in the States: A Look at Progress Fifteen Years after the Winter Commission", *Public Administration Review*, 68 (1), pp. 50–57. 2008.

Nyhan, R. "Increasing Affective Organizational Commitment in Public Organizations: The Key Role of Interpersonal Trust", *Review of Public Personnel Administration*, 19 (3), pp. 58–70. 1999.

Nyhan, R. "Changing the Paradigm-trust and Its Role in Public Sector Organizations", *The American Review of Public Administration*, 30 (1), pp. 87–109. 2000.

Nyhan, R., and H. Marlowe. "Development and Psychometric Properties of Organizational Trust Inventory", *Evaluation Review*, 21 (5), pp. 614–638. 1997.

O'Brien, G. "Participation as the Key to Successful Change—A Public Sector Case Study", *Leadership and Organization Development Journal*, 23 (8), pp. 442–455. 2002.

Pandey, S., and J. Garnett. "Exploring Public Sector Communication Performance: Testing a Model and Drawing Implications", *Public Administration Review*, 66 (1), pp. 37–51. 2006.

Park, S. "Toward the Trusted Public Organization: Untangling the Leadership, Motivation, and Trust Relationship in U.S. Federal Agencies", *The American Review of Public Administration*, 42 (5), pp. 562–590. 2012.

Perry, R. "The Relationship of Affective Organizational Commitment with Supervisory Trust", *Review of Public Personnel Administration*, 24 (2), pp. 133–149. 2004.

Pfiffner, P. "Political Appointees and Career Executives: The Democracy-bureaucracy Nexus in the Third Century", *Public Administration Review*, pp. 57–65. 1987.

Pitt, D. "Leadership, Empowerment, and Public Organizations", *Review of Public Personnel Administration*, 25 (1), pp. 5–28. 2005.

Rainey, H. *Understanding and Managing Public Organization.* Danvers, MA: Jossey-Bass. 2009.

Rainey, H., S. Pandey, and B. Bozeman. "Research Note-public and Private Managers' Perceptions of Red Tape", *Public Administration Review*, 55 (6), pp. 567–574. 1995.

Rosen, B., and T. Jerdee. "Influence of Subordinate Characteristics on Trust and Use of Participative Decision Strategies in a Management Simulation", *Journal of Applied Psychology*, 62 (5), pp. 628–631. 1977.

Rubin, E. "The Role of Procedural Justice in Public Personnel Management: Empirical Results from the Department of Defense", *Journal of Public Administration Research and Theory*, 19 (1), pp. 125–143. 2009.

Sayre, Wallace. "The Triumph of Technique Over Purpose", *Public Administration Review*, 8 (Spring), pp. 134–147. 1948.

Selden, S., G. Brewer, and J. Brudney. "Reconciling Competing Values in Public Administration: Understanding the Administrative Role Concept", *Administration and Society*, 31 (2), pp. 171–204. 1999.

Selden, S., P. Ingraham, and W. Jacobson. "Human Resource Practice in State Governments: Findings from a Survey", *Public Administration Review*, 61 (5), pp. 598–607. 2001.

Shafritz, Jay, Albert Hyde, and David Rosenbloom. *Personnel Management in Government, 3rd ed.* New York: Marcel Dekker, Inc. 1986.

Shapiro, S. "The Social Control of Impersonal Trust", *American Journal of Sociology*, 93 (3), pp. 623–658. 1987.

Simon, H., D. Smithburg, and V. Thompson. *Public Administration.* New York: Alfred A. Knopf. 1950.

Smith, E. "The Role of Tacit and Explicit Knowledge in the Workplace", *Journal of Knowledge Management*, 5 (4), pp. 311–321. 2001.

Sowa, J., and S. Selden. "Administrative Discretion and Active Representation: An Expansion of the Theory of Representative Bureaucracy", *Public Administration Review*, 63 (3), pp. 700–710. 2003.

Spreitzer, G., and A. Mishra. "Giving Up Control without Losing Control: Trust and Its Substitutes' Effects on Managers' Involving Employees in Decision Making", *Group Organization management*, 24 (2), pp. 155–187. 1999.

Sproull, L. and Kiesler, S. "Reducing Social Context Cues: Electronic Mail in Organizational Communication", *Management Science*, 32. 1986.

Stazyk, E., and H. Goerdel. "The Benefits of Bureaucracy: Public Managers' Perceptions of Political Support, Goal Ambiguity, and Organizational Effectiveness", *Journal of Public Administration Research and Theory*, 21 (4), pp. 645–672. 2011.

Svara, J. "The Myth of the Dichotomy: Complementarity of Politics and Administration in the Past and Future of Public Administration", *Public Administration Review*, 61 (2), pp. 176–183. 2001.

Thompson, F. "Professionalism, Mistrust of Politicians and the Receptivity of Civil Servants to Procedural Buffers: The Case of Personnel Officials", *The American Review of Public Administration*, 13 (3), pp. 143–156. 1979.

Thompson, J. "Reinvention as Reform: Assessing the National Performance Review", *Public Administration Review*, 60 (6), pp. 508–521. 2000.

Thompson, J. "State and Local Governance Fifteen Years Later: Enduring and New Challenges", *Public Administration Review*, 68 (1), pp. 8–19. 2008.

US Civil Service Commission. *History of the Federal Civil Service 1789 to the Present.* Washington, DC: US General Printing Office. 1941.

US Office of Personnel Management. *Position Classification: A Guide for City and County Managers.* Washington, DC: US Government Printing Office. 1979.

Van Riper, Paul. *History of the United States Civil Service.* Evanston, IL: Row, Peterson and Co. 1958.

Van Wart, M. "Sources for Ethical Decision Making for Individuals in the Public Sector", *Public Administration Review*, 56 (6), pp. 525–533. 1996.

Waldo, D. *The Administrative State: A Study of the Political Theory of American Public Administration.* New York: Ronald Press Co. 1948.

Waldo, Dwight. *The Enterprise of Public Administration.* Novato, CA: Chandler and Sharp Publishers, Inc. 1981.

West, J. "Georgia on the Mind of Radical Civil Service Reformers", *Review of Public Personnel Administration*, 22 (2), pp. 79–93. 2002.

White, Leonard. *The Jacksonians.* New York: Macmillan. 1954.

White, Leonard. *The Republican Era.* New York: Macmillan. 1958.

Wolf, A. "Policies that Were Tried and Trashed a While Back Resurface", *Times Higher Education Supplement*, 30 (July), p. 13. 2004.

Wright, B., and S. Kim. "Participation's Influence on Job Satisfaction: The Importance of Job Characteristics", *Review of Public Personnel Administration*, 24 (1), pp. 18–40. 2004.

Yang, K., and A. Kassekert. "Linking Management Reform with Employee Job Satisfaction: Evidence from Federal Agencies", *Journal of Public Administration Research and Theory*, 20 (2), pp. 413–436. 2010.

Yang, K., and S. Pandey. "How Do Perceived Political Environment and Administrative Reforms Affect Employee Commitment?" *Journal of Public Administration Research and Theory*, 19 (2), pp. 335–360. 2009.

CHAPTER 4

Budgeting Practices

BUDGETING IN GOVERNMENT

The budget process presents a variety of problems for the public manager. The manager must not only recognize the importance of investing ample time in the development of the budget but also must be cognizant of the restrictions budget enactment may place on the organization's operations. For the agency manager, a budget is not simply a technical document. Rather, it is the political and policy document that compiles the myriad decisions on funding levels negotiated during the budget process and establishes the shape and character of governmental activities.

Understandably, the channels through which these governmental decisions are processed are quite complex. The budgeting process consumes many months and involves numerous individuals and departments as well as interested publics. Final budget figures can be influenced by the insistence of the public, influential politicians, and bureaucrats; by variations in presentation style, budget formats; or by the expectations and performance of the agency anticipating the funds. Any of these influences may operate independently but, more than likely, will combine with several others to act in concert in influencing the final outcome. The final version of any budget can only be understood as an end product of some combination of all these influences.

The budget is also critical as a document that constrains and controls public managers charged with expending allocated funds. From a micro-perspective, understanding the influences which ultimately delineate the size of budget allocations is imperative. A micro-perspective is concerned with the challenges of managing within the constraints established in the budget and examines how administrators choose to make use of the resources they have received in order to carry out their organizational responsibilities. The corresponding macro-perspective, while not underestimating the strategic roles that public administrators assume as information providers and interim decision makers, includes the larger political elements of the budgeting process.

This chapter explores both perspectives, but, before undertaking that analysis, a review of the historic evolution of budgeting is in order. After placing the budgeting process in historical context, the next section explores various macro-viewpoints. (Much of this section is drawn from the work of long-time budget scholar John Wanat [1978] and utilizes his seven-fold classification to define the macro-viewpoint.) The final section will explore the challenges of the micro-viewpoint from the much more "bureaucratic" or managerial perspective of implementing the budget rather than shaping it.

BUDGETING IN HISTORIC PERSPECTIVE

Multiple Budgets

The constant debate between the executive and legislative branches over "The Budget" obscures several important historical points about budgets. First and foremost is that governments rarely have a single budget. Even if we consider the simple distinction between capital outlay and an operating budget, the obvious point is that most governments use more than a single budget to set fiscal policy.

In the earliest period of our political history, the budget for any particular period of time was simply the accumulation of the funding requests of the various agencies to the legislature. There were as many budgets as there were agencies of government. This haphazard approach extended to the revenue stream needed to fund the programs. When it became apparent that revenues would not match expenditures at any particular point in time, a new source of revenue was sought (most often in early history, a lottery). This piecemeal procedure was especially true when new programs or special projects such as roads and bridges were initiated, or, in the case of the federal government, when new military programs such as the building of sailing ships were undertaken. Politically, a pattern of treating certain efforts as unique and, therefore, somewhat apart from the regular, ongoing programs of government, emerged. This is the procedural precursor of the capital budget which is separated from "regular" budget decisions due to the modes of funding (bonds, often paid for by taxes dedicated to the specific program) or by the singular nature of the project (still likely to be a new highway, bridge, or building).

This utilization of multiple budgets can still be observed in the federal government practice of enacting several budgets, divided by agency. This linkage of budgets to an agency or cluster of agencies, however, has unfortunate consequences for the politics of budgeting. The original direct connections between revenues and specific expenditures have been lost. Multiple budgets mean that no single budget can be directly linked to its revenue requirements as was the case in earlier times. What ensues is somewhat of an administrative sleight-of-hand routine. The potential to trade off one program against another to bring the budget in line with expenditures is partially lost because some programs and agencies have been funded before revenue problems become apparent. At best, programs within a narrow range of agencies may bear the brunt of the budget-cutting axe. This has the unfortunate effect of dampening the drive for innovation and change in programs. The more bland, uncontroversial, and similar to prior budgets the current request is, the more likely that early approval can be achieved and thus avoid a later budget squeeze.

Executive Budgeting

It is also important to remember that the notion of a budget as an executive branch document is fairly recent. Throughout the eighteenth and nineteenth centuries, state and federal budgeting was a process undertaken by agencies and legislatures. Gubernatorial and presidential influence was considerably less than it is today because no *formal role* existed for chief executives. It was widely assumed that budgeting would never become an instrument of conscious policy until it could become a more unified process. The best way to accomplish this was to bring the budget process under the control of the chief executive, thus permitting a single policy perspective (i.e., that of the mayor, governor, or president) to dominate the process of setting budget levels. This view implicitly assumes that legislative majorities were too ephemeral to hold to any consistent policy perspective.

Regardless of the cogency of this distinction between the executive and legislative facility to set coherent policy, the idea of an executive budget was a strong political motivator during the first two decades of the twentieth century. Prior to 1921, agencies still followed the tradition of preparing their estimates and transmitting them to the Treasury Department, which passed them over to Congress without analyses. Agencies sometimes overspent their appropriations, leaving Congress obligated to appropriate overspent amounts. The president did not participate in the budget process and there was no overall Executive Branch Plan (Lynch, 1995). Beginning with the Taft administration, however, reforms were initiated, motivated substantially by progressive era initiatives and the expense of World War I. Often by constitutional mandate, control of the budget was gradually tilted toward the executive by requiring that all budgetary submissions (often as part of a "unified" operating budget) be cleared through the chief executive. The Budget and Accounting Act of 1921 first provided for a national budget, instituted independent auditing of government accounts (the Act established the General Accounting Office), and established the Bureau of the Budget (BOB)—strengthening the executive's power to control budgetary negotiations. In 1937, the Brownlow Commission recommended strengthening the BOB, and the Reorganization Act of 1939 transferred BOB to the Executive Office of the President. The Hoover Commission in 1947, the Second Hoover Commission in 1955, and the President's Commission on Budget Concepts in 1967 continued to strengthen the executive role in the budget process. Today, only remnants of the earlier system remain. Two states, Arkansas and Texas, continue to have agencies submit requests directly to the legislature (a single committee reviews the budget and then forwards it to the floor as a single, unified budget). The mandate for the president to submit a budget (actually fourteen budgets) comes from a statute, not a constitutional mandate.

The shift to an executive budget, in adding a second political actor, made the now three-way budget process (agency, chief executive, and legislature) more political. The public sees the budget as a tug-of-war between the governor or president and the legislature. No side completely controls the budget process, though public perception is that the agencies are caught between the executive and legislative branches. As discussed later in the macro-perspective section, the politics of the budget process are far more complex than the ordinary pulling and hauling between chief executive and legislature. Rather, the sense that the budget is both political and "politicized" is very accurate.

Budget Documentation

Auditing and accounting procedures have always been part of the budget process, albeit for many decades the procedures were extremely rudimentary, involving little more than straightforward bookkeeping to track expenditures and facilitate auditing. These budgets included but a single line of expenditures for an entire agency.

The reform movement of the latter part of the nineteenth century focused on eliminating "corruption" in government. A key goal was the reform of budgeting procedures to control how monies were spent. This is the beginning of the line item budget—expenditures were restricted to exactly (and only) the amount approved in a line item! But this level of control was only the first step toward limiting the discretion of government officials. Almost at the same time, procedures to facilitate the audit of a budget were introduced. The key to understanding these developments is that the central purpose was to prevent corruption and misuse of public funds, that is, a mechanism of control. The budget as a control mechanism is discussed in more detail below as part of the discussion of the macro-perspective on the budget.

Each of the above elements of change in the budget process influences how we prepare budgets today. As we move to a discussion of the macro-perspective on budgeting, it is important to remember that the changes just discussed shaped the macro-perspective, defining it for the last half of the twentieth century. It is also worth noting that more change is inevitable. Our perspectives will change further as a result of contemporary demands and developments. The macro-perspective described below is valid *only* for the last half of the twentieth century. Thus, even as we are tied to the past, the key to understanding these perspectives is in recognizing their changeability.

MACRO-BUDGET PERSPECTIVES

In exploring the many different perspectives that may help us understand the budget process and the decisions that create a budget, we must acknowledge that none of these perspectives adequately explains budgeting in and of themselves. The budget process simultaneously circumscribes a set of institutional or organizational relationships, while serving at the same time as the chosen means to decide how resources should be allocated on behalf of society. Each of these perspectives helps us to appreciate the numerous practical and academic viewpoints found in the practice of public budgeting. Each of the various actors involved in the budgeting process brings a unique perspective. For example, agency attorneys see budgeting activities as a semi-judicial process during which agencies plead their case to the legislative committees, much as they plead their clients' cases in court. Accountants, on the other hand, believe the main purpose of budgeting is accountability and control. Politicians see the budget as an instrument of policy; agency administrators may see it as a management tool or plan for action. Agency clients bring yet another set of perspectives and priorities to the process (Lynch, p. 3). It bears repeating that we do not assume any single perspective to be correct or incorrect. Likewise, no single perspective can sufficiently describe the enormous complexity of budget process dynamics. The key to understanding lies in learning how each perspective contributes to the broader processes of determination of the overall size of the budget, departmental allocations, and even specific program decisions.

The Budget as an Allocator of Social Resources

Because people cannot always acquire all the goods and services that they need for themselves, they must rely on others for help. In contemporary societies, the allocation of goods and services is provided through two mechanisms: the private market system and the government system. Government allocates society's resources by mandating that taxes be collected and then by deciding where those taxes are spent.

Allocations are necessary in part because the market mechanism is not adequate to serve all societal needs. Services and goods that cannot be divided or assigned a cost to individuals, collective goods as they are called, will not be provided by a profit driven market (Bator, 1958)—the classic example of a collective good is national defense. Also, where price is not a good indicator of the value of a service, the private sector is unlikely to provide the service. Educational programs for the mentally handicapped fit into this category. Similarly, goods and service provisions where extraordinary risks are involved will not find free enterprise operating except in partnership with the public sector. Finally, the case where natural monopolies occur, where only one producer of a good or service can reasonably operate (such as with public utilities), mitigates against the operation of a free market. In all of these situations, the government is expected to use its power to ensure that certain resources are allocated to provide those services.

Government also allocates resources because society believes that we ought to, as a society, pursue positive goals—not just remedy the deficiencies in the market system. For example, government uses its power to command that monies be allocated for reducing unemployment, for attempting to relieve poverty and to discourage antisocial behavior. All of this redistribution occurs because the citizenry insists it wants these issues attended to.

The most immediate means by which government allocates financial resources is through the budget process. However, the budget is not the only means by which to allocate resources. The decision to support an initiative through tax decisions (called tax expenditures) is often the chosen means to decide how resources should be allocated on behalf of society. The central point here is the philosophical choice of government involvement in resolving a social problem. The budget allocation process from this perspective is one that determines the overall size of government and the government's level of participation in private-sector endeavors.

The Budget as a "Game"

Our attempt at an explanation of budgeting process behavior can be assisted by an understanding of the various roles assumed by budgeting participants. These roles are strongly influenced by the nature of the participant's constituency, by the fiscal or programmatic orientation the individual holds, and by the professional or political outlook of each participant. John Wanat succinctly outlines a series of distinct perspectives that illustrate the potential disparity in apprehension that is possible when budget actors conceptualize their responsibilities and obligations to the budgeting process. Wanat (1978) suggests seven such budgetary perspectives in the following list:

1. As an allocation mechanism, whereby a significant proportion of the nation's resources are channeled into efforts decided upon in the governmental sector
2. As a process that organizes the appropriation of money by elected leaders for specific purposes
3. As a stylized interaction among groups of governmental elites, all of whom have specific interests, stakes, and motivations for seeing particular budgetary outcomes
4. As a technical tool for controlling expenditures, for managing agencies, for planning programs
5. As a ritual in which many political and governmental figures go through their paces leading to a nearly foreordained conclusion
6. As plain and simple politics, by which is meant "who gets what, when, and how"
7. As a measurement of certain outputs of the governmental system

(p. 10)

Both in the way that internal perceptual understandings lead up to the presentation of the chief executive's budget in a particular style or format and in the legislators' choices of how to reshape that budget proposal, the role perceptions of the participants frame their attitudes and behaviors. Typically, it is only at the agency or program level and in the congressional committee where strong support for substantial budgetary increases ever exists. The role definitions of most of the other budget actors suggest a budget-cutting stance.

CHART 4–1

Budget Practices

Definition

A budget practice is a procedure that assists in accomplishing a principle and element of the budget process. It is appropriate for all governments and in all circumstances and situations. Budget practices can be hierarchical—that is, one practice can help accomplish another practice. The Council has avoided a practice hierarchy of more than one level. A budget element typically has multiple practices associated with it.

Budget practices must be clearly related to activities identified in the budget process definition. A practice is not a budget practice unless it specifically contributes to the development, description, understanding, implementation, and evaluation of a plan for provision of services and capital assets. For example, a policy statement on debt capacity is included in a set of budget practices since debt is a component of the budget and the budget decision-making. However, a practice encouraging competitive sales of debt is not a budget practice. More specific methods of accomplishing a budget practice are usually categorized as tools and techniques. There also may be alternative ways to accomplish a practice. Different governments may find one tool or technique works better for them than another. Budget practices do not identify a specific time frame, but tools and techniques may do so.

Element 1— Assess Community Needs, Priorities, Challenges, and Opportunities

Description:
A government should develop an understanding of the condition of the community, and trends and issues that may affect it in the future. This process requires an examination and assessment of stakeholder issues, concerns, needs, and desires. Also, factors that affect the community, stakeholders, and the government should be identified. These include the state of the economy, the composition of the population, technology, legal or regulatory issues, intergovernmental issues, and physical or environmental issues.

Practices of Element 1:

Practice 1.1— Identify Stakeholder Concerns, Needs, and Priorities

Practice 1.2— Evaluate Community Condition, External Factors, Opportunities, and Challenges

Element 2—Identify Opportunities and Challenges for Government Services, Capital Assets, and Management

Description:
A government should undertake an assessment of its own operations, including the services it currently provides, the assets it owns, its management structure, and the opportunities and challenges that may affect them. A government should review existing services and assess how well services address community needs and changes that may be necessary to respond to opportunities and challenges. There should also be a corresponding review of existing capital assets. Note that this element provides only for an evaluation of services and capital assets and does not address decisions as to whether to provide or maintain them. Since internal management practices can affect achievement of goals, issues such as organizational structure, information flow, and employee motivation should be reviewed to determine whether changes will be needed to achieve goals.

Practices of Element 2:

Practice 2.1— Assess Services and Programs, and Identify Issues, Opportunities, and Challenges

Practice 2.2— Assess Capital Assets, and Identify Issues, Opportunities, and Challenges

Practice 2.3— Assess Governmental Management Systems, and Identify Issues, Opportunities, and Challenges of Budget Practices

Element 3—Develop and Disseminate Broad Goals

Description:
A government should identify and disseminate broad goals. Broad goals should be related to the needs, challenges, and opportunities confronting the government and take into account the services operated by the government, its capital infrastructure, and its management systems. A government should also provide for dissemination and review of goals to ensure stakeholder understanding of the direction in which the government is moving.

Practices of Element 3:

Practice 3.1— Identify Broad Goals

Practice 3.2— Disseminate Goals and Review with Stakeholders

Element 4—Adopt Financial Policies

Description:
A government should develop a comprehensive set of financial policies. Financial policies should be consistent with broad government goals and should be the outcome of sound analysis. Policies also should be consistent with each other and relationships between policies should be identified. Financial policies should be an integral part of the development of service, capital, and financial plans and the budget. All other adopted budgetary practices of a government should be consistent with these policies.

Practices of Element 4:

Practice 4.1—	Develop Policy on Stabilization Funds
Practice 4.2—	Develop Policy on Fees and Charges
Practice 4.3—	Develop Policy on Debt Issuance and Management
Practice 4.4—	Develop Policy on Debt Level and Capacity
Practice 4.5—	Develop Policy on Use of One-Time Revenues
Practice 4.6—	Evaluate the Use of Unpredictable Revenues
Practice 4.7—	Develop Policy on Balancing the Operating Budget
Practice 4.8—	Develop Policy on Revenue Diversification
Practice 4.9—	Develop Policy on Contingency Planning

Element 5—Develop Programmatic, Operating and Capital Policies and Plans

Description:
A government should develop policies and plans to guide service provision and capital asset acquisition, maintenance, replacement, and retirement. These policies and plans give direction to the government regarding the level of services and types of capital assets to be provided, and the manner in which the services and capital assets will be provided. They should be integrated with the government's broad goals and its service and capital needs. They may include the development of standards for service provision and capital asset condition and maintenance. Policies and plans also should be consistent with each other. The practices associated with this element and those of Element 6 are closely related and will involve an iterative process.

Practices of Element 5:

Practice 5.1—	Prepare Policies and Plans to Guide the Design of Programs and Services
Practice 5.2—	Prepare Policies and Plans for Capital Asset Acquisition, Maintenance, Replacement, and Retirement

Element 6—Develop Programs and Services That Are Consistent with Policies and Plans

Description:
A government should develop and evaluate programs, services, and capital assets. Because there may be times when a government's policies and plans are best achieved by having other entities besides the government provide services or capital infrastructure, an analysis of service delivery and capital acquisition alternatives is an integral part of the program evaluation process. Performance measures should be developed to determine whether program and service goals are being met.

Practices of Element 6:

Practice 6.1— Develop Programs and Evaluate Delivery Mechanisms

Practice 6.2— Develop Options for Meeting Capital Needs and Evaluate Acquisition Alternatives

Practice 6.3— Identify Functions, Programs, and/or Activities of Organizational Units

Practice 6.4— Develop Performance Measures

Practice 6.5— Develop Performance Benchmarks

Element 7—Develop Management Strategies

Description:

A government should develop appropriate management strategies to enhance its ability to successfully execute the budget and to achieve long-range goals. Management strategies are necessary to facilitate achievement of both programmatic and financial goals, and to promote budgetary compliance. The choice of budget type and manner of presentation affects the information available to management and other decision makers, issues that will be raised, and level of control.

Practices of Element 7:

Practice 7.1— Develop Strategies to Facilitate Attainment of Program and Financial Goals

Practice 7.2— Develop Mechanisms for Budgetary Compliance

Pracitce 7.3— Develop the Type, Presentation, and Time Period of the Budget

Element 8—Develop a Process for Preparing and Adopting a Budget

Description:

A government should establish an administrative structure that facilitates the preparation and approval of a budget in a timely manner. Procedures should be established for ensuring coordination of the budget process. A process is also needed to develop and communicate the policies and guidelines that will guide budget preparation. In order for the budget to be adopted in a timely manner, processes should be developed to assist stakeholders in understanding tradeoffs and to help decision makers make choices among available options. The processes should include reporting to, communicating with, involving, and obtaining the support of stakeholders.

Practices of Element 8:

Practice 8.1— Develop a Budget Calendar

Practice 8.2— Develop Budget Guidelines and Instructions

Practice 8.3— Develop Mechanisms for Coordinating Budget Preparation and Review

Practice 8.4— Develop Procedures to Facilitate Budget Review, Discussion, Modification, and Adoption

Practice 8.5— Identify Opportunities for Stakeholder Input

Element 9—Develop and Evaluate Financial Options

Description:

A government should develop, update, and review long-range financial plans and projections. The information obtained from these plans and projections is used in determining the resource and expenditure options available for the budget period and the implications of those options. This element does not address decisions on a specific set of programs and services to be funded through the budget.

Practices of Element 9:

Practice 9.1— Conduct Long-Range Financial Planning

Practice 9.2— Prepare Revenue Projections

Practice 9.3— Analyze Major Revenues

Practice 9.4— Evaluate the Effect of Changes to Revenue Source Rates and Bases

Practice 9.5— Analyze Tax and Fee Exemptions

Practice 9.6— Achieve Consensus on a Revenue Forecast

Practice 9.7— Document Revenue Sources in a Revenue Manual

Practice 9.8— Prepare Expenditure Projections

Practice 9.9— Evaluate Revenue and Expenditure Options

Practice 9.10— Develop a Capital Improvement Plan

Element 10— Make Choices Necessary to Adopt a Budget

Description:

A government should prepare and adopt a budget. The proposed and adopted budget should be a comprehensive operating and financial plan. The budget document should communicate key fiscal and policy decisions, issues, and tradeoffs. In order to facilitate stakeholder understanding of the choices that have been made, it is essential that materials be prepared in a format that is clear and comprehensible.

Practices of Element 10:

Practice 10.1— Prepare and Present a Recommended Budget

Practice 10.1a— Describe Key Policies, Plans, and Goals

Practice 10.1b— Identify Key Issues

Practice 10.1c— Provide a Financial Overview

Practice 10.1d— Provide a Guide to Operations

Practice 10.1e— Explain the Budgetary Basis of Accounting

Practice 10.1f— Prepare a Budget Summary

Practice 10.1g— Present the Budget in a Clear, Easy-to-Use Format

Practice 10.2— Adopt the Budget

Element 11— Monitor, Measure, and Evaluate Performance

Description:

A government should monitor and analyze the performance of its service programs, its capital programs, and its financial performance. Performance should be based on stated goals and budget expectations. The analysis should also include customer and other stakeholder satisfaction and should include the impact of external factors affecting the government such as the economy, demographic and social factors, intergovernmental changes, weather, and other relevant factors.

Practices of Element 11:

Practice 11.1— Monitor, Measure, and Evaluate Program Performance

Practice 11.1a— Monitor, Measure, and Evaluate Stakeholder Satisfaction

Practice 11.2— Monitor, Measure, and Evaluate Budgetary Performance
Practice 11.3— Monitor, Measure, and Evaluate Financial Condition
Practice 11.4— Monitor, Measure, and Evaluate External Factors
Practice 11.5— Monitor, Measure, and Evaluate Capital Program Implementation

Element 12—Make Adjustments as Needed

Description:
From time to time, a government may need to adjust programs, strategies, performance measures, the budget, and goals based on the review and assessment of program, budget, financial condition measures, stakeholder satisfaction, and external factors. Processes are needed to ensure that these adjustments are formally presented to decision makers and other stakeholders and receive adequate consideration.

Practices of Element 12:
Practice 12.1— Adjust the Budget
Practice 12.2— Adjust Policies, Plans, Programs, and Management Strategies
Practice 12.3— Adjust Broad Goals, if Appropriate

Source: National Advisory Council on State and Local Budgeting: Government Finance Officers Association. www.gfoa.org/services/nacslb/

The executive branch's orientation to budgeting is characterized by professional personnel with a strong programmatic orientation based on a specific constituency. These actors consequently seek budget expansion; they believe the programs they administer are good for society. Chief executives, serving broad constituencies and coming from political backgrounds, must balance conservative fiscal demands with programmatic priorities of their own. Consequently, they both allow and seek higher funding levels for some agencies but also cut back on the desires of others. Departmental personnel must act to meet the programmatic demands of the agencies and at the same time meet the financial revenue constraints imposed on them by higher officials. Because senior department personnel have both political and professional backgrounds as well as diverse constituents inside and outside of government, their budgetary stance is variable. One of the least ambiguous roles is that of personnel in the central budget offices. They have only one constituent, the chief executive officer, and must take on that individual's programmatic and fiscal concerns. Revenue specialists are fiscally oriented and from professional backgrounds, and, like central budget office personnel, they serve the chief executive officer.

At the budget approval phase, action by legislators is also made more understandable by consideration of their constituency, background, and fiscal programmatic orientation. In general, legislators are dominated by their general constituency, which seeks reduced spending (unless it offers a recognizable advantage to them). As politicians, they will generally attempt to please their constituency, though just who that constituency is may vary with different legislative roles. The constituency of members of the appropriations committees, for example, are the rest of the legislators (Gist, 1978). They, too, seek low levels of spending because lowering overall budget totals is popular among legislators. Only where it can be shown that the programs would directly benefit them, or their constituencies does the norm of lowering budgets fail. Budget actions by legislators tend to find resolution by allowing some increase over what the agencies were allowed to spend in the previous year yet not as much as they had requested for the upcoming fiscal cycle.

For almost a half century, this legislative appropriations process was a model of almost predictable stability. Beginning in the 1960s, however, decisions on taxing and spending have been characterized by instability, experimentation, and compromise. The Budget and Impoundment Control Act of 1974 was a major statutory change challenging the executive branch's authority to accumulate budgetary reserves and fundamentally altering the established balance between the legislative and executive branches (Fisher, 1992). The increasing constraints of deficit politics through the late 1970s and early 1980s led to the passage in 1985 of the Balanced Budget and Emergency Deficit Control Act (known as Gramm-Rudman-Hollings), one of the most far-reaching and controversial acts of Congress ever initiated. Besides raising serious constitutional issues on separation of powers and the relative roles of Congress and the president in guiding the fiscal affairs of the nation, Gramm-Rudman-Hollings has been charged with exacerbating "expediency" in the budgeting process. (Critics insist that a $10-billion cushion allowed in the law, ostensibly to account for any "estimation errors" or "economic changes," was added simply to allow for a larger deficit!) Rather than making Congress more attuned to deficit reduction as its proponents claimed, Gramm-Rudman-Hollings has allowed Congress opportunities to indulge short-term institutional perspectives and has permitted it to avoid accountability on particularly controversial budgetary deliberations (LeLoup, Graham, and Barwick, 1992).

Finally, the frustrations of deficit politics since the 1980s have resulted in proposals to amend the US Constitution to require a balanced federal budget. A policy goal such as the balanced budget amendment suggests a popular perception that government can no longer be depended upon to achieve deficit reduction without specific rules. This perception is based, of course, on the subjective judgment that balanced budgets are unconditionally superior to deficits and that the political process systematically produces inferior results. The case for rules rather than discretion in policy making has been given vitality by "rational" expectations, but the case for such rules has not been demonstrated to unequivocally speak for constitutional amendment. Rules can be followed (priorities can be incorporated into the budgeting process) without constitutional amendment. To incorporate such a rule into the US Constitution without adequate justification would clearly be hasty and premature (Keech, 1992).

"Politics" of Budgeting

The budget is the ultimate political tool. It is the budget, not legislation, which affirms the priorities and policies of a government. The politics of the budget get played out in several venues and several time frames. For example, budgets can be presented in several formats. The most common are:

- Line-item
- Technically based (ZBB, PPBS)
- Performance-based

Because each of these formats conveys different information, they direct decision-making toward different choices in both the short term and the long term. The line item budget is the most traditional of budgets. It is most effective at tracking expenditures over time within the context of single-purpose, well-defined, programs. It is not good at communicating the priorities among competing and overlapping functional areas. It makes "incremental" funding choices easier to understand. Yet it also makes program effectiveness difficult to measure. Legislatures often favor line-item budgets because they simplify oversight at least for stable programs.

As early as the 1950s a variety of budget "reforms" were introduced to replace the line-item budget. Program budgeting was first proposed as a companion to performance budgeting by the Hoover Commission, appointed by President Truman in 1949. Three decades later the idea of zero-based budgeting was proposed by President Carter. These techniques emphasized the separation of current expenditures from proposed and anticipated budgets. They generally emphasized more long-term or strategic analysis of expenditures. The use of these techniques often paralleled the political tug-of-war between the executive and legislatives branches over who would have final say in expenditures. Legislatures have rarely been supportive of these "reforms" because they saw them as little more than thinly disguised efforts to hide the policy intentions of the executive.

"Performance-based budgeting" has been at the heart of public-sector budget reform for five decades. Seemingly, performance budgeting is old enough that it is in "fashion" again (see discussion of performance budgeting in Bland and Rubin, 1997, pp. 14–17). The notion of performance budget is deceptively simple. Lynch (1995) describes performance budgeting (and the related program budgeting) as the rational allocation of money based upon grouping activities and defining the outcomes of those activities (p. 43–44). The problem is that the outcomes by which performance is measured may be in dispute. Who controls the definition, controls the evaluation of performance. This is an age-old statement in government that invokes all the elements of the political and philosophical conflict between the legislature and the executive. Thus, even in this sub-field there are numerous difficulties in establishing performance measures that can then be used in budget analysis. Joyce (1993) enumerates the following:

- The difficulty in agreeing on objectives and priorities of agencies is an enduring obstacle to performance measurement, and this problem is perhaps particularly acute in the federal government.
- Even where objectives and priorities can be agreed upon, developing the measures themselves is challenging.
- Local and state governments have had limited successes in using performance measures beyond the individual agency level, particularly for budgeting.
- Past federal efforts to link performance to budgeting were not successful, and repetition of these mistakes should be avoided.
- Since federal agencies currently use performance measures for only limited purposes, which rarely include budgeting, the task is a challenging one. In particular, responsibilities vary widely from agency to agency; therefore, it is important not to treat the federal government as a monolithic entity.
- Any performance measurement effort must confront the issue of the appropriate combination of executive and legislative branch action.

- The pace of reform may be an important factor in its potential for success. The complexity of the endeavor suggests that a deliberate approach is better than adopting a set of uniform, and immediate, requirements for all federal agencies.
- It is important to understand how performance measures might influence the budget process, which requires understanding their limitations.

(p. 336)

The Politics of Budgetary Decision-Making

Since the budget is the life-blood of any program, the budget is the ultimate policy tool (Wildavsky, 2004). Control of the budget means:

- Expenditure control
- Program control
- Outcome control

As suggested above even the form and format of the budget document can become a highly charged political issue. The various forms and formats begin from an assumption of who should control the budget process. The reform efforts discussed above are frequently championed by different groups within government because the form gives that particular group control of the flow of information upon which budget decisions rest. Thus, legislators prefer a line-item budget because it better fits the compromise- and consensus-driven deliberations of legislative bodies (Wildavsky, 2001). Political executives (and the agencies which report directly to the executive) prefer a technically based budget because the preponderance of technical competencies rest within the executive. Agencies prefer either a technically based or a performance-based budget, whichever form gives the functional agencies greater control over the flow of information to the political executive and/or the legislature. Mid-level managers prefer a performance-based budget because it provides the richest source of data to judge organizational operations.

As suggested earlier the typical budget format remains the line-item budget because it best suits the legislature. On the other hand, political executives often pursue post-budget enactment controls through the line-item veto and authority to restrict expenditures based upon revenue contingencies.

Until overtaken by macro concerns about deficits, the central debate among academics concerning public budgeting was over the quest for an alternative to "incrementalism." Based upon Lindblom's theory of decision-making, it suggests that decisions about future expenditures are based upon small (incremental) changes from current expenditures. Incrementalism is criticized for being "irrational" because budget changes are seemingly divorced from agency performance and effectiveness. It is criticized for being too conservative (status quo is "right"); funding for new initiatives often get squeezed out as older programs continue (sometimes well beyond the time when they should be terminated). Furthermore, it implies political control over technical-professionals. In fact, it continued existence is precisely because political institutions, but particularly legislatures, prefer the greater control it affords them. The two theorists most associated with incrementalism, Aaron Wildavsky and Charles Lindblom, both argued that rather than being irrational, incrementalism is a *rational* response to the need to decide with inadequate information and little time for introspection.

MICRO-BUDGET PERSPECTIVES

Given the incredible complexity, political volatility, and professional vulnerability the budgeting process encompasses, it is not surprising that few managers look with much favor upon it. The budget consumes enormous amounts of time in preparation (line managers rarely support academically initiated reforms to rationalize the budget because they often result in more paperwork), often with precious little positive result—and more recently, often with negative consequences. Despite the problems, managers must recognize the importance of devoting time to budget development and, moreover, be prepared to adjust their organizational operations to fluctuating budgetary priorities. These fluctuating priorities demand that the agency manager develop an astute sense of how to coordinate, negotiate, and manipulate the various players in the budgeting subprocess, especially at the micro-level. Assessing which elements of the ever-changing budgetary environment demand the most attention and in what order can be a daunting task for the manager. This section explores some of the more critical elements as they operate within the agency context.

The Budget Cycle

The process of determining how much any particular agency receives in any given year is one that may take nearly three years to complete. This reality presents a number of problems for the manager. Planning as part of budget review is difficult because the anticipated amounts of money available for future budgets are always far from certain. The expenditures being planned are two years away, and the amounts to be spent in the interim are not even finalized. In environments where expenditures are generally stable, this may not be a significant problem. However, where the organization is experiencing programmatic or budget volatility, planning becomes infinitely more difficult.

At the other end of the cycle, the time available for budget analysis and review is deceptively short. Much of the lead time before budget enactment is reserved for policy makers, whether they work for the chief executive or are in the legislature. The time required to complete a budget review obviously detracts from the time available for day-to-day agency operations. Complicating the situation even further, the timing of any rebuttal or rejoinder to decisions occurring outside the agency is necessarily quite close to the end of a fiscal year or at the start of a new fiscal year. (From the standpoint of agency operations, this could not be a worse time.) Further, decisions made about those future budgets will have implications, both positive and negative, for current operations.

Budget Restrictions

It is never an easy task to interpret budget changes. While the US Congress often provides some information about funding-level decisions, it is quite rare for state legislatures to provide such information. Decisions as to how to allocate resources granted by the legislature are possibly the most significant choices administrators make. The manager's knowledge of politics and ability to negotiate and mediate among policy makers can be of more importance than technical skill in agency operations. This is especially true where there is disagreement among policy makers. The question of budget interpretation is possibly the best illustration of the effect that a management subprocess can have on one's ability to manage.

Texts on budgeting often suggest that the budget is simultaneously a highly structured process of analysis (budget preparation) and a highly controversial and political process (budget enactment). In the first part of the process, the agency manager plays a major role. In the second part of the process, the manager is relegated to the sidelines while politicians and policy makers decide an agency's fate. These descriptions are, at best, only partially correct. They fail to reflect the role of the manager adequately in defining and defending program allocations during executive department deliberations and, somewhat more covertly, during legislative deliberations. Texts on budgeting rarely examine the line manager-budget office battle in any depth and treat the budget enactment process as though only the legislature and the chief executive are involved.

The agency manager is invariably caught up in the process of negotiating and bargaining over the allocations of funds (Sharkansky, 1968). This is not a conflict based on analyses of program output so much as it is about perceptions. (Will the legislature accept a large increase in this agency? Does this program reflect the chief executive's agenda? Does the public approve of this program?) Program performance is, of course, related to these concerns, but a well-run but unpopular program will still find it difficult to acquire new monies. The agency manager must appreciate these political realities and address efforts for new funds to these perceptions.

A final point concerning negotiations is to remember that they take place in two different arenas: within the executive branch and then in the legislative branch. The concern of the branches with regard to an agency may be different or even in conflict (LeLoup and Moreland, 1978). In the final analysis, the manager's assertiveness in negotiating between the branches may ultimately shape the overall success the agency achieves in overall growth and funding requests approved by the legislature.

Post Audit and Review

The question of how well monies are spent is one which again brings the manager and legislature together. The issues of expenditure need not rest on narrow technical concerns of whether expenditures were made from the proper line item or on the timeliness and exactitude of the paperwork. These are critical questions but no longer the only ones being asked of the manager. The increasing number of state legislatures using audit bureaus and the shifting emphasis at the US Government Accountability Office (an arm of the US Congress) to managerial rather than accounting audits reflects a concern that how well a program is run has more to do with the political correctness of the policy area than with the accuracy of the balance sheets (Sharkansky, 1965).

A modern government agency manager can expect far closer scrutiny of why, when, and where funds were spent than ever before. Again, the reconciliation of political controversy and policy choices falls to the manager. The need to justify the decisions to re-allocate funds will be a critical responsibility for the manager.

The successful manager is often the one who can make programmatic changes without budget change. It is not merely a case of doing more with less (though that may be one result). It requires a skill in accepting the pace of incrementalism by making changes in practice, procedure, or program output at the same pace. This implies having people doing more than one job during that slow transition, but, since it is the nature of the process, there is rarely much more that can be done.

The successful manager must simultaneously use the extended budget process for mid-range planning. Since the budget process starts nearly two years before the start of the fiscal year, the budget can be used to encourage planning. Thinking in terms of the current year or even merely next year is a sure formula for staying behind.

In addition, the successful manager must recognize the politics of the budgeting process, particularly the politics played within the executive branch. Once the budget enters the executive review process and most certainly by the time it goes to the legislature, the budget parameters are fairly well established. The political playing field begins at the agency and department levels. The notion of a budgetary fair share is often set at the department level, not in the legislature. Selling the merits of a program to budget examiners and senior managers may be the most important lobbying activity of a manager. Further, moving programs into the budgetary "base" as quickly as possible is another intradepartmental process. A program that cannot establish a base and define a fair share within its department is a candidate for abolition in times of budget cutback, or at best, it will have to tolerate a boom-bust cycle of funding that may be impossible to manage (Hale and Douglas, 1977).

Lastly, it must be remembered that the execution phase of the budget begins with decisions on the apportionment of funds. Holding on to a fair share may be as difficult (more difficult during cutbacks) when apportionment decisions are made. Many a program that did not have an established base yet cleared all the budget deliberations hurdles all but disappeared during apportionment. Apportionment decisions are made more difficult when certain program activities are front-loaded or back-loaded. The successful manager must first hold on to a fair share but also gain enough flexibility in allocations that "lumps" in the expenditure cycle can be covered.

FOUR PLUS DECADES OF GLOBAL FISCAL CRISIS

Public Administration as an academic discipline and as professional practice is built on the three pillars of economy, efficiency, and effectiveness. Especially in the American version, the foundations of public management in the first half of the twentieth century looked to functional analyses (Gulick, 1937a, 1937b) and newly developing management practices (Taylor, 1911; Urwick, 1937b; Follett, 1996), primarily emphasizing economy and efficiency. Briefly in the 1960s the academics across the world in the field of public administration proposed a new focus on the effectiveness of public organizations. The optimism and high expectations of the post-World War II era were dashed in the 1970s by much rockier economic and, therefore, budgetary circumstances.

In the US the academic response was to explore "cut-back" management and "retrenchment" (Levine, 1980). In the UK and elsewhere the emphasis was on budget control and reform that would evolve into what is now known as the New Public Management (Pollitt, 1995; Hood and Dixon, 2013). The "solutions" to the fiscal problems of the late 1970s seem both familiar and yet oddly quaint some forty years later as cut-back management in the US morphed into first privatization, next reinvention, and then the New Public Management. While there are occasional echoes of other viewpoints through an emphasis on improving quality of services, the political and organizational responses to reinvention were a shift toward an "efficiency and economy" perspective (see the comments on the Gore Commission in Hill and Lynn, 2009, p. 84).

By the beginning of the twenty-first century the idea of fiscal stress was labeled as a "permanent" aspect of American politics and governance (Hutchinson and Osborne, 2004). That a Labour Government under Tony Blair would adopt and even extend the fiscal and managerial policies initiated by Margaret Thatcher and the political success of right-of-center governments from France to Sweden were the order of the day, affirmed Europeans' attraction to governments that promised less government. These concerns were exacerbated by the demise of communist control of eastern European countries. The new regimes of the early 1990s embraced the idea of privatization as an anecdote to the intrusive and heavy-handed control of those regimes (McKevitt, 1998; Peters, 2010). Making government "work" meant removing programs from government control and radically reducing economic regulations. The horror of the authoritarian regimes under communist control seemingly was easily corrected, by eliminating the functions and activities of government workers. Charges of waste and corruption that may have been theoretical complaints in Western Europe and the USA were very real in Eastern Europe. The reality of the corruption in Eastern Europe and the reduction in government from the bloated behemoths of the communist era became proof of the relationship between waste and big government asserted by public choice economists. Western European governments, but especially the US government, would be more economical and efficient if they followed the lead of those former eastern bloc countries. Deregulation and privatization solved all problems. The only slightly more moderate precepts of the New Public Management were touted and embraced in Japan, Canada, Singapore, New Zealand, and elsewhere.

What changed over the time from the cut-back management period to that of the New Public Management? First is the sense that a fiscal crisis required a shift from a "managed" response by the public sector into one in which the private-sector approach is viewed as the *only* way to get things done (in fact through privatization, or in spirit through the adoption of private-sector methods). Second is a change in public perception from one in which fiscal distress is an "event" in time to one in which fiscal distress is the steady-state. Third is that the ideas of the New Public Management were deeply ingrained in the rhetoric and practice of politics (Pollitt, 1995). All three of the elements, but especially the third element, contribute to the incapacity and incapability (i.e. political infeasibility) of governments addressing problems related to improving the quality of public service. The potential results are a broken system in which revenue growth is not used for policy realignment, but for budget cuts and in which decisions by one government are treated as though those decisions have no consequences for people outside that government's narrow jurisdiction.

> Part of the reason why cross-national studies have not been able to go far in answering the basic question of whether or how far NPM reforms succeeded in cutting costs is that the data needed to answer that question are not to be found in the sort of cross-national datasets that many comparative scholars of public management reform rely on. . . . In the face of such problems, the best way of answering the question seems to be by a form of "consilience" . . . . Consilience means putting evidence together from several sources, no one of which is perfect on its own, but which if combined provide more powerful evidence than any one element would do on its own if those various sources point in the same direction.
>
> (Hood and Dixon, 2013, p. 116)

This review is an exercise in consilience. In a preliminary way it begins to pull some of the analyses from across the globe to bear on the central themes of this study; the extent to which the sense of the new normal of fiscal distress is accepted by the public as both normal and possibly even normative and, therefore, does not require reform or change. Certainly, it would appear that across the world, against the evidence, the ideology of the governments as failures pervades politics. To explore this topic in more detail, it is first necessary to take a step back and look at the evolution of the literature on public management in both theory and practice and then examine the fiscal implications of that perspective.

Fiscal Conflict in the American System

In parallel with changing understandings of American public administration has been an evolutionary (de-evolutionary?) change in the public policy as an intergovernmental endeavor. By the 1970s public finances were so intertwined that no government truly had the exclusive policy responsibility for, or the exclusive capability to implement policy (Miller and Cox, 2014). These changes were a manifestation of the evolution of public administration, not politics. Program development, analysis, and implementation required a level of professionalism not previously acknowledged. The renaissance of the states was a public administration revolution (Cox, 2009; Miller and Cox, 2014).

While the revenue generation systems in the United States were never self-consciously tied together, by the last quarter of the twentieth century certain assumptions and expectations dominated intergovernmental relations. These links were part of the solution to the policy expansion of the 1950 and 1960s, but also fiscal problems of the 1970s. This arrangement was fragile (Cox, 2009; Miller and Cox, 2014). It was dependent on funding sources to continue, jointly or independently, to maintain the funding stream (Cox, 2009). Unfortunately, this was not to be. The politics of the end of the twentieth century and beginning of the next century changed from one of partnership to one where the governments refocused their attention on their own interests and goals. Governments were much more interested in their own bottom line than in sharing revenues (Casselman, 2014). The interactions among governments that had been marked by cooperation began to disintegrate. The new relationship was to be defined by the conflict and controversy associated with "unfunded" mandates (Miller and Cox, 2014).

Many of the policy mechanisms that helped address the fiscal crisis in US cities and states in the 1970s and 1980s are no longer available, but more critically the public support for significant public action by state and local governments also is gone. The current situation began against a backdrop that Hutchinson and Osborne (2004) starkly describe as one of the ever-increasing costs of health care and public safety needs, an aging population, pension plans, continuing resistance to major tax increases, and an increasing demand and need for public assistance programs that have placed new stresses on state and local governments.

Over the last three plus decades, policy choices have increasingly become self-referential. The safest political path when faced with fiscal problems was to cut monies transferred to other governments. These cuts meant that the deliverer of the services paid the political price for the withdrawal of funds, not the governments who funded the services. The public choice mantra that public managers are incompetent and wasteful is invoked to justify budget cuts that are the product of economic malfunctions. The progressive era notion of economy and efficiency, coupled with a heavy dose of privatization, has become the norm. But more critical for this analysis is that the political objective of the public choice perspective requires a constant drum beat of crisis and fiscal stress. These become problems that are unsolvable. Government is the problem, and, therefore, all government solutions (except privatization) will fail.

Realigning the American Fiscal System

The late 1950s and into the early 1980s is a period of renaissance for state government. Never an important fiscal actor and not particularly important on national issues after the Civil War, the states reform, reorganize, and reshape themselves as partners for both the federal and state government on a variety of fiscal policy issues. Five reforms in this period are indicative of the changes occurring in the states:

- Massive increases in state funding for public education
- A systematic policy of expansion of post-secondary public education
- Assumption of both the cost and administration of the "local" share of social services
- Major re-organizational and restructuring reforms
- Transformation of state tax policy to generate funds to finance the above and other new initiatives across a wide range of policy

For the purposes of this commentary we need not explore all of the above reforms. For our purposes it is the last item that is most important. Just as the federal government never could become an important part of the expansion of social services in the twentieth century without a shift from unreliable and inconsistent revenues from customs duties to the graduated personal income tax as the prime revenue source, the states could not remake themselves without creating a more equitable and reliable revenue system. From the mid-1950s to the mid-1970s states debated, refined, and expanded their tax systems, focusing on two issues: tax equity and revenue redistribution. While in 1950 relatively few states used an income tax as a source of revenue, by 1975 more than 40 states used that method. Furthermore, states sought wherever possible to substitute state dollars raised through sales and income taxes to replace regressive local property taxes. The basis for the shift was a belief that taxation should be as equitable (i.e. progressive) as possible and that revenue systems should be elastic.

Tax Elasticity and Tax Progressivity

Economists classify tax systems in a number of ways. One is the extent to which the tax system has the capacity to generate a revenue stream that grows proportionally larger as it increases. This is referred to as elasticity. Certain taxes, but most particularly graduated income taxes, are elastic. Taxes that are inelastic grow (or potentially even decline) at the same rate as the growth in the monies being taxed. Real estate taxes, consumption taxes (cigarettes, fuel), and fees are examples of taxes that are generally considered inelastic.

A related issue is the fairness or equity achieved through the tax. While not exactly the same thing, we associate tax equity with tax progressivity. Graduated income taxes are progressive because those who are most capable of paying the tax are subject to higher tax rates and, therefore, presumptively contribute a higher portion of their income in taxes. Thus at least in the case of a graduated income tax it is both progressive and equitable.

State Tax Reform

As noted above much of the focus on the restructuring of state taxes in the '50s, '60s and '70s was driven by a desire to ensure that the increases in taxes also were progressive, equitable, and elastic. During those decades, states shifted away from other taxes and kept sales taxes low by using the income tax as the prime generator of new revenues. I remember sitting in on legislative floor debates in Massachusetts in which the issue of the relative merits of different tax increases were argued based upon progressivity and equity.

By the middle of the 1980s the states had become the lynchpin in the intergovernmental system. The federal government remained the primary funder of cross-national activities, but the role of the states had changed to that of an important service delivery partner for the federal government and the major source of intergovernmental dollars for local governments. The addition of a federal revenue sharing program during the Nixon administration and the steady growth of federal support for state and local governments and states for municipalities are the hallmark of the 1970s.

Informal Tax Redistribution

While the revenue generation systems in the US were never self-consciously tied together, by the last quarter of the twentieth century certain assumptions and expectations dominated intergovernmental relations. These assumptions and expectations were:

- In the name of effective tax administration, tax capacity and equity revenue collections should be pushed upward through the intergovernmental system, sometimes twice (local to state and state to federal). Unofficially and informally "they" were collecting money for "us."
- The money collected "above" was returned/redistributed based upon shared expectations that reflected mutually agreed upon policy goals. The sense was that this was *our* money being collected by *one of us* and then returned.
- Policy implementation represented broad policy goals with the ability at the local level to tailor the funding to reflect specific needs within the goals.

While the tri-lateral relationship among local, state, and federal governments has remained the same over the last two decades, increasingly the politics of those relationships and the fiscal dynamics of those relationship have changed. The interactions among governments which had been marked by cooperation began to disintegrate. The new relationship was to be defined by the conflict and controversy associated with "unfunded" mandates.

Realigning the Tax Structure

The 1980s did not get off to an auspicious start. A recession that would push unemployment to 10 percent by December 1982, the cancellation of the last vestiges of federal revenue sharing, and a series of statutes and initiatives to limit the capacity of state and local to increase taxes changed the relationship, if not yet significantly, of the dollars flowing through the intergovernmental system.

Critical for the fiscal system, the public attitude about government had shifted. While there was never much public support for state and local government, the trust in the federal government born in the Depression had evaporated. More importantly it was the private sector, which had little interest in tax equity or the intergovernmental system, that drove pushes for corporate tax cuts and rate reductions at the higher end of the tax scale (i.e. making the income tax less progressive). The federal tax cuts of 1982 focused on reducing the top end of the tax structure. A flat rate income tax (introduced by "liberal" US Senator Bradley) was seriously debated by the US Congress. Even when tax increases were needed (as in 1986, 1992, and 1998) the tax debate was of a very different character than in the '60s and '70s. Increases were as likely to affect middle-class Americans as they were the poor or the wealthy. Deductions for health-care expenditures were curtailed by applying a net income deduction, but deductions for income tax payments and mortgage interest on multiple homes were preserved. The result of the tax changes in the 1980s and 1990s was a federal personal income tax system that was less progressive, yet it was still targeted as too high at the top end of the scale.

The debate in the states was even more stilted. Beginning with Proposition 13 in California and Proposition 2.5 in Massachusetts, the capacity of states and local governments to increase taxes and/or an outright cap on tax rates was instituted. In other states the focus was almost exclusively on retrenchment and reductions of business taxes. In parallel the new model for economic development was the offer of "tax incentives" to convince businesses to relocate. Quite literally tens of millions of state and local taxes were not collected. Funding for a wide variety of programs, and especially in the programs that were the crowning achievement of the state renaissance—social services, public education, and local government revenue sharing—was cut or at least limited in growth. "Reform" became synonymous with program and tax cuts.

Fiscal Policy in the New Century

Where then were we as this century began? Every politician knows that to even suggest a tax increase is to incur the wrath of the general public and is presumed to be a sure way to lose the next election. For most of the decade public opinion was decidedly against any government action. Even as the nation entered a second recession of the decade in 2008, public sentiment and legislative actions favored even further cuts.

In the public mind there is little or no connection between "revenues" and "expenditures." Budgets are the limitations placed (rightly and wrongly) upon services by politicians who have a different "agenda" than everyday people. In December 2017 Congress enacted and the president signed into law revisions to the federal tax code that offered significant cuts to wealthy people in general and changed the tax regulations on certain types of investments that reduced the tax rate to below the lowered rate for "regular" income. Some of the rate cuts were offset by programmatic cuts, but the program reductions are far smaller than the revenue losses. While the numbers are difficult to calculate, the consensus is that the cuts will increase the overall deficit, even as we have experienced a decade of historically high federal deficits against revenues coming into the federal coffers. The tax cuts were only marginally popular with the general public and that support has dropped to the point where the majority of Americans think the cuts will not help the economic growth. That lack of broad support may suggest that the rather pessimistic view of the public's attitude is changing. A better gauge will be whether efforts to correct the disparity between revenues and expenditures become part of the public discourse in the states in the next couple of years.

The disconnect extends into the other levels of government. Particularly at the local level the disconnect of the public is reflected in the response of city councils and state legislatures to the budget. While all will affirm the importance of the requirement of a balanced budget, the debate in the council and legislature often is about expenditures without regard to existing budget commitments. Assertions that the deficit can be fixed by simply eliminating "waste" is accepted and applauded.

Increasingly funding is controlled by rules that are beyond the control of those who must deliver services. Administrative decisions and court rulings that mandate expenditures for programs rarely consider budgetary or tax constraints. The courts do not consider that a community may be "capped" in terms of its authority to increase taxes. Court rulings and administrative decisions are made sequentially and independently of all other actions. The consequences are not relevant to the decision maker.

A Broken System

The last two decades of the twentieth century was been an economic and financial disaster for all levels of governments, but especially the states and municipalities.

The willingness of the public to support tax change, other than tax cuts is nonexistent. Each level of government operates on the basis that there are no fiscal consequences for others in the fiscal policy decisions they make. The federal government cuts taxes even though the lost revenues create still larger deficits. Intergovernmental transfers have become a "luxury" that cannot be afforded because of deficits, created in part by tax cuts. The states, although rarely allowed to operate with a deficit, nonetheless follow the same practices as the federal government. Multi-year tax cuts are enacted, which create deficits, which have to be corrected by program cuts. Funding for local governments and public education become luxuries that must be sacrificed to meet the mandate of balanced budgets. The downward spiral of budget cuts goes beyond the expectations of doing more with less and seemingly have a momentum of their own. Most devastating for "recipient" governments is that these cuts occur in programs that are most visibly their responsibility—schools, roads, public safety. The public's displeasure is felt by those closest to them—the local government.

The Continuing Fiscal Crisis

Ray Sheppach, the Executive Director of the National Governors Associations (NGA), has argued that the public sector has entered an era of "perpetual fiscal crisis." He described the convergence of forces swelling to buffet public finance as "a perfect storm" (Hutchinson and Osborne, 2004). We must keep in mind that Sheppach was describing the situation as the country was emerging from the economic downturn of 2001–2002, not the economic crisis of 2008–2010.

We entered the situation ill-prepared economically and politically to address the problem. The situation began against a backdrop that Hutchinson and Osborne (2004) described as one of ever-increasing cost of health care and public safety needs, an aging population, pension plans, continuing resistance to major tax increases along with and increasing demand and need for public assistance programs that have placed new stresses on state and local governments. They go on to note that state governments were passing their problems down to cities and counties, with deep cuts in local aid, while the federal government has been digging a fiscal hole so rapidly that future cuts and unfunded mandates for states and localities are inevitable (Hutchinson and Osborne, 2004). Even a much less severe economic downturn may have triggered the crisis of 2008–2010.

Where are we today? The fragile equilibrium of the intergovernmental system has collapsed. The funding sources, which supported the system, have made radical cuts in, or simply stopped, funding programs. There is no longer a margin for error. Thirty years of doing more with less has left little capacity to keep up with the demand for services even though there is no tolerance for increasing resources to provide those services.

As massive as the federal stimulus package of 2010 was, it is notable for two things: first, the system is so bound up in regulations that the only way to redistribute monies is through existing programs, and second, despite how small the reduction in the deficits of the states and municipalities, the public sees it as having "solved" the problem. The continuing problem of deficits again becomes one of (in the public's mind) mismanagement and waste. When local and state governments are floating in even more red ink, the public will have little sympathy, because we already addressed the problem.

The Depression spawned an entire new system of intergovernmental partnerships and a multi-decade long discourse on effectiveness and equity in tax policy. The last four decades have been a period of retrenchment. The informal understandings that served as the basis for tax policy shifted back to a more independent perspective that in reality was feasible only because of the tax policy system the new arrangement rejected.

What should concern us all is that there is no sense of need to reform the system. The most important fiscal crisis of the twentieth century radically remade the fiscal relations among all levels of government. The first great fiscal crisis of the twenty-first century has produced little sense of long-term peril, but rather a belief that the sooner we get back to the "way it was" the better.

CONCLUSION: THE MANAGEMENT SUPPORT SYSTEM

Our brief examination has demonstrated that managers employ a large number of techniques to increase their budgetary flexibility and discretion. Administrators make policy despite or often perhaps because of the absence of legislative and executive guidance. While we are aware that our survey is not exhaustive and does not go into the countless possible variations, we hope we have described the essential mechanisms and dynamics that explain the budgetary process actors and the manager's place in the action.

As complex as budgeting and budget reform seem, the need to address the fiscal policy elements of budgeting are more complex. Seemingly, in nations across the globe the fiscal tools that are permitted by the public and the fiscal tools that make sense as a governance exercise are at odds. After more than four decades of fiscal instability, most governments are no further along (and some seem to be going backwards) with regard to getting their individual fiscal houses in order. Budget reform is all but meaningless under such circumstances.

DISCUSSION QUESTIONS

- What has been the affect on executive-legislative relations by the shift to an executive budget?
- Can budget reform that presumes that politics can be removed from the budget work?
- How does the budget relation to policy analysis and policy implementation?
- Critique zero-based budgeting.
- Does incremental budgeting actually work?
- Way is budgeting so deeply imbedded in politics?
- Why can't governments successfully implement program budgeting (or maybe they do)?
- How can budget staff best support managers and decision-makers?

BIBLIOGRAPHY

Bator, Francis M. "The Anatomy of Market Failure", *Quarterly Journal of Economics*, 72 (3), pp. 351–379. August 1958.

Bland, Robert, and Irene Rubin. *Budgeting: A Guide for Local Governments*. Washington DC: ICMA. 1997.

Casselman, B. "Public Schools are Hurting More in the Recovery than in the Recession." [Online], (Retrieved June 10, 2014, www.fivethirtyeight.com/economics).

Cox III, Raymond W. "Seeding the Clouds for the Perfect Storm: A Commentary on the Current Fiscal Crisis", *State and Local Government Review*, 41 (3), pp. 216–222. 2009.

Fisher, Louis. "Ten Years of the Budget Act: Still Searching for Controls", in Albert C. Hyde (ed.) *Government Budgeting, 2nd ed.* Pacific Grove, CA: Brooks/Cole Publishing, pp. 135–153. 1992.

Follett, M. P. "The Essentials of Leadership", in P. Graham (ed.) *Mary Parker Follett: Prophet of Management*. Boston: Harvard Business School Publishing, pp. 163–177. 1996.

Gist, John R. " 'Increment' and 'Base' in the Congressional Appropriations Process", *American Journal of Political Science*, XXI (2), pp. 341–352. May 1977.

Gist, John R. "Appropriations Politics and Expenditure Control", *The Journal of Politics*, 40, pp. 163–178. 1978.

Gulick, Luther. "Notes on the Theory of Organization", in Luther Gulick and Lyndall Urwick (eds.) *Papers on the Science of Administration*. New York: Institute of Public Administration, pp. 3–46. 1937a.

Gulick, Luther. *Papers on the Science of Administration*. New York: Institute of Public Administration. 1937b.

Hale, George E., and Scott R. Douglas. "The Politics of Budget Execution: Financial Manipulation in State and Local Government", *Administration and Society*, 9 (3), pp. 367–378. November 1977.

Harkness, Peter. "Tying Federal Funding to Regional Cooperation", *Governing*. September 2009. Web. 25 October 2009.

Hill, Carolyn, and Laurence Lynn, Jr. *Public Management: A Three-Dimensional Approach*. Washington, DC: CQ Press. 2009.

Hoene, Christopher, and Michael Pagano. "Research Brief on America's Cities: City Fiscal Conditions in 2009", *National League of Cities*, pp. 1–11. September 2009.

Hood, Christopher, and R. Dixon. "A Model of Cost-Cutting in Government? The Great Management Revolution in UK Central Government Recon-

sidered", *Public Administration*, 91 (1), 114–134. 2013.

Hutchinson, Peter, and David Osborne. "Introduction", In Hutchinson and Osborn (eds.) *The Price of Government: Getting the Results We Need in an Age of Permanent Fiscal Crisis*. New York: Basic Books, Inc, pp. 1–15. 2004.

Joyce, Philip G. "Using Performance Measures", in: "Using Performance Measures for Federal Budgeting: Proposals and Prospects", *Public Budgeting & Finance*, 13 (Winter), pp. 3–17. 1993

Keech, William R. "A Theoretical Analysis of the Case for a Balanced Budget Amendment", in Albert C. Hyde (ed.) *Government Budgeting*. Pacific Grove, CA: Brooks/Cole Publishing. 1992.

LeLoup, Lance T., Barbara L. Graham, and Stacey Barwick. "Deficit Politics and Constitutional Government: The Impact of Gramm-Rudman-Hollings", in Albert C. Hyde (ed.) *Government Budgeting*. Pacific Grove, CA: Brooks/Cole Publishing, pp. 154–168. 1992.

LeLoup, Lance T., and William Moreland. "Agency Strategies and Executive Review: The Hidden Politics of Budgeting", *Public Administration Review*, 38 (3), pp. 232–239. May-June 1978.

Lemov, Penelope. "How to Win and Income-Tax Hike", *Governing. Governing Magazine*, 21 October 2009. Web, 25 October 2009.

Levine, Charles H. *Managing Fiscal Stress*. Chatham, NJ: Chatham House. 1980.

Lynch, Thomas D. *Public Budgeting in America, 4th ed.* Englewood Cliffs, NJ: Prentice Hall. 1995.

Lynch, Thomas D. *Public Budgeting in America, 5th ed.* Upper Saddle River, NJ: Prentice Hall. 2004.

McKevitt, David. *Managing Core Public Services*. Malden, MA: Blackwell. 1998.

Miller, David Y. and Raymond W. Cox III. *The Metropolitan Region: Governing America's New Frontier*. Armonk, NY: M.E. Sharpe.

Peters, B. Guy. *The Politics of Bureaucracy, 6th ed.* London: Routledge.

Pollitt, C. "Justification by Works or by Faith? Evaluating the New Public Management." *Evaluation*, 1 (2): 133–54. 1995.

Pound, William T. *State Tax Update: July 2009*. Denver, CO: National Conference of State Legislatures. 2009.

Sharkansky, Ira. "An Appropriations Subcommittee and Its Client Agencies: A Comparative Study of Supervision and Control", *The American Political Science Review*, 59 (3), pp. 622–628. September 1965.

Sharkansky, Ira. "Agency Requests, Gubernatorial Support and Budget Success in State Legislatures", *The American Political Science Review*, 62, pp. 1220–1231. 1968.

Taylor, F. *The Principles of the Scientific Management.* New York. Harper Brothers. 1911.

Urwick, Lyndall. "The Function of Administration: With Special Reference to the Work of Henri Fayol", in Luther Gulick and Lyndall Urwick (eds.) *Papers on the Science of Administration.* New York: Institute of Public Administration, pp. 115–130. 1937b.

Wanat, John. *Introduction to Budgeting.* North Scituate, MA: Duxbury Press. 1978.

Wildavsky, Aaron B. *The Budget for All Seasons?* Boulder, CO: Westview Press. 2001.

Wildavsky, Aaron B. *The New Politics of the Budgetary Process, 5th ed.* New York: Longman. 2004.

CHAPTER

5

Administrative Law

Public and administrative law is the one aspect of public administration most influenced by the formal structures of government. Even the language is different. Broadly, parliamentary systems use the term public law to reflect both formal enactments of the parliament and the rules and regulations promulgated by government agencies. New rules and regulations are presumed to be the logical consequence of the enactment of new laws. Presidential systems separate law from rulemaking, both as a label and as a statement of institutional origin. What organizational unit of government is constitutionally eligible to enact laws as opposed to promulgating rules is a matter of contention, most particularly in the American systems of government. When, how, and even if rules can be developed are steeped in political controversy, both at the national level and in the states. Therefore, the discussion below will have a distinctly American cast. As will be apparent, the very existence of "administrative" law was questioned and was a matter of court adjudication. The process shifts from one of should administrative law exist, to whether the actions of agencies fit with the unique American arrangement, and then to the scope of rulemaking. The twisted path toward the modern administrative state in presidential systems is worth a look, because even as it is different, there are lessons for those whose only experience is in parliamentary systems.

THE EVOLUTION OF AMERICAN ADMINISTRATIVE LAW

The issue of delegation of powers to administrative agencies was an important concern from the very beginning of the administrative state in 1887. Without the power to issue rules and regulations, administrative agencies would be impotent. Almost at once, regulated industries and concerned political theorists questioned the legitimacy of the agencies, and their questions were of two sorts. First, did Congress have the authority to establish entities with the power to make rules (legislate), to implement administrative decisions (execute), and to resolve disputes (adjudicate)? Two of these functions were not given to Congress by the Constitution but actually rested with the other branches of government. If Congress could not itself either execute or judge, how could it delegate these powers to another government agency? The second question was even more fundamental: even if Congress could justify delegating authority, were not the resulting agencies in violation of the basic Constitutional doctrine of separation of powers? The controversy waged for decades before it came to a head in 1935, when the Supreme Court confronted the constitutionality of delegation in *Schechter Poultry Company v. United States* (295 U.S. 495 [1935]). It was on this issue of delegation that Roosevelt's New Deal rested.

The Sick Chicken Case

The year 1935 was not a good year for Roosevelt's New Deal. The Supreme Court had repeatedly ruled against his program; the "nine old men" found time after time that Roosevelt's cherished welfare programs or business regulations were unconstitutional. That spring, a New York City shopper stopped at the Schechter Poultry Market to purchase a live chicken for her Friday Sabbath dinner. She examined the chickens in the partially filled coop carefully, finally selecting one that looked healthier and fatter than the rest. "That one," she said, pointing, and the clerk grabbed it out, thereby violating the Code of Fair Competition for poultry sales, established under the auspices of the National Recovery Administration. The code forbad selecting particular chickens: the customer had to take "run of the coop" to give every customer an equal chance at a plump, healthy bird. For this and other violations, the four Schechter brothers received jail sentences and were fined $7,425. Before the Schechter case was over, the president faced a major constitutional crisis, the Supreme Court stopped challenging the New Deal, and anti-government conservatives were armed with weapons that even today could cripple the administrative apparatus of the federal government.

As often happens in legal cases, what was at issue here had little to do with the facts of the case. No one in government, then or now, cared about the actual health of the chicken, or whether "run of the coop" was fair. The issue raised here was much more serious: Did the United States Congress have the authority to establish a federal agency to regulate, among other things, poultry sales? There was no question that Congress could itself regulate interstate commerce; the Constitution explicitly gives Congress that power. The question was the delegation of power to an agency. Anti-regulatory businessmen argued that because the Constitution gives Congress the power to regulate commerce, only Congress can exercise the power. Given the proliferation of administrative agencies in the New Deal, it was obvious that a decision in Schechter against the government could cripple Roosevelt's program.

The court ruled that the National Recovery Administration (NRA) had been established by an unconstitutional exercise of congressional power. If Congress established administrative agencies, the court said, it must give explicit guidelines for agency operations; the vague directives mandated for the NRA surrendered the congressional obligation to legislate.

This decision and several others which followed on its heels led to the famous "court packing" efforts of Roosevelt. The public uproar over this ploy, generated more by Roosevelt's deviousness in proposing it than by the proposal itself, caused Roosevelt to withdraw his plan to pack the Court. The Court took the hint and no longer thwarted Roosevelt's New Deal. However, *Schechter* was never overturned and is still good law. A conservative court could easily resurrect the *Schechter* rule and use it to demolish existing federal regulatory agencies. Such action was made less likely when in 1997 the US Congress enacted legislation that gave the Congress the authority to review recently enacted regulations (within the prior year) to determine if those rules and regulations fit the intent of the original Congressional mandate. In 2017 several regulations from federal agencies were deemed to exceed the Congressional mandate and thus were abolished.

DEFINING ADMINISTRATIVE LAW

More was at stake in *Schechter* than the issue of delegation; also, at issue was the legitimacy of the administrative state and the special approach to public law that had grown up around it. In the early years of the republic, three kinds of law were important: criminal law, concerned with offenses of individuals against society; civil law, which regulated behavior between individuals; and constitutional law, concerned with the form and function of government itself. When the administrative agencies began to exert their influence at the end of the nineteenth century, lawyers and political scientists were unsure how to categorize the legal issues that arose. They could not agree on how to define this new field of law, who should practice it, where and how it should be taught, or even if it were a separate branch of law at all. Thus, the history of the development of the legal field itself is important. The conception of the field is still changing, and to understand where it may go in the twenty-first century, we must first understand where it has been in the twentieth.

In the very early years, three men came to dominate the study of administrative law: Frank Goodnow, a political scientist; Ernst Freund, a law school professor; and Felix Frankfurter, a law professor who later became an associate justice of the Supreme Court.

Frank Goodnow was a political scientist primarily interested in public administration. He is noteworthy as the first scholar in the United States to recognize the increasing importance of administrative law, although his vision was a narrow one. He divided public law—all the law that was neither criminal nor civil—into two fields: constitutional law, which sets out the broad scope of permitted governmental activity such as regulating commerce, and administrative law, which governs the implementation of the more general constitutional mandate.

Goodnow's early views of administrative law were very influential in establishing the ground rules for the theoretical debate that followed. His mechanistic approach to administrative law hampered intellectual attempts to address both the political value of discretionary actions by administrators and the qualitative impact of various substantive policy areas on legal development. For many years, scholars asserted that the law was applied equally in all areas of public administration, and there was no important administrative difference between, for example, regulating railroads and organizing national parks. Just as public administration was to be politically neutral and to avoid policy making, so administrative law was only properly concerned with the "organization and . . . the competence of the administrative authorities" (neutral competence) and the individual's "remedies for the violation of his rights" (judicial oversight of improper use of administrative authority) (Goodnow, 1893, pp. 8–9). There was no concern for the policy impact of administrative decisions and no control of the inevitable discretionary decisions.

Ernst Freund, a contemporary of Goodnow, wrote more directly about administrative law. In 1894, he asserted that administrative law was a burgeoning field for which general principles could be found. Freund foresaw the development of subfields in public law that were specific to particular policy areas:

> with the growth of administrative tribunals, and particularly of a practice of publishing reports of administrative decisions and of abiding by precedents, there is every reason to suppose that such a body of commission or departmental administrative law will gradually establish itself.
> (Freund, 1930, pp. 454–455; quoted in Kraines, 1974, p. 71)

Freund was influential in the establishment of the University of Chicago Law School at the turn of the century. He tried without success to include in the law school curriculum such subjects as criminology, railroad transportation, banking, government and industry, accounting, and psychology. He also bitterly opposed the use of the case method being preached by the faculty at the Harvard law school, believing that the case method obscures the vital concerns of political context and substantive policy implications of legal cases. For a short time, Freund prevailed at Chicago for his own courses in administrative law, but his victory was short lived. The Chicago school indeed adopted the case method of legal instruction, acceding to Harvard's demands that all other law schools adopt the teaching methods in vogue at Harvard. As a result, legal education in administrative law used only case law and judicial opinions, and scholars who examined administrative law often ignored political factors.

The third person to wield great influence over the early years of the discipline of administrative law was Felix Frankfurter. In 1927, he openly rejoiced that administrative law had at last become recognized: "And so," he wrote, "this illegitimate exotic, administrative law, almost overnight overwhelmed the profession, which for years had been told of its steady advance by the lonely watchers in the tower" (Frankfurter, 1927, p. 616). Much of Frankfurter's impact came from the bright young lawyers he sent to Roosevelt's New Deal and from his opinions as a Supreme Court Justice. Frankfurter viewed administrative law as a field deeply interwoven with constitutional law whose task was to implement social policies while protecting individual freedoms. His definition of administrative law was not the static definition of legislative control of agencies; instead, administrative law was fluid and "markedly influenced by the specific interests entrusted to a particular administrative organization, and by the characteristics—the history, the structure, the enveloping environment—" of the agency (Frankfurter, 1927, pp. 619–620).

Frankfurter recognized, as did Freund, that the substantive policy under consideration has a great impact on the administrative law and judicial review governing that policy. His advanced views had no legitimate forum until after World War II because the delegation issue was unresolved.

Judicialization

The confusion of definitions finally reached some resolution in the years just prior to the New Deal. On one side, scholars such as Freund regretted that the non-constitutional aspects of administrative law received such limited treatment (Freund, 1932). However, the academic legal establishment would not accept any subject that was not part of the law school curriculum. Practicing attorneys and judges favored the establishment view as well. The two sides compromised:

> Administrative law ceased to be the law that administrative agencies made and became instead the rules that governed when, where, and how courts would review agency findings and the rules governing the procedures of agencies.
> (Kraines, 1974, p. 105)

This definition shifted the emphasis in administrative law away from the agencies and toward the courts for several reasons. First, it directed attention to the interface between courts and agencies. Second, since the courts largely define the rules for judicial review, and these rules are found in judicial opinions, law students could continue to study administrative law through the case method, and the field became merely another sub-discipline of law. Finally, by producing a definition of administrative law which was the law of *procedure*, the study of administrative law remained respectable; this "procedural focus tended to leave in some sort of non-legal limbo the substantive policies and decisions of administrative agencies" (Kraines, p. 105–106).

This perception of administrative process and of administrative law did not remain static. One influence for change was found in the simple process of judicial attrition. A second influence for change in the 1930s was the new view of the administrative process itself. Richard Stewart (1975) calls the early view of the administrative process the "transmission belt theory": a traditional model that sees the agency as a "mere transmission belt for implementing legislative directives in particular cases" (p. 1675). The new emphasis on the judiciary, incorporated with the law school compromise, led to an increased judicialization of the administrative process. By 1933, this theory of how the administrative process ought to work was firmly entrenched in the judicial mind. It excluded discretionary action; it ignored the substantive aspects of agency decisions; and it provided a basis to defend the judicial hegemony of the formative years of administrative law.

However, the New Deal years saw the creation of agencies with control over previously unregulated sectors of national life, leading to serious questions about the fairness and regularity of agency procedures. The Depression emphasized the need for regulation, and Roosevelt's New Deal provided it. Even before the stock market crash of 1929, regulation of business had begun. Not unreasonably, the business community was nervous. Equally concerned were some students of government who saw a trend away from the constitutional protections of individual liberty. Law made by administrative agencies through their rulemaking powers (as opposed to laws made by legislative bodies) were perceived as illegitimate. The lack of a forum for proposed and new regulations to be brought to public attention, the lack of public debate, and the assumption by the agencies of such potentially dangerous powers as the right to subpoena led the legal community to lobby for some sort of legal and preferably judicial control over the new processes.

The Administrative Procedure Act[1]

In 1934, the second year of the New Deal, the American Bar Association (ABA) formed an administrative law committee that issued annual reports stressing the reduced power of the judicial branch. Joining these critical voices were the conservatives who used complaints about fairness, due process, and conformity to common law to cloak their opposition to Roosevelt's economic and social policies. Some of the critics, however, were genuinely concerned about what they perceived as threats from the administrative process to traditionally protected rights. Their basic question was how the political system could maintain justice and the constitutionally mandated separation of powers if one person or agency acted as legislature (making rules), prosecutor (investigating infractions), judge (conducting hearings), and enforcing agent. As it became increasingly clear that the agencies were involved in making policy as well as interpreting legislative policy, concerns about the substantive law increased as well.

The Special Committee on Administrative Law of the ABA managed in 1935 to engineer the passage of the Federal Register Act. The Federal Register provided a daily record of the administrative activities of the executive branch; it contained texts of executive orders, proposed final, and final rules. Encouraged by this success, the Special Committee lobbied successfully for an administrative procedures bill passed by Congress in December 1940.

Although the bill passed Congress, President Roosevelt vetoed it. Opponents of the bill charged that the act was nothing more than a blatant attempt to wrest control of the administration from the president. "The proposal before me is one of the repeated efforts by a combination of lawyers who desire to have all processes of government conducted through lawsuits and of interests that desire to escape regulation" (H.R. 986, p. 3).

Roosevelt had another reason for his veto. The Final Report of the Attorney General's Committee on Administrative Procedure was almost complete. The work of this Committee was unique; instead of merely taking testimony and generating a report, it conducted primary investigations and produced legislation. For the first time, the administrative process was studied on the

> basis of knowledge rather than of hypothesis or preconceived ideas. . . . [The Committee] studied the administrative establishment from the inside, thoroughly and dispassionately. Its acute discussion of the characteristics of the administrative process, its conclusions as to defects existing in the process, and its proposals to remedy them all sprang from and were buttressed by facts laboriously ascertained and carefully weighed.
>
> (Woltz, 1968)

The Attorney General's Report affirmed the necessity for and value of the administrative process. It found that agencies were an inevitable development that were essential for effective management of modern, industrial government. The majority felt that the substantive issues dealt with by the various agencies were so complex and idiosyncratic that no uniform code could govern them all; the minority disagreed, and it is their recommendations that actually provided the basis for the APA.

Although extensive hearings were held in the summer of 1941 on the proposed Administrative Procedure Act, America's entry into World War II delayed further consideration. Close to the end of the war, the ABA began again to agitate for legislation, and in 1946, the Administrative Procedure Act was passed.

The Act codified existing practice and law; in other words, it found a common ground among the agencies. One sign of the amazing success of the APA is how little it has been amended since 1946. Section 552 contains most of the amendments, and they are primarily adjustments to the basic APA rather than changes to the law's essential structure. Section 552 is the Freedom of Information Act; Section 552(a) is the Privacy Act of 1974, and 552(b) is the Government in the Sunshine Act.

Rulemaking

The third section of the APA is perhaps the most important. It provides the guidelines for the federal rulemaking procedures. The definition of rule is quite detailed:

> "[R]ule" means the whole or a part of an agency statement of general or particular applicability and future effect designed to implement, interpret, or prescribe law or policy or describing the organization, procedure, or practice requirements of an agency and includes the approval or prescription for the future of rates, wages, corporate or financial structures or reorganization thereof, prices, facilities, appliances, services or allowances thereof, or of valuations, costs, or accounting, or practices bearing on any of the foregoing.
>
> (5 U.S.C. §551(4))

It is important to distinguish between rulemaking and adjudication. Rulemaking is the administrative equivalent of legislation: It is sometimes called "secondary legislation." Rulemaking establishes *future* standards of *general* applicability. Adjudication is the administrative parallel to the judicial process: It deals with a particular case. Rulemaking prescribes the activity before it happens; adjudication takes place after some activity has occurred. Agencies can make policy through either rulemaking or adjudication; courts prefer them to use rulemaking because rules announce guidelines for individual behavior, and persons subject to rules have a better basis for decision-making.[2]

The courts are more likely to review rules on procedural due process grounds than substantive due process. Regulations and rules must stay within the statutory authority given to the agency by the legislature, but this authority is often vague and leaves a great deal to the agency's discretion. The rules must have a reasonable basis; that is, they may not be arbitrary, capricious, or involve an abuse of discretion, and they must be promulgated in accordance with the APA and with the restrictions laid down in their own enabling or organic act.

Types of Rules

There are three types of rules: substantive (legislative), procedural, and interpretive.

Substantive rules implement or prescribe law or policy, for example, safety requirements for nuclear power plants. They are legally binding and can be enforced in court as though they were primary legislation. The amount of authority that an agency has to promulgate rules varies with the enabling legislation. Some agencies have very broad authority; for example, NEPA states:

> The Administrator is authorized to allow appropriate use of special Environmental Protection Agency research and test facilities by outside groups of individuals and to receive reimbursement or fees for costs incurred thereby when he finds this to be *in the public interest.*
>
> (42 U.S.C. §4379, emphasis added)

Since "in the public interest" is not defined in the statute, the Administrator has been given very broad powers. Other agencies find their authority quite restricted; for example, the Endangered Species Act of 1973 requires that:

> [T]he Secretary shall make a finding as to whether the petition presents substantial scientific or commercial information indicating that the petitioned action may be warranted. If such a petition is found to present such information, the Secretary *shall promptly* commence a review of the status of the species concerned. The Secretary shall promptly publish each finding made under this subparagraph in the Federal Register.
>
> (16 U.S.C. §1533(b)(3)(A), emphasis added)

Here the statute requires action if certain conditions are met; the Secretary has no discretion.

Procedural rules "describe the organization, procedure or practice requirements of an agency." For example, they may define who is allowed to intervene in an agency adjudication and under what circumstances. APA does not apply to procedural rulemaking, and indeed, an agency is allowed to go beyond APA and its own organic act in restricting the procedures under which it operates. However, an agency is required to honor these rules once they have been issued.[3]

Interpretive rules are "statements issued by agencies that present the agency's understanding of the meaning of the language in its regulations or the statutes it administers" (Cooper, 2007, p. 145). They are exempt from APA requirements but must be published in the Federal Register. They do not add or subtract any information from existing law; they simply give the public a more detailed idea of how the agency intends to act. In this sense they are the administrative equivalent of advisory opinions. It is not clear how binding an interpretative rule is on the agency. On occasion the courts have ruled that an interpretive rule was deemed as substantive and therefore binding on the agency that had issued it. The safest approach is for the agency to assume that a court will find the rule binding but for the affected party to assume it is not. Why would an agency bother with such an ambiguous process? It allows the administrative agency to make small adjustments to policy without going through the cumbersome rulemaking procedures.

Rulemaking Procedures

There are three basic procedures for making rules: informal rulemaking, formal rulemaking, and hybrid rulemaking.

Informal rulemaking is informal only in contrast to the formal rulemaking. It is also called Notice and Comment Rulemaking and is governed by §553 of the APA. The informal rulemaking procedure requires the agency to publish a notice of the proposed rule in the Federal Register. An exception is allowed if everyone subject to the proposed rule is individually notified, but this exception is rarely used. There are several necessary components of the notice. It must give the time, place, and nature of the rulemaking proceedings and refer to the legal authority under which the rule is made. The notice either provides the term or substance of the proposed rule, or it gives a description of the subjects and issues involved. Finally, the notice includes an opportunity for written or oral (and sometimes both) comment by interested parties.

Once the agency has fixed upon the rule, it must publish the text of the rule, and a general statement of its basis and purpose, in the Federal Register at least thirty days before the effective date to allow affected parties to come into compliance. Even then, interested persons have the right to ask for an "issuance, amendment, or repeal" of the rule.

This sort of rulemaking is relatively simple and informal. There is no formal hearing in which evidence and testimony about the rule is heard. The timeline is short; an agency might complete the rulemaking process in less than sixty days if the rule is simple and not controversial. There is no record required: The agency merely announces its intention, receives comments, and issues the rule. In contrast, formal rulemaking is much more complex.

The distinguishing characteristic of formal rulemaking is the administrative hearing that is required. Several statutes require full hearings as part of the rulemaking process, and a hearing must be held only if the statute explicitly requires one. There is, however, nothing to prohibit an agency from having one voluntarily. Administrative hearings are conducted under the regulations spelled out in Sections 556 and 557 of the APA. An administrative law judge presides over these hearings, and his or her opinion is conveyed to the administrator charged with making the final rule. The opinion must be considered, although it is not binding. Any final rule must be based on the "substantial evidence" criterion: the agency must demonstrate that its position is upheld by "reliable, probative, and substantial evidence" (§556[d]).

There are many arguments that favor the formal process over the informal. The formal record that is generated by the hearing process provides a pedigree for the development of the new regulation. There is full opportunity for public participation, and, because there are rules of evidence (although not the same rules of evidence as apply in a criminal trial), all information can be verified. The burden of proof rests with the agency, and the formal hearing provides a record for the interested parties to be sure that the weight of the evidence is sufficient to support the rule.

There are also many counter-arguments. Formal rulemaking is costly in terms of both money and time. Flexibility of the administrators is reduced—an evil that the administrative process is designed to avoid. And the process itself, resembling a court trial, is increasingly judicialized. For example, the original APA created independent "hearing examiners" who had specialized knowledge in their own regulatory fields. These hearing examiners have metamorphosed into "administrative law judges" who are attorneys with at least seven years' experience presenting cases before federal courts or agencies.

Hybrid rulemaking uses a combination of informal and formal procedures; the impetus for hybrid rulemaking came from the judiciary. Federal courts prefer administrative agencies to use their rulemaking powers to make policy rather than to use case-by-case adjudicatory powers, because judicial review is simplified when a rule is the basis of the administrative decision. However, the informal process does not require establishment of a reviewable record, and the lack of a formal record complicates the judge's task when reviewing agency action. As the administrative agencies continued to utilize their rulemaking powers and the need for regulation increased, the courts found their job increasingly complex. Deference to administrative expertise was a nice concept, but a court had difficulty judging the "substantial" basis of a rule that was technically complex and lacked a formal record.

Partly in self-defense, the agencies began to generate records of the informal rulemaking processes, and the courts, followed by the Congress, applauded. The keystone of the hybrid process is the record before the administrator. This record allows not only judicial review, but it also allows peer preview, legislative oversight, and public criticism. Surprisingly, it also increases administrative flexibility because it simplifies changing rules to meet changing circumstances.

Congress has followed the judicial lead, and most rulemaking legislation in the past thirty years has included hybrid rulemaking requirements. For example, the Toxic Substance Control Act of 1976 requires hybrid rulemaking:

> Any rule under subparagraph (A), and any substantive amendment or repeal of such a rule, shall be promulgated pursuant to the procedures specified in section 553 of [APA], except that (i) the Administrator shall give interested persons an opportunity for the oral presentation of data, views, or arguments, in addition to an opportunity to make written submissions, (ii) a transcript shall be kept of any oral presentation, and (iii) the Administrator shall make and publish with the rule the finding described in subparagraph (A).
>
> (15 U.S.C. §2604(b)(2)(c))

Generally, hybrid rulemaking follows informal rulemaking procedures with several additions on the record: the basis and purpose of the rule with supporting documentation; evidence that adequate notice was given or made available to all interested parties; sufficient time for comments and alternative interpretations; evidence that the agency did consider and respond to comments; and the reasoning followed by the administrator.

A recent refinement in federal rulemaking is negotiated rulemaking. To reduce the likelihood of lengthy challenges to a rule, stakeholders negotiate the language of the rule before the proposed rule reaches the Federal Register. Although the negotiation process is announced in the Federal Register, the process is often criticized as limiting public participation and creating expectations among stakeholders of particular results before the rule is open for public notice and comment. Use of this method of formulating rules is encouraged by the Negotiated Rulemaking Act of 1990 (Cooper, pp. 161–165).

Substantial presidential efforts have been made to take control of the regulatory process, particularly as industry frequently complains that the cost of regulations are not properly considered when new regulations are issued.[4] Carter created the Regulatory Analysis and Review Group (RARG), replaced by Reagan's Executive Order 12291 (and later Executive Order 12498) that required agencies to conduct a benefit-cost analysis of all proposed rules and to choose the least costly alternative. George H. W. Bush "found the contention [over Executive Order 12291] too politically costly and quietly backed away from Reagan's aggressive enforcement policies" (Rosenbaum, 2005, p. 143). In 1993, President Clinton issued Executive Order 12866, revoking Reagan's Executive Order 12291. His order required consultation with state, local, and tribal agencies and required agencies to impose the "least burden on society" in promulgating regulations. During Clinton's administration, both Democratic and Republican Congresses passed stiffer benefit-cost analysis requirements. President G. W. Bush left Clinton's Order 12866 largely unchanged (Cooper, p. 171). The use of benefit-cost analysis for regulatory rulemaking is now routine, except in those few areas such as the Clean Air Act where the law prohibits consideration of economic effects.

Administrative Adjudication

The fourth section of the Administrative Procedure Act deals with adjudication. The specific kind of adjudicatory procedure required in agency processes varies from relatively informal, oral hearings to very structured procedures that resemble formal civil trials. Some statutes require hearings, and it is only these statutes that automatically trigger the full hearing described in the APA. In some circumstances, the courts have mandated adjudicatory hearings based on constitutional requirements. Finally, the agencies themselves may have rules independent of their enabling legislation or court decisions that require them to hold hearings.

There are five central components of any administrative hearing: notice of the hearing given to all interested parties; the opportunity to be heard by an impartial examiner, to present evidence and to challenge opposing evidence; to receive a reasoned decision based on a written record; and the right of appeal. These requirements are spelled out in sections 554–557 of the APA, although the precise nature of a hearing varies with the enabling statute, previous judicial interpretations, and agency regulations.

Judicial Review

The sixth section of the APA deals with judicial review of agency actions. Some agency actions are not subject to review. The Supreme Court does not have jurisdiction over all agency actions because the Congress has the power to exempt some activities: "In all the other cases before mentioned, the Supreme Court shall have appellate Jurisdiction, *both as to Law and Fact, with such Exceptions, and under such Regulations as the Congress shall make*" (United States Constitution, Article III, §2[2], emphasis added).

Section 701 of APA, which defines the application of judicial review of agency actions, exempts actions where the "statutes preclude judicial review" or that have been "committed to agency discretion by law." However, Section 706 (2)(A) of the act forbids arbitrary and capricious action and abuses of discretion. The reviewing courts must determine when an action is committed to agency discretion and when these actions are reviewable under Section 706. The overall effect of these two seemingly contradictory sections is to encourage agencies to maintain records of their actions and interactions.

Some agencies have a great deal of discretion conferred by their enabling statutes. Since 1984 the Chevron doctrine has provided some protection from judicial review of discretionary action. In *Chevron U.S.A. Inc. v. Natural Resources Defense Council* (1984), the court was examining EPA's interpretation of "stationary source" in applying the Clean Air Act. The Court articulated a two-part test: If the statutory language or the intent of Congress is clear, the agency must follow them. If not, the agency's interpretation need only be reasonable (not subject to the test of "arbitrary, capricious, or an abuse of discretion") to pass judicial muster.

Courts do not have an unlimited license to oversee agency activities. The scope of judicial review for administrative actions is defined in Section 706:

> To the extent necessary to decision and when presented, the reviewing court shall decide all relevant questions of law, interpret constitutional and statutory provisions, and determine the meaning or applicability of the terms of an agency action.

The court may "compel agency action unlawfully withheld or unreasonably delayed" as well as "hold unlawful and set aside agency action, findings, and conclusions" that are arbitrary, capricious abuses of discretion and violations of constitutional rights or that exceed statutory authority, violate due process, or are unsupported by substantial evidence.

For adjudicatory decisions, the primary judicial question is whether the agency position is supported by substantial evidence. Since most adjudicatory hearings are adversarial and therefore may produce conflicting evidence, a court often has a difficult time determining which evidence is applicable. In formal rulemaking, the scope of review also rests on substantial evidence, while review of informal rulemaking is limited to the "arbitrary and capricious" standard. In hybrid rulemaking, the scope of review is determined by the authorizing statute. For example, the Toxic Substances Control Act gives as part of the standard of review:

> Section 706 of [APA] shall apply to review of a rule under this section, except that—
>
> (I) in the case of review of a rule under [several sections of the Act] of this title, the standard for review prescribed by paragraph (2)(E) of such section 706 shall not apply and the court shall hold unlawful and set aside such rule *if the court finds that the rule is not supported by substantial evidence in the rulemaking record.*
>
> (15 U.S.C. §2618 (c)(1)(B), emphasis added)

The years that followed the close of World War II were eventful in administrative law. The Administrative Procedure Act, while left essentially intact, was amended. For example, in 1966, the Freedom of Information Act amended Section 3 of APA to require public access to agency records unless otherwise prohibited. In 1974, Section 552 was amended to reduce undue agency secretiveness, and also in 1974, the Privacy Act added Section 552a to control disposal of government records on individuals. In 1976, the "Governmental in the Sunshine" Act added Section 552b which required open meetings except where exempted. Sections 561–569 are the Negotiated Rulemaking Act, and Sections 601–612 (Regulatory Flexibility Act) protect the interests of smaller organizations when new rules are adopted. In addition, some agencies have been removed from the reach of the Administrative Procedure Act: For example, the Immigration and Naturalization Service is exempted from the hearing requirements of APA when holding a deportation hearing.

CONCLUSION: THE MANAGEMENT SUPPORT SYSTEM

Public agencies and therefore administrative law have been blamed for every modern administrative failure from the Challenger disaster to Katrina. At the heart of these criticisms is the problem of administrative discretion. One virtue of the administrative process is the ability to respond to crises more quickly than legislative processes. The danger, of course, is that when administrative actions fail, legislators from both the left and the right find it easy and politically expedient to lay the blame squarely on the shoulders of the administrators. Although the agencies are rarely blameless,[5] they are often pawns of larger political forces. Unfortunately, bureaucrats are an easy target (Goodsell, 2003). In the 1970s, public administration came under attack from both the left and the right. President Carter created the Senior Executive Service, a move that made senior bureaucrats professionally vulnerable to politically motivated personnel decisions. The Reagan administration was overtly hostile to public bureaucrats; the infamous "Maleck Manual" even suggested that political appointees deliberately mislead bureaucrats in their agencies to improve the chances of achieving policy change. Bureaucrats did not fare much better under the Democratic administration of Bill Clinton as "privatization or contracting out, the use of market-oriented strategies in place of regulation and negotiated strategies to avoid enforcement or legal decisions were to be preferred" (Cooper, p. 114). The Bush-Cheney administration continued the trend with an anti-regulatory bias and a massive realignment of federal agencies, justified in part by the administration's need to respond to the terrorist attacks on the World Trade Center and other American targets.

> The current period is a time of significant change as efforts such as the new public management and more recently the governance approach have challenged traditional administrative law processes. . . . [It] seems clear, as we settle into the twenty-first century, that a host of forces are at place that will render administrative law quite different than it has been over the past 50 years.
>
> (Cooper, p. 121)

To think of administrative law merely in terms of the tripartite definition or substantive law or discretion is to continue to ignore how administrative law is conceptualized. Is it simply case law on a particular topic, neatly indexed by Shepard and West? Does it include the hearings held before the agencies and decided by administrative law judges? Probably both views may be included without much controversy since they both contain the trappings of the law and because the courts may ultimately review the hearing results. Does administrative law include the rules and regulations published, as required by law, in the Federal Register? Probably so; especially as these may be viewed as secondary legislation, and legislation is clearly law. Does administrative law include the decision process by which these rules and regulations are made? Perhaps. This is political activity, and some academics and lawyers cling to the illusion that politics is antithetical to law. In one sense, any legitimate government activity is law, and any differentiation between kinds of law is partly artificial and designed to induce clarity and order where none exists in fact. But to include any bureaucratic activity as administrative law is to define the field out of existence.

As noted at the beginning of this chapter this is the most American of the discussions in this work. Administrative law is an artifact of American politics and the American Constitution. Yet as a support system public and administrative law have a considerable procedural and substantive influence on the management of agencies. The creation of rules and regulations, or the more complex process of adjusting those rules both affect organization effectiveness and influence the very practices of the agency. Managers need not be experts in public and administrative law, but managers must be attentive to the substantive implications of new rules and must seek input on when and how rules must be interpreted and potentially be amended.

DISCUSSION QUESTIONS

- What are informal rules?
- Why is judicial review of administrative decisions necessary?
- While it would seem that managers make little use of administrative law expertise they are deeply embedded in personnel systems (think grievance procedures). How are administrative law and personnel practices intertwined?
- What is substantive administrative law?
- What are some of the political issues associated with developing rules for the implementation of new statutes?
- What is red tape?

NOTES

1. This section is excerpted from *Understanding Environmental Administration and Law, 3rd ed*, by Susan J. Buck, Copyright © 2006 Island Press. Reproduced by permission of Island Press, Washington, DC.
2. Agencies can also make policy by informal actions, such as the suspension action taken by EPA in 1979 when it banned 2,4,5-T (dioxin) on an emergency basis just before the spring crop spraying season.

CHAPTER 5 Administrative Law

3. For example, during the Watergate investigation US Attorney General Elliot Richardson appointed Archibald Cox as Special Prosecutor and at the same time issued a procedural rule giving the Special Prosecutor the authority to contest claims of executive privilege. When Cox tried to get President Nixon's tapes and rejected Nixon's claims of executive privilege, Nixon ordered him fired. The first two attorneys general that he ordered to fire Cox refused; the third was Robert Bork, who complied with Nixon's order. The DC District Court invalidated the firing on the grounds that the procedural rule was binding. This action is one reason Bork was not confirmed as Associate Justice of the Supreme Court.

4. Unless otherwise noted, this material is from Walter A. Rosenbaum, *Environmental Politics and Policy*, 6th ed. Washington, DC: CQ Press, 2005, pp. 140–155.

5. For example, it is difficult not to blame FEMA for the debacle in New Orleans, although one might argue that some responsibility lies with the Army Corps of Engineers and with the decision of the Bush administration to shift FEMA to the Department of Homeland Security after the World Trade Center bombings.

BIBLIOGRAPHY

Buck, Susan J., ed. *Understanding Environmental Administration and Law, 3rd ed.* Washington, DC: Island Press. 2006.

Cooper, Phillip. *Public Law and Public Administration, 4th ed.* Belmont, CA: Thomson Wadsworth. 2007.

Davis, Kenneth Culp. *Administrative Law: Cases-Text-Problems, 6th ed.* St. Paul, MN: West Publishing Co. 1977.

Davison, J. Forrester. "What is Administrative Law?" *George Washington Law Review*, 7. April 1939.

Freund, Ernst. "The Law of Administration in America", *Political Science Quarterly* 9. 1894.

Freund, Ernst. "Administrative Law", *Encyclopedia of the Social Sciences*, 1. New York: Macmillan. 1930.

Frankfurter, Felix. "The Task of Administrative Law", *University of Pennsylvania Law Review* 75. May 1927.

Goodnow, Frank J. *Comparative Administrative Law.* New York: G.P. Putnam's Sons. 1893.

Goodsell, Charles. *A Case for Bureaucracy, 4th ed.* Washington, DC: CQ Press. 2003.

Kraines, Oscar. *The World and Ideas of Ernst Freund.* University, AL: University of Alabama Press. 1974.

Plater, Zygmunt, Robert Abrams, William Goldfarb, and Robert Graham. *Environmental Law and Policy: Nature, Law, and Society, 2nd ed.* St Paul, MN: West, 1998.

Rosenbaum, Walter A. *Environmental Politics and Policy, 6th ed.* Washington, DC: CQ Press, 2005.

Stewart, Richard. "The Reformation of American Administrative Law", *Harvard Law Review*, 88. June 1975.

Woltz, Charles K. *Preface to Administrative Procedure in Government Agencies (Attorney General's Committee Report).* Charlottesville, VA: University Press of Virginia. 1968. Facsimile edition of Senate Document No. 8, 77th Congress, 1st Session. 1941.

CHAPTER

6

Policy Analysis

While the formal study of policy is not quite two hundred years old, and, indeed, in its present form is barely ninety, governmental policy has been studied and organized at least since the eighteenth century B.C., when the Code of Hammurabi was recorded. This Code set out criminal and civil laws clearly so that uniform justice was dispensed by government officials. Indian and Chinese officials organized codes of behavior; the Confucian system included normative guidelines for correct behavior in both government policy and official behavior. In the fourth century B.C. Aristotle taught principles of governmental policy to young Alexander of Macedonia, before Alexander began to conquer the world. And in the fifteenth century A.D., Machiavelli tutored his prince in the political realities of government (Dunn, 1981).

The word *policy* comes from the Greek *polis* (city-state), the Latin *politia* (state), and the Middle English *policie* (the conduct of public affairs). This similarity of words continues to muddle the distinctions between political science, public administration, and policy analysis. As policy analysis continues to receive increasing proportions of research funding, both public administration and political science have tried to lay claim to the field. However, as we shall see, the roots of modern policy analysis lie in a variety of social science disciplines, not the least of which is sociology.

WHAT COMES AFTER COUNTING?

Very late in the eighteenth century, reformers and politicians began to concern themselves with the astonishing concentrations of people descending on the urban centers of Europe and England. The industrial revolution, especially in England, and the political unrest on the continent had dispersed the manageable feudal communities and sent a burgeoning working class into the cities. Policy makers needed information about these new populations. Between 1791 and 1799, Sir John Sinclair published his *Statistical Account of Scotland*, thus marking the first use of the term statistics or "state mathematics." In 1801, Parliament instigated the first

British census, primarily to count Englishmen; it seems extraordinary that prior to then, no one either knew or cared how many people inhabited the country. In the United States, the Constitution requires a census, but this was primarily motivated by political compromises arising out of the Constitutional Convention: The number of delegates each state could send to the House of Representatives was based upon population. Social parameters were added later.

The first real social statistician was Adolphe Quetelet (1796–1874) who collected data on the Netherlands in the 1820s. Unlike Marx and Comte, whose data collection was unsystematic, Quetelet collected his facts in an orderly progression and then created generalizations about social conditions in the Netherlands. Soon afterward, Quetelet moved to London, where he tutored Prince Albert and helped found the Statistical Society. Prince Albert later became a patron of the Society, which changed its name to the Royal Statistical Society. This society sponsored research projects and served as an inspiration for the social reformers of England. Some of the work was, by our standards, rather laughable. Henry Mayhew, who conducted studies of London's poor in 1851, was so misled by the effects of poor nutrition, miserable sanitation, and filth that he concluded that the street people of his day were of a different race than the rest of Anglo-Saxon England (Glazer, 1959, p. 56)!

Data collection methodology, and the mathematics to support it, advanced rapidly. In 1855, Frederic Le Play published *Les Ouvriers Europeens*, a cross-cultural comparison of worker income and expenditure. However, despite significant continental contributions such as that of Le Play, the English received the credit for developing the technique of utilizing firsthand field research to generate empirical data for statistical analysis.

What drove the English to counting and beyond? Daniel Lerner (1959), taking a somewhat cynical view, identified the great problems of the industrial age: How much do workers need for maintenance? How much savings do they need? How much can they earn before there is a surplus to tax? That manipulative motive is, in part, true. However, the English concern was also partly scientific and partly reform:

> The immediate interest of the [statistical] societies was the condition of the new masses in the cities. Organized, as they were, by men who were close to the new industrial interests . . . they were concerned at times to demonstrate that the effects of industry and the cities upon the workers and their children was not as fearful in all respects as the landed interests, and their propagandists, insisted. But their concern was only partially apologetic: they had an honest interest in reform; and, beyond any other interests, they were concerned with science, with gathering facts, independent of the arguments they could serve. They had a deep belief in the saving power of the fact as against the theory.
>
> (Glazer, p. 51)

Some of these facts led to successful reform. For example, Charles Booth's *Life and Labour of the People of London* (1891–1903) described poverty in mathematical terms. His work on the aged poor in 1894 led directly to changes in the old-age pension laws of England. His work and the work of other reformers was an inspiration to Americans such as Lincoln Steffens. When the industrial revolution reached the United States, following on the heels of the Civil War and the official closing of the American frontier, the tools of social reform and control were already at hand.

THE PROGRESSIVE ERA

With the exception of the New Deal years, probably no modern period was more tumultuous in the United States than the progressive era at the turn of the century. The industrial revolution was well established, the political machines were under attack, and the application of science to everything—to inventions, to business management, to government—was transforming the way Americans viewed their country.

Public administration began to emerge as a distinct field at this time, partly because the politics-administration dichotomy allowed the administration side to be approached "scientifically." The field focused on American government and began to lose the comparative flavor of Goodnow and Freund's earlier work. The writers of the day—who thought of themselves as political scientists—had three approaches: scientism, which stressed political process and avoided any semblance of prescription; activism, which built on the European tradition of academic involvement in public affairs; and education for citizenship (Ranney, 1968). It was no accident that "scientism" was first.

In 1887, H.B. Adams's report for the Bureau of Education, *The Study of History in American Colleges and Universities*, encouraged "expansion of the statistical offices as the key to good government, and the provision of such education as the primary role of political science in the universities" (Crick, 1959, p. 34). The discipline—and the government—paid attention to Adams's strictures. Charles Beard wrote in 1908:

> It was not the function of the student of politics to praise or condemn institutions or theories, but to understand and expound them; and thus, for scientific purposes [the study of politics] is separated from theology, ethics and patriotism.
>
> (Beard, 1908, p. 75)

A. Lawrence Lowell's 1909 APSA presidential address stressed, among other things, statistics and functionalism, while in his 1910 address as president of APSA, Woodrow Wilson said that political science is properly concerned with the development of public policy (Somit and Tanenhaus, 1967). The Bureau of the Census was established in 1909, and its duties soon increased to include collecting information on agriculture, commerce, and schools. The Department of Labor and Agriculture had their own research units. The Agricultural Experiment Stations and the Extension Service, found in this period, relied heavily on the work of rural sociologists. The data gathered by social scientists in these and other bureaus helped to fuel the progressive movement through surveys and statistical analysis.

This data was used—or intended to use—as empirically as possible. Scientism, as this new approach was called, was

> The belief that the methodology generally associated with the natural sciences can be fruitfully used to attack problems of fundamental concern to a given discipline. . . . [It assumes] that regularities or laws can be developed which have explanatory and predictive utility.
>
> (Somit and Tanenhaus, p. 27, note 16)

The new academic approach was gratefully received by the policy makers. Some authors agree that, in America, empirical research was as much a tool for control as a tool for reform, needed by new labor-intensive businesses to justify their working conditions and to control nascent unrest.

> Modern science and technology did not shape the growth of the new centralized system of political control and government policy making; it was the other was around. . . . The growth of new methods of inquiry was . . . an attempt by dominant social groups to use products of scientific research for purposes of political and administrative control.
>
> (Dunn, pp. 14–15)

Even the prominent social scientists who were willing to accept some of the tenets of scientism had their doubts. William Elliott thought the number of potentially important variables was too large ever to allow a useful formulation of governmental activity, and both he and Edward Corwin, the famous constitutional law scholar, lamented the exclusion of values in scientism's calculations. Charles Beard, who was an early and enthusiastic endorser of scientism, could not acknowledge a morally neutral political science. Of course, they were correct. American scientism was wedded to Dewey's pragmatism and to American business, and these in turn were inextricably bound up with the Protestant work ethic and the idea of democracy. The progressive era, which established as its slogans the concepts of initiative, referendum, and recall, was as ideological as any other political movement, but it naïvely—and probably unconsciously—masked its ideological goals with the rhetoric of value-free science, neutral competency, and administrative expertise. The administrators, who under this program must surrender their political and administrative discretion to make policy, were supposedly compensated by the deference which would be paid to their scientific expertise. The offices of city manager and county manager developed in this era of neutral administration; the Pendleton Act, consciously designed to emulate the "neutral" British Civil Service, began to curtail patronage. What happened, of course, was the first step in diminishing administrative responsibility:

> Perhaps the tragedy of the Progressive Era was that the doctrine of intelligent public administration based on technical standards began more and more to supersede the doctrine of personal responsibility.
>
> (Crick, p. 82)

TOWARD THE NEW DEAL

The policy studies of the progressive era were "intellectually premature and scientifically innocent . . . almost entirely lacking in rigor and in anticipation of consequences" (Truman, 1968, p. 279). However, they did provide the early impetus for behavioralism, a robust multidisciplinary approach to the social sciences that was the intellectual basis for the policy studies of the 1960s and beyond. During World War I, those social sciences that were quantitative made great strides: The "disciplines which possessed quantitative methods were the ones that rose most rapidly in influence. . . . [Economists] had method. And they were quantitative. They could manipulate data in the light of a system of general postulates, laws, and hypotheses" (Laswell, 1951, p. 5). Psychologists were used to evaluate recruits in this war as they used in World War II. After World War I, there were two significant developments in the study of public policy.

First, conditions were favorable for an increased emphasis on the social sciences in general. There was a strong predisposition toward increasingly more sophisticated and systematic approaches to problems and data. More funding, especially from private foundations, was available, so that between 1921 and 1930 private foundations gave $27 million to social science research (Crawford and Biderman, 1969, p. 5). In the same decade, several privately financed social science institutes provided information to the government. In 1928, the National Bureau of Economic Research, the Institute for Government Research, and the Institute of Economics joined to form the Brookings Institution, still one of the foremost social research centers in the United States. There was a critical mass of social scientists able to generate students, classes, grants, and projects. Graduate education increased dramatically: In 1921, about six hundred doctorates were awarded in all fields, but in 1938 the number was close to three thousand. About one-sixth of these were in the social sciences, and although the percentage had not increased, the total quantity was up. Over five hundred new scholars, eager for advancement, were seeking research funding.

Second, the disciplines were becoming more sophisticated. This was a mixed blessing. Specialization increased as the numbers of social scientists grew, and their studies became fragmented. They lost a common perspective, and concern for public policy diminished. This is not surprising as the rewards in academia come from theoretical contributions, and practical contributions are viewed with suspicion, especially by narrow-minded academics who lack administrative experience. This in turn reduced the apparent relevance of their work to public officials, and it was not until the desperate days of the New Deal that public administration and the social sciences again became partners.

The impact of scientism continued well past the 1920s. Several substantive research reports were published. Examples include Harold Gosnell's *Negro Politicians* (1935) and William Ogburn's *Recent Social Trends* (1933), sponsored by the President's Committee on Social Trends established by Hoover in 1929. Another development seems strange to present-day students accustomed to sophisticated computerized data analysis: "[w]hile the use of time series, partial correlations, factor analysis, and tests of significance was hardly common, by the late 1930s it was no longer a rare phenomenon" (Somit and Tannenhaus, pp. 4–5). Finally, professional advancement became increasingly dependent on research productivity.

Charles Merriam, himself an indifferent user of science, was the prime advocate of a science of politics. He urged the combination of statistics and psychology to enhance governmental control. He was the first chair of the Social Science Research Council, founded largely at his instigation in 1923. This council tried to regularize social science methodology by stressing the interdisciplinary nature of policy sciences. Under its sponsorship in 1924, Merriam and Harry Barnes edited *A History of Political Theories: Recent Times*, including lawyers, anthropologists, geographers, historians, economists, political scientists, and social philosophers.

But just as Freund's earlier efforts to broaden administrative law were doomed to failure, so was Merriam's effort at the same school doomed twenty years later. Merriam's enduring contributions have been in his students, and in the organizations such as the Social Science Research Council and the National Resources Planning Board that he founded rather than in his own work. From the first,

> Merriam envisaged the "science of politics" as a "policy science." Political scientists, he felt, should be concerned with, and involved in, public issues. By the early 1930s practically every leading exponent of the new politics had come around to the same position.
>
> (Somit and Tanenhaus, p 139)

The "science of politics" became the fashionable approach to studying government and governance. National Conferences on the Science of Politics were held in 1923, 1924, and 1925. Political scientists began tabulating the voting patterns of Supreme Court justices. Several important books were released. *Political Parties of Today* (Holcombe, 1925) categorized congressional districts to aid in analyzing party politics. Stuart Rice wrote *Farmers and Workers in American Politics* (1924), which uses statistical techniques to correlate data, a task that is casually performed by students today for routine course assignments but that was a dramatic advance in 1924. In the same year, Merriam and Gosnell wrote *Non-Voting, Causes and Methods of Control*, which was one of the first projects to use survey data collected by trained interviewers. Finally, in 1931, the Social Science Research Council published *Methods in Social Science*, which summarized the most advanced empirical techniques of the day.

However, after 1929, interest in scientism waned. Americans were preoccupied with the economic and social conditions of the Great Depression. The emphasis on political science shifted to citizenship and political education. Other social scientists were called to Washington to help implement Roosevelt's New Deal, and their science was put to immediate and practical uses in government programs to alleviate social ills. The Depression and the New Deal led to an expansion of the government's welfare and regulatory functions with a concurrent need for social data. Between 1931 and 1937 the number of social scientists in government agencies jumped from 680 to 2,150 (Crawford and Biderman, p. 7). It is here that public administration and political science begin to go their separate ways and to consider themselves separate fields.

For social scientists, World War II continued the New Deal patterns. Links between the universities and the government were increased and strengthened, and government funding was still a primary source of research dollars. Many university personnel found government posts: It was accepted that all kinds of brains—even academic ones—were necessary to win a total war. However, political scientists who had become interested in issues of citizenship and political education were at a disadvantage. They "were generally not trained in statistics or accounting, . . . they usually had no substantive field competence (e.g., labor, finance, transportation, production, etc.) and . . . they ordinarily had little prior experience in, or with, governmental agencies" (Somit and Tanenhaus, p. 141). Nevertheless, even governmental activity not directly related to the war effort expanded and the social scientists involved prospered: In 1942 the Department of Commerce began publishing national income data, and such information as the Gross National Product (a term first used by Roosevelt in 1944) began to have an effect on government planning.

For the policy sciences, the war years differed from the New Deal in two respects. First, the sheer number of social scientists involved in the war effort was much greater than had been used in the New Deal. Second, the war opened new areas of inquiry such as psychological warfare, morale, and the diffusion of propaganda. The impact of recruit intelligence tests and aptitude tests on psychology alone was enormous, and the spinoffs for business management incalculable. Modern intelligence agencies were first organized during this war, and the social data used by these agencies were substantial. The Central Intelligence Agency recruited young political scientists trained in quantitative methods for intelligence data analysis; the agency sends personnel specialists to political science conferences around the country.

After the war, political science returned to its behavioralist interests. Researchers lost their pioneering focus and began to search for oversimplified, testable, behavioral laws. Stress was on ranking variables rather than correlating them; for example, was socioeconomic status a better predictor of party preference than gender? By focusing on sub-systems, researchers could avoid the less-rewarding interdisciplinary studies. They looked increasingly for easy-to-measure, gross variables and lost sight of the predicting and engineering facet of policy studies. Why did this happen?

First, there was widespread dissatisfaction with the discipline as it existed in the postwar years. The war had showed the large gap that existed between theory and practice. European social scientists who fled to the United States to escape the war brought with them a capacity for empirical research unmatched in the United States. Second, methodology was improving: Survey techniques were better, statistical techniques were more powerful, and the potential for really elaborate mathematical analysis by computer was becoming apparent. Few people could have predicted the technological advances that would make the large government computers obsolete and place faster, smaller, more powerful computers at the desk of any university professor, but it was clear that something spectacular was in the offing.

Finally, there was money. Foundations would fund quantitative research of almost any quality, but money for theoretical qualitative research was in scarce supply. Fewer of the wartime programs for natural sciences were dismantled; the Cold War and, later, Sputnik ensured their survival. Competition for social research dollars was intense, especially as much of the policy analysis conducted after the war was a result of the activities of engineers, operations researchers, systems analysts, and applied mathematicians who could speak the language understood by their fellow scientists on the grant review boards. The National Science Foundation (NSF), established in 1950, had no social science programs until 1958. In order to be competitive with the natural sciences, social sciences had to look as scientific as possible. This involved following the scientific method, as far as the discipline would allow, and in eschewing any mention of values, norms, or prescriptions. The behavioralists concerned themselves with process over content. Had they begun to consider content, they would have found themselves mired in normative issues.

In addition, understanding content requires expertise in the content area, and this entailed a training that few university social scientists had. If nuclear engineers could design nuclear power for peace or for war, because "science is neutral," so the policy analysts could analyze without concern for the consequences. As Joe Friday said on *Dragnet*: "The facts, ma'am, just the facts." Grant seekers have only been partially successful. In a sense this conflict parallels the procedural vs. substantive administrative law debate (see Chapter 5), and in that debate as in the policy debate the process (quantitative) view won out.

The same criticisms that held true for scientism in the early decades of the twentieth century were true for behavioralism. There were too many complicated variables, and values cannot be excluded from policy analysis. Even the natural scientists recognized the impossibility of perfect quantification of political behavior. Cybernetic pioneer and mathematician Norbert Wiener (1948) wrote:

> Our investigations in the social sciences . . . will never be good to more than a very few decimal places, and, in short, can never furnish us with a quantity of verifiable, significant information which begins to compare with that we have learned to expect in the natural sciences. We cannot afford to neglect them; neither should we build exaggerated expectations of their possibilities. There is much which we must leave, whether we like it or not, to the un-"scientific" [sic] narrative of the professional historian.
>
> (p. 148)

In reaction, Harold Laswell and others, such as Yehezkel Dror and Daniel Lerner, proposed a new behavioralism that they labeled *policy sciences*. This was a multidisciplinary approach that had a greater focus on policy issues and on individual choice to maximize value. There were five major elements that contributed to the social and intellectual background of the policy sciences movement:

1. Development first of general systems analysis [e.g., the work done at RAND] and then of applied systems analytical thinking
2. The emphasis on governmental effectiveness, or outputs, as contrasted to line-item costs or inputs
3. The concept of government policy as applied social science and of government programs as social experiments
4. The "social indicator" or measurement movement
5. The concepts of cybernetics and the development of an information exchange capacity following an information explosion crisis

(Lane, 1972, pp. 71–72)

In 1951, Lerner and Laswell published *The Policy Sciences*, which was the "first systematic appeal to develop policy analysis as a special orientation within established social science disciplines" (Dunn, p. 19). Their emphasis was that policy sciences were to enhance democratic values. Hence, as the originators of modern policy analysis envisioned, it was *not* value-neutral. When alternatives were chosen, the democratic outcomes should receive special consideration. In 1951, Laswell predicted that in coming years, the

Emphasis will be upon the development of knowledge pertinent to the fuller realization of human dignity . . . the "policy sciences of democracy."
(1951, p. 10)

In addition, policy analysis should be active:

From a manipulative standpoint, the social sciences are better designated as *policy sciences*—their function is to provide intelligence pertinent to the integration of values realized by and embodied in interpersonal relations. We conceive of political science as one of the policy sciences—that which studies influence and power as instruments of such integration. . . . Integration of the manipulative and contemplative standpoints implies, among other things, that political science research must give due weight to the emerging future, rather than dealing only with the more or less casual and haphazard data from the past.
(Laswell and Kaplan, 1950, p. xii)

In fact, the policy analysts succeeded all too well in removing historical concerns from their inquiries. Norbert Wiener's grudging acceptance of historical research was forgotten; in the late 1980s the discipline was once again concerned with the use of history in policy analysis and with lamenting an over-reliance on mathematical technique without understanding the complicating political variables.

Yehezkel Dror, writing in 1968, was still optimistic, looking forward to the development of a *policy science* that would significantly improve the quality of public policy making if it is fully used (1968). Perhaps Dror was mistaken, or it is possible that policy science has not been "fully used" as he intended. Certainly, great changes occurred in American in the 1960s. The United States was still reeling from Vietnam, the counter-culture movement—which grew too quickly into the drug culture—Kennedy's assassination, and the space program. Johnson's Great Society and the War on Poverty changed the structure of government in Washington. In 1966, HEW was assigned the task of setting up social indicators to monitor progress in combating poverty. The "environmental decade" began with Earth Day in April 1970, and an enormous regulatory bureaucracy was set up to take care of the environment. Dispute resolution, environmental law, citizen participation—all led to an optimistic view of policy analysis that could not be realized: The "decade of the 1970s was, with minor exceptions, a time of exuberant oversell, burgeoning activity, and limited performance" (Brewer and deLeon, 1983, p. 8).

Fragmentation and specialization increased, and policy analysis was not able to maintain an identity as a separate discipline. By the mid-1970s, each discipline had its own policy organization, many of which had their own journals, such as *Policy Sciences*, *Policy Analysis*, or *Policy Studies Journal*. Many separate schools for the study of public policy were established in the late 1960s and 1970s, but the graduates of these schools find jobs in departments of political science, where they often must struggle to justify their research. The 1990s was a time of renewed interest in the policy studies. Often spun off from economic analysis, new public policy programs encouraged renaissance in the study of policy from a social science (economic) perspective. The interest in performance measures as a tool of management spawned new research on both management and decision-making.

LOCATING POLICY ANALYSIS

The Conundrum of Expertise

The role of the policy analyst and policy analysis methods are problematic. To extend this examination of policy analysis the work of two quite distinct perspectives must be explored in more depth: that of Aaron Wildavsky in his exploration of the evolution and emergence of public policy analysis as an academic discipline and *profession*; and that of Hannah Arendt in her development of the distinctions between knowledge and understanding. Taken together these works will yield what is labeled as the conundrum of expertise; the dilemma of a technological-driven process that yet must accommodate to the politics of decision-making.

Speaking Truth to Power is Wildavsky's (1979, 2007) extended discourse on an appropriate mission and curricula for a School of Public Policy. Critically, he notes that "Truth" is fragmented and incomplete (multiple sources [and versions] of truth—see Bok). Therefore,

> policy analysis must go beyond the task of calculating the best solution, considering the constraints and the objects, to the task of selecting the constraints in the first place and formulating a statement of the objectives. Whereas the first task requires technical competence, the second requires an equally rare composite of intelligence, judgment and virtue.
>
> (Wildavsky, 1979, p. 388)

Wildavsky (1979) spoke about the need for the analyst to have "values" by which he meant an adherence to the principles of democratic governance and public ethics.

Decisions are directed toward the outcomes for a wider public, but a follower may have a quite different understanding of the consequences. Professional training and job roles push the follower toward another-directedness that is much narrower than the public *at large*. Professionally defined responsibilities and practices establish the constituency for the work output. "Doing it right" may become more of an assessment of the application of methods, rather than a statement of ethics. The complaint often expressed in the classroom, *we* did it right but the politicians (or the higher ups in the department) changed it, is at its core an argument about relevant constituencies.

In a commentary about policy analysis but focused on the application and utility of tacit knowledge, Dror (2001) notes

> a more advanced type of professional knowledge, which can be used with significant benefits for the benefit of public decision-making is needed in today's policy analysis process. There should be an extensive reliance on tacit understanding, Gestalt-images, qualitative models and qualitative methods (instead of main emphasis on explicit knowledge and quantitative models and tools). This involves imaginative thinking, systematic integration of trained intuition into policy analysis, development of qualitative tools and construction of broad qualitative models of complex issues in cooperation with social scientists and other professionals.
>
> (p. 253)

The policy analyst who falls into the trap of adherence to methodological dogma distorts policy analysis and cannot "speak truth to power" (Wildavsky, 1979). This is an analyst who rejects Wildavsky's assertion that problems have the same status as solutions, whereby analysis is preceded by the task of selecting the constraints and formulating a statement of the objectives (Wildavsky, 1979, p. 338).

In an argument that parallels the analysis-objectives discussion, Arendt (2003) asserts that thinking and judging are interrelated, but separate. Thinking is the result of forming abstractions (much like analysis). Judging is the first step toward deciding (deciding to decide as it were). It is the product of understanding the situation in its fullest sense.

Rules and regulations, hierarchical relationships, in fact the entire range of structural-functional understandings of modern organizations emerge from *thinking* about organizational design and process. The decision is the result of the process of thinking. The classic model of policy analysis in which the *optimal alternative* is uncovered is an example of this form of decision-making. There can only be one decision; therefore, the analysis yields the answer.

C.P. Snow (1961) noted that science and government were two distinct worlds that inevitably clashed. Among other things the "culture" of these worlds creates different understandings of time and method. The people that make up an organization "see" problems through the lens of their organization or profession; scientists are trained to see things narrowly and deeply; administrators are trained to see things broadly (64–65). Snow's entire career was predicated on trying to reconcile those cultures. In a sense the outlook of the scientist is like that of Plato's guardian class. Even though this understanding has been rebutted by, among others, Waldo (1948) and Appleby (1952), the debate continues.

Despite Wildavsky's angst about policy analysis, most policy analysts are trained to be the exemplar of the guardian class: As traditionally conceived, policy analysis uses what House (1982) refers to as the "technological guidance approach." The danger is not a lack of rigor in applying the techniques of analysis, but in the *hubris* to believe that a perfectly neutral instrument exists. Still more problematic is that those without knowledge of the limitations of the techniques are led to believe that these techniques generate "true" answers. When the "answer" of the supposedly neutral analyst and the decision of policy makers are compared, rarely is the policy decision cast in a favorable light.

This brings us back to Arendt and the importance of understanding. Ethical decisions will emerge as the leadership-followership is played out and "imaginative thinking and the systematic integration of trained intuition" (Dror) yield "values" which adhere to the principles of democratic governance and public ethics (Wildavsky).

What can be said about policy sciences and policy analysis as disciplines and fields of study? The term *policy sciences*, despite being an American coinage, is rarely used. *Policy analysis* is the more popular. It is distinct from *program evaluation*. We have not discussed evaluation in this chapter, primarily because it is narrower in scope than analysis. Public policies affect large numbers of people through governmental actions; Dunn (1981) defines policy analysis as:

> an applied social science discipline which uses multiple methods of inquiry and argument to produce and transform policy-relevant information that may be utilized in political settings to resolve policy problems.

(p. ix)

Policy analysis is a prospective activity rather than a retrospective one. It is but one of several management support processes, a tool to help define alternatives and choose among them. Evaluation, in contrast, checks how successful a particular policy has been. It is a narrower endeavor in one sense, because usually evaluation is conducted at some end point in the policy process. Evaluation itself is often categorized as either formative or summative. Formative techniques are applied prior to the finalization of an implementation strategy for a policy area. Essentially the formative evaluation techniques are very similar to other forms of policy analysis. The second type of evaluation is summative evaluation. This is the classic end-of-program review that is most identified as program evaluation. Evaluators look at the stated goals and attempt to measure how well the program that implemented the policy met the goals. The academic theories and models that define program evaluation, but especially summative evaluation, are not the same as those that define policy analysis. The level of analysis is different: Typically, evaluation is program evaluation, and the distinction between policy and program is analogous to that between goal and objective. Both policy and goal are broad, while program and objective are narrow, more easily bounded and measured, and usually have less total impact.

The proper role of policy analysis is the clarification and surfacing of problems. In one sense, policy analysis has been a boon to the extremists of all political persuasions precisely because of its quantification. Many people are in awe of numbers and do not understand the incorrect uses—both conscious and unconscious—to which they may be put. For example, in calculating the cost-to-benefit ratio for federal projects, analysts must choose a discount rate. This is a percentage that corrects for inflation and for prevailing interest rates over the life of the project, so that the dollar cost of today may be easily compared to the dollar benefits of tomorrow. We make roughly the same internal calculation when we figure out that our buying power has decreased: A dollar of salary buys less now than it did ten years ago. Obviously, the size of the discount rate will change the value of future benefits; hence, any cost-benefit analysis is automatically affected by whatever factors led to the choice of the discount rate. Analysts who favor a particular project simply choose the lowest possible discount rate; those that have concerns about the program choose a higher discount rate over a longer period of time (essentially all new proposals can be rejected based upon this technique). What the consumer of the analysis sees is an ostensibly value-neutral comparison of costs and benefits over the long term.

Policy Analysis at EPA

Under Director Scott Pruitt and at the behest of President Trump the rules and regulations that support the US Clean Air Act (42 USC 7401) have been challenged. In October 2017 a "Final Report on Review of Agency Actions that Potentially Burden the Safe Efficient Development of Domestic Energy Resources under Executive Order 13783+ was released by the Environmental Protection Agency. Its conclusion reads:

> Multiple ways exist for EPA to protect the environment and public health while supporting the President's policy to promote economic growth and energy independence. The four key initiatives identified herein will advance the

goal of reducing unnecessary regulatory burdens on the development and use of domestic energy resources in accordance with E.O. 13783. These initiatives also illustrate meaningful progress towards fulfilling Administrator Pruitt's efforts to satisfy EPA's core mission through increased transparency, public participation, and cooperative federalism

(EPA, 2017, p.7).

In June 2018 the EPA announced that the formula by which the economic effects of EPA regulations would be changed. Defended as a technical correction the EPA would no longer consider secondary health effects in setting (or in this case revising) EPA regulations. Only directly linked activities (for example coal dust) would be examined for health effects. Thus, related effects (the creation of pollutants from the interaction with the air) would no longer be regulated. The statute need not be changed for the method of analysis would change, as would the direction and scope of rule enforcement.

Some writers naïvely suggest that policy analysis is inherently democratic and that authorization regimes are inhibited by social science (Lerner, 1959). The opposite would seem to be true (Fischer, 2009). Carefully wielded, social science is a powerful tool for control of even literate, middle-class populations: witness the environmental groups in the southern states pacified by the water resource model. Even democratic regimes may be seduced by the call of science:

These developments [the study of every aspect of American life] have been possible only in a society that placed a high value on continuous self-improvement through self-study. Otherwise the prying into personal lives which such studies require would not be tolerated.

(Lerner, p. 23)

There is no such beast as neutral analysis. The best any analyst can hope for is to make his or her biases as explicit as possible so the policy makers, who must rely on this analysis, can evaluate the results fairly. This explication of bias can be very difficult; often we are not even aware of our own prejudices. An analyst who is risk-averse will choose very conservative statistical techniques to minimize the probability of error; an optimistic analyst may overestimate the good will of a political adversary. It is also tempting to draw the same absolutist conclusions about policy analysis results that natural scientists claim to be able to draw about their controlled laboratory experiments.

With the natural conservatism of policy analysis, which must take the *status quo*—institutions, wage structures, and so on—as given, it is not surprising that policy analysis has diverted social science from "radical and fundamental kinds of analysis [such as] Plato's question (Plato, 1992): What is justice? Policy analysis is not the domain of political science or of public administration alone. In many places it is dominated by economics and its hybrid offspring, public choice. This approach to policy analysis is dangerous because of the underlying assumptions of economic analysis. Not only is it conservative, it also presumes that humans are motivated entirely by economic considerations; one school of public choice asserts that altruistic behavior *never* occurs.

While no research is easy, poorly done quantitative analysis is relatively simple to camouflage as profound thinking. Policy makers must learn to evaluate policy analysis and to use it as simply one tool of many. This is a very difficult concept for many technical people to grasp. A civil engineer may know "the" correct route for a highway; however, political considerations may require the road to go elsewhere. The civil engineer may be forced to accept the decision, but she will never agree with it; she will always think of it as a poor choice tainted by politics.

Fortunately, policy analysis as a discipline is continuing to turn toward explicit consideration of normative and political dimensions. Garry Brewer and Peter deLeon (1983) write: "Policy sciences is not a simple, incremental modification of any of the standard disciplinary or professional approaches. It is a fundamental change in outlook, orientation, methods, procedures, and attitude" (p. 8).

CONCLUSION: THE MANAGEMENT SUPPORT SYSTEM

As in administrative law, analysts have realized that a knowledge of substantive content is essential to understanding a policy. The use of historical analysis is also increasing. Graham Allison's brilliant book of models of the policy analytic process, *Essence of Decision* (1971, 1999), used the Cuban missile crisis to illustrate how identical facts may be interpreted differently by analysts who have differing theoretical perspective: All are right, and none are. A more formal approach to historical policy analysis comes in Neustadt and May's book, *Thinking in Time* (1989), in which they point out the ways historical analysis may change public policy for good or ill. All three authors are connected with the Kennedy School at Harvard, where applied policy analysis is actually put to use in Washington.

The title of Aaron Wildavsky's book on policy analysis says all there is to say about policy analysis. The role of the ethical analyst is to speak the truth as he or she sees it, after studying the issues as thoroughly as the craft will allow. Policy analysis is not, and never can be, an exact science: Like other endeavors that touch the human experience, policy analysis is art. Finally, the analyst should never forget that the power to decide rests not with the analyst but rather with the political decision maker.

DISCUSSION QUESTIONS

- In other discussions about policy analysis the problem of "expertise" is introduced. How is this a problem? Why is it a problem?
- As with many other technical analytic tools policy analysis is caught in the conflicts associated with measurement. What are the problems associated with measurement?
- Wildavsky's book about public policy is entitled *Speaking Truth to Power*. Who is the speaker and to whom is the conversation directed?
- Is policy analysis political? Should it be cognizant of politics?
- Does policy analysis have to be quantitative to be accurate?
- What do you think of House's challenge to policy analysis?

BIBLIOGRAPHY

Allison, Graham. *Essence of Decision*. Boston: Little, Brown and Co. 1971.

Allison, Graham, and Philip Zelikow. *Essence of Decision, 2nd ed.* New York: Longman. 1999.

Appleby, Paul H. *Morality and Administration in Democratic Government*. Baton Rouge: Louisiana State University Press. 1952.

Arendt, Hannah. *Responsibility and Judgment*. New York: Schocken Press. 2003.

Beard, Charles. *Politics*. New York. 1908.

Brewer, Garry, and Peter deLeon. *The Foundations of Policy Analysis*. Homewood, IL: Dorsey. 1983.

Choo, Chun Wei. "Sense-Making, Knowledge Creation and Decision Making: Organizational Knowing as Emergent Strategy", in C. W. Choo and N. Bontis (eds.) *The Strategic Management of Intellectual Capital and Organizational Knowledge*. New York: Oxford University Press. 2002.

Crawford, Elisabeth, and Albert Biderman. "Editors' Introduction", in Crawford and Biderman (eds.) *Social Scientists and International Affairs: A Case for a Sociology of Social Science*. New York: John Wiley & Sons. 1969.

Crick, Bernard. *The American Science of Politics: Its Origins and Conditions*. Berkeley, CA: University of California Press. 1959.

Dror, Yehezkel. *Public Policy Making Reexamined*. San Francisco: Chandler. 1968.

Dunn, William. *Public Policy Analysis: An Introduction*. Englewood Cliffs, NJ: Prentice Hall. 1981.

Fischer, Frank. *Democracy and Expertise*. Oxford: Oxford University Press. 2009.

Glazer, Nathan. "The Rise of Social Research in Europe", in Daniel Lerner (ed.) *The Human Meaning of the Social Sciences*. New York: World Publishing. 1959.

Holcombe, Arthur E. *The Political Parties of Today 2nd ed*. New York: Harper and Brothers, 1925.

Hird, John A. *Power, Knowledge and Politics: Policy Analysis in the States*. Washington, DC: Georgetown University Press. 2005.

House, Peter W. *The Art of Policy Analysis*. Beverly Hills, CA: Sage. 1982.

Hummel Ralph E. *Working*. Unpublished paper. 2005

Lane, Robert E. "Integration of Political Science and the Other Social Sciences through Policy Analysis", in Charlesworth (ed.) *Integration of the Social Sciences Through Policy Analysis*. Philadelphia: American Academy of Political and Social Science. 1972.

Laswell, Harold. "Policy Orientation", in Daniel Lerner and Harold Laswell (eds.) *The Policy Sciences*. Stanford, CA: Stanford University Press. 1951.

Laswell, Harold, and Abraham Kaplan. *Power and Society*. New Haven: Yale University Press. 1950.

Lerner, Daniel. "Social Science: Whence and Whither?", in Daniel Lerner (ed.) *The Human Meaning of the Social Sciences*. New York: World Publishing. 1959.

Lindblom, Charles. "Integration of Economics and the Other Social Sciences through Policy Analysis", in Charlesworth (ed.) *Integration of the Social Sciences Through Policy Analysis*. Philadelphia: American Academy of Political and Social Science. 1972.

Neustadt, Richard E., and Ernest R. May. *Thinking in Time*. New York: Free Press. 1989.

Plato. *The Republic* (trans. C.M.A, Grube) Indianapolis, IN: Hackett Publishing. 1992

Ranney, Austin. "The Study of Policy Content: A Framework for Choice", in Austin Ranney (ed.) *Political Science and Public Policy*. Chicago: Markham. 1968.

Somit, Albert, and Joseph Tanenhaus. *The Development of American Political Science*. Boston: Allyn & Bacon. 1967.

Truman, David. "The Social Sciences: Maturity, Relevance, and the Problem of Training", in Austin Ranney (ed.) *Political Science and Public Policy*. Chicago: Markham. 1968.

Waldo, D. *The Administrative State: A Study of the Political Theory of American Public Administration*. New York: Ronald Press Co. 1948.

Wildavsky, Aaron. *Speaking Truth to Power: The Art and Craft of Policy Analysis*. Boston: Little, Brown and Co. 1979.

CHAPTER

7

Program Evaluation

The last chapter discussed the practices and techniques of policy analysis. Those practices were contrasted with those of program evaluation. Simplistically these are separated by time more than technique. Evaluation checks how successful a particular policy has been. It is a narrower endeavor in one sense, because usually evaluation is conducted at some end point in the policy process. Usually evaluators look at the stated goals and attempt to measure how well the policy meets the goals. The academic theories and models that define program evaluation are not the same as those that define policy analysis. The level of analysis is different: Typically, evaluation is program evaluation, and the distinction between policy and program is analogous to that between goal and objective. Both policy and goal are broad, while program and objective are narrow, more easily bounded and measured, and usually have less total impact.

In this chapter that distinction is further refined by examining two aspects of program evaluation; first the historical basis for evaluation and second the core problem in evaluation, performance measurement.

PROGRAM EVALUATION

Beginning in the late 1960s the United States Federal government began a concerted effort to review federal grant programs to ensure that they were efficiently and effectively administered. Why do we evaluate programs? In the broadest sense it is to determine whether or not we are meeting the previously established goals and objectives of a specific program or activity at a specific time. Wildavsky views program evaluation as a form of organizational learning.

> The ideal organization would be self-evaluating. It would continuously monitor its own activities so as to determine whether it was meeting its goals or even whether these goals should continue to prevail. When evaluation suggested that a change in goals or programs to achieve them was desirable, these proposals would be taken seriously by top decision makers. They would institute the necessary changes; they would have no vested interest in continuation of

154

current activities. Instead they would steadily pursue new alternatives to better serve the latest desired outcomes. . . .

Evaluation should not only *lead to the discovery of better policy programs to accomplish existing objectives but to alteration of the objectives themselves.* Analysis of the effectiveness of existing policies leads to consideration of alternatives that juxtapose means and ends embodied in alternative policies. The objectives as well as the means for attaining them may be deemed inappropriate.

(emphasis added, Wildavsky, 1972)

Traditional evaluation techniques follow a pattern of application that in many ways is similar to traditional policy analysis. Most critical is the assumption of the validity of the status quo. The program, as established, and as functioning, is presumed to be correct. It is an evaluation of current practice, not an evaluation of the appropriateness of program goals. Also, there is an assumption that there is a rational and logical connection between program goals and program activities. However, this need not be the only valid approach to program evaluation. The approach shared by strategic management and Total Quality Management techniques look at evaluation quite differently. The evaluation process is one that distinguishes TQM from other management improvement initiatives. Very often an enthusiastic manager will introduce several new management initiatives. What is not thought through, especially in the rush to get things started, is the *criteria for success*. This is especially critical if several changes are introduced, because it becomes impossible to determine what is working and what is not working. There is no point of reference by which to judge "success."

The concept of continuous process improvement cannot exist without monitoring and problem-solving mechanisms. This should not be a great surprise since it has been a central feature of the management change literature for nearly two decades. But what sets "continuous improvement" apart from more straightforward evaluation mechanisms is the idea that improving operations is not linked to a specific operation element, but, rather is linked to overall operations. When the evaluation criteria are associated with a specific activity the question is "are we still on track?" If the evaluation results indicate that everything is going well, then you continue as before. Changing procedures is an indication of a problem in the way the project was conceptualized. In fact, the most likely experience of government officials with the evaluation process is to have a consultant come in after a project is over to tell the officials what they should have done. Continuous process improvement takes the opposite approach. The evaluation process is intended to reject rather than affirm the status quo. The goal is to change procedures, not keep them as they were. One can "muddle through" with an inadequate evaluation of a project. Without a rigorous monitoring and evaluation scheme, no "improvement" is possible, and the very idea of TQM ceases.

The difficulty is that a rigorous evaluation process requires a significant commitment of resources. It is expensive in both time and money, yet it is not an activity that can be avoided or done in a half-hearted manner. Those in the "trenches" will be asked to go the extra mile, but also it is critical that senior managers support this effort with the monies necessary to do it "right" (Cox, 1995).

Program Efficiency and Effectiveness

What is efficiency? Any basic economics textbook can supply the answer. This is a concept that is critical to public administrationists, as well as economists. Yet, should it be paramount?

> The design and maintenance of organizations is often a straightforward engineering proposition. When the goals of the organization are clear-cut, and when most choices can be made on the basis of known and objective technical criteria, the engineer rather than the leader is called for. His work may include human engineering in order to smooth personal relations, improve morale, or reduce absenteeism. But his problem remains one of adapting known quantities through known techniques to predetermined ends.
>
> From the engineering perspective, the organization is made up of standardized building blocks. These elements, and the ways of putting them together, are the stock-in-trade of the organization engineer. His ultimate ideal is complete rationality, and this assumes that each member of the organization, and each constituent unit, can be made to adhere faithfully to an assigned, engineered role. Furthermore, the role assigned does not stem so much from the peculiar nature of *this* enterprise; rather, the roles are increasingly generalized and similar to parallel roles in other organizations. Only thus can the organization engineer take advantage of the growth of general knowledge concerning the conditions of efficient administrative management.
>
> (Selznick, pp. 137–138)

The assessment of the efficiency (no waste) of a program activity is determined by one of two forms of program evaluation: formative evaluation and summative evaluation. Formative evaluation is, as the name implies, conducted before the final adoption of a program. It has many of the characteristics of traditional policy analysis; it is essentially program-specific policy analysis. Summative evaluation can be divided based upon the goal of the evaluation. In a chapter appropriately entitled, "The Art and Method of Process Evaluation," Sylvia, Meier, and Gunn (1985) explore the differences between an outcome evaluation and an evaluation designed to uncover the deficiencies in an ongoing program.

A central issue in the debate between the outcome and process evaluation is in the defining of goals. Outcome evaluators believe that defined and measurable goals are a prerequisite to evaluation. In contrast, process evaluators argue that goals cannot be firm because organizations are constantly evolving in response to changing conditions in the environment. The important point is that programs do not begin at zero. Most programs are well established and ongoing. Theoretical and program goals were established in the near or distant past. Strategies for implementing the goals will have been adapted, new missions will have been tacked on to existing organizational structures, and the staff will have long since ceased to occupy itself with questions of mission and mandate.

For these reasons the skills of the process and outcome evaluator are different. The outcome evaluator focuses on program outputs that are assessed against those clearly defined program goals. The outcome evaluator must be familiar with research design and be sophisticated in data gathering and analysis and in report writing. The analyst processor should know something about the theory and practice of public program management and about the program under study.

Outcome evaluation uses defined goals to develop systematic measures of program outputs. A process consultant might use the goals to analyze the organization of agency activities, to assess the allocation of organization resources, or to assist in the redesign of delivery systems in line with agency goals.

The differences between the process and outcome approaches go beyond goal definition and include the research designs employed. Research designs appropriate to outcome evaluations were discussed previously. The next step is to turn to the methodologies appropriate to process evaluation.

Like the entire strategic management process, a process evaluation will differ in specific application, depending on the nature of the problem, the time available to conduct the evaluation, or the resources that can be brought to bear on the evaluation. Under most circumstances a process evaluation occurs in four phases: problem identification, solution development, implementation, and feedback. Put most simply, the evaluation would emerge as follows:

1. Phase I: Problem Identification
   a. The process consultant meets with program officials and engages in a series of problem identification activities.
   b. The consultant presents identified problems to program staff.
2. Phase II: Solution Development
   a. Program officials and the consultant select a course of action to resolve agency problems.
3. Phase III: Implementation
   a. The solutions are put into operation, with specific individuals taking responsibility for various components of the strategy for change.
   b. Management control systems are put in place to see that agreed-on changes are scheduled and carried out.
4. Phase IV: Feedback Evaluation
   a. The consultant and/or program staff engage in systematic assessments of the impacts of the changes on the organization and program implementation
   (Sylvia, Meier, and Gunn, p. 137)

Flexibility is the key to a successful process evaluation. The emphasis is on problem-solving. In that sense a process evaluation shares ultimate responsibility for the success of the program since the quality of the evaluation will to some extent control how effectively the program is implemented. This "bias" is the most significant point of departure between an outcome and process evaluation.

PROGRAM MEASUREMENT

As was noted in Chapter 4, one of the fundamental principles of the management literature of the last three decades has been that we must be able to measure what we do to establish a baseline for change and improvement. Yet, that deceptively simple notion that "things" can be measured is at the core of the failure of governments (and private enterprise) to sustain reform efforts. Taking a somewhat broader perspective Gerry Gabris (1986) ponders

> whether current management techniques used by public administrators often create more problems than they solve. Do rational management techniques, designed to increase organizational effectiveness, actually work? Or do they simply create new burdens? . . .
>
> All too often, agencies at the federal, state and local levels adopt rational management tools that look good in theory and become dysfunctional or problematic in practice. Public administrators often assume that new techniques will automatically increase organizational effectiveness, without first thinking through the unanticipated consequences. While management techniques can improve organizational productivity, they also contain the potential for decreasing organizational performance through faulty application and implementation. This dysfunctional potential represents a major paradox in the use of management techniques as tools for increasing organizational effectiveness.
>
> (p. 101)

It is not that those in government do not want to change. To the contrary, long before the public became enamored with privatization and reinvention, many in government and the academy struggled with means of transforming governmental operations (Stanley, 1964; Bennis et al., 1976; Hatry, Winnie, and Fisk, 1981).

One problem is there is no agreement on what can, or should, be measured. Nor is there consensus on how best to develop such measures. For that matter there is not complete agreement on a definition of performance measurement. Epstein recommended that measurement "is a general term that covers any systematic attempt to learn how responsive a local government's services are to the needs of the community, and to the community's ability to pay" (1988, p. 2). He goes on to suggest that numerous techniques and practices are part of performance measurement, such as "efficiency [studies], productivity [analysis], cost effectiveness, cost benefit analysis and program evaluation" (Epstein, p. 3). In other words, performance measurement is one of those management techniques for increasing organizational effectiveness. The question is whether performance measurements also "contain the potential for decreasing organizational performance through faulty application and implementation." Such "mechanical" approaches are indicative of "good theory," but not good "practice." Philip Selznick more than four decades ago shaped the problem thusly,

> There is a strong tendency not only in administrative life but in all social action to divorce means and ends by overemphasizing one or the other. The cult of efficiency is administrative theory and practice is a modern way of overstressing means and neglecting ends. This it does in two ways. First, by fixing attention on maintaining a smooth-running machine, it slights the more basic and more difficult problem of defining and safeguarding the ends of an enterprise. Second, the cult of efficiency tends to stress techniques of organization that are essentially neutral, and therefore available for any goals, rather than *methods peculiarly adapted to a distinctive type of organization or stage of development*.
>
> (emphasis added, Selznick, 1957, pp. 134–135)

Often, for reasons that will be explored below, we find ourselves in a loop in which we define performance measures, not on the basis of a relation to task, outcome, or result, but upon how well we can quantify and, therefore, "measure" an element. Thus, for example, we establish rules which require benefit-cost analyses be conducted as part of formal decision-making, because that process supposedly provides an "objective," unbiased, and "measurable" means of judgment that makes comparison across alternatives easier. Yet, we acknowledge that the task of assigning values to the benefits and costs are subjective. The means (benefit-cost analysis) becomes more important than the end sought (quality decisions).

Performance measurement is a tool that is fraught with pitfalls. In ignoring those pitfalls, we risk providing inaccurate and false information to decision makers. We are not suggesting here that performance measurements should not occur, but we are suggesting that the limits and weaknesses of the method must be better understood, if they are to be used properly. In other words, performance measurement methods must be "peculiarly adapted to a distinctive type of organization or stage of development" (Selznick, p. 135). This paper will review the use of performance measurements in a variety of local government settings to uncover the biases that often creep into their use. The goal is to examine the "how, what, and why" of performance, as it affects measurement. Performance measurement is a tool used in a variety of settings and in a variety of forms. To better understand the extent to which performance measurement suffers from the dysfunction noted by Gabris, those various forms must be examined. Thus, the first step is to create a snapshot of performance measurement and related techniques, such as policy analysis and program evaluation, in various contexts. To help place that snapshot in some context, several case examples of practices and procedures will be presented. Then to address the admonition of Selznick that the distinct type of organization (the public sector) be considered, the third section of the paper will look at two issues—the politics of public-sector decision-making and current perspectives on "best practices" in public-sector management. The conclusion of the review is to suggest practices and procedures to ensure that we measure those things that contribute to performance improvement, not simply those things that are easily measured.

The "State of the Art" in Performance Measurement

Performance measurement is not a single tool or practice. Rather, it is a cluster of tools with a common foundation that is applied to different practices such as policy analysis and performance appraisal. The goal of performance measurement is to establish a baseline of activity (benchmarks) by which future activities and in particular change in activity can be evaluated and judged. Forty years ago, David Stanley noted that this measurement process can be classified at three levels, impressionistic, presumptive, and proven (Stanley, 1964). Most academic examinations of performance and performance measurement have focused on the technical, or proven, methods of evaluation. Books on performance measurement and the related techniques focus on "technical" methods, leaving the impression that "impressionistic" and presumptive techniques are less useful and certainly less "accurate." This reinforces the bias toward mechanical techniques.

Performance measurement is a tool created by science for use by government. The dilemma then is in the conflict of cultures. The expectation in how, when, and why measurement is applied is rarely resolved precisely because those questions are grounded in fundamentally different "basic assumptions." The challenge is to transcend the barrier of presumption to create measures that meet the expectations of science and of government. Earlier in this discussion it was noted that Wildavsky associated program evaluation with organizational learning. But the concept of organizational learning does not fit readily into traditional approaches to program evaluation, which tend to emphasize technical attributes and methods over result (or more accurately, science presumes that "proper" methods yield correct results). The problems? Citing a Congressional Budget Office study, Joyce enumerates the following:

- The difficulty in agreeing on objectives and priorities of agencies is an enduring obstacle to performance measurement, and this problem is perhaps particularly acute in the federal government.
- Even where objectives and priorities can be agreed upon, developing the measures themselves is challenging.
- Local and state governments have had limited successes in using performance measures beyond the individual agency level, particularly for budgeting.
- Past federal efforts to link performance to budgeting were not successful, and repetition of these mistakes should be avoided.
- Since federal agencies currently use performance measures for only limited purposes, which rarely include budgeting, the task is a challenging one. In particular, responsibilities vary widely from agency to agency; therefore, it is important not to treat the federal government as a monolithic entity.
- Any performance measurement effort must confront the issue of the appropriate combination of executive and legislative branch action.
- The pace of reform may be an important factor in its potential for success. The complexity of the endeavor suggests that a deliberate approach is better than adopting a set of uniform, and immediate, requirements for all federal agencies.
- It is important to understand how performance measures might influence the budget process, which requires understanding their limitations.

(Joyce, p. 336)

This list could be repeated for virtually every use of performance measurement. In each instance the tool or technique has become more valued than the practice it was designed to aid. Thus, the academic community continues to teach the efficacy of performance budgeting without grasping its limitations. Seemingly, it is easier to continue to apply the technique and thus repeat the mistakes of the past in the development of measures, than it is to honestly assess the limits of the tool or to acknowledge the complexity of decision-making in the public arena. Unless we fully understand the implications of the use of performance measures upon political processes, we will continue to have this problem.

As House (1982) points out, the assumptions of the "technological guidance approach" are flawed. The presumption that the methods themselves are "neutral" and that the analysts are without bias are inaccurate. The danger is not a lack of rigor in applying the techniques of analysis, but in the hubris to believe that a perfectly neutral instrument exists. As critical is the danger that those without knowledge of the limitations of the techniques are led to believe that these techniques generate "true" answers. When the "answer" of the supposedly neutral analyst and the decision of policy makers are compared, rarely is the policy decision cast in a favorable light. The biases of the policy maker are presumed; the biases of the analyst are ignored. Both methods of decision-making are biased. Thus, for example, the seeming attraction of benefit-cost analysis is its simplicity and ease of comparison, but at what price? In the 1980s, the US Federal government introduced rules that required a benefit-cost analysis to be conducted on the decision to develop new rules. Obviously, the framers of this rule understood that a benefit-cost analysis can be made to say whatever you want; in this instance to halt regulatory activity in selected federal agencies. *Objectivity in analysis was not the desired outcome.* Rather, it was the very flexibility and subjectivity of the tool that was the point of its use. How could this be? How could a tool be thought to be objective, yet in reality be subjective? The secret to the illusion of objectivity is the ability to measure. By assigning a dollar figure to all activities, the focus of attention shifts to the resulting ratio, and away from the subjective and even deceptive decision of the assigned figure. People argue over whether the benefit-cost ratio is 3 to 2 or 7 to 4, when it is the bases for those numbers that should be scrutinized. All performance measurement endeavors suffer from this deficiency.

Case Examples

To help provide some perspective in this analysis the section that follows offers a variety of experiences in the use of performance measurements, which cast light on the weaknesses in traditional performance measures.

Lauderhill (Florida) Police Department

In 1997, the author assisted the City of Lauderhill in preparing several grants for the Department of Justice Community Policing program. One of the grant proposals sought to study the investigatory techniques of officers to determine if culture played a role in the ability of officers to gather evidence. The City of Lauderhill had changed dramatically over the years. In the 1950s and 1960s, it was the western most development in Broward County (the greater Fort Lauderdale area). While its demographic profile was, as were other such communities in south Florida, skewed toward an older, white population, Lauderhill boasted of several good golf courses and was in general more wealthy than other suburbs. The population peaked and then stabilized by the early 1980s as wealthy suburbs sprang up further south and west of Lauderhill. The population began to age rather rapidly in the mid-1980s. Schools were being closed and consolidated. Around 1990 a very significant shift occurred. A large contingent of Haitian immigrants began to move into the community. These new immigrants were attracted by the price of the 1950s-sized homes and condominiums. Lauderhill's forty- to fifty-year-old homes were smaller and, therefore, more affordable than those in surrounding communities. Within a few years the population was nearly 50 percent Haitian. Also, schools were soon bursting, as the small ranch-style homes that had catered to older couples now were home to families with three, four, or more children. One of the dilemmas for city officials was that the new residents were considerably less wealthy than those they replaced. And, as with many communities experiencing change, the new residents suffered through increases in crime. In 1957 the city had opted to contract with the County Sheriff to provide police services in the city. The Sheriff's deputies assigned to Lauderhill reflected the overwhelmingly white character of the county at large. Furthermore, that department still reflected some of the rural and southern traditions and style of law enforcement. By the 1990s, such a police force was less acceptable to the community and government officials. In 1991, the city took the unprecedented and expensive step of terminating its contract with the County and recreating its own police force. One of its goals was to mirror the community. It was in this context that the department began to recognize that the traditional interrogation and investigation procedures taught at the police academy were not functional in a city in which those who were most likely to experience crime had little if any knowledge of "American" policing. The legal tradition with which they had experience was based upon the French tradition overlaid with many years of brutality and corruption. The police were considered as "criminal" as the criminals. Cooperation with the police was not done. The American concepts of police professionalism and community policing were to say the least "foreign" to the new residents of Lauderhill.

By all standard measures, the shift from the County to a city police department was a failure. Crime was on the rise and the ability of the department to close cases was dropping. The Police Chief of Lauderhill recognized that waiting several years until Haitian recruits could move up the ranks was not a viable option. In its proposal to the US Justice Department, the department did not recommend the typical solutions of special recruitment, rapid promotion, and more training in traditional methods. The department proposed to look at developing a new definition of community policing that emphasized understanding the community, rather than simply engaging the community. It proposed collecting data, as part of its investigations, on which methods and techniques seemed to work best. They proposed using local citizen "translators" to accompany officers to crime scenes, citizen satisfaction surveys targeted to those who were involved in any facet of an investigation (victim and "criminal"), and they proposed developing social service programs out of the station to begin the process of "engaging" a community that was otherwise reluctant to get involved. None of these activities would help the "bottom-line" of more closed cases. By addressing the intangibles, rather than the standard measures of analysis, the department risked compounding its poor "record." The department proposed a quite radical step. Rather than focus on standard measures and crime statistics to judge the department, it was proposing that it be judged by its relationship to the community it served. The proposal was, in fact, too radical for the COPS program, but it does offer insight on the question of performance and measurement. The famous motto of the Los Angeles Police Department is "To Protect and Serve." Most large police departments have a slogan that is quite similar. Yet, if we defined this motto/slogan as a mission statement, what types of activities would it invoke? While there is no direct answer to this question, it is very likely that standard police practices of patrol and react would not be the answer. That implies that the standard measures of performance do not result in mission success. At that point it must be asked if we are measuring the correct performance.

Government-Mandated Program Evaluation

Beginning in the late 1960s, the United States Federal government began a concerted effort to review federal grant programs to ensure that they were efficiently and effectively administered. To ensure that such projects were evaluated objectively, outside consultants (often university faculty) were hired to conduct the evaluation. In the absence of clearly defined rules for evaluation, or even agreed-upon mission and goals statements for many of these projects, such evaluations were rarely the objective analysis sought. As a young legislative staffer in the early 1970s, I was caught up in the "Catch-22" that can be program evaluation. As part of the contract requiremrnts a university professor was hired. As part of that work he was directed to interview pertinent individuals involved in the program. I had been one of the staff members with responsibility for drafting the legislation at the direction of the legislative committee. Thus, I was one of the persons interviewed. The professor had done a great deal of work before getting to me (talking to anyone in the legislature probably was an afterthought). He reported on his preliminary findings in which he was highly critical of the program for not meeting its "objectives." I thought it was a successful program. The differences in our views were over the program objectives. His definition of the purpose of the program and my view of the purpose were diametrically opposite. I tried, in vain, to suggest that as author I might have some insight into the purpose of the program. He argued that as a PhD researcher he could read. The program was roundly criticized in his final report.

The other side of the coin was the famous (infamous) evaluations of the Head Start program conducted by the Nixon administration in 1972 and the Reagan administration in 1983. The Head Start program was a program of early intervention for at-risk pre-school children. The stated goal of the program was to bring at-risk children up to the same education level as other students by the fourth grade. The measurement for this status was to be a standardized examination for fourth graders used in various parts of the country. There were, we now know, several problems with this goal. First, politicians and educations were not yet aware of the cultural and socioeconomic bias in these standardized examinations. Second, the decision to pick the fourth grade as the measurement point had nothing to do with child development, pedagogy, or other factors related to the children to be tested. Why the fourth grade? It was very simple; the standardized test already existed and was widely used. The program evaluation in 1970 examined only a single cohort of students. The conclusion was that the program had failed to meet its objectives. The program was not abolished, in part because it was recognized that the evaluation methodology was defective (Posavac and Carey, 1997). The next major evaluation occurred in the Reagan administration. Again, the program did not meet its objectives. The program was not abolished, but no new funds were made available. By the late 1980s, during the Bush (senior) administration, periodic reviews still did not show that Head Start students achieved academic "parity" by grade four, but they did show something else. In tracking students beyond the fourth grade, it became apparent from an examination of the longitudinal data that those Head Start children never "caught up" in terms of test scores and grades, but were doing something more significant; they were graduating from high school at rates comparable to the other students. Head Start did not help with grades, but those kids graduated from high school—a major milestone in terms of future employment and lifetime income. In other words, the program failed its goal, but it did something more significant. We had been measuring the wrong goal. These revelations resulted in major funding increases for the program throughout the 1990s.

Performance Appraisals Under Civil Service

An interesting case study of how we conduct performance measurement is in its use as part of employee evaluations and appraisals (see also Chapter 3). At various times the author was involved in the revision of the performance appraisal instruments used in an agency. The first time was as part of the mandate of the US Civil Service Reform Act of 1978. The second was as part of a comprehensive position classification study for a municipality in Florida. Although twenty years separated the two projects, many of the same issues emerged in revising the performance appraisal processes. Two problems emerged as problematic: first, the considerable resistance by workers and managers to include team and organizational factors in the evaluation and second, the tendency of managers to use simple, numerically based factors to judge performance. The former problem is partly cultural. Americans are uncomfortable in situations where their individuality is not acknowledged (try to grade students on the basis of a group project and hear the complaints about how much "harder" the student worked than everyone else!). It is not relevant that we recognize that we are dependent upon others to accomplish our work. Hummel would argue that workers intuitively understand that their work activities are unrelated to organizational goals. To have part of their performance appraisal based upon the accomplishment of organizational goals is to automatically give them a failing performance rating. Since it is the managers who have a major responsibility for goal displacement, evaluating workers on the basis of organizational goals will make known this simple fact. The use of numerically based measures is simply an affirmation of the goal displacement. The argument that performance appraisals are "qualitative" was a deeply troubling revelation for many managers (particularly the engineers). To them a qualitative judgment was biased and "wrong." Only a quantitatively formulated appraisal process, whereby the sum of a set of numbers yielded a result, was appropriate. As performance measures were proposed, I would ask a simple question, "Can this measure be answered with a 'yes' or a 'no,' or must it be judged on a scale?" If the measure could be answered with a "yes" or "no," then it was rejected (clerical staff were often given a scaled ranking on whether or not work was submitted on time, or "neatly"!). The managers did not want to be a "judge." They wanted the numbers to be the judge, so that they could not be held "responsible" for the rating. This abdication of responsibility in the name of objectivity is a prime example of goal displacement. Performance appraisals were not a way to improve organizational performance and develop employees; they were simply a "task" to be performed with as little time and thought as possible.

If we are unwilling and unable to develop measures by which to judge the performance of colleagues and peers, how can an organization expect these same persons to develop appropriate measures by which to judge *organizational* performance? The obvious answer is that they cannot. But once performance appraisals of the individual are separated from any relationship to organizational performance, then both activities can be conducted without recognizing the incongruity of the practices.

Crime Statistics and Youth Gangs

The problem of youth gangs is hardly new, though the nature of the crimes and problems of gangs evolved from the "juvenile delinquency" of the 1950s (as epitomized by the play "West Side Story") to the tragedy of drug use and violent crime in the 1980s; the American public put increasing pressure on police departments to address this issue. One of the ideas that emerged in the late 1970s in the largest cities of America and spread to many smaller communities in the 1980s, was the creation of specialized youth gang units within municipal police departments. Because of the public perception, spurred by newspaper stories, of the migration and expansion of youth gangs from Los Angeles into the State of New Mexico, there was a big push in the larger cities of that state to create youth gang units. The city of Las Cruces, New Mexico was the first community to establish such a unit, followed shortly thereafter by Santa Fe, New Mexico. Following good management procedures, and in anticipation of getting federal law enforcement monies for the units, these police departments began to collect separate crime statistics on all youth gang related crimes. Within a couple of years Las Cruces, and to a lesser extent Santa Fe, had the data to justify major grant applications to the US Department of Justice. More importantly, they had the indicators, which helped pinpoint problems and suggest courses of action to address the youth gang "problem." What was found was that youth gangs, and youth in general, were responsible for a disproportionate percentage of crime in the community. The good news was that those crimes were in general confined to "non-violent" such as auto theft and burglary. The youth gangs that were identified were "locals." The great fear of infiltration by the violent gangs of Los Angeles was not yet a reality. Furthermore, preliminary results suggested that the unit was having a positive affect as a deterrent. It was a classic and very effective application of performance measurement and program evaluation techniques.

While these statistics demonstrated a definitive need for the additional funding, the new statistics had a very different effect on the public. The publication of the crime statistics *heightened*, rather than reduced, the public's fear of youth gangs. But still more problematic was that Albuquerque, New Mexico, which had a serious youth gang problem (according to a State Police and FBI report on the existence of a Los Angeles gang in Albuquerque), chose not to create a youth gang unit. This decision was made in part because the police department did not want to be subjected to the public scrutiny and criticism that they saw being applied to the Las Cruces Police Department. In fact, they realized that it created a plausible "deniability" about youth crime. Since Albuquerque did not have a youth gang unit, there were no separate crime statistics to contradict the city's claim that there was no problem. The issue became untenable in Las Cruces, when the city of Albuquerque and the Bernalillo Chamber of Commerce began to try to lure new businesses to Albuquerque by pointing out the "gang problems" in Las Cruces made it a much less desirable place to set up a company. The business community in Las Cruces immediately began to pressure City Hall and the Police Department to drop the youth gang unit. That group went so far as to lobby the City to drop the federal grant application. Ultimately, the City caved in to the pressure. The youth gang unit was disbanded and the crime statistics folded back into the broader city statistics. The unit fell to political pressure despite having done everything "right." Given more time the police department might have been able to demonstrate that their efforts were effective in reducing youth gang crime. But, ultimately, the mere fact of creating the unit and, therefore, the measure of analysis, was its downfall.

The lesson of these stories about program evaluation is that goals, like other processes, are mutable. To continue to use a single measure of performance (even one in the preamble to the law) may not capture the "truth" about a program. Even projects done "by the book" may suffer adversely from unanticipated consequences. We need to carefully map out the mission and goals of a program as the basis for program evaluation. At the same time, the result of an evaluation may well be an indication that our performance measures are wrong, not that the program is wrong. Finally, the lessons above suggest that performance measures should be viewed as internal management tools, not as the basis for public debate. This is not a suggestion to "hide" information from the public. Rather it is a suggestion that judgments about policy be made on the basis of policy information, not management information. Otherwise, the discussion may focus on the efficacy of the management practices, not the policy practices.

Borrowing from the varied literature on OD, TQM, strategic management, chaos theory, and then overlaying the need for introspection, reflection, and learning, yields a framework for "right management thinking." The successful manager's actions must incorporate the following:

- Future orientation
- Uncertainty as the only "certainty"
- Empowerment and
- Collective, rather than individual, vision

How might these leadership/management practices be related to performance measurement? An orientation toward the future is straightforward. The very purpose of performance measurement is to examine the past to help guide the future. However, as has been suggested above, the future is not something that can be controlled. The decisions we make about the future are educated guesses, but still guesses. More importantly, we look to the future with the intention of making it different than the present. The essence of a future-oriented process is a rejection of the status quo. It is the desirability of a new future that impels action. A performance measurement process, which is designed to limit or control the future, is in opposition to this notion of a future orientation.

In much the same way that a future orientation is critical, it is necessary to acknowledge uncertainty. This is a difficult perspective if a "rational analytic" perspective is applied. The very concept of measurement seems the antithesis of uncertainty.

However, if the starting point is that the increasing *inability* to measure with accuracy is to be expected and, therefore, desirable, performance measures center on the changing character of events and policy consequences. When measurement is no longer possible with any level of certainty, then it is time to rethink the goals and objectives that helped shape the performance measures in the first place. It is not the time to scramble to "get back on track." To do so is to create more "chaos." The central reality of uncertainty is that no one, no matter how skilled, can "control" the future. Limiting measurements to those things that are "measurable" merely creates the illusion of control. In the long run, events will become more and more inexplicable. Again, Gloria Grizzle summarized this perspective quite well.

> [P]erformance measurement should not be confined to those events over which a program manager has near-total control. Doing so would ignore the questions about program outcomes that the public and their elected officials most want answered. Instead, outcomes, though often not controllable by a single actor, should be measured and the question of accountability approached by developing the concept of joint responsibility.
>
> Second, the distortion of effort resulting from performance measurement is likely to be most severe when measurements focus upon program activities rather than program outcomes. Measuring outcomes has the additional advantage, then, of providing the organization with an incentive rather than a disincentive to achieve stated goals.
>
> (Grizzle, 1982, p. 135)

There is another, and more critical, lesson here. The distinction between program activities and program outcomes is not trivial. Outcomes are derivative of the mission and goals of the organization. The activities and tasks of the organization should logically flow from those goals. As Weber and a score of other researchers have warned for many years, goal displacement is quite common in hierarchical organizations (Rainey, 1997). Rules to facilitate organization goals over time become rules to facilitate work tasks. Paperwork, forms, and procedures are geared to make internal operations easier, even as they create more distance from the original purpose of the organization (Hummel, 1994). The focus on program activities in performance measurement (number of forms processed, clients met, students enrolled, etc.) is an example of goal displacement. More problematically, the act of measurement gives these activities more credibility and strengthens the focus on *activities*. As the organization looks inward, it produces measurements to affirm this changed focus. The mission and goals of the organization are lost in a blizzard of paper affirming that performance is getting "better."

How does the concept of empowerment relate to performance measurement? Surprisingly, this concept is vital to effective measures. Fundamental to the concept of empowerment is the straightforward notion that the persons most directly connected to work activities know best how to organize that work (Hummel, 1994). The delicate balancing act is to know what activities can be transferred. Empowerment is not about willy-nilly abdicating responsibility/authority. Rather it is transferring responsibility for tasks to those who best understand those tasks. The distinction here is that the establishment of goals (those things which will be measured) is left to management, but the actual work is left to others. The management staff, in conjunction with the public and the legislative branch and the myriad others who have a say in setting policy in a representative democracy, sets the goals to be measured. But it is the "workers" who know best how to measure. In other words, defining the appropriate measures can be left to others. This allocation of responsibility protects the organization from goal displacement and leaves to those most able to be responsive and flexible with the task of measuring.

A Different Approach to Measurement

As suggested elsewhere, Morgan (1986) suggests that each of us uses metaphors by which to define how we think an organization should operate. When we observe an organization in action, we tend to see what we want to see. In other words, we see organizations operating as they "should." Because of education, experience, and culture, each of us has preferred metaphors. The metaphors that dominate our thinking about organizations are what we observe. If we think of an organization as a machine, we see a machine. But also, we will want it to operate as a machine (i.e. workers are parts, not people). We will define an effective organization based upon how closely it mimics our preferred metaphor. We will measure those aspects of organizational activity that can confirm or deny our expectations. The long ago "Hawthorne Experiments" (Roethlisgerger, 1939), particularly those related to illumination in the workplace, are good examples of performance expectations (i.e. there is an optimal level of illumination in the factory that will optimize output).

One lesson is the changed understanding of the *purpose* of formative evaluation. In standard evaluation methodologies, formative evaluation is designed to determine if the project is "still on track." The lesson of Strategic Management and TQM is that evaluations should ask a different question, Is this the right track? The point is that, over time, as we gain experience, we may see new opportunities and new directions. Getting back on track is precisely the wrong thing to do. It does not matter how precise our measures are, if the wrong activity is being measured. Performance measures should undergo the same scrutiny. Simply because this is the measure that has "always" been used, or because it is in the law, does not mean that it provides a useful indicator.

The primary points of conflict rest on differing perspectives on the approach to problem-solving (is it primarily a task of problem definition or alternative analysis?) and the expectation of the ability to come to some kind of closure on a problem (are we offering a temporary respite from the problem, or are we determining an end solution?). Parenthetically, it might be added that democratic decision-making is a more "human" and thus more idiosyncratic exercise.

CONCLUSION: THE MANAGEMENT SUPPORT SYSTEM

Can we measure moving targets? Traditional analytic methods would, of course, say no. But, if the purpose of measuring performance is to give us warning about change, then we need performance measures as an "early warning system," not as a control mechanism. Just as the lessons of chaos theory and best practice management shift our attention to the future, the role of performance measurement is to do the same. Under this scenario, performance measurement becomes an adjunct of organizational management. It also reinforces the need to look *back* to goals and the public values that underlie those goals and *forward* to new outcomes.

> The setting of institutional goals cannot be divorced from the enunciation of governing principles. Goal-setting, if it is institutionally meaningful, is framed in the language of character or identity, that is, it tells us what we should "do" in order to become what we want to "be." A decision to produce a new product or enter a new market [or begin a new public program], though it may set goals, is nevertheless irresponsible if it is not based on an understanding of the company's [government's] past and potential character. If the new venture, on analysis, requires a change in distinctive competence, then that becomes the new goal. Such a goal is bound up with principles because attaining and conserving a distinctive competence depends on an understanding of what standards are required and how to maintain them.
>
> (Selznick, p. 144)

This greater flexibility also addresses the age-old problem of the interface between technical administration and policy making. When performance measurements are used as a mechanism of control, flexibility is impossible. But, if current measures of outcome are used as harbingers of change, then such measures fit the more experimental, skeptical stance that is part of political decision-making. As Grizzle comments, "one cannot isolate performance measurement system design and development from systems politics. Neither can one keep the information that the performance measurement system generates from being used in the political process" (Grizzle, p. 135).

To be successful, performance measures must serve the institution, not the organization. In doing this it elevates the sights of the measurement process away from organizational "results" to the mission and goals of the institution.

> Organizations are technical instruments, designed as means to definite goals. They are judged on engineering premises; they are expendable. Institutions, whether conceived as groups or practices, may be partly engineered, but they have also a "natural" dimension. They are products of interaction and adaptation; they become the receptacles of group idealism; they are less readily expendable.
>
> (Selznick, pp. 21–22)

Organizations look inward while institutions look outward. Measuring institutional performance should be an outward-looking process, i.e. one that is focused on mission. The shift from evaluation as a tool to affirm the status quo to one that encourages new directions was first introduced in TQM. Performance measures should follow the same approach. Benchmarks and planned evaluation should be done with the intention of making changes, not of "staying the course." The goal is to reject current practice and to seek new performance goals. Performance measures must change with each evaluation cycle. If they do not, then one might question whether or not "progress" is in fact being made. This may require the exploration of new methods and strategies for developing measures and analyzing measures. For example, Robert Yin has noted that "case studies are the preferred strategy when 'how' and 'why' questions are posed, when the investigator has little control over events and when the focus is contemporary phenomena with some real-life context" (Dreussi, 2001, p. 95). While Yin was referring to policy analysis, the comment equally applies to program evaluation and performance measurement. Can a better description be found for the circumstances under which performance measures are created and collected than the above? As a recent doctoral student found in conducting a program evaluation study, the only effective tool for evaluating the various projects was the case study. The best method for assessing what program practices worked and therefore how to create a workable and effective program came from the depth and quality of the interviews, not the program analysis data (Dreussi). This suggests that one of the tools for performance measurement may be the case study.

The mind-set of the person to develop performance measures is similar to Wildavsky's "evaluation man."

> The ideal member of the self-evaluating organization is best conceived as a person committed to certain modes of problem solving. He believes in clarifying goals, relating them to different mechanisms of achievement, creating models (sometimes quantitative) of the relationships between inputs and outputs, seeking the best available combination. His concern is not that the organization should survive or that any specific objective be enthroned or that any particular clientele be served. . . .
>
> Evaluation should not only lead to the discovery of better policy programs to accomplish existing objectives but to alteration of the objectives themselves. Analysis of the effectiveness of existing policies leads to consideration of alternatives that juxtapose means and ends embodied in alternative policies. The objectives as well as the means for attaining them may be deemed inappropriate. But men who have become socialized to accept certain objectives may be reluctant to change. *Resistance to innovation then takes the form of preserving social objectives.* The difficulties are magnified once we realize that objectives may be attached to the clientele . . . with whom organizational members identify. The objectives of the organization may have attracted them precisely because they see it as a means of service to people they value. They may view changes in objectives, therefore, as proposals for "selling out" the clients they wish to serve. In their eyes evaluation becomes an enemy of the people.
>
> (emphasis added, Wildavsky, p. 275)

In the context of the discussion of organizational culture, Wildavsky's "social objectives" become embedded in the basic assumptions (i.e. unexamined, preconscious assumptions) of the organizations. It is no longer a matter of capacity to serve a clientele, but an imperative to serve. Not surprisingly, we establish measurements that assure that we will adhere to the interests of that clientele.

How can the problem of resistance to innovation be overcome? The first step is to recognize that performance measurement is a tool of government. That implies two things: first, its use must reflect the culture of government and second, as a tool, it is essentially a "neutral" devise. We should measure that which is *there*, not what we want or expect to be there. In other words, its application must be directed toward the unexpected, not the expected.

To summarize, it is suggested that the best approach to performance measurement begin with a stance that is tilted toward the flexibility of participative management and chaos theory. Thus, measures should be flexible and experimental. Second, borrowing from Grizzle, Wildavsky, Selznick, and current management practice, the goal should be to create measures that are expendable. Performance measures should change over time, because the organization, its goals, and its operating techniques and processes will change. Third, performance measures should help the organization operationalize the values of government and of governance, not the internal concerns of the organization. Thus, the measures should reflect broad, transcendent policy goals, not narrow organizational goals or the results of tasks. Performance measures should be less about current activities and practices and more about future results. Fourth, different techniques such as triangulation and case studies may be useful methods of evaluating and analyzing performance. Fifth, performance measurement should be subject to the same consensus-based decision process as other public policy matters. Measurement and analysis are not "superior" to politics and political analysis; they are adjuncts to them. Sixth, performance measures can in this context be attempted in the full knowledge of its limitations. Performance measurements are vital elements of policy analysis, program evaluation, performance appraisals and even strategic management. However, the first step toward proper and effective use of those measures is appreciating that knowing what those measurements do not imply is as critical as knowing what they do imply. Finally, performance measures are one of many tools to aid in decision-making, not the method of making decisions. The chief of police, in seeking to create a police force that was at once sensitive to cultural differences and able to conduct investigations without dividing the community, reflected the values of policing, not the internal operational norms of crime statistics; the continuation of Head Start, because it helped a generation of students have a chance at a successful work career, even though it never achieved its statutory goal; the creation of performance appraisal methods that encourage growth and development, rather than an artificial scale of performance; and the use of measurements to create a baseline of data to aid decision-making and not to support a political agenda are all examples of adapting performance measures to broader values and principles. This is the approach toward which we should strive.

DISCUSSION QUESTIONS

- What are the differences of technique, perspective or practices between policy analysis and program evaluation?
- Why is measurement a problem?
- How is program evaluation different from the program assessment in strategic management?
- What are the differences between formative and summative evaluations?
- How does organizational culture influence program evaluation?
- How does political ideology influence program evaluation?

BIBLIOGRAPHY

Bennis, Warren G., Kenneth Benne, Robert Chin, and Kenneth Corey. *The Planning of Change, 3rd ed.* New York: Holt, Rinehart and Winston. 1976.

Bennis, Warren, and B. Nanus. *Leaders: The Strategies for Taking Charge.* New York: St. Martin's Press. 1985.

Bland, Robert, and Irene Rubin. *Budgeting: A Guide for Local Governments.* Washington DC: ICMA. 1997.

Brudney, Jeffrey L., F. Ted Hebert, and Deil S. Wright. "Reinventing Government in the American States: Measuring and Explaining Administrative Reform", *Public Administration Review*, 59 (1), pp. 19–30. 1999.

Burns, James McGregor. *Leadership.* New York: Harper Collins. 1978.

Cox III, Raymond W. "Getting Past the Hype: Issues in Starting a Public Sector TQM Program", *Public Administration Quarterly* Spring, 19 (1), pp. 89–104. 1995.

Cox III, Raymond W. "Organizational Development and TQM", in Halachmi and Bouckaert (eds.) *Public Productivity: The Challenge of Total Quality and Strategic Management.* Amsterdam: Russell, IIAS/IOS. 1997.

Cox III, Raymond W., Susan Buck, and Betty Morgan. *Public Administration in Theory and Practice.* Englewood Cliffs, NJ: Prentice Hall. 1994.

Cox III, Raymond W., and Ralph P. Hummel. "A Declaration of Independence for Congress: Why Politics Cannot and Should Not Be Managed", A Paper Presented at the American Political Science Association. August 30–September 2. 1988.

Dreussi, Amy. *A Multimethodological Impact Analysis of Urban Development Action Grants for Projects Related to the Steel Industry.* PhD Dissertation University of Akron. 2001.

Epstein, Paul D. *Using Performance Measurement in Local Government.* New York: National Civic League Press. 1988.

Forester, John. *Planning in the Face of Power.* Berkeley, CA: University of California Press. 1989.

Frant, Howard L. "Dangers, Chimeras Ahead: Commentary on Terry", *Public Administration Review*, 59 (3), pp. 268–271. 1999.

Frederickson, H. George. "Public Ethics and the New Managerialism", *Public Integrity*, 1 (III) (Summer). 1999.

Gabris, Gerald T. "Recognizing Management Technique Dysfunctions: How Management Tools Often Create More Problems Than They Solve", *Public Productivity Review*, 19 (Winter), pp. 3–19. 1986.

Gawthrop, Louis C. "Public Entrepreneurship in the Lands of Oz and Uz", *Public Integrity*, 1 (I) Winter, pp. 75–86. 1999.

Gerth, Hans H., and C. Wright Mills, ed. *From Max Weber.* New York: Oxford University Press. 1946.

Grizzle, Gloria A. "Measuring State and Local Government Performance: Issues to Resolve Before Implementing a Performance Measurement System", *State and Local Government Review*, 14 (September), pp. 132–136. 1982.

Gruber, Judith E. *Controlling Bureaucracies.* Berkeley, CA: University of California Press. 1987.

Hatry, Harry, Louis Blair, Donald Fisk, and Wayne Kimmel. *Program Analysis for State and Local Government, 2nd ed.* Washington, DC: The Urban Institute Press. 1987.

Hatry, Harry, Richard C. Winnie, and Donald Fisk. Practical *Program Evaluation for State and Local Governments, 2nd ed.* Washington, DC: The Urban Institute Press. 1981.

House, Peter W. *The Art of Policy Analysis.* Beverly Hills, CA: Sage. 1982.

Hummel, Ralph P. "Bureaucracy, Democracy and Politics: Are They Compatible?", unpublished paper. 1986.

Hummel, Ralph P. *The Bureaucratic Experience, 4th ed.* New York: St. Martin's Press. 1994.

Joyce, Philip G. "Using Performance Measures", in: "Using Performance Measures for Federal Budgeting: Proposals and Prospects", *Public Budgeting & Finance*, 13 (Winter), pp. 3–17. 1993.

Kanter, Rosabeth Moss. "The Architecture of Culture and Strategic Change", in J. Steven Ott Classic (ed.) *Readings in Organizational Behavior, 2nd ed.* Fort Worth, TX: Harcourt Brace College Publishers, pp. 487–505. 1996.

Kiel, L. Douglas. *Managing Chaos and Complexity in Government.* San Francisco: Jossey-Bass. 1994.

Kouzmin, Alexander, and Judy Johnston. "An International Symposium on Auditing Australian Public Sector Innovations: From Public Administration to Public Management", *Public Productivity and Management Review*, 21 (4), pp. 344–351. 1998.

Lindblom, Charles E. "The Science of Muddling Through", *Public Administration Review*, 19, pp. 79–88. 1959.

Lynch, Thomas D. *Public Budgeting in America, 4th ed.* Englewood Cliffs, NJ: Prentice Hall. 1995.

Maor, Moshe. "The Paradox of Managerialism", *Public Administration Review*, 59 (1), pp. 5–18. 1999.

McGregor, Douglas M. *The Human Side of Enterprise.* New York: McGraw Hill Book Company. 1960.

Morgan, Gareth. *Images of Organization.* Newbury Park, CA: Sage. 1986.

Posavac, Emil J., and Raymond Carey. Program *Evaluation: Methods and Case Studies, 5th ed.* Upper saddle River, NJ: Prentice-Hall. 1997.

Price Waterhouse Change Integration Team. *The Paradox Principles.* Chicago: Irwin Professional Publishers. 1996.

Rainey, Hal G. *Understanding and Managing Public Organizations, 2nd ed.* San Francisco: Jossey-Bass. 1997.

Roethlisgerger, Fritz J., and Dickson, W. J. *Management and the Worker.* Cambridge, MA: Harvard University Press. 1939.

Schein, Edgar H. "Defining Organizational Culture", in J. Steven Ott (ed.) *Classic of Organization Theory, 4th ed.* Fort Worth, TX: Harcourt Brace College Publishers, pp. 430–441. 1996.

Selznick, Philip. *Leadership in Administration.* Berkeley, CA: University of California Press. 1957.

Simon, Herbert A. *Administrative Behavior.* New York: Free Press. 1948.

Smith, Michael P. "Barriers to Organizational Democracy in Public Administration", *Administration and Society*, 8 (3) November, pp. 275–317. 1976.

Stanley, David T. "Excellence in Public Service—How Do We Really Know?", *Public Administration Review*, 24, pp. 170–174. 1964.

Stillman II, Richard J. *Preface to Public Administration.* New York: St. Martin's Press. 1991.

Svara, James H. "Complementarity of Politics and Administration as a Legitimate Alternative to the Dichotomy Model", *Administration and Society*, 30 (6), pp. 676–705. 1999.

Sylvia, Ronald D., Kenneth J. Meier, and Elizabeth M. Gunn. *Program Planning and Evaluation for the Public Manager.* Monterey, CA: Brooks/Cole Publishing. 1985.

Taylor, Frederick. *The Principles of Scientific Management.* New York: Harper and Brothers. 1934.

Terry, Larry D. "Administrative Leadership, Neo-Managerialism and the Public Management Movement", *Public Administration Review*, 58 (3), pp. 194–200. 1998.

Tichy, Noel M., and David O. Ulrich. "The Leadership Challenge- A Call for the Transformational Leader", in J. Steven Ott (ed.) *Classic Readings in Organizational Behavior.* Pacific Grove, CA: Brooks/Cole Publishing. 1989.

Tinder, Glenn. *Tolerance.* Amherst, MA: University of Massachusetts Press. 1976.

Trice, Harrison M., and Janice M. Beyer. "Changing Organizational Cultures", in Jay M. Shafritz and J. Steven Ott (eds.) *Classic of Organization Theory, 4th ed.* Fort Worth, TX: Harcourt Brace College Publishers, pp. 473–484. 1996.

Waldo, Dwight. *The Administrative State, 2nd ed.* New York: Holmes and Meier. 1984.

Weber, Max. "Politics as Vocation", in Gerth and Mills (eds.) *From Max Weber.* New York: Oxford University Press. 1946.

Weick, Karl. *Social Psychology of Organization, 2nd ed.* Reading, MA: Addison-Wesley Publishing. 1979.

Wildavsky, Aaron. "The Self Evaluating Organization", *Public Administration Review*, 32 (September-October), pp. 509–520. 1972.

Wolin, Sheldon S. "Democracy and the Welfare State", *Political Theory*, 15(4) November, pp. 467–500. 1987.

Yates, Douglas. *Bureaucratic Democracy.* Cambridge, MA: Harvard University Press. 1982.

Yates, Douglas. "Hard Choices: Justifying Bureaucratic Decisions", in Moore (ed.) *Ethical Insight Ethical Action.* Washington, DC: International City Management Association. 1988.

CHAPTER

8

Organizational Dynamics and Change

The preamble of the US Constitution mandates that the government "promote the general welfare" as well as seek "justice" and "liberty." Constitutions around the globe place similar demands upon the government. The implicit assumption in such statements is that government is the chosen vehicle by which to redress societal problems. Broadly conceived, then, the role of government is to introduce change. In essence, the government is in the business of planned change. However, the reality is that having the mandate for change and having the capacity or capability to achieve change are two quite different things. The nature of politics can be summarized in that difference. We have traditionally agreed on the broad outline of change (we accept the mandate of change), but we frequently disagree about the scope and specification of such change. Politics is about defining the capacity and capability to change.

Much of the responsibility for achieving change falls on public administrators. Change after all is both external and internal. Not only must the public manager take the lead in the implementation of the strategies that emerge from the policy development process, but additionally, implementation requires internal change to ensure that the personnel and financial resources are in place to carry out such implementation efforts properly and fully. Change runs the gambit from thinking about and defining problems to effectuating solutions to those problems. Further, change implies altered policy (or services) as well as altered practices and procedures.

In parallel with the development of macro-change tools such as strategic management (see Chapter 12), were the development of techniques and interventions to improve personal and organizational practices. This chapter will examine several techniques that are available to managers to improve the internal functioning of the organization. These techniques, and especially Organization Development, are often introduced into and potentially implemented by non-agency personnel or outside consultants.

PLANNED CHANGE AND GOVERNMENT ACTION

While we hardly find it surprising that governmental change initiatives are rarely premised on academic initiatives, there is still something to be learned from an examination of the planned change literature. The key point to remember in examining this literature is that change can be understood either as a phenomenon that is the result of individual change or as the result of systemic or organization (government) level change. Obviously, the means for achieving such change are different depending on the focus of the change.

Thus, for example, those concerned with individual change focus on means of influencing those specific persons they wish to change. Those interested in systemic change must seek change in broadly held values and, therefore, seek to shape opinion and societal values that will ultimately yield the behavioral change sought. Societal or systemic level change often has more to do with what might be considered politics, or at least, broad policy concerns (e.g. should the government establish an unemployment compensation fund or a new ethics code). For the purposes of this chapter it is individual change that is most pertinent.

The central point of the discussion that follows is to explore the character of change efforts initiated by government. Those changes may be either individual or systemic in orientation (and more likely include elements of both orientations). The common denominator is that all are government-sponsored efforts to induce change by the public or public agencies (state and local governments, for example). To fully understand government-sponsored change, three issues will be discussed: (1) the public administrator as instigator of change (as a change agent), (2) the individual systemic change in the context of intergovernmental relations, and (3) the problems associated with successfully achieving change. Before looking as those change practices it is first necessary to examine the assumptions about innovation and change that influence the strategy and therefore are built into the policy choices made.

THE DIFFUSION OF INNOVATION

One of the leaders in the study of the diffusion of innovation is Everett Rogers. For Rogers the concept of innovation is quite broad: It is any idea that is perceived as new. Thus, while the idea may have existed in other places, that does not alter the impact upon the person who encounters it for the first time and perceives it as new. Perception is the key concept in the broad application of Rogers's diffusion of innovation propositions.

Four central elements delimit all diffusion and adoption processes: the innovation itself, the communication of the innovation, the social system in which the process occurs, and the time factor (Rogers and Shoemaker, 1971; Rogers, 2003).

Innovation

Lauer summarizes the five major characteristics of the innovation as follows:

1. The relative advantage of the innovation. The more people perceive the innovation to enhance their advantage, relative to the existing situation, the more they will tend to adopt the innovation. The obverse is also true; the relative disadvantage, or lack of advantage of an innovation, will inhibit adoption.

2. A second perceived characteristic of an innovation is its compatibility with existing values and needs. A new method of birth control may diffuse through a system where there is a value on family limitation but is unlikely to diffuse where religious values condemn artificial birth control. Professionals, as well as lay people, resist innovations that are incompatible with their values (as opposed to rejection on technical grounds). For example, professional therapists were found to be less accepting than lay people of a community mental health ideology. The ideology was no doubt contrary to some of their own ideologies of therapy; however, it was also contrary to their self-interests.
3. The rate of adoption of innovations will be affected by their perceived complexity. Some innovations will be perceived to be very difficult to understand and utilize. Thus, they will be adopted more slowly and, possibly, even be rejected.
4. Innovations are more or less adopted on the basis of their "trial-ability": the extent to which it is possible to institute them on a trial basis.
5. The rate of adoption is affected by the communicability of the innovation. The more frequently a potential adopter can observe the effects of the innovation, the more likely he or she is to adopt it. Further, the more easily an innovation can be explained or demonstrated, the more likely it is to be adopted.
(Lauer, 1982, p. 171)

Communication

The way in which an innovation is communicated (how and by whom) has an impact on the rate of adoption. The essence of the process is human interaction by which one individual communicates a new idea to one or more other individuals. Reduced to the most basic level, the diffusion process consists of (1) new ideas, (2) an individual with knowledge of the innovation, (3) a second individual who is unaware of the innovation, and (4) some process by which the two individuals communicate. Importantly, the nature of the social relationship between the two individuals determines the conditions under which the first will or will not communicate the idea to the second; and, further, it influences the impact of the communication on the second (Rogers, 2003).

Various ways of communicating an innovation to a target population or client group exist, and the method chosen will affect the rate of adoption. Rogers argues that both the purpose of the communication and the nature of the client group must be considered in selecting a channel. If the purpose is merely to inform, the mass media may be the best channel; for the media allows us to reach a large population both rapidly and efficiently. However, if the purpose is to persuade, interpersonal channels are necessary; an individual is more likely to be persuaded by a face-to-face discussion with another person than by a newspaper or radio or TV report.

Social Processes

It is important to remember that the diffusion process is a social process. The structure of the social system can have an important influence on the dissemination of new ideas. The social structure of the system may impede or facilitate the rate of

The Diffusion of Innovation **177**

diffusion and adoption of new ideas. The norms, social statuses, and hierarchy of a social system influence the behavior of individual members of the system.

A number of facets of a social system are of importance. The three most critical ones are norms, opinion leaders, and change agents.

1. Norms influence the individual's reaction to innovations and have been found to be even more important than certain individual characteristics, such as level of education or cosmopolitan outlook.
2. Opinion leaders are the second important aspect of the social system that bears upon the fate of innovation. Opinion leaders are capable of influencing others because of their competence, their conformity to norms, and their status. In other words, opinion leaders have influence independent of their relationship to any particular innovation. Thus, when they promote an innovation, it is more likely to be adopted.

   Opinion leaders are not necessarily those who first adopt an innovation. An individual who is an opinion leader in one area is not necessarily a leader in a different area. Typically, any individual opinion leader is considered expert in only a few areas. Further, opinion leaders are more likely than others in the social system to utilize a broad variety of sources of information, to be cosmopolitan in orientation, to have higher levels of social participation, to have higher status, and to be more innovative (although they are not necessarily the innovators).
3. The third aspect of the social system is the change agent. In contrast to the opinion leader, who is a member of the social system into which the innovation is introduced, the change agent is an outsider who attempts to exert the kind of influence defined as desirable by a change agency. The change agent frequently uses an opinion leader within a system to facilitate his or her work. The most intensive efforts of the change agent occur in the early stages of adoption, when the rate of adoption is low.

(Lauer, pp. 170–171)

Time

Time is an element in the diffusion process and can be divided into three dimensions: (1) the innovation decision process, (2) the innovativeness of the individual adopters, and (3) the rate of adoption of the innovation within the social system.

The innovation decision process is the series of mental steps through which an individual passes from first knowledge of an innovation to a decision to adopt or reject it. This process is composed of four stages: knowledge, persuasion, decision, and confirmation. The knowledge function occurs when the individual is first exposed to the innovation's existence and acquires some understanding of its functioning. The persuasion function occurs when the individual forms an opinion (favorable or unfavorable) about the innovation. The decision function occurs when the person undertakes activities which force a choice between adoption and rejection. The confirmation function occurs when the individual seeks reinforcement of the decision made, although he or she may reverse a previous decision if conflicting messages about the innovation are received (Rogers and Shoemaker, p. 27).

178 | **CHAPTER 8** Organizational Dynamics and Change

Innovativeness is an individual's propensity to adopt innovations earlier than other members of his or her social groups. The adopters may be categorized in the following manner: (1) innovators, (2) early adopters, (3) early majority, (4) later majority, and (5) laggards.

> How many people are we talking about in each of these categories? Rogers defines the first 2.5 percent of adopters as innovators, the next 13.5 percent as early adopters, the next 34 percent as early majority and another 34 percent as late majority, and the last 16 percent as laggards or late adopters. The term "laggard" is probably an unfortunate choice, incidentally. Rogers himself recognizes that not every innovation, not even every innovation that is adopted, is beneficial for people. In some cases, then, the "laggards" may be the only people who are pursuing a healthy course. As we noted earlier, technology is not the savior, and every technological innovation is not beneficial per se for all people.
>
> (Lauer, pp. 172–173)

If the data above are plotted, a bell curve of innovation adoption is obtained. The attractiveness of this feature of Rogers's work held sway for many years in a good number of federal agencies. The debate inevitably focused on whether the federal officials should concentrate on early adopters or the early majority. The reality of such a curvilinear distribution or its application to institutions rather than individuals was an issue that was suppressed. The fact that over time an innovation is adopted in a social system in a bell-curve distribution does not explain who will innovate and who will not. Research could replicate the fact of the bell curve; it could not serve as a predictor of where a particular person or institution fell within the curve on any particular innovation. Yet the argument was often made that the federal role was to foreshorten the time between adoption by innovators and adoption by others. Sorting out just who the appropriate "other" was remained problematic.

The processes of innovation diffusion and adoption are complex. Lauer (1982) selected the following generalizations from Rogers; work to represent best the breadth of these efforts.

1. Innovativeness of individuals is related to a modern rather than a traditional orientation
2. An individual's innovativeness varies directly with the norms of his or her social system on innovativeness
3. *Relatively later adopters are* more likely to discontinue innovations than are earlier adopters
4. Awareness occurs at a more rapid rate than does adoption
5. The relative advantage of a new idea, as perceived by members of a social system, affects its rate of adoption
6. Earlier adopters have more opinion leadership than later adopters
7. Change agents have more communication with higher-status than with lower-status members of a social system

(p. 168)

THE CHANGE AGENT

The change agent plays a critical, pivotal role in any change process as he or she must "orchestrate" that change. We wonder if these activities imply a value structure that impels change agents to certain types of change processes or objectives. For instance, a value structure (i.e., social equity) underlying the efforts of the new public administration is obvious. Whether such a value orientation exists, is necessary for, or is even critical to the activities of any change agent is more problematic.

Huse (1989; see also Cummings and Worley, 2005) suggests three different styles associated with change agentry:

1. The "people-change-technology" type (PCT): This type of change agent works for management to change the way in which organizational members behave . . . the assumption underlying the PCT approach is that if individuals change their behavior, the organization will change, especially if enough individuals (or the right ones) change.
2. The "analysis-from-the-top" type (AFT): This approach relies primarily on the rational, Socratic approach. . . . The focus may be on changing the organizational structure or technology so as to improve output and efficiency. Approaches might include computerized information-processing systems and the development of new task groups to operate the innovations.
3. The "organization-development" type (OD): The OD model grew out of such areas as sensitivity training, survey data feedback, and team building. . . . The realization has grown that each of the techniques associated with the OD approach embodies only a partial truth. As a result, change must involve multiple techniques and may also require a complete organizational redesign.
   (pp. 441–442)

It would seem from the above summary that each type of change agent has a different goal orientation. The AFT change agent would seek increased organizational output and efficiency as a primary goal. While the PCT and OD agents have multiple goals, both seem to be concerned with improving the quality of organizational problem-solving.

What type of person is this change agent? Cummings and Worley, following Huse, suggest that the effective change agent is a "marginal person." The marginal person stands at the boundary (or margin) between two groups who hold differing values, goals, or viewpoints.

> Those who are good at marginal roles seem to have personal qualities of low dogmatism, neutrality, open-mindedness, objectivity, flexibility, and adaptable information processing. Rather than being upset by conflict, ambiguity and stress, they thrive on it. Individuals with marginal orientations are more likely than others to develop integrative decisions that bring together and reconcile viewpoints between opposing organizational groups and are more likely to remain "neutral" in controversial situations. Thus, the research suggests that marginality can have positive consequences when a boundary-spanning role is filled by a person with a marginal orientation. Such a person can be more

objective and better able to perform successfully in linking, integrative, conflict-laden roles.

(Huse, 1980, p. 446)

The "Marginal Agent" of Intergovernmental Relations

In relating the previous description of the change agent to the process of intergovernmental relations, several problems emerge. For example, who is to be the change agent? What level of organizational change is being sought? And, what is the appropriate role for political leadership in stimulating change? The answers are not simple. The problem of the perspective of the analyst underlying the distinction between national and nationwide problems is often a major stumbling block in answering these questions.

For example, one traditional federal model of the change agent might be an administrator at the Department of Health and Human Services, Housing and Urban Development, or elsewhere who approves categorical grants. As the change agent, this federal official would be primarily concerned with the uniformity and orderliness with which a predetermined problem solution is applied throughout the country. The major vehicle for change is the regulations promulgated by the agency. The "marginality" of the bureaucratic role is in mediating between interest groups as part of the process of rulemaking, or in smaller programs of preparing application guidelines such as Requests for Proposals (RFPs) or program solicitations.

Governments face the critical governance task of addressing the dual problems of identifying/selecting both a change agent and implementing institutions. This task is clearly more difficult than simply ranking similar programs. National programs start with a presumption that the "best way" of achieving change has been determined by the federal bureaucrat/change agent, and it is only in the quality of execution that state and local governments differ. In the second category of programs, decisions are less clear-cut. Direction from Washington is less precise; no one, whether in Washington or in the locality, knows what will work. The goal is change, but only a general idea of the direction of that change is known beforehand. Further, it is the people within the locality who are in the best position to recognize change opportunities; that is, the change agent is found within the organization, not in Washington.

If we look at the literature on planned change, we find that for a non-categorical program guidance in selecting institutions is at best ambivalent. Social change literature (Benne, Bennis, and Chin, 1976) is pertinent to the Washington program manager. However, for the change agent in the state or local government, the guidance of organization development and diffusion of innovation is more to the point. This does not mean that the Washington program officer need not be familiar with this literature; rather he or she must work within both bodies of literature to do the job. The problem of Washington bureaucrat is one of knowing the job of change agent without ever exercising the responsibility of that position.

This rather odd confluence of ideas of change (seeking institutional change by funding institutions but relying on the ideas of individual change to carry out the work) has produced a somewhat unique theoretical underpinning for the many intergovernmental programs. While seeking institutional change, the focus is necessarily individual, not organizational. Thus, the literature on the diffusion of innovation (Rogers, 2003) that concerns the response of individuals to change came to be the centerpiece of theory for a program seeking institutional change. Similarly, the anomalies which occur within programs may be best viewed as the product of the combination of change theory from both perspectives rather than an outright rejection of diffusion theory.

IMPLEMENTING CHANGE

Rogers provides only part of the answer in explaining the process of change. The motivation to change and the structural aspects of change have been the province of social psychologists such as Kurt Lewin and Warren Bennis. The focus here is an organizational change that is the product of individual change. As such, it represents a different perspective than Rogers, who was concerned with the adoption of innovation among a class of people (farmers or doctors, for instance). Lewin looked to ways to help people change because of the organization change it could impart.

Benne and Chin offer a rather interesting examination of the dominant modes of analysis in planned change. Under their categorization, Rogers represents the rational-empirical strategy of change, while Lewin represents the normative-re-educative strategy. The distinction drawn is significant. While most programs of the federal government use the rational-empirical model, others (especially in the state governments) operate under the Lewin model. Each of these models, and particularly the premises underlying them, require further development.

Benne and Chin succinctly draw the distinction between these strategies when they postulate that rational-empirical strategies have an underlying assumption that people are that rational. Individuals will follow their rational self-interest once it is revealed to them. A change is proposed by someone who recognizes in a situation an opportunity which is desirable, effective, and in line with the self-interest of the person or group to be affected by the change. Because of the assumption of rationality and self-interest as a motivator, it is assumed that a proposed change will be adopted if that change can be rationally justified and the change shown to be of benefit to the affected group.

The normative re-educative approach is built upon different assumptions of human motivation.

> The rationality and intelligence of men are not denied. Patterns of action and practice are supported by sociocultural norms that are supported by the attitude and value systems of individuals—normative outlooks which undergird their commitments. Change in a pattern of practice or action, according to this view, will occur only as the persons involved are brought to change their normative orientations to old patterns and develop commitments to new ones . . . changes in normative orientations involve changes in attitudes, values, skills, and significant relationships, not just changes in knowledge, information, or intellectual rationales for action and practice.
>
> (Bennis et al., 1976, p. 23)

Some of the common elements of this approach are the following: The first is an emphasis on the client system and clients' involvement in working out programs of change and improvement for themselves. The way the client sees herself and her problem must be brought out as the basis of the relationship between the client and the change agent. Second, the problem confronting the client cannot be presumed to be solved by the provision of technical information. The problem may lie in attitudes, values, norms, or the external or internal relationships of the client; and, therefore, may require alteration or re-education of these as a condition of solution. Third, the change agent must learn to intervene mutually and collaboratively along with the client in the efforts to both define and solve problems. Fourth, nonconscious elements that may hinder problem solution must be brought out, examined, and reconstructed. Fifth, the methods and concepts of the behavioral sciences are resources that must be used selectively, relevantly, and appropriately in learning to deal with similar problems as they arise in the future (Benne et al., 1976, p. 33).

In other, subtle ways government makes assumptions about how to institute change. For example, the idea of the tax expenditure emerges from a rational-empirical notion that if individuals are offered incentives in the form of tax breaks (for home mortgages, for example), they will change their behavior (for example, buy homes rather than rent). In other instances, changes are made in the law to reflect how people should act in hope that they will come to accept the new behavior as better. Civil rights laws, in the face of strong opposition in some parts of the country, certainly followed this normative re-educative pattern.

It can also be assumed that change efforts may fail because the change strategy is faulty. While it may have been nothing more than wishful thinking, many political leaders at the close of the eighteenth century believed that the abolition of the importation of slaves would eventually lead to the demise of the entire practice of slavery. This normative re-educative attempt was based on assumptions that proved quite false.

It can also be assumed that the change agent will affect the success of a program. Laurence Lynn's early study of the interconnection between leadership style and opportunity for change can be thought of as a study of the role of change agents (in this case, political appointees in the Reagan administration). The persons Lynn describes who were not successful were thus unsuccessful as change agents (Lynn, 1987).

The variables in change efforts seem almost endless. The introduction of new policies by government may succeed or fail on the merits of the policies. But also, those policies may succeed or fail because of the approach or strategy of change selected or because of the change agentry abilities of the public official in charge of the program.

This more complicated view of the practice of planned change helps explain why so many public programs never quite live up to public expectations. Given the limitations of the change strategy, a program may be accomplishing all that should be expected; but that, nonetheless, is less than the public expects. In the last few decades we have come to expect public schools to solve a range of social and economic concerns quite apart from their mandate to educate our people. In some instances, it may simply be that we have not allowed enough time for the change to take hold, or we have found the change produced was different than what we thought it would be. The Head Start program was nearly abolished within a few years of its inception because significant change in the grades of Head Start children had not occurred. What we found several years later was that grades never changed significantly, but what did change was that children who had been in Head Start stayed in school and graduated from high school in significantly greater numbers than those who were never part of Head Start.

Most government initiatives are planned change efforts. As this chapter has suggested, change is a complex process, and while our theories of change tell us a great deal about how change may occur, how to define the most appropriate strategy for change is less clear. Our knowledge of change simply does not extend that far. Therefore, planned change in practice is a much less certain process than it would seem. We select change strategies and change agents in the hope that the desired results will emerge, but we certainly should not be overconfident of those results.

Many of the management and decision-making activities of government are premised on the all too shaky foundations of our knowledge of planned change. To gain confidence in our decisions and management practices designed to yield change, other practices are introduced before decisions are made. Thus, policy analysis (discussed in Chapter 6) is a mechanism for evaluating the effectiveness of policy alternatives. One possible way to evaluate an alternative is to examine the theoretical premises of change that underlie the policy. Organization development (OD) is a means of looking at changing the management practices of an organization so that it is more effective in achieving its goals. If change agentry and leadership are related activities, then the ability to introduce change through OD is predicated on the leadership within the organization. It is OD to which we turn next to complete the review of organizational change.

ORGANIZATION DEVELOPMENT

While many of the techniques of OD rely upon theoretic and practical applications of psychology and social-psychology, they are rooted in rational-analytic practices of organizational assessment. Organization development efforts are preceded by diagnostic and data collection stages. These two stages provide definition to the OD intervention strategies by delimiting what problems are to be focused upon and what characteristics and features of the organization (structure, culture, processes, people) are to be changed.

Diagnosis

Lippitt, Langseth, and Mossop (1985) advocate a seven-step diagnostic model for defining organizational problems. Huse and Cummings (1985, 1989) suggest a 3 x 3 matrix model for diagnoses (Table 8.1). These models will be described below. What must be recognized is that the models are simply different ways of addressing the same problem. What is common to both is an emphasis on the collaborative nature of diagnosis. Whether the diagnosis is to uncover the causes of specific problems or to assess overall performance, it is a task that must be undertaken by both management and the OD change agent. Specific knowledge of norms and practices in an organization that only those within the organization possess is essential for a proper diagnosis.

Seven-Level Analysis

The Lippitt, Langseth, and Mossop model of organizational analysis fits best where the goal is to broadly examine the performance of an organization. The seven levels of analysis are as follows:

1. Context of organizational operations
2. Type of outputs (both organizational and psychosocial)
3. Organizational culture
4. Task requirements
5. The nature of the formal organization (structure and processes)
6. The people
7. Physical and technological setting

The context of organizational operations refers to the purpose of the organization, as well as to the internal and external environment of the present. Much as we saw with the strategic management steps of mission and Strengths-Weaknesses-Opportunities-Threats (SWOT) analysis, this step is an attempt to better understand the social, political, economic, and temporal position of the organization.

The outputs of the organization concern not only the product or service that is the central mandate of the organization but also the psychosocial context of the organization. The first output analysis addresses the question of whether or not the organization is effective in implementing the policies and programs over which it has responsibility (Are people served? Is the trash collected?). The second output analysis concerns the people of the organization. Is the organization experiencing quality control problems? Is it experiencing personnel and labor relations problems?

The concept of organization culture is more difficult to define. Ott (1989) defines organizational culture as follows:

> it means something similar to the culture in a society and consists of such things as shared values, beliefs, assumptions, perceptions, norms, artifacts, and patterns of behavior. It is the unseen and unobservable force that is always behind organizational activities that can be seen and observed.
>
> (p. 1)

Because the forces that define the culture are "unseen and unobservable," any cultural analysis must be the result of connecting outward behavior to inner perceptions. The behaviors that are examined most often relate to norms, rituals (SOPs), even the folk wisdom that passes among employees. Also critical are certain structural and technological factors that seem to "type cast" an organization (banks are conservative, high tech firms are entrepreneurial, etc.). The organizational analyst looks for breakdowns in the transmission of norms or disagreements as to rituals. These are signs of a culture in transition.

The task requirements of the organization most closely relate to a description of how work actually gets done in an organization. The key questions relate the match between employee skills and the tasks to be done, and the connections and links that join tasks together into a coherent program.

The formal organization is sometimes overlooked in organizational analysis because of the emphasis on human relations and interpersonal and psychological factors. The simple truth may be that the organizational structure needs to be altered. The key questions concern formal communications to facilitate problem-solving and the general coordination of work (do the right people report to each other?).

The need for the right kind of people often stops with an analysis of the skills of the employees, supervisors, and junior managers. At least as important is an analysis of the support for change by senior management. No OD effort can be successful if support from the top management echelon is lacking.

The physical and technological setting, like the issue of structure, is often overlooked. The physical and technological setting can have a significant effect on productivity (imagine the Social Security Administration trying to do its job without computers!).

The Huse Matrix

The matrix developed by Edgar Huse incorporates the three levels of problem analysis (individual, group, and organization) with three aspects of operations (inputs, design components, and outputs). The assumption is that if there is a good "fit" between the inputs and the design components, then the operations should be effective (Table 8.1).

TABLE 8.1

The Huse 3 x 3 Matrix

Inputs	Design Components	Outputs
	Technology	Organization
Strategy	Structure	Effectiveness
Task Environment	Measurement Systems Human	(e.g., market share return on investment
Organization	Resource Systems	environmental impact)
Design	Culture	Group Effectiveness
Organization Design	Task Structure Composition Performance Norms Interpersonal Relations	(e.g., quality of decisions, teamwork,
Group Design		cohesiveness)
Personal Characteristics	Skill Variety	Individual Effectiveness
	Task Identity	(e.g., quantity and quality of performance, absenteeism, job satisfaction,
	Task Significance Autonomy	learning, and personal development)
	Feedback about Results	

Source: Edgar F. Huse and Thomas G. Cummings, *Organization Development and Change*, 3rd ed. (St. Paul, MN: West Publishing, 1985, p. 39)

A key to the usefulness of this method of analysis is in the use of levels of analysis. In differentiating operations by the three levels, a greater degree of specificity in locating the problem may result. The depth of detail and richness of information that is the hallmark of the Lippitt, Langseth, and Mossop model is compensated for by this opportunity to target the problem. Of course, if problems exist at all three levels of the organization, then this ability to specify the problem area is lost.

For our purposes it is not necessary to examine in more detail the nine cells of the Huse diagnostic model. The concern for level of analysis will reemerge in subsequent discussions of the application of OD techniques.

Data Collection

The ability to design a successful OD strategy is premised on the ability to gather valid and reliable data. Several issues that contribute to validity and reliability include (1) the relationship between the data collector and organization members, (2) the methods of data collection employed, and (3) the processes for feeding back the data.

Huse sees three benefits deriving from careful attention to data collection:

The first and most immediate objective is to obtain valid information about organizational functioning. . . .

When employees trust the consultant, they are likely to participate in the diagnostic process and generate energy and a commitment for organizational change. . . .

Finally, data collection helps develop the collaborative relationship necessary for effecting organizational change.

(p. 65)

The actual methods of collection are the standard practices of social science data collection. The most commonly applied techniques are questionnaires, interviews, observations, and unobtrusive measures.

The final element of data collection is the process of clearing or feeding back data to organization members. The key point to the feedback process is first to assure oneself that the context is accurate, verifiable, valid, and useful, and second to use the opportunity of feeding back information to set the stage for the implementation of the OD program.

Data Analysis

The process of analysis can be thought to occur in three forms, by two different groups. The first two forms of analysis are undertaken by the management group or consultant responsible for the data collection. These qualitative and quantitative analyses are two ways of approaching the data, although certain forms of data are more amenable to one type of analysis. For example, of the four types of data gathering techniques, interviewing is the least suited to quantitative analysis because of the difficulty in coding and interpreting that data. The application of qualitative techniques such as force field analysis and role analysis are best under such circumstances. While questionnaires and observations are better suited to quantitative analysis, it is still possible to apply qualitative techniques to such data.

The third form of analysis is to bring together a task force or team from within the organization to conduct the analysis. Lippitt, Langseth, and Mossop suggest this approach at the point where the implications of the data are at issue. The types of questions that such a team would ask include cost, benefits, feasibility, control, timing, time scale, discreteness, and interdependence (pp. 91–92).

These questions go to the heart of data analysis. Rather than the question "What can we learn about existing operations (and therefore possible problems)?" the question is "How do we address the problems that we now face?"

OD PRACTICE: THE INTERVENTION

Much of the literature on OD pays scant attention to planning for the implementation of an OD change. This deficiency is also noted in strategic management and policy analysis. Given the less sophisticated nature of the environmental analysis that occurs in OD as compared with a strategic management effort, this defect may be more glaring. The course of change is subject to numerous affects, both anticipated and unanticipated. Not planning for these affects is to invite failure. There is much more to implementation planning than simply selecting the "best" alternative.

One approach to more conscious planning for implementation is to borrow from Huse's concept of levels of intervention that are part of this model for planned change noted above. While this does not guarantee a better implementation plan, it does refine the direction and character of the intervention.

Levels of Intervention

The level of intervention is associated with the part or feature of the organization affected by a change effort. Very roughly, these levels relate to the three perspectives on human behavior. The three levels of intervention are: the organization, the group, and the individual. As before, these classification schemes are useful to conceptualize the practice. However, they should not be regarded as rigid distinctions. While certain types of intervention are linked to only the level of affect, certain other interventions potentially influence other levels.

What is the value in a distinction by level of affect? Such a distinction is a useful tool for understanding the nature of the intervention in fairly traditional terms (time, cost, complexity, etc.). In addition, such a distinction is important for ethical reasons. Most researchers and consultants who use this distinction do so with the intent to prioritize interventions. The assumption is that the less intrusive into the work life of the individual the intervention is, the "better" it is. Thus, given a choice between an organization-level change effort and a group-level change effort, the organization-level change should be attempted first. Another logic reinforces this choice. Structural and technical change can more easily be controlled and directed than changes that are necessarily based on the motivations and behaviors of many individuals.

188 | **CHAPTER 8** Organizational Dynamics and Change

Organization-Level Intervention

The primary interests at this level concern matters relating to the structure, technology, and work environment of the organization. The types of tasks performed, and the strategic assumptions that underlie the work design are key variables. The aspects of the organization most likely to be affected by a change effort are the formal structure, the technologies used or possibly to be used, the basic human resources structure (recruitment, selection, training, job specifications, pay, etc.), and the organizational culture. Obviously, the culture is the most difficult to change, because it necessarily touches upon the other levels of affect.

Group-Level Intervention

The work group is often thought of as the lowest common denominator in the performance of organizational activities and tasks. The norms of behavior affect productivity as well as the general work atmosphere. A major concern is that of communications: the ability to reach common understandings both within the group and across groups.

The kind of questions to be addressed through intervention include

1. Does the task structure permit the group sufficient freedom to be an effective problem-solving team?
2. Is the right mix of job skill and experience present in the work group?
3. Are the norms of performance of the group directed at task accomplishment or toward social and interpersonal concerns?
4. Are there interpersonal problems in the work group?
5. Is there a norm of conflict suppression rather than one of confrontation and resolution of conflict?

Individual-Level Intervention

This level of intervention involves the intention to change the behaviors, attitudes, or skills of the individual worker. These are traditional management responsibilities. These problems can be attacked from two directions: by changing the work environment through job redesign and other quality of work life techniques or by changing the individual skills in job performance and skills in interpersonal relations.

The types of questions to be asked in analyzing these data are

1. Does the job design reflect the skills, capabilities, and potential of the workforce?
2. Do the jobs permit appropriate levels of autonomy and the potential for growth?
3. Do employees have a good sense of the connection between their individual responsibilities and the broader task?
4. Are there interpersonal problems that reflect biases or attitudes that affect performance?

The examination of the level of intervention gives us a partial picture of the intervention process. We now know some of the questions to ask. The next step is to link those questions to potential intervention practices. Matching the level and type of intervention is the best chance for producing a workable OD change effort. In looking at these interventions, it must be remembered that this analysis is not foolproof. What is being made is an educated guess at what changes to pursue. That is why it is necessary to begin with the least intrusive forms of change. Only if that level and type of intervention fails is a "deeper" penetration necessary.

In rough order by choice of intervention, the following major types of intervention are possible:

1. A change in overall strategic direction
2. A change in the technological and structural aspects of the organization
3. A change in the human processes links
4. A change in fundamental human behaviors and skills

Strategic Change

Strategic changes have the most in common with the concept of strategic management (see Chapter 12). These are changes that are most commonly organization-wide. The central purpose of such change is to reorganize the fiscal and human resources of the organization to better meet the goals and missions assigned to the organization. This effort may include either a new plan for meeting goals or a change in the values or norms that energize the people in the organization or both.

There are any number of different means of addressing strategic change. Connor and Lake (1988) suggest two: an organization culture approach and a product or service approach. The primary distinction here is between the attitudes and beliefs that shape performance and the performance per se. The type of strategic endeavor undertaken will emerge from the analysis of which approach seems to be the source of difficulty.

In either instance, the goal is improved performance. Each starts with some image or vision of what the organization should be accomplishing. From there it is a matter of deciding whether the problem lies in the technical system or the human system.

The human problems are the more critical to confront because they are more difficult to define. Technical system problems are relatively straightforward. Determining the exact nature of human problems presents special challenges—especially if one of the organization's disorders is an unwillingness to face human problems. Risk aversion and opposition to change represent double problems because they foster an unwillingness to act. Often these and many other types of difficulties are lumped together as problems of organizational culture. Where the culture is the problem, only a change in the culture (never an easy or quick task) will yield the appropriate change in behavior.

Technical and Structural Change

This change has much in common with technical system strategic change. When the focus is on overall organizational design, that connection is quite direct. But technical and structural change may have a smaller, more human side. That is, when the concern is for the worker or the man-machine nexus. The best known of these approaches is the quality of work life movement (Chart 8–1). This movement addresses such questions as, "What are the conditions under which various types of rewards and reward systems prove most effective?" and "What are the structural and other constraints that influence a supervisor's behavior?"

Human Process Interventions

One of the fundamental tenets of management since the days of the Hawthorne experiments has been that the work group has a significant impact on job performance. This impact may be either negative or positive. The idea behind this level of OD intervention is to make use of the positive aspects of group behavior (cohesiveness, common goals) and to reduce or eliminate the negative aspects (poor cooperation, intergroup conflict). A wide variety of interventions, including the use of T-Group, process consultation, third-party interventions, and team building, are indicative of this type of OD change effort. Each of these four interventions is deserving of a brief description because of the frequency of their use.

The use of T-Groups, or sensitivity training, is a practice that predates the concept of organization development. The basic premise of the T-Group is that with the assistance of an outside facilitator, a group (often of strangers) learns to explore the social dynamics that are a product of learning about each other. There are many goals of such an activity, although the basic goal is to have a better understanding of oneself by seeing yourself as others see you. From this starting point, an individual can better understand the various roles he or she plays in the group and how to use that understanding to improve the relationships, attitudes, and performance in the group.

Process consultation is an intervention designed to help the group understand its problems and make better use of its own skills and resources to resolve those problems. Depending on how broadly or narrowly the "group" is defined, a process consultation may occur at any level of intervention. The primary foci of the process are

1. Communications
2. Roles and functions of group members
3. Group problem-solving
4. Group decision-making
5. Group norms
6. Leadership and authority
   (Huse and Cummings, p. 99)

Third-party interventions are introduced when interpersonal conflicts emerge between two or more persons in the organization. The nature of the conflict may be as broad as labor-management relations or as narrow as problems of bias or simple misunderstanding. In addition to the question of the nature of the conflict,

CHART 8–1

What is "Quality of Work Life"?

1. **Adequate and fair compensation**—Does pay received meet socially determined standards of sufficiency or the recipient's subjective standard? Does pay received for certain work bear an appropriate relationship to pay received for other work?

2. **Safe and healthy**—That employees should not be exposed to physical conditions or work arrangements that are unduly hazardous or unhealthy is widely accepted. In the future, when health will be less the issue than comfort, more stringent standards than today's will possibly be imposed. They may include minimizing odors, noise, or visual annoyances.

3. **Development of human capacities**—To varying degrees work has become fractionated, deskilled, and tightly controlled; planning the work is often separated from implementing it. So jobs differ in how much they enable the worker to use and develop skills and knowledge, which affects his or her involvement, self-esteem, and the challenge obtained from the work itself.

4. **Growth and security**—Attention needs to be given to (a) the extent to which the worker's assignments contribute to maintaining and expanding the worker's capacities rather than leading to his or her obsolescence; (b) the degree to which expanded or newly acquired knowledge and skills can be utilized in future work assignments; and (c) the availability of opportunities to advance in organizational or career terms that peers, family members, or associates recognize.

5. **Social integration**—Whether the employee achieves personal identity and self-esteem is influenced by such attributes in the climate of the workplace as freedom from prejudice, a sense of community, interpersonal openness, the absence of stratification in the organization, and the existence of upward mobility.

6. **Constitutionalism**—What right does the worker have and how can he or she protect these rights? Wide variations exist in the extent to which the organizational culture respects personal privacy, tolerates dissent, adheres to high standards of equity in distributing rewards, and provides for due process in all work-related matters.

7. **The total life space**—A person's work should have a balanced role in his or her life. This role encompasses schedules, career demands, and travel requirements that take a limited portion of the person's leisure and family time, as well as advancement and promotion that do not require repeated geographical moves.

8. **Social relevance**—Organizations acting in a socially irresponsible manner cause increasing numbers of their employees to depreciate the value of their work and careers. For example, does the worker perceive the organization to be socially responsible in its products, waste disposal, marketing techniques, employment practices, and participation in political campaigns?

Source: J. Richard Hackman and J. Lloyd Suttle, ed., *Improving Life at Work* (Santa Monica, CA: Goodyear Publishing Co., 1977, pp. 3–4)

there are other issues that must be addressed before an appropriate intervention can be designed. The most difficult problem is that the conflict may be hidden, because it is either unrecognized or being suppressed. Further complicating the diagnosis of conflict is that the cause of conflict may only represent a symptom of deeper conflicts and problems. Finally, conflict is not always a "problem." Tension and conflict are the inevitable result of change. The problem for the consultant is to know when to intervene and halt the expansion of conflict and when to allow the conflict to work itself out within the other changes that occur.

Team building is an intervention strategy designed to help people work together more effectively (Parker, 2008). The primary focus of team building is in helping management groups become more effective. While the "team" that is helped may be a defined group, it is not necessary that the group that is assisted even have common work responsibilities. That is often the case with management teams. The key is to increase cooperation and coordination across parts of the organization that otherwise have little in common—that, after all, is the most likely place for problems to arise.

Human Skill and Behavior Change

One of the basic tenets of OD is that a worker responds to the incentives for growth and development made available through the organization by superior performance. While at one level those incentives are closely linked in time and place to that performance (merit pay, bonuses, and other rewards), there is another level of incentive that is more closely linked to long-term concerns (such as career development). It is these latter change efforts that are examined here.

Two long-term approaches associated with OD are career planning and stress management. Both are directed toward the employee's attitude in contemplating a long-term commitment to an organization. In the first instance, the opportunity to enhance skills and have those new skills recognized and utilized is important for the continued commitment of the employee to the organization. (A few occupations, such as city management, involve changing jobs and communities to "move up" the career ladder. In most governmental organizations, however, careers can be successfully completed within one agency or organization.) In the second instance, the goal is to avoid or ameliorate the negative effects and health problems associated with stress. If the organizational conditions that cause stress are addressed, then the stress experienced can be reduced. Further, many techniques for coping with the stress that seems to be part of so many jobs have been developed in the last decade.

These two forms of intervention are often used together. It serves no purpose to establish career paths that lead to jobs that are so stressful that few hold on to their health once having reached such positions. The goal is to create a work environment in which human growth and development is enhanced. Under such conditions, people can perform to their fullest.

Evaluating OD Interventions

As with any change effort, the chance to step back and assess what has occurred is critical. That assessment has two purposes: (1) to ensure that the level and type of intervention was appropriate and correct and (2) to lay the groundwork for institutionalizing the OD practices into the routine of the organization. In other respects, the nature of the evaluation is not much different from the one described in Chapter 12 on strategic management.

ORGANIZATION DEVELOPMENT IN THE PUBLIC SECTOR

In 1985 Robert Golembiewski offered an insightful analysis of why OD seemed to be more common in the private sector, even though he thought it was more critical to the public sector. In a 1989 double issue symposium in *Public Administration Quarterly* Golembiewski was somewhat more optimistic about the pace and scope of OD use in the public sector. Both his earlier concerns and his later slight hopefulness are instructive for understanding OD in the public sector. These are the topics for this final portion of the analysis of organization development.

Constraints on Public Sector OD

Golembiewski suggests two broadly related aspects of public-sector organizations that limit the applicability of OD to that sector. Those factors are (1) the general structural and institutional features of the public sector and (2) the norms of management and interpersonal relations that are part of the ethos of public-sector management theory (Golembiewski, 1989b, 1989c, 2003).

Institutional Constraints

Golembiewski defines two aspects of institutional constraint. The first aspect relates to the unique structural features of government. The second aspect is what Golembiewski calls "the habit background" (or what Weber called "organizational norms" and Allison "organizational process").

A number of structural features in the public sector constrain the effective use of OD. Four of the more significant ones are

1. Multiple access to multiple authorities
2. Variety of interests and reward structures
3. Command linkages and competing identifications/affiliations
4. Weak linkages between political and career levels

This array of structures limits any OD effort in several ways. First, the level of trust and cooperation across agencies and across branches is low because there are few, if any, incentives to cooperate. Only where task assignments overlap can there be an incentive to cooperate. Yet many agencies of government have little or nothing to do with the task environment of another (except in the clash over budget share). In studies of metropolitan and regional governments (Miller and Cox, 2014) both these circumstances were borne out. Getting disparate communities in a region to come together to form a regional governing mechanism is difficult because many wealthy suburbs see no reason to share resources. On the other hand, there are many regionally based single function districts (water districts, irrigation districts, mosquito abatement districts, and on and on) that are created because it is easier to organize around the common cause of a singular problem.

In this context, it should not be surprising that the smaller the organization or sub-organization, the more likely that OD can be attempted. Yet, the ability to effect broad change simultaneously diminishes in this move "down" the organizational ladder.

Further, the changing character of public-sector practices suggests a moving target for planned change. Administrative arrangements vary even within organizations, as well as over time. The easily defined target of goals and mission found in the private sector are inevitably missing in the public sector. Except in the very narrowest terms, concepts such as organizational goal achievement and even organizational effectiveness are quite elusive (see the discussion of the use of performance measures throughout the book but especially Chapter 6).

The effort to adhere to the "Weberian" bureaucracy as well as the unique means of policy making and control have created patterns or habits of behavior within the public sector that restrict the operator of any OD change effort. Each of these patterns and habits conflict with the goals of OD. Those constraints are

1. Limited delegation and layering
2. Legalities and legalism
3. Need for security or secrecy
4. Procedural regularity and caution
5. Lesser sense of professionalism as a manager

The ability to solve problems through the assertion of the individual or group is more difficult under the above norms. Further, the habit of the mind described above does not lend itself to the risk of outlining new norms. It must also be added that it is the habit of these behavior patterns that must be addressed. Few who give serious consideration to public-sector practice advocate these behaviors, even when these patterns are still necessary (as in the need for secrecy under some circumstances, and the continued need for the equality of treatment that is partially achieved through routinization). Like any other habitual behavior, it must be examined and re-examined to determine if the reasons that gave rise to its introduction still exist. As suggested above, some reasons for such habits still exist. For others, there remains little reason beyond habit and those habits should be changed.

Managerial Constraints

The differences between the public and private sectors have been examined by innumerable authors. Wallace Sayre was famous for the comment that business administration and public administration were alike in all the *unimportant* respects. These differences are important because the philosophy and outlook of organization development is closer in orientation to business administration thinking. Since these are the important respects, it should not be surprising that the fit between OD and private-sector practices is better than the fit between OD efforts and public-sector practice. The solution is not to impose business practice through OD on the public sector, but, rather, it is in the difficult search for OD interventions that fit public-sector values, norms, and practices. That, however, is for a later discussion.

Golembiewski (1989a) suggests that the managerial environment in the public sector is qualitatively different in at least three respects: the parameters of inter-organizational relations, the differences in working conditions, and the differences in organizational culture. Little has changed in the last three plus decades to alter this view, though as suggested in Chapter 1 the effort to make government more "businesslike" has been the vogue for that same time.

In a variety of respects, the way that problems are defined, and who can participate in that process of problem definition, is far more complicated in the public sector than in the private sector. Thus, for example, the public-sector manager must attempt to address policy concerns over which considerable disagreement still exists. How that policy is defined is to some extent out of the manager's hands. Further, performance is more likely to be judged on the basis of the evaluator's definition of policy than the manager's definition. Without a clear understanding of goals, it is assumed that management is impossible; yet that is an everyday operating condition for the public manager.

Managers in the public sector work under conditions of change and uncertainty. Golembiewski suggests four such conditions that limit and define management practice in quite different ways from the private sector. The day-to-day work life of the public manager necessitates

1. Dealing with goals and purposes set or influenced by multiple *external* authorities
2. Operating within structures mandated or designed by distant authorities
3. Working with persons whose career and possibly even current job performance are beyond the manager's control or ability to influence
4. Facing the need to achieve goals in relatively short time frames (one to two years)

The norms and expectations of management behavior in the public sector are often fixed so that change is avoided or, at least, quite difficult to implement. Four features of public-sector management that lead to this norm are

1. More limited discretion in the range of acceptable practices, reinforced by patterns of "bureaucratization" and "routinization"
2. Less support for risk-taking and innovation because of the prohibitions against failure when using "someone else's money"
3. The emphasis on looking for ways not to act before seeking ways to act
4. The need to establish accountability standards (records) as a priority

We are not suggesting that the above would be wrong (necessarily) in all instances. The culture of the public sector did not develop in some perverse way to ensure failure. It is the extremity of these practices that becomes a problem. A public culture should encourage accountability standards, but not at the risk of never accomplishing the task. An aversion to risking public funds is not misplaced (except when it becomes an excuse to do nothing).

The Future of OD in the Public Sector

The discussion above may well lead the reader to conclude that OD efforts in the public sector are a waste of time. The list of constraints and inhibitions seem insurmountable. Yet, those very difficulties are the justifications for a search for a better pairing of OD techniques and public-sector management practice. As we suggested earlier, there is some evidence that the use of OD change techniques is on the rise, particularly at the level of agencies or bureaus. Ted Poister's 1989 work is of great significance in examining departmental-level change efforts where the department has ceased to perform at anything close to acceptable levels. Also encouraging are Golembiewski's conclusions that OD efforts in the public sector (even in economically deprived third-world governments) are almost as successful as private-sector ventures as is the related fact that OD interventions may be less culture-bound (and sector-bound) than previously thought.

Poister's summary concerning the steps in the effort to revitalize a public agency are instructive in how to make use of OD in the public sector.

1. At the outset of attempts to turn around public-sector agencies at the bottom of the performance curve, OD strategies, and particularly the interaction-centered OD techniques, may not be appropriate or even feasible due to the mix of internal and external conditions that mandate revitalization in the first place.
2. Other more traditional management approaches may be necessary to get the turnaround "on track" and to produce quick results, but taken too far or implemented in ways that are insensitive to the needs of employees, such strategies may have detrimental by-products and be counterproductive in the longer term.
3. Later on in the revitalization effort, OD interventions may help undo some of the psychological damage of initial measures and strengthen organizational capacity to move on to higher levels of productivity

(1989, p. 69)

The point of Poister's analysis is that an organization in trouble may be in so much trouble that traditional OD techniques may not work. This makes sense if one thinks of the many constraints of structure, habit, and management practice we have described. An agency that suffers from poor management, low morale, loss of public support, and little public credibility is one that has fallen into the habits and behavior patterns described above, and furthermore, can see no way out from such behaviors. The readiness of the organization to accept the changes implied by OD is necessarily preceded by a change in these destructive habits and behaviors. In particular, the leadership needed to see an OD intervention through to institutionalization is likely absent from an agency that is in such serious need of revitalization. OD interventions are part of the second phase of a revitalization process; to introduce them earlier is to risk failure.

This puts a somewhat different light on the constraints Golembiewski defined. The question is not so much how to introduce OD interventions in the face of these constraints, but rather how to overcome some of these constraints before an OD intervention can be viable.

A second approach to the use of OD in the public sector is to examine OD's fundamental values to direct the change effort toward support of the *basic* tenets of representative government. The two concepts do have points in common. Participative management is founded in the same assumptions of human nature as representative, democratic government. A corollary to this is the need to address OD to both the politicians and the professionals in the organization, simply because the two are inseparable. The successful public professional must simultaneously be a successful politician. Thus, it is not a question of addressing one or the other set of needs. In a public setting, both are of one cloth. The goal must be to improve the overall capacity of the organization to be effective—which is itself both a managerial and a political judgment. The OD process must be oriented toward meeting both definitions as established by the organization. Interventions that are deemed to carry a political message or reflect the political views of the OD change agent are inappropriate. In reality, such a stance would constitute a denial of the very precepts of openness and participation that are the core of OD because it replaces the political choices of government with the preferences of the OD change agent. The simple choice is to not become involved in the OD intervention and to exercise the right of all citizens to challenge public policy through such means as letters and the ballot.

CONCLUSION: THE MANAGEMENT SUPPORT SYSTEM

The discussion above offered suggestion for practice for both consultants and managers. It would not have been inappropriate to include this chapter in Part III. The tipping point in placing it in Part II is that first the adoption of certain planned change techniques or theoretical frameworks are implicit in the organization's creation and operations. These are perspectives that managers inherit in becoming a manager rather than the product of the manager's choice. Second, the OD interventions are inevitably done with the aid of consultant-change agents. Larger agencies may have these change agents as part of the personnel office.

While a wide variety of techniques fall under the concept of planned change, they all point to a single central goal: the improvement of an organization's effectiveness. The assumption is that through the introduction, adoption, and institutionalization of these planned change efforts, OD can help any organization better adapt to the changing demands of the public outside of the organization.

Several features of the generic OD process were examined. The two most critical features are to recognize that OD interventions can be categorized by the level of intervention (organization, group, and individual) and by the type of intervention (strategic, structural, human process, and human behavior).

The final and most critical point is to recognize how the OD intervention process works in a public setting. The many complicating factors that make public-sector management more difficult also make the introduction of OD change efforts more difficult. Those factors must be addressed if OD efforts are to have the desired effect. Furthermore, any OD effort must be structured to conform to the basic values, approaches, and structures that are derivative of representative democratic government. With these two caveats having been met, OD can be successful in the public sector.

DISCUSSION QUESTIONS

- Why do governments seem to rely upon normative re-educative models of change?
- How did Rogers define innovation? Why is that definition important for understanding his idea of diffusion?
- Why are the distinctions among levels of OD intervention important?
- Why has it been difficult to successfully introduce OD programs in the public sector?
- How would you use the Huse Matrix in developing a change management strategy?
- What is process consultation?
- Why do change techniques begin with an organizational assessment? What can come from that assessment?
- What are some of the attributes of early adapters?
- Why does Rogers emphasize communication?

BIBLIOGRAPHY

Benne, Kenneth D., Warren G. Bennis, and Robert Chin. "Planned Change in America", in Bennis, Benne, Chin, and Corey (eds.) *The Planning of Change, 3rd ed*. New York: Holt, Reinhart and Winston, pp. 13–21. 1976.

Bennis, Warren G., Kenneth D. Benne, Robert Chin, and Kenneth E. Corey, eds. *The Planning of Change, 3rd ed*. New York: Holt, Reinhart and Winston. 1976.

Connor, Patrick E., and Linda Lake. *Managing Organizational Change*. New York: Praeger. 1988.

Cummings, Thomas G. *Handbook of Organizational Development*. Los Angeles, CA: Sage. 2008.

Cummings, Thomas G., and Christopher G. Worley. *Organization Development and Change, 8th ed*. Mason, OH: Thomson/South-Western. 2005.

Golembiewski, Robert T. *Humanizing Public Organizations*. Mt. Airy, MD: Lomond Publications, Inc. 1985.

Golembiewski, Robert T., ed. "Perspectives on Public Sector OD IV", *Public Administration Quarterly*, 13 (1) and 2 (Spring). 1989a.

Golembiewski, Robert T. "OD Applications Under Economic Deprivation", *Public Administration Quarterly*, 13 (1) (Spring), pp. 31–65. 1989b.

Golembiewski, Robert T. *Organization Development: Ideas and Issues*. New Brunswick, NJ: Transaction Publishers. 1989c.

Golembiewski, Robert T. *Ironies in Organizational Development, 2nd ed, Revised and Expanded*. New York: Marcel Dekker, 2003.

Hackman, J. Richard, and J. Lloyd Suttle, eds. *Improving Life at Work*. Santa Monica, CA: Goodyear Publishing Co. 1977.

Huse, Edgar F. *Organization Development and Change, 2nd ed*. St. Paul, MN: West Publishing. 1980.

Huse, Edgar F., and Thomas G. Cummings. *Organization Development and Change, 3rd ed*. St. Paul, MN: West Publishing. 1985.

Huse, Edgar F., and Thomas G. Cummings. *Organization Development and Change, 4th ed*. St. Paul, MN: West Publishing. 1989.

Lauer, Robert H. *Perspectives on Social Change, 2nd ed*. Boston: Allyn and Bacon. 1982.

Lippitt, Gordon L., Peter Langseth, and Jack Mossop. *Implementing Organizational Change*. San Francisco: Jossey-Bass. 1985.

Lynn, Laurence. *Managing Public Policy*. Boston: Little, Brown and Co. 1987.

Ott, J. Steven. *The Organizational Culture Perspective*. Pacific Grove, CA: Brooks/Cole Publishing Company. 1989.

Parker, Glenn. *Team Players and Teamwork: New Strategies for Developing Successful Collaboration*. San Francisco: John Wiley and Sons. 2008.

Poister, Theodore H. "Public Agency Revitalization: How and When Does Organization Development Fit In?" *Public Administration Quarterly*, 13 (1), pp. 66–90. Spring 1989.

Rogers, Everett. *Diffusion of Innovation, 4th ed*. New York: Free Press. 2003.

Rogers, Everett, and Floyd Shoemaker. *Communication of Innovation, 2nd ed*. New York: Free Press. 1971.

Stacey, Ralph, and Douglas Griffin, eds. *Complexity and the Experience of Managing in Public Sector Organizations*. London and New York: Routledge. 2006.

PART

III

The Managerial Toolkit

In the previous part we examined public administration from the perspective of the activities and professional practices that contribute to the management of public organizations. Another way to understand public administration is to explore it from the various outlooks and theoretical perspectives that shape how we see and understand public management. In this endeavor we borrow from the work of Dwight Waldo, whose early work showed how America as a "business society" developed public administration as a variation on business practices, and from numerous sociologists who suggested that one's preconceived notions about organization theory and behavior shape how we understand human interaction in the workplace. These views are such that many of the theories of public administration are like looking at public administration through the lens of a telescope. The instrument helps us see far. It brings far away objects into focus, but it does so by narrowing our sight. We can see further by blocking out everything else. It is our perspective that over time public administration has been examined through many lenses. But as each lens gives us more depth and detail, they also require us to discard much. Public administration is more than the sum of the parts. But until we "see" those parts we cannot even begin to understand public administration in theory or in practice.

Structuring government operations is only a part of the puzzle of governance. Managing and leading those offices and agencies are quickly recognized as important.

More than a century before academics would begin to define the concept of organization theory, government officials in the United States were faced with the difficult task of structuring and controlling government. This was critical for the new national government, particularly as it spread across a larger area than all but two or three nations in the world. There were few models. The politics of European nations was too intrusive in administrative affairs to be acceptable in the American political culture. The practices of the Swedes and Prussians would not work in the United States because they were too colored by the existence of monarchies. The private sector of the eighteenth century was dominated by what Adam Smith called shopkeepers. The industrial revolution had come to few nations in the 1820s and

1830s. Yet, the United States government already had thousands of field offices (mostly post offices and land offices) stretching across thousands of miles of territory. Government agencies, whether federal or state, were being "managed" even before the concept of the manager as a distinct function and role existed.

What emerged in that period was a unique combination of the political and the administrative. Driven by political considerations and the need to respond to the public, the core processes of government organization of the 1830s were becoming increasingly bureaucratic. The primary concerns were for centralized control, division of labor, standardized procedures, and written reports. These same concepts would dominate thinking about governmental organizations for over a century. Even now governments are assumed to be built on a foundation of hierarchical control. "The bureaucracy" means to people across the globe "government." Centralized control was (and occasionally still is) the primary feature of public management. But the first efforts to decentralize came in the 1930s as state governments began to disperse for the personnel system and then other activities. Since then the debate about the relative value of centralization versus decentralization has continued. The world-wide interest in the New Public Management was at its core an attempt to decentralize decision-making by locating it with a wider range of management. Even those with misgivings about the NPM were comfortable with the decentralization of decisions. Letting the managers manage was very attractive. For those in agencies that are still strongly hierarchical, command and control based, the attractiveness of more latitude for managers is in the ability to use central control as needed but to emphasize the behavioral aspects of management theory to make these organizations more effective. Essentially, since the 1970s or 1980s, management theory has advocated a style of practice in which the behavioral and interpersonal elements of management are paramount.

The next five chapters examine the skills needed to be an effective manager. The chapters examine the managers' toolkit to address trans-organizational and intra-organizational management issues. The first discussion focuses on the manager in transboundary roles. Public managers engage those outside their immediate organization with considerable frequency. Intergovernmental relations is a critical feature of governments across the globe. Policy implementation is often a multi-organizational process. As such, understanding the need for and the methods of inter-organizational collaboration is fundamental to management and program success.

Chapter 10 returns to a topic introduced in Chapter 3 (Personnel Practices). Cultural competence is both an aspect of personnel training and professional development, but also a critical management perspective. The more diverse the organization, the more capacity to innovate. Getting past the barriers of prejudice and bias is important, but such training simply opens the organization to the possibility and opportunity of appropriate decisions. Valuing diversity is the first step toward enhancing the information that circulates in an organization prior to decision-making.

Chapter 11 gives us a somewhat different view of diversity. Citizen engagement opens the organization to the possibility of fully involving the public at various points in the decision process. It is another form of boundary expansion. The lessons of collaboration that are part of intergovernmental management are re-envisioned as processes for public involvement.

Chapter 12 discusses the same concepts discussed in the first three chapters of this part, but in the context of strategic or long-term approaches to problem-solving. Managing an organization is not merely about tactics. Managing an organization requires an understanding of the implications and consequences of the choices we make for the life or duration of the problem we are attempting to resolve. Strategic thinking is closely associated with ethical reasoning and as such is foundational to good management.

Chapter 13 wraps up this discussion through an exploration of the idea of leadership. Leadership in organizations is essential to the change process, whether it is in fostering "instability" or in envisioning the future as a starting point for cultural transformation. Helping an organization follow an unknown path of change and innovation is not an easy task. It takes a manager of insight and courage.

The sum of these chapters is a toolkit of the perspectives and practices of good management. Public managers work in a complex and difficult environment. More so than their counterparts in the private sector, public managers are more likely to be second-guessed, to be criticized and challenged. These tools help a manager understand the work environment to be successful.

Learning Outcomes

At the conclusion of Part III a student should be able to:

1. Be able to identify the attributes of persons who successfully work at the margins.
2. Explain what the most common transboundary interaction at the local government level.
3. Defend diversity of perspective as a critical value in modern organizations. In such an explanation, identify both organizational and interpersonal components.
4. Identify the characteristics of an organization or program which explains why culture competence would be regarded as a critical concern.
5. Understand the institutional and political importance of citizen engagement.
6. Understand why listening is more important than merely having access to give voice.
7. Explain the differences between strategic management and long-term planning.
8. Understand why ending a program to go in a completely new direction is a necessary option in strategic management.
9. Explain the inter-relationship between leaders and followers.
10. Understand the importance of consensus building.

CHAPTER
9

Transboundary Interactions

Much of the work of government officials at the local and regional levels can best be described as operating at the margin or edge of the organization. Whether it is relating to those above and below in the organization, or with peers in similar organizations, inter-organizational management may well be the most common experience of most in bureaucracy. Few government endeavors fall neatly within the purview of a single government agency and, therefore, there is the inevitable duty of reconciling the capacities and resources of multiple different agencies to address a task. The same is true of collaboration across jurisdictions (think how complicated things would be if something as straightforward as a mutual aid pact among several fire departments did not exist). The practices and behaviors of the managers involved are quite different.

Transboundary interactions are central to the work of most managers. Whether it is coordinating with field offices, working with peers from similar agencies but working for a different jurisdiction, working across agencies which share responsibility for implementing a program, or working across the executive-legislative divisions, managing these activities is the ultimate test of government managers. Complicating matters is that the management skills in these transboundary experiences are different and may require different management styles.

As governments have grown in the twentieth century, and especially as the emphasis in governments shifted to social services for individuals and families, the need for public access to those responsible for such programs meant that small, functionally specific government offices were scattered across a country's geography. As will be examined in more detail below, in a case study of field office-central office relations in an agency in the State of Ohio, close communications convey what is being done, not via stale reports, but as the measure of success and organizational effectiveness. The key question to be addressed is whether rigid uniformity is critical or a get-the-job-done-given-the-circumstances approach may work. Both choices are permitted, and both have consequences.

Peer relationships are carried out in the context of narrow, expert-driven, and capacity-enhancing endeavors. The choices available are often well understood and reflect a professional ethos. Again, multiple fire department negotiating a mutual aid pact is a good example. In many ways this is the most straightforward of the transboundary relationships. All the parties to the negotiation share a common technical language and therefore there is limited misunderstanding. The expectation is that an outcome is a technical problem that can be resolved by the application of agreed-to tools. The mishaps in such relationships come from the changes in technology that fluctuate the understanding of compatibility or changes of mission which complicate implementation.

The more complicated and parenthetically the most common interaction involves agencies at different levels of government which share responsibility for the implementation of a program or who come together to collaborate on a shared problem(s). Examples of such activities range from coordination between a national government and a local government, to the operations of multi-government regional organizations, and to large international efforts (for example the European Union or the United Nations).

The last set of relations involves the interaction of the executive and legislative branches. Another way to frame this is to see this as the political aspect of management, whether that is a city manager or department head interacting with a city council, or a large national agency interacting with the national assembly. These interactions are different, because the rules of the game and the outcomes sought may differ among those involved. This topic will be discussed in much more detail in Chapter 10.

This chapter will review in some detail the types of management practices pertinent to each of these four versions of transboundary interactions. The mind-set and managerial style appropriate to each will be discussed.

FIELD OFFICE-CENTRAL OFFICE RELATIONS

In an often overlooked comment in his study of bureaucracy, Wilson (1981) stressed the importance of physical distance as a determinant in the reliance upon rules (especially written rules) to regulate behavior. He noted that police supervisors use the *expectation* of rule compliance as a substitute for direct supervision. Interestingly, in a book written a number of years before, Matthew Crenson (1975) suggested that the impetus for the bureaucratization in the Jackson presidency was the need to control individual behavior in far-flung government offices (particularly the Land Office, but also the Post Office and Customs). The goal of the introduction of written reports and other "red tape" in the 1830s was driven by a desire to make government interactions with citizens more uniform and equitable (Crenson, 1975).

The simple reality is that as organizations expand beyond the physical boundaries of a specific location, the organizational response is to de-emphasize management as interpersonal (leadership) and emphasize management as old-fashioned, Tayloresque, control. Seemingly the desire to centralize the management of the organization is a direct response to the physical decentralization of operations. The concern for equality of treatment of the citizen leads to the paradox of less latitude and discretion for those in the field (who presumably know better what is equitable). Presumably, equal treatment trumps equitable treatment, or at least becomes an issue beyond the discretion of the "street-level" (Lipsky, 1980) public servant.

While it is overly simplistic to suggest that the conflict between the push for de-centralization and the pull for centralization is one of who should exercise discretion (Cox, 2000, 2005; Cox, Hill, and Pyakuryal, 2008), the felt need to control decisions whether at the center, or on the street, is at the heart of this tug-of-war. The nearly century old literature on centralization and decentralization has missed a salient point—that field operations even under highly structured control structures operate with considerable latitude. Central administrators rely upon the reports and records of field operations to affirm that they (central administration) are in charge. Field operations more often than not operate on a "need-to-know" basis when keeping central administrators informed. As long as things seem to be going well, both sides are content in their mutual misunderstanding.

Over the last four decades academics have strongly endorsed efforts at decentralization. The New Public Administration (Marini, 1971) stressed efforts to push *downward* both the capacity and authority to act. The advocates of the New Public Administration saw in grants authority to "street-level" bureaucrats a return to an emphasis on equitable treatment as a core public service value. Theories such as Total Quality Management, although coming from the private sector, nevertheless carried on the academic tradition of favoring greater authority at lower levels of the organization. While the New Public Management (Kettl, 2005; Pollitt, 1995, 1998) favors central management decision-making, for the most part, this theoretical framework has not been widely accepted by the academy (Rosenbloom, 1989, Terry, 1998). The "re-invention" movement (Osborne and Gaebler, 1992), while linked to the NPM, is very much in the middle. Certainly, the emphasis on "customer service" created the opportunity for de-centralized (street-level) decision-making. From the perspective of local government, especially city manager governments, reinvention strongly favors manager-driven decision-making, which means central control. In larger governments, reinvention pushes down into the agencies decision-making creating a quasi-decentralized organization. The tenor of the times is such that both academics and public-sector "management" consultants are likely to look first for ways to decentralize organizations and emphasize the professionalism of lower-level managers and supervisors.

The question for us in this analysis is to explore what happens when a widely dispersed organization chooses to "reinvent" itself. What is the reaction to reforms which seemingly empower those field offices? Under such circumstances it would seem likely that those who most benefit from decentralization would be the strongest advocates of such "reform." This would also seem to be a reform effort which could be implemented quickly, because those responsible for implementation (field offices) have so much to gain from that implementation.

The reorganization and reform of the Ohio state liquor control activities in the late 1990s represents an interesting study in the dynamics of the relationship between a central office and field offices in attempting to introduce a management reform agenda. If there was a management reform initiative that had a good chance of success, this was it. Yet at the macro-level an organizational cultural transformation did not occur, because the field offices found little reason or need to change.

This was not a matter of displaced goals or inter-organizational conflict (Pressman and Wildavsky, 1973). Nor was there a lack of leadership (Burns, 1978). This was not a good idea gone wrong. The lesson of this study is that organizational structure, at least in the form of a field operation, changes the organizational change equation. This was a program developed by senior management in the Columbus state office. Despite budget issues (which in fairness affected all of state government), there was leadership at the top to support change. While not everyone at the state office had field experience, there was a shared culture, mission, goals, and organizational perspective. Since there was no real opposition to the development of CODE 2000, it would have to be said that there was a consensus on the goals and objectives of the change. Finally, the central office conscientiously created a performance tracking system (albeit a poorly structured system) and made those measures the centerpiece of agency annual reports. This was a well-planned and thoughtfully conceived change effort.

Why then was the result less than could have been expected? The dynamic of the "knowledge gap" between the expectations and understandings of the central office and the reality of practices in the field offices is at the core of the problem. The simplest answer is that the central office was attempting to change what had already changed. Probing more deeply several things become apparent:

- Field reports serve the lowest common denominator of being timely and in the proper formation. They rarely serve as a useful part of a *management* information system.
- Field reports address the questions *asked*, not the questions that *should have been* asked.
- Uniform reporting criteria are not the same as uniformity of service delivery or work result.
- Form follows function.
- Managing operations is more situation specific and results based rather than generic and output based.
- The idiosyncratic character of field offices must be accounted for before restructuring and reform is implemented.

(Cronin and Cox, 2007)

The changes in the Liquor Control organization offers interesting insight into the management issues associated with this internal form of transboundary relationship. First is that the impetus to create rules and processes as a substitute for direct interaction, first implemented in the Jackson administration almost two centuries ago prove inadequate. It is not that rule-based monitoring is wrong, but rather that the organizational cultures of field offices and central offices are different. Communications are incomplete. Reporting systems are based upon the desire of the central offices to gather the data the central office needs, not to find out "what is going on in the field." The Ohio changes failed, not because the field offices resisted the changes being mandated but because the field offices were already doing much of the work using those management precepts. The "reform" was for the field operatives a reporting exercise, designed to permit the central office to lay claim to being innovative. The reports going to the central office did not convey the work being done, but rather simply offered data to affirm what the central office desired (Cronin and Cox, 2007).

The management issue before us is that the communications gap that prevails between central offices and field offices is more complex than acknowledged. Field offices reluctantly provide reports to central offices in part because they do not see those reports as reflective of the work being done. This—I need to tell you what we do, rather than filling in the boxes on a report—is a persistent problem for managers in the central office. Capturing the reality of the activities in the various field offices is critical information. Field offices, which communicate upward, view such reports as judgments of performance, and will not view the central office with favor. Those reports have a single purpose and that is to transmit information upward beyond the central office. This is not an effective tool for understanding what is happening. Managers who fail to understand this are doomed to make the mistakes made in Ohio—initiating reforms at the field level that were already being done in the field.

PEER-TO-PEER RELATIONSHIPS

The second version of transboundary relations is peer-to-peer relations. Broadly this is the most common type of transboundary interaction. These are interactions between and among persons with similar work responsibilities but who work in different governments. These are relationships that may be formal, such as in regional (for example, a water district or fire district) or informal such as in professional associations (county or state city manager groups). The central feature here is that the persons come together because of common interests and common responsibilities. The process may begin informally through a professional association and then become formal. Police and fire department mutual aid pacts emerged over the decades before becoming the norm by the 1980s.

The central purposes of such relationships are two-fold: professional development and effective service delivery. Both purposes have value. From a management perspective, providing time for others (and oneself) to participate in professional associations and encouraging collaboration across governments are important. Innovation and effective service delivery often emerge from such activities. The tendency of many governments to cut travel, training, and to view collaboration as a waste of time is problematic.

While in the last few years there has been a focus on networks and collaborative efforts (see for example Agranoff, 2006; Agranoff, 2017; LeRoux and Carr, 2005), the focus here is on the foundational influences of peer-to-peer interactions. Not every opportunity for collaboration is a success (O'Toole, 2012, nevertheless the beginning of a successful relationship is the existence of a prior social relationship. We tend to talk to acquaintances, not strangers.

Special districts and regional governing organizations are the most common form of formal peer-to-peer relationship for service delivery. Although they exist in every part of the country, the most common formats of such structures are in urban or metropolitan areas. As a sociological term, "city" is interchangeable with "metropolitan region" in that both terms mean an urbanized area with many jobs and people living therein. When "city" is used in a politico-legal sense, the terms are not interchangeable, even though the need to make more public decisions at the regional level is becoming self-evident. Today's metropolitan regions have nascent characteristics of the politico-legal city (Miller and Cox, 2011, 2014). There are several reasons for this approach. First, the metropolitan region has replaced the city as the conceptual unit in which people live and business is conducted. Second, it permits a better frame for discussion of the structured relationship between the institutions of government and governing. By that we mean there is a vertical relationship, in terms of the governing context created by the state in which the metropolitan region exists, and a horizontal dimension or the relationship between the institutions of government that exist within a metropolitan region (discussed in more detail below).

The study of the governing of metropolitan regions is framed by acknowledging a conceptual distinction between government and governance. There have been broad societal changes over the last half century that have had pronounced effects on how we think about and operate in our world. As those changes relate to the public sphere, we are moving from a paradigm centered on government to one centered on governing or governance. Governing is the act of public decision-making and is no longer the exclusive domain of governments. Indeed, governments at all levels, nonprofit organizations, and the private sector now work together in new partnerships and relationships that blur sectoral lines. Private businesses, under contract to governments, deliver a wide variety of governmental programs. Conversely, governments are often managing more private-sector firms than public-sector employees. Nonprofit organizations, often representing organizations of governments, are partnering with governments, private firms, and other nonprofits to deliver services. Private foundations in many metropolitan regions utilize revenues generated from the private sector to finance public, private, and nonprofit organizations in addressing important regional public problems.

There is a structure to the patterns of relationships that exist within metropolitan regions (Miller and Lee, 2011). This structure has three primary dimensions. The first is a vertical dimension. Most of the activity falls within the domain of the state. The states have adopted a wide range of strategies in their treatment of local governing institutions. Some states take a relatively hands-off approach and leave much of the design and execution of local governing in the hands of localities. Other states take a relatively authoritarian approach and more directly control the design and function of local governments. A second dimension is horizontal and involves the fundamental relationships between the municipalities within a metropolitan area. Municipalities are relatively equal in the eyes of the law and custom. They have grants of authority to undertake a number of functions, the power of taxation to implement the desires of its citizens, and the land-use authority to control the nature and direction of development within the community. Municipalities are the building blocks of metropolitan areas and their relationship (or lack thereof) to each other is the key variable in determining whether meaningful regional decision-making can occur and how it will occur. The third is also horizontal but involves the fundamental relationships between important governing institutions within a metropolitan area. As such, it captures the emerging notion of metropolitan governance (see Foster, 1997; Foster and Barnes, 2012). In addition to local governments it includes the other principal types of local governments, such as counties, special districts, and school districts. Of the three, some county governments come closest to municipalities relative to function, taxation, and land-use authority. That said, and there are exceptions to the rule, county government seldom has the same degree of freedom as that of municipalities. The districts, special or school, will often lack at least two of the features associated with municipalities. They seldom have a broad functional role as they are usually confined to a very narrowly defined service. Special districts may or may not have taxing authority and they seldom have significant land-use authority. Although special districts are qualitatively distinct, they are nonetheless as much a part of the fabric of metropolitan America as are municipalities.

In addition to traditional forms of local government, there has emerged over the last sixty years an institution born out of the "metropolitanizing" of America that has been named the Regional Governing Organization (Miller and Cox, 2014). It is usually a single institution within a metropolitan area constituted primarily by local governments increasingly recognized as the place where regional issues and problems can be discussed and, hopefully, resolved. Such an institution exists in every metropolitan region under a wide variety of titles with varying degrees of responsibility. Even though state and federal policies have driven the formation of the RGO, local actors and the willingness of local governments to accept its authority determines its role.

Taken together, these three dimensions play out differently in each metropolitan region, resulting in a wide variety of metropolitan governing structures throughout the United States. This attempt to define and understand the practical relations among the actors in a region is complicated by the conflicted nature of local governments. Indeed, there are two distinct and diametrically opposed visions of local government. One holds local governments to be creatures of their citizens and the other to be creatures of the state. Currently, a battle is playing out in a winner-take-all war wherein one vision will beat out the other. This is a senseless war because local governments are neither. Rather, they move back and forth between the two visions. Indeed, we want them to be both. That they can move back and forth is both necessary and essential to the success of local governing. The key to regional governing in America is the successful management of the competing visions they create separately and the tension they create collectively between them (Miller and Cox, 2011, 2014).

INTERGOVERNMENTAL RELATIONSHIPS

In many states local governments can do anything collectively that they can do individually. Because such actions are voluntary, it means the agenda will be restricted to only a few sets of activities that can generate unanimity of action. Further, they can and will act collectively only when it is in their individual private interests. In his critique, Frug (2002) argues that creating a functional division of power based on the idea that governmental functions can be divided between those that serve a parochial conception of self-interest and those that serve the greater good is a formula for failure. Such a model merely enables localities to advance a privatized notion of self-interest. Bollens's (1997) study of special district formation in southern California concludes that representation on regional policy boards by local government officials does not create regional politicians and constituencies but allows local governments to operate in a regional forum to protect and enhance local interest even at the expense of regional goals. The notion of two-tiered government presumes that the tension between the local and regional can be solved through indifference. Rather than address the relationship between local and regional, the strategy is to divorce them and create separate domains.

Creating regional institutions that are divorced from local governments, or are created in spite of local government institutions, is an equally flawed approach. As the distance grows between the regional organization and the local governments within the region, the regional institution lacks the underlying credibility necessary to be effective.

The metropolitan region exists within an older and more established framework of intergovernmental relations in which state and local governments have operated since before the founding of the United States. Think of a state government and the local governments within its borders as a complex network of parts and wires that somehow are supposed to work together, much like a sound system on which we listen to music, if all the wires are connected correctly. These systems are similar in that they are complex sets of dynamically intertwined and interconnected elements. Each includes inputs, processes, outputs, feedback loops, all within an environment in which they operate and with which they continuously interact. Any change in any element of the system causes changes in other elements. The interconnections tend to be complex, constantly changing, and often unknown. This systems perspective is the overarching framework that will be used to explain state, local, and regional government in the United States.

One way to begin sorting through this dilemma is to think of metropolitan regions as networks. Such a perspective accommodates both foundational principles and represents a way of thinking about how we govern as opposed to the study of governments (Agranoff, 1990; Agranoff and McGuire, 1999; Agranoff, 2001; McGuire, 2002).

For instance, H. George Frederickson in the John Gaus Lecture at the American Political Science Association (1999) noted the growing use of inter-departmental agreements across municipalities. Under this arrangement department heads, whether public works, parks and recreation, police, or fire, would develop formally or informally cooperative agreements with their counterparts in other communities within a region. This behavior was attributed to the need to create economies of scale to make certain services more affordable and/or to improve the overall quality of service delivery. While "mutual aid" agreements for public safety units have been in place for several decades, Frederickson noted two aspects of this practice that he defined as new or innovative: one was that the impetus for the arrangements came from within the departments, not from the political side of government, i.e. it was viewed as simply an extension of "good" service delivery, and two was that the arrangements were viewed by the city managers as economically vital for their individual communities. This "regionalization" of services was touted as a significant step, precisely because it came from within the professional community. It was argued that it avoided the political contentiousness that other regional proposals often engendered, and it permitted those who could benefit from cooperation to do so without getting the permission of those who might be opposed to the arrangements (Thurmaier and Wood, 2002). In counterpoint, O'Toole, Laurence, and Meier (2004) expressed concern about the dark side of these management-dominated arrangements, i.e. that the socially and politically powerful have an advantage.

These arrangements are of interest in part because they take for granted most of the foundational principles of the economic vision of the metropolitan area. It is self-interest as often as better services which drives this practice (Howell-Moroney, 2008). And, even when the search for better service is the goal, it is done through a search for like-minded departments and governments. It becomes a way to sell the "uniqueness" or "distinctiveness" of a community even as it cooperates with others. It ducks the entire issue of governance and presumes that what is being done is some kind of politically neutral professionally driven administrative practice.

The tactics for expanded intergovernmental cooperation continue to straddle the line between the visions of the metropolis. As has been true for much of our history, the economic model predominates. Concerns about that model abound, if for no other reason than its historic links to polycentric models that challenge the need for *metropolitanization* of any type.

In 1999 Agranoff and McGuire suggested that there were seven "metaquestions" to be addressed concerning networks. While that list included issues that we have touched upon including collaboration, cohesion, and accountability, we may be adding two more:

- The importance of the definition of "place" as it relates to community
- The perceived relevance of "geography"

The boundaries of a network are a necessary element in the success of the network. Shared interests, shared problems, and shared history are part of the definition of place. This in itself is enough to bring people "to the table," but it is not sufficient to get them to agree to act (Fisher and Ury, 1981). The barrier is that the emphasis on markets seemingly provides justification to *not* act. The arrangement becomes a network whose purpose is to obfuscate and delay. The idea of geography similarly influences the ability to act. Many regional and metropolitan efforts are "top-down." They are defined by geography, but oddly do not acknowledge geography. The region becomes the sum of who will meet (or are required to meet), not a sense of geographic imperative. In this sense the EU could slowly work its way toward regional governance because the concept of Europe as a distinct geographic entity already existed (the unease about how "European" Eastern-bloc nations, and more pointedly Turkey, are at the root of the controversy over their admission to the EU). If we base metropolitan regions on historically and socioeconomic, but nonetheless *artificial*, criteria (federally defined MSAs) then we get the geography wrong.

Unlike Frug (2002), who utilizes the EU voting system to empower a new regional legislature that is more like a foundational principle, transforming an existing institution can be derived from either foundational principle. The existing regional institution is a collective of local public economies, and to empower those representatives to make decisions that are binding on the whole regional economy is a balanced compromise between the two principles.

The important question is what inducements, incentives, or events might trigger a transformation to move off its adversarial stance? Clearly, the easiest policy route would be for state legislatures or federal legislation to mandate or incentivize the development of super majority voting rules. The easiest political route is a much more complicated question. Perhaps the best route is to frame the discussion around satisfying both of our foundational principles. It could be seen as a win-win scenario. Strong local government advocates see local governments as the building blocks of regional institutions, while those advocating regional decision-making see institutional capacity for needs of the region to have weight. In so doing, we are committing to the importance of both foundational principles, not to the victory of one or the other. The lesson in the divergent responses of Florida and Ohio are important. The two states perceive similar problems, but in one shared concerns became the basis of the development agenda, in the other protecting "turf" became the watchword. In Florida there was value in cooperation and coordination that was proven through continued economic growth. In Ohio the coordination and cooperation was sporadic and generally the product of idiosyncratic relationships between center cities and counties.

Local officials are looking for new ways to balance their local interests with what they know to be the interests of the region taken as a whole. What they lack are alternatives that can satisfy those needs to balance the local and regional.

CROSS BRANCH RELATIONSHIPS

The oldest form of trans-boundary management is the relationship between different branches of government, most particularly the relations between the executive and legislative branches. Unlike the relationships described in the prior sections, these are relationships that are founded in two characteristics: first, these are political relationships and therefore are grounded in political perspectives, and second, these are relationships that are founded in the fundamental differences between the two branches. The focus of Chapter 14 is on politics and administration. Therefore, that topic will be left for a later time.

Executive-legislative relations are important because as managers progress in their careers their role shifts from one that is dominated by a service orientation toward a policy orientation. As managers are assigned responsibility for advising others on policy or setting policy the nexus between the executive and legislative branches becomes more critical. The first point is that the goals, processes, and structures of the two branches are different. A simple example is that for legislators the end point of policy making is a legislative enactment (a new or amended law or ordinance); for an administrator the law is the foundation upon which an implementation strategy is hung. One of the sources of conflict in American-style governments is this disconnect between administrators and legislators. This is not to deny the considerable overlap between the two branches in policy making, but it does reflect a mind-set about policy making. A well-conceived and widely supported law nevertheless may be difficult to implement. The legislator (and chief executive) seeks to achieve success through a political decision process in which consensus is a tool. Administrators often turn to more rational analytic methods. As was discussed in the chapter on policy analysis the "best" outcome derived from rational analysis may not be politically feasible. As managers advance within the organization they find that the problem to be solved is as much one of political feasibility as it is technical assessment. One of the most difficult transitions for public service professionals is the shift from a program and process focus to a policy-making political focus.

MANAGING AT THE MARGIN

Each of the different types of transboundary relationships calls for a different management outlook, because the context and environment of each is different. The internal demands of the field office-central office are interesting because the dispute is between persons who presume that they have the same goal and outlook because they work within the same organization. Yet the management lesson concerns communications and perspective. The assumption that "we have the same goals" is at least partly wrong. The easy assumption that everyone knows what and why things are done is also wrong. Open communication even about what is assumed to be obvious is necessary because the uses of information are different and, therefore, the form and shape of information transfer is different. In this sense, managing in a peer-to-peer relationship is more straightforward, even though it involves persons in other agencies and jurisdictions. Typically, peer-to-peer relationships are voluntary, but also driven by a shared professional ethos. Managing such relationships are as much about time management as anything. The single caveat is that certain regions and areas have different histories with such relationships. In areas where such relationships have been unsuccessful, a manager may encounter resistance from other jurisdictions or from political leadership in the community.

Intergovernmental relations often have the characteristics of peer-to-peer relationship, particularly in the technical silos of special districts, but because they are both horizontal and vertical they are more complicated. Depending on the policy type being implemented, such relations may have some of the characteristics of the field office-central office dynamic. Also because of the political dimension to vertical relationships, there may be an antagonistic rather than cooperative history in the relationship. In addition, this type of relationship reflects the complex political relationships and history of government jurisdictions. Creating regional governance organizations is the most difficult of all intergovernmental relationships.

Politics infuses the transboundary process more than may first be apparent. This is not so much a problem as it is a warning to recognize that the rules of the game in the relationship are often far removed from simple, technical, professional exchanges. Mastering the dynamic interplay of politics may be the most critical for the manager navigating the boundary.

DISCUSSION QUESTIONS

- What are the attributes of persons who successfully work at the margins?
- Why do transboundary interactions seem to occur most frequently at the local government level?
- Why don't central offices and field offices work as closely as one might expect?

- What are the institutional and interpersonal problems associated with peer-to-peer relationships?
- Using the peer-to-peer inter-relationship, explain the failure of regional governance.
- What are the challenges in working vertically? Horizontally?

BIBLIOGRAPHY

Agranoff, Robert. "Managing Federalism Through Metropolitan Human Services Bodies", *Publius*, 20 (1), pp. 1–22. 1990.

Agranoff, Robert. "Inside Collaborative Networks: ten Lessons for Public Managers", *Public Administration Review*, 66 (1), 56–65. 2006.

Agranoff, Robert. "Managing within the Matrix: Do Collaborative Intergovernmental Relations Exist?" *Publius*, 31 (2), pp. 31–56. 2001.

Agranoff, Robert, and M. McGuire. "Big Questions in Public Network Management", *Journal of Public Administration Research and Theory*, 11 (3), pp. 295–326. 1999.

Benjamin, Gerald, and Richard Nathan. *Regionalism and Region: A Study of Governments in the New York Metropolitan Area*. Washington, DC: Brookings Institution Press. 2001.

Burns, James McGregor. *Leadership*. New York: Harper Collins. 1978.

Cox III, Raymond W. "Seeding the Clouds for the Perfect Storm: A Commentary on the Current Fiscal Crisis", *State and Local Government Review*, 41 (3), pp. 216–222. 2009.

Cox III, Raymond W., and Kelly Cronin. "Instituting Innovation: A Model of Administrative Change in a State-level Liquor Control Board", in C. L. Jurkiewicz (ed.) *Social and Economic Control of Alcohol: The 21st Amendment in the 21st Century*. New York: Taylor and Francis, pp. 189–207. 2007.

Cox III, Raymond W., Michael L. Hill and Sucheta Pyakuryal. "Tacit Knowledge and Discretionary Judgment," *Public Integrity*, 10 (2): 153–166. 2008.

Cox III, Raymond W. "Administrative Discretion: The Conundrum Wrapped in an Enigma", in van Baalen, P., E. Schwella, and M. Burger (ed.) *Public Management and Governance: The Seventh Winelands Conference*. Stellenbosch, SA: University of Stellenbosch, pp. 249–263. 2000.

Crenson, Matthew A. *The Federal Machine: Beginnings of Bureaucracy in Jacksonian America*. Baltimore, MD: Johns Hopkins University Press. 1975.

Emerson, Kirk, and Tina Tabatchi. *Collaborative Governance regimes*. Washington, DC: Georgetown University Press. 2015.

Feiock, Richard, ed. *Metropolitan Governance: Conflict, Competition and Cooperation*. Washington, DC: Georgetown University Press. 2004.

Feiock, Richard, and Jered Carr. "Incentives, Entrepreneurs, and Boundary Change: A Collective Action Framework", *Urban Affairs Review*, 36 (3), pp. 382–405. 2001.

Foster, K. A., "Regional Impulses", *Journal of Urban Affairs*, 19 (4), pp. 375–403. 1997.

Foster, K. A., and W. R. Barnes. "Reframing Regional Governance for Research and Practice", *Journal of Urban Affairs*, 48 (2), pp. 272–283. 2012.

Fisher, Roger, and William Ury. *Getting to Yes: Negotiating Agreement Without Giving In*. Boston: Houghton Mifflin Company. 1981.

Frederickson, H. George. "The Repositioning of American Public Administration", John Gaus Lecture, American Political Science Association, Atlanta, GA (September 3). 1999.

Frug, G. "The City as a Legal Concept", *Harvard Law Review*, 93, pp. 1059–1154. 1980.

Frug, G. "Beyond Regional Government", *Harvard Law Review*, 115 (7), p. 1763. 2002.

Howell-Moroney, Michael. "The Tiebout Hypothesis 50 Years Later: Lessons and Lingering Challenges for Metropolitan Governance in the 21st Century", *Public Administration Review*, 68 (1), pp. 97–109. 2008.

Ledebur, L., and W. Barnes. *All In It Together: Cities, Suburbs and Local Economic Regions*. Washington, DC: National League of Cities. 1993.

LeRoux, Kelly, and Jered Carr. "The Social Structure of Interlocal Cooperation in Metropolitan Areas", Paper presented at the annual meeting of the Midwest Political Science Association. April 7–10, Chicago, IL. 2005.

Lubell, Mark, and John Scholz. "Cooperation, Reciprocity, and the Collective-Action Heuristic",

American Journal of Political Science, 45 (1), pp. 160–178. 2001.

Kapucu, Naim, Maria-Elena Augustin, and Vener Garayev. "Interstate Partnerships in Emergency Management: Emergency Management Assistance Compact in Response to Catastrophic Disasters", *Public Administration Review*, 69 (2), pp. 297–313. 2009.

Kettl, Donald F. *The Global Public Management Revolution, 2nd ed.* Washington, DC: Brookings Institution Press. 2005.

Marini, Frank (ed.) *Toward a New Public Administration.* Scranton, PA: Chandler. 1971.

May, Peter J. "Can Cooperation Be Mandated? Implementing Intergovernmental Environmental Management in New South Wales and New Zealand", *Publius*, 25 (1), pp. 89–113. 1995.

McGuire, Michael. "Managing Networks: Propositions on What Managers Do and Why They Do It", *Public Administration Review*, 62 (5), pp. 599–609. 2002.

McGuire, Michael. "Intergovernmental Management: A View from the Bottom", *Public Administration Review*, 66 (5), pp. 677–679. 2006.

Meek, Jack, and Kurt Thurmaier (eds.) *Networked Governance: The Future of Intergovernmental Management.* Washington, DC: CQ Press. 2011.

Miller, David Y., and Raymond W. Cox III. "Reframing the Political and Legal Relationship between Local Governments and Regional Institutions", in Meek and Thurmaier (eds.) *Networked Governance: The Future of Intergovernmental Management.* Washington, DC: CQ Press, pp. 97–126. 2011.

Miller, David Y., and Raymond W. Cox III. *The Metropolitan Region: Governing America's New Frontier.* Armonk, NY: M.E. Sharpe. 2014.

Miller, David Y., and J. H. Lee. "Making Sense of Metropolitan regions: A Dimensional Approach to Regional Governance", *Publius,* 41 (1), pp. 126–145. 2011.

Osborne, David, and Ted Gaebler. *Reinventing Government.* Boston: Addison-Wesley. 1992.

O'Toole, Jr., J. Laurence, and K. J. Meier. "Desperately Seeking Selznick: Cooptation and the Dark Side of Public Intergovernmental Networks", *Public Administration Review*, 64 (6), pp. 681–693. 2004.

Pollitt, C. "Justification by Works or by Faith? Evaluating the New Public Management." *Evaluation*, 1 (2), pp. 133–54. 1995.

Pollitt, C. "Managerialism Revisited", in B. G. Peters and D. Savoie (eds.) *Taking Stock: Assessing Public Service Reforms.* Montreal: McGill–Queens University Press, pp. 45–77. 1998.

Post, Stephanie R. "Metropolitan Area Governance and Institutional Collective Action", in Feiock (ed.) *Metropolitan Governance: Conflict, Competition and Cooperation.* Washington, DC: Georgetown University Press. 2004.

Pressman, Jeffrey L. and Aaron Wildavsky. *Implementation: How Great Expectations in Washington are Dashed on Oakland or Why its Amazing Federal Programs Work at All.* Berkeley, CA: University of California Press. 1973.

Swanstrom, T. "What We Argue About When We Argue About Regionalism", *Journal of Urban Affairs*, 23 (5), pp. 479–496. 2001.

Syed, A. *The Political Theory of American Local Government.* New York: Random House. 1986.

Terry, Larry D. "Administrative Leadership, Neo-Managerialism and the Public Management Movement", *Public Administration Review*, 58 (3), pp. 194–200. 1998.

Thurmaier, Kurt, and Curtis Wood. "Interlocal Agreements as Overlapping Social Networks: Picket-Fence Regionalism in Metropolitan Kansas City", *Public Administration Review*, 62 (5), pp. 585–598. 2002.

Vogel, Ronald K., and Norman Nezelkewicz. "Metropolitan Planning Organizations and the New Federalism: The Case of Louisville", *Publius*, 32 (1), pp. 107–129. 2002.

Walker, D. B. "Intergovernmental Relations and the Well-Governed City", *National Civic Review.* March–April 1986.

Wilson, James Q. *The Politics of Regulation.* New York: Basic Books, Inc., 1981.

Yoo, Jae-Won, and Deil S. Wright. "Public Administration Education and Formal Administrative Position: Do They Make a Difference? A Note on Pope's Proposition and Miles' Law in an Intergovernmental Context", *Public Administration Review*, 54 (4), pp. 357–363. 1994.

CHAPTER 10

Cultural Competence

The foundations of public management were for decades rooted in simple notions of command and control, or for that matter Theory X and Theory Y. Precepts of governance that were once the realm of political theory are now at the core of management theory. Government agencies, bureaus, and offices, no less than nations are shaped and thrive by the application of concepts such as participation, engagement, shared authority, and diversity.

Cultural competence reflects that changing viewpoint in that, as will be presented here, cultural competence is the tool by which those ideas are implemented in the workplace. Cultural competence is a more than a set of practices, it is also attitudes and procedures that enable agencies, organizations, and people to effectively interact with other cultures. Some of the components of cultural competence include cross-cultural skills, personal worldview of one's own culture, view of cultural differences, and knowledge of other cultural practices (www.reference.com/article/cultural competence). Stated most simply, cultural competence is the skill by which managers appreciate and apply the diversity of viewpoints available to the organization because of a diverse workforce. According to Seibert, Stridh-Igo, and Zimmerman (2002)

> United States of America demographic profiles illustrate a nation rich in cultural and racial diversity. Approximately 29% of the population are minorities and demographic projections indicate an increase to 50% by the year 2050. This creates a highly mobile and constantly changing environment, revealing the need for new levels of cultural awareness and sensitivity. These issues are particularly critical in the medical community where medical professionals must understand the impact cultural differences and barriers can have on evaluation, treatment, and rehabilitation (p.146).

The Cultural Competence literature is divided into two categories—practitioner and academic perspectives. Much of the practitioner approaches emerged out of public health and the pressing need to bridge the gap between health-care professionals and the racially diverse clientele who were receiving health-care services (Betancourt et al., 2005; Campihna-Bacote, 2002). It was not enough to just have "diverse faces" in positions of service delivery, a new transition was, and still is, necessary to help health practitioners overcome their own cognitive and behavioral biases that impacted connecting with marginalized clientele. Furthermore, a systemic change was necessary to transform the organizational mind-set that all clientele is valuable. The value of racially diverse clientele was operationalized within public health agencies through policy, organizational, and delivery service changes which helped health-care professionals identify and overcome cultural myths and cultural differences in communication and understanding one another. This section will give a brief historical background of cultural competence, examine cultural competence models, and discuss cultural competence within public administration (Wallace, 2018).

Cultural competence derives from having a skill set or knowledge or ability to be effective in cross-cultural situations, including learning new behavior patterns and applying them in appropriate circumstances (Rice, 2015). However, when used across disciplines and professional fields, this definition continues to evolve. Cultural competence picks up where concepts like pluralism, multiculturalism, and cultural and racial diversity leave off. However, there are several assumptions where all models of cultural competence converge. Cultural competence

- Is a process not a destination.
- Consists of five constructs, which are cultural awareness, cultural knowledge, cultural skill, cultural encounters, and cultural desire.
- Understands that more variation appears within ethnic groups than across ethnic groups.
- Is a direct relationship between the competence level of a public servant and the level and the ability of the public servant to be culturally responsive.
- Is essential in rendering effective, culturally responsive services to ethnically diverse clients. Most of the cultural competence literature is told from a provider perspective within the provider/client perspective within health professions.
- Is outcome based and focuses attention on obvious language differences in consultation with clients and agency representatives.

(Wallace, 2018)

In addition, cultural competency highlights the communication of distress and help-seeking practices. These factors influence procedures and policies for showing respect for patients' cultural beliefs and attitudes and an expression of genuine interest to learn about "other cultures" (Rice, 2006). Research brought more clarity to cultural competency, and distinguished cultural competence from cultural awareness. The current perspective assumes that cultural awareness is the recognition that different cultural groups tend to

> focus on the outward cultural characteristics such as physical appearance, food, art, religious practices; while cultural sensitivity involves internal changes in attitudes and values. Cultural competence moves from being a concept to being realized when information about cultural differences are integrated in a way that transforms knowledge about specific groups or individuals transforms knowledge about individuals and groups into specific standards, policies, practices, and attitudes . . . to operate effectively in distinct cultural contexts.
>
> (Rice, 2006, p. 7)

CULTURAL COMPETENCE MODEL CONSTRUCTS

In recent years a number of studies added to the development of cultural competence models. Many of these studies modified or created new models to operationalize. The rationale behind these models was establishing a framework for training their referenced audience, evaluating current implementation models, or bench-markings. Bhui, Bhugra, Edonya, McKenzie, and Warfa (2007) identified several new models and applications of cultural competency for the training of physicians, medical students, nurses, local and state government officials, and organizations, along with some interdisciplinary research. Importantly, these studies have been instrumental in exploring and explaining how the models are useful across fields of endeavor where there is direct personal contact between professionals and individuals from distinct cultural backgrounds. Balcazar, Suarez-Balcazar, and Taylor-Ritzer (2009) identified at least 18 unique cultural competence models. Bhui et al. (2007) examined models of cultural competence that included a participation component. Some of those models include:

1. Ferguson's Community Curriculum Model was used to set curriculum standards for cultural diversity in 1999 and 2000. The referenced population was a group of 15 medical schools in New England and New York. This model consisted of three modules: cultural competence and the role of the physician, teaching skills of cultural competence, and moving beyond cultural awareness.
2. Siegel's (2003) cultural competency model was a two-phase construct. Phase one defined the five-step framework of cultural competence performance measures of cultural competence. These five steps were (a) needs assessment and information exchange, (b) services, (c) human resources, (d) policies and plans, and (e) linkages to outcomes. Phase two examined the framework domains on three levels: (a) administrative (state mental health authority or a managed care entity), (b) service delivery entity, and (c) individuals involved in direct delivery of care (Bhui et al., 2007). The study examined performance measures benchmarked in these organizations providing health-care services to diverse groups of people.
3. The Diversity Competency Model was the result of a study that utilized a mixed method approach. Using focus groups and gathering quantitative data from documents from the nursing organization, Frusti et al. (2003) devised their version of a diversity competency model. This model comprised five prongs included drivers, linkages, cultures, and measurements, with commitment being the cohesive element. The purpose of this model was to create a practical and generalizable culturally competent mechanism that increased staff performance and workload capacity that was grounded in "understanding and respect for each person's uniqueness" (Frusti et al., 2003, p. 32). Cultural Competency Agencies, Programs, and Services were services responsive to the racial and ethnic differences of populations they serviced. Stork et al. (2001) conducted a case study that assessed five states' implementation of culturally competent provisions in behaviorally managed care contacts. This study's thesis focused on federal cultural competence regulations that go back to the 1990 Disability Act and the Civil Rights Act. This study discovered that cultural competence implementation translated into translation services

and language assistance, quality assurance rules, grievance procedures, disciplinary mix, geographic distribution.

4. The US Department of Health and Human service (HRSA) developed an assessment profile for health-care organizations. This model outlined nine domains. These domains are:
   a. Values and attitudes
   b. Cultural sensitivity
   c. Communication
   d. Policies and procedures
   e. Training and staff development
   f. Facility characteristics
   g. Intervention and treatment model
   h. Family and community participation
   i. Monitoring, evaluation, and research

(Bhui et al., 2007)

These domains provided an overall framework for health-care organizations in the United States to operate within a structure with outcome indicators of organizational cultural competency. Bhui et al., 2007) further stated the models they identified in their study had commonalities in their cognitive and behavioral components. Attracting a lot of attention after the 1960s and well into the 1990s, many professional organizations such as rehabilitation counseling and psychology have revised their code of ethics to include respect for cultural diversity. Cultural competency guidelines are interwoven into many professional standards for education, training, research, and practice (Balcazar et al., 2009, p. 1154).

Cultural competence is undergirded by the larger belief that people should not only appreciate and recognize other cultural groups but also be able to work effectively with them. Cultural competence is perceived to be more holistic than assimilation and pluralism (Sue, 1998). Cross (2010) builds on this notion further by suggesting that cultural competency may be the third wave of diversity. This perception is based on the idea that those who embrace cultural competence become willing participants in understanding the cultural, language, social, and economic nuances of people (Wallace, 2018).

CULTURAL COMPETENCE AND PUBLIC ADMINISTRATION

Cultural competency should not only focus on giving public servants the "transferable technical skills" but it should also challenge the personal motivation of people who make up these organizations serving the public. Cultural competence at its core seeks to help people understand differences by identifying and tackling their biases that conflict with being a sensitive, fair, and just public agent (Wallace, 2018).

Cultural competence in theory and practice is still new to public administration, and the field continues to struggle with finding a usable framework. Rice (2015) observes that "the focus on cultural competency in public administration and public service delivery is evolving slowly" (p. 190). Moreover, since racially diverse groups of people have not been "highly regarded topics in the study of the administrative state" (Rice, 2015, p. 190), the field is grappling with how to frame this concept of cultural competence.

Betancourt et al. (2005) describe cultural competence within public administration as a practice that acknowledges and incorporates (at all levels) the importance of culture, assessment of cross-cultural relations, vigilance toward the dynamics that result from cultural differences, expansion of cultural knowledge, and adaptation of services to meet culturally unique needs. Studies around cultural competency have been slow in development. First, the study and practice of cultural competence within public administration in the field sees cultural differences and cultural variations in public service delivery and public agencies as invisible, illegitimate, and negative (Adler, 1991) and a focus on cultural differences/cultural variations does not fit the neutrality/equality principles (treat all clients the same with neutral feelings) advocated in textbook scenarios in relation to specific client needs in public service delivery. Secondly, the agreement around cultural competence legitimacy is not consistent, if at all acknowledged. This is because cultural competence is viewed as a "soft science" (Betancourt et al., 2005), lacking an evidence-based scientific approach for both application and utility in public and social service programs (cited in Rice, 2006). In other words, the cultural competence had not yet emerged as a concept within public administration as legitimate and easy to fold into the context of public service delivery. Moreover, moving past "face diversity" to embrace cultural competence as a worthwhile field of study lacked empirical evidence, a defined framework and definition, and a practical context. Nevertheless, cultural competence continued to emerge slowly as a concept, a framework, and eventually a worthwhile foundation to embrace as part of the public service mission (Wallace, 2018).

The movement to adopt cultural competence accelerated when the accreditor of public affairs and public administration masters' programs reframed the programmatic expectations and mission to include culturally competent objectives (Rubaii and Calarusse, 2012). Within public administration agencies, culturally competent behaviors are recognized as individuals or agencies that are comfortable with their own culture and experiences, and recognize their biases that come along with their culture; a keen sensitivity to and thoughtful response to varying cultures of others (Gaynor, 2014). Public administrators would see concepts like multiculturalism and diversity as foundational building blocks for competent cultural agencies. Four key components of culturally competent agencies are: (1) an inherent value for diversity, (2) evaluation, assessment, and accountability measures, (3) consciousness inherent in the organizational culture around the dynamics of two different cultures interacting, and (4) an organizational culture of "institutionalized and growing knowledge" (Wallace, 2018).

Public administration graduate programs have a responsibility to collaborate with public agencies to prepare graduates that are ready to seamlessly move from student to employee with a sound cultural competency skill set to work with diverse groups of people. One of the biggest hurdles that public administration faces in embracing and operationalizing cultural competency is that each organization and institution must take into consideration the groups of people that make up that organization and the clientele they are servicing. This perspective assumes that cultural competency is a transferable skill set (Wallace, 2018). Others question the transferablity of cultural competence skills. Carrizales (2010) argues that cultural competence is a not an independent skill set, but rather it is one that is to be integrated. These skills are meant to produce a public servant that is understanding of him/herself, their culture, their biases in the context of their respective organizations' mission of service. Pulling from Carrizales's (2010) study on culturally competent based curricula, the key components of integrating cultural competence within the classroom setting are based on four components: (1) knowledge based, (2) attitude based, (3) skill based, and (4) community based. Knowledge-based cultural competency includes common knowledge, common vocabulary—definition and terms—local and national demographics, examination of disparities, and policy and legal implications. Attitude-based competencies include self-reflection, examination of societal biases, and organization culture and change; skills-based competencies are defined in terms of communication, curriculum development, program assessment, and the use, integration, and access to technology; while the community-based component serves as a guide for public policy and public affairs programs to adopt and incorporate into their curriculum. Carrizales's approach aligns with Gay's (2000) definition of culturally competent or culturally responsive pedagogy as a pedagogy that is validating, comprehensive, multidimensional, empowering, transformative, and emancipatory. Embracing cultural competency within the curriculum is key to producing public servants ready to deal with a diverse population. Thus, cultural competence skills are learned through dynamic interaction with students, facts, knowledge, and the instructor or professor as the class facilitator. Teel and Obadiah (2008) expand the definition of cultural competence by including the idea of a cultural competence continuum. This continuum has eight aspects ranging from a comfort level with students, student academic engagement, personal connection with students, the level of academic expectation, acceptance of responsibility for student performance, relationship with parents, self-evaluation/reflection, and culturally relevant lessons (Teal and Obadiah, 2008, p. 146).

The purpose of this chapter is not to discuss the introduction and implementation of cultural competence programs into an organization. While that task is critical, it is part of the responsibility of the personnel/human resources department and as such is covered in Part II. Rather this chapter is about operationalizing the lessons of cultural competence into management practice. It is creating a work environment in which diversity is not merely accepted as a reality but is recognized as advantageous. Four themes will be explored to better understand the role of cultural competence in management practice. Those themes are:

- Interpreting cultural values
- Diversity in an organization
- Diversity as a contributor to decision-making
- Managing and fostering a diverse organization

INTERPRETING CULTURAL VALUES

Fundamental to the effective knitting together of people in any organization is in ensuring and enacting respect for different cultures. People in an organization must first be aware of cultural differences. Race and ethnicity are the main cultural differences that influence attitudes and behaviors. A person's nationality often defines their beliefs, thoughts, interests, and outlooks. Religion, economic status, and even sexual orientation are also integral parts of people's identities and belief systems. Showing sensitivity to differences and inviting others to share their cultural experiences can be an effective way to foster cultural awareness and feelings of inclusion (www.reference.com/article/cultural competence).

Cultural sensitivity is important for organizational leaders to understand as well. In a diverse workplace, companies need to promote a culture where people tolerate unique and varying views of people from many cultures. Some organizations even go as far as to offer initial or ongoing training for employees on cultural sensitivity. Language, customs, mannerisms, and etiquette are among the factors that influence someone's level of cultural sensitivity (www.reference.com/article/cultural competence).

DIVERSITY AS AN ORGANIZATIONAL ATTRIBUTE

As noted above, the American workplace (and those in most of Europe) has grown more diverse. While there is a long way to go to overcome prejudice and discrimination, the government workplace especially reflects the demographic diversity of the population. This change began as part of the civil rights movement of the 1960s. At the time these were primarily socio-political efforts. While individual discrimination remains a serious problem, many of the institutional barriers that were common through the 1960s are disappearing. The institutional stance of government and business are that discrimination and bias are unacceptable. Thus,

> In the workplace, cultural competence is closely related to an emphasis on diversity. Valuing diversity includes acknowledging the different ways in which members of various cultures communicate, think and behave and integrating those differences in a way that makes underrepresented members feel valued and included within an organization. Practicing cultural competence creates better communication despite speech barriers and fosters culturally aware motivation strategies and a better understanding of others' perspectives and behaviors.
>
> (www.reference.com/article/cultural competence)

While this seems straightforward, the reality of the workplace is that most senior managers (who are likely older and "monochromatic") push back on such notions. The "diversity is our strength" mantra is belied by organizations in which good old boy networks exist and, more insidiously, the mentoring process promotes such behavior. As noted by Seibert, Stridh-Igo, and Zimmerman (2002) prejudice and bias exist. They call it a "fact of [organizational] life." Interestingly, those who deny it are most afflicted (think of the pushback against being "politically correct"). To accomplish cultural awareness, managers must first understand his or her own cultural background and explore possible biases or prejudices toward other cultures. "Upon close examination of prejudice, bias, and their sources, it appears that fear is the foundation. Work to overcome these fears; education will facilitate the process" (Seibert, Stridh-Igo, and Zimmerman, 2002, p. 146).

DECISION-MAKING IN DIVERSE SETTINGS

Theories and practices of organizational decision-making have evolved as theories of leadership have evolved (see Chapter 13). Participation, engagement, and collaboration are presumptive elements of management and leadership. The more diverse the workplace the more imaginative and effective the decision-making.

Managing organizations is a difficult task at the best of times. The interplay of theory and practice of leadership has followed a somewhat dialectic path. The emphasis shifts from a primarily organizational perspective to an individual and/or interpersonal perspective. Current leadership theories exist on the parallel planes of the organization and the individual (Cox, Plagens, and Sylla, 2010). Traditionally, leadership or a leader in an organization is viewed as a person who has the capacity and the power to lead followers or subordinates. Well into the twentieth century, leadership was seen as the result of the singular will of the leader: Julius Caesar (I came, I saw, I conquered). The central understanding of leadership was based on the notion that the leaders actively lead and the followers or subordinates, passively and obediently, follow. The basic premise of this style of leadership is that leaders give orders (commands) to homogeneous followers.

This conception of leadership was developed in the early twentieth century. The "Scientific Management" theory introduced by Frederick Taylor (1911), the charismatic and authoritarian leader evoked by Max Weber (1946), and the command approach in administrative or bureaucratic organizations, and in government (Gulick, 1937), all generated a kind of control and power from the top down, and the subordinates in these organizations were practically under the submission of the leader.

From the beginning there were those who doubted and challenged this approach. Exemplars of these critiques of the accepted views on leadership were Follett (1996) and Barnard (1968). The vision of the leaders expressed here is that of a conciliator and facilitator. A half century later these writers would provide the basic frame of reference for advocates of a more "follower-centric" approach to leadership.

Follett's view on the giving of orders presages future works of much later scholarship. It is in her work on orders that the emphasis on individualism and the dignity of the work come through most clearly. Follett firmly believed that orders, like control, involved a reciprocal, integrative activity. Compliance with orders was not simply the product of the authority of the issuer of the orders (Follett, 1996).

Barnard's *The Functions of the Executive* (1968) has influenced generations of organization theorists. His emphasis on cooperation, leadership, and the informal group represents a major departure from the structural and authoritarian assumptions characteristic of classical organization theory.

During the middle and later decades of the twentieth century (and into this first part of the twenty-first century) concern for the worker both as an individual and as part of a group becomes paramount. This is a time when the human element in organizations becomes defined as the most important factor in an organization's success. Concerns as varied as individual motivation to managerial capability to lead are facets of human relations in the organization. The basic premise of this "group-based" style of leadership is that leaders must work with followers who are heterogeneous and respond to quite different internal and external "stimuli." A dissatisfied or unmotivated worker will make little use of a well-structured facility, and a motivated employee will be able to do better under adverse physical conditions.

> The Hawthorne experiments were the emotional and intellectual wellspring of the organizational behavior perspective and modern theories of motivation. The Hawthorne experiments showed that complex, interactional variables make the difference in motivating people—things like attention paid to workers as individuals, workers' control over their own work, differences between individuals' needs, management willingness to listen, group norms, and direct feedback.
>
> (Roethlisberger, 1939, pp. 28–29)

Criticism of the group dynamics perspective came from both those who were unwilling to relinquish the traditional views of leadership and from those (primarily psychologists) who found the focus on group dynamics did not leave sufficient room to explore individual relationships.

Maslow first presented his views on human motivation in 1943. In that work he presented his now famous hierarchy of needs. Those needs are: physiological, safety, love, esteem, and self-actualization. First, it is important to understand the interrelationships among these needs. Second, satisfaction need not be complete before the needs of a higher level are addressed. Third, and probably most important, is that these needs are generally unconscious. While higher-level needs can be brought out in each of us and therefore become conscious, this is not often the case. Fourth is that all behavior is motivated; some behavior is an expression of personality and experience rather than needs.

All this suggests that goals are the central principle within the concept of motivation. Gratification through the attainment of goals is the basic process for determining a shift to other needs (and therefore goals). The point is that the work setting must be taken into account if the manager is to create a work environment where achievement of higher needs is possible (Fiedler, 1967). For Fiedler, the differences are likely to be found in the flexibility and adaptability of management style of the respective manager.

Another psychological approach comes in the exploration of the role of "power" and/or authority in defining the relationship between leaders and followers. The more commonly applied approach is that of French and Raven (1959), who explored the role of "power" in structuring and defining relationships in an organizational setting. French and Raven offer five different forms or types of power:

- Reward
- Coercive

- Legitimate
- Referent
- Expert

The idea of power and influence in organizations represents a logical starting point for a broader study of leadership in organizations. This perspective differs from that which we have just described, in that it is more socio-psychological rather than psychological.

> Leadership in organizations has become more difficult since the 1980s for a variety of reasons. . . . First, the rate of change in organizations increased substantially almost universally and has actually accelerated again with the advent of the Great Recession in 2008. Public and non-profit organizations are still adjusting to the movement from a traditional bureaucratic paradigm to a post-bureaucratic paradigm that integrates much higher levels of customer service, devolution, coproduction, and competition. This makes the job of leadership more interesting, but also more confusing and risky. . . . Second, the range of leadership activities required of leaders is simply greater. . . . This is hard work. Third, in a more cynical age it is more difficult to be a leader. Followers are not only more cynical about institutions. . . , but also more likely to be cynical about individuals who lead them.
>
> (Van Wart, 2017, p. 313)

In 1999 Agranoff and McGuire suggested that there were seven "meta-questions" to be addressed concerning networks. That list included *collaboration*, *cohesion*, and *accountability*. In a longer treatment on this idea in 2003 they described the American government as being in an "Age of Collaboration."

They describe the attributes of governmental collaboration as:

- Trust
- Mutual benefit
- Shared goal/outcome
- Pooled resources

Or, as they cleverly noted, familiarity breeds cooperation (Agranoff and McGuire, 2003, p. 20).

Realities of Collaborative Behavior

Policy making has always been a shared responsibility whether between councils and managers in a city or across levels and types of governments. Shared governance is not a conveyor belt; it is an iterative and self-reinforcing process of feedback and response. If organizations are to be successful, both the formal and the informal aspects of the organization must be predicated on the following understandings of trust: Trust should affirm the organizational-interpersonal link; trust should promote cultural values such as respect, vision, diversity, and empowerment; trust should be built through the application of the skills of talent searching, communicating, deciding, self-assessing, enabling, culture creating, and culture affirming.

Miller and Cox (2014) posit that the boundaries of a network emerge as individuals or governments recognize shared interests, shared problems, and shared history. This in itself is enough to bring people "to the table," but it is not sufficient to get them to agree to act. The barrier is that the emphasis on markets seemingly provides justification to not act. The arrangement becomes a network whose purpose is to obfuscate and delay.

Decision-making is based upon the intricate relationships that are both horizontal and vertical. In both orientations the assumption is that decisions are collective affairs. The stumbling block to success seems to be the unwillingness to relinquish control. This is not merely the preference for a hierarchically based command and control approach to management and decision-making but also the assumption that teams and collaborations are based upon being "like-minded." Forgotten are the lessons of politics and the need to understand problems before defining them and solving them. Politics is premised on bringing people together to seek common interests and values. The shared perspective is the outcome of the political process, not the beginning. The politics of exclusion and division assume that only those who are alike can decide. The politics of modern governments struggle with this problem when problem identification and problem-solving are turned over to small groups. The failure of regional governments in the face of narrow self-interest is an example of this dynamic. Until we recognize that politics is about bringing people together because they are not alike before defining a problem or solving it, we will continue down a path in which diversity and collaboration is dismissed as not being helpful for decision-making.

MAKING IT WORK: MANAGING A DIVERSE ORGANIZATION

In a discussion presented by Landry (2018), lessons gleaned from observations in a range of organizations (mostly private and nonprofit) on managing a diverse workforce were provided. This discussion is worth offering in some detail.

> Some managers and teams have a hard time acknowledging they have a culture problem, instead pitting the blame on a high turnover rate or change in leadership. Ignoring the issue, however, can come with consequences.
>
> The Society for Human Resource Management (SHRM) reports that culture impacts productivity, explaining that "employees from different backgrounds are motivated by different incentives and react differently to various management and communication styles." For example, Swedish management tends to be decentralized and democratic, whereas American managers are collaborative, yet tend to prioritize their own interests and career. Acknowledging and reconciling those subtle differences can improve communication and lead to a more motivated workforce.
>
> For those who aren't sure where to start, [it is recommended to begin by] performing an audit of all internal communications. What's the mission of your organization, and how are you defining your company values? Are your mission and values inclusive? Have you taken your team's various cultures into account?

From there, undergo a data collection exercise and survey employees. Take the time to dig in and understand what's most meaningful to the team and connect that to your communications. By gathering employee feedback, you can better determine how the current organizational culture is being received and strategize ways to create a more inclusive environment where different perspectives and cultures are valued and embraced. This feedback helps those in the organization recognize who they are and who they are speaking to.

It's important to get to know colleagues on a personal level and find common ground—particularly in an age of video conferencing, email, and other virtual communication tools, where teams aren't always interacting in person or observing their peers' daily behaviors.

"There's not a clear path or one model that's going to fit every situation," Goodman says. "It's more taking the time and going through the inquiry process and, in the midst of that, recognizing the types of questions that need to be asked and what communication needs to be adjusted."

(Landry, 2018)

Developing Cultural Awareness of Self

The emphasis in the above discussion is understanding ourselves, not merely those around us. An understanding of our own cultural system may be an important first step toward correcting biases that affect interactions with others. Self-awareness can be defined as verbal discrimination of our own behavior. Culture can be described as common behaviors related by comparable learning histories, social and environmental contingencies, contexts, and stimuli, so self-awareness might also include verbal discrimination of these aspects of personal experience (Seibert, Stridh-Igo, and Zimmerman, 2002).

Cultural discrimination often is the by-product of a lack of self-awareness. UNESCO indicates that discrimination often is commonly directed at ethnic minorities within the society, organizations, or institutions. Religious hate, tribalism, and racism are the most common forms of cultural discrimination. Cultural discrimination that results from social stereotyping leads to poor communication and interpersonal relationships. Cultural discrimination manifests itself through unfair hiring, unjust firing, or sexual harassment. When such discrimination is deeply embedded in the organizational (and social) culture, such behaviors are difficult to uproot even though it is illegal.

Cultural awareness is the ability to notice and respect these differences. Showing consideration for the cultural norms of others makes a person more hospitable in a home country, and better equipped to fit in when traveling abroad. Cultural awareness involves recognizing different beliefs, values, and customs that other people have that are based on their origins or upbringings. Cultural awareness positions people to be more successful in both personal and professional relationships.

Practicing cultural awareness means extending respect to people from different cultures. Cultural awareness also involves making adjustments and adaptations as necessary in different social and professional situations. Using sensitivity and flexibility helps people navigate diverse social and professional situations to avoid offending others. Workers must utilize sensitivity for the influence of culture on both communication and etiquette. Cultural etiquette often has significant differences, which present challenges for people who are trying to work together. Recognizing cultural differences and accepting these differences in a respectful and affirming manner helps everyone to feel valued. The ability to have positive verbal and nonverbal communication with others who have different backgrounds and beliefs broadens perspectives and enhances the ability to collaborate effectively.

Cultural sensitivity means being aware and accepting of the differences that exist among people with different cultural backgrounds. Being culturally sensitive enables a person to approach interactions with people from different cultures in a respectful manner, both in workplace and interpersonal interactions. Cultural sensitivity is important for organizational leaders to understand as well. In a diverse workplace, companies need to promote a culture where people tolerate unique and varying views of people from many cultures. Some organizations even go as far as to offer initial or ongoing training for employees on cultural sensitivity. Language, customs, mannerisms, and etiquette are among the factors that influence someone's level of cultural sensitivity (www.reference.com/article/cultural competence) (see Figure 10.1).

Although the cultural sensitivity and awareness checklist included here was written for public health professionals, the list offers a perspective that is useful for a manager in a public or nonprofit setting. There are three features of this checklist that are worth highlighting in this discussion:

1. Language Barriers
2. Trust
3. Bias and Prejudice

Governments across the globe have struggled with the issue of language. Language is often the basis for national identity and becomes critical to a people's understanding of themselves and their government. Many mandate the use of a single language for all government endeavors. Others seek different accommodations. Belgium has two official languages in government, often with separate government offices to serve the people. The employees of the national government of Canada are required by law to be bilingual, but the provinces are not (the primary language of the Province of Quebec, including its public school system, is French).

The distinction that must be made here is the level and type of service available to those for whom the primary language is other than that of the government. Most government services are available to all those who reside within a jurisdiction, not merely to those who have citizenship. While much is made of this distinction in US politics in this era (2018), the reality is that those who are not citizens (and therefore, likely to have more limited language skills) are the most likely to encounter government employees, because they are potentially from relatively vulnerable groups (children and the elderly). The critical issue is to remember that the goal of language and communication is to successfully convey information to which the participants have a similar understanding. The management task is to ensure that people who seek service fully understand their rights and eligibility. To not attend to the comprehension of the person seeking service is tantamount to denying the service.

1. Communication method: Identify the patient's preferred method of communication. Make necessary arrangements if translators are needed.

   Miscommunication occurs frequently between health-care professionals and patients, a problem that is intensified by language barriers. About 14 percent of the USA population does not speak English at home. Of the people who speak a language other than English at home, 47 percent say they have difficulty speaking English. Assuring information is conveyed and received as intended must consistently be a top priority.

2. Language barriers: Identify potential language barriers (verbal and nonverbal). List possible compensations.

   Nonverbal communication plays an essential role when people are exchanging information. Like the old adage indicates: *you cannot, not communicate*. Communication experts routinely emphasize the significance of understanding the intricacies of nonverbal communication. Most of what we understand is conveyed by nonverbal cues—it is not what we say but how we say it. All of us use these cues to aid clarification during complicated situations. We should all learn how *we* convey information nonverbally to avoid expressing personal biases.

3. Cultural identification: Identify the patient's culture. Contact your organization's culturally specific support team (CSST) for assistance.

   The CSST is composed of people who are able to represent various cultures and ethnic groups, preferably people who are actually members of the specific groups. This group's role is to help educate caregivers about the target culture's customs and possible associated needs that will play a role in recovery. The CSST also helps to ensure understanding in essential interactions with patients and families. The CSST collects and provides information about community resources that might be useful for a particular culture or ethnic group's needs. Translators are usually an integral part of this team.

4. Comprehension: Double-check: Does the patient and/or family comprehend the situation at hand?

   Remember, nodding and indicating some type of affirmative response does not necessarily guarantee understanding has been achieved. Re-explaining is useful and facilitates comprehension, particularly during times of stress. Effective communication launches effective care. One useful technique is to gently ask the patient or family member to convey the information, in his/her own words, before concluding that he/she understands.

5. Beliefs: Identify religious/spiritual beliefs. Make appropriate support contacts.

   Religious/spiritual beliefs play an important and powerful role in recovery. We found in our study of superior recovery that religion/spirituality is one of the characteristics that contributes to a successful recovery. Patients and families often attribute successful recovery, as well as survival, to these types of beliefs.

6. Trust: Double-check: Does the patient and/or family appear to trust the caregivers? Remember to watch for both verbal and nonverbal cues. If not, seek advice from the CSST.

   A study by the brain injury rehabilitation unit (BIRU) at Liverpool Hospital in Australia found that "good communication leading to the establishment of trust" seemed to be more important to the participants than the expertise of the professional. "A good professional is one you can trust." Lack of trust can impede achieving the best possible outcomes because the patient and family might withhold essential health-related

---

FIGURE 10.1

The Cultural Sensitivity and Awareness Checklist

230 **CHAPTER 10** Cultural Competence

information. Another trust-related impediment occurs when patients and families fail to follow crucial instructions or do not believe recovery can be achieved.

7. Recovery: Double-check: Does the patient and/or family have misconceptions or unrealistic views about the caregivers, treatment, or recovery process? Make necessary adjustments.

    Give those involved enough time to process information received and to gain familiarity with the situation. Later, allow more time for any questions that will help clarify the circumstances. Patients and their families routinely experience misconceptions or form unrealistic expectations that can impair the ability to make the wisest decisions. Help guide appropriate conceptions.

8. Diet: Address culture-specific dietary considerations.

    Certain cultures and ethnic groups include very specific dietary regulations. As nutritionists have long stressed, appropriate nutrition is vital to optimum recovery. Simple dietary modifications can be made that will respond to these needs. As an added bonus, this action will convey respect for the particular culture or ethnic group, thus raising comfort level and trust.

9. Assessments: Conduct assessments with cultural sensitivity in mind. Watch for inaccuracies.

    Be aware of potential differences in culturally accepted emotional expression and verbalizations of private information. For cognitive assessments, tests must be analyzed to identify culturally specific questions and modified accordingly. Even subtle differences can profoundly influence assessments.

10. Health-care provider bias: We have biases and prejudices. Examine and recognize yours.

    It is a fact of life that prejudice and bias exist. Those who deny it are most afflicted. Identifying and recognizing this will help control its expression. To accomplish cultural awareness effectively "the health-care professional must first understand his or her own cultural background and explore possible biases or prejudices toward other cultures." Upon close examination of prejudice, bias, and their sources, it appears that fear is the foundation. Work to overcome these fears; education will facilitate the process.

Source: P.S. Seibert, P. Stridh-Igo, and C.G. Zimmerman (2002). "A Checklist to Facilitate Cultural Awareness and Sensitivity." *Journal of Medical Ethics* (28):143–146

FIGURE 10.1
(Continued)

The need for persons to trust those in government and for those in government to trust people (with the obvious exceptions of those who commit unlawful acts). Trust is closely linked to the idea of organizational integrity. Integrity has two behavioral aspects. The most basic definition involves trustworthiness (Six and Huberts, 2008), but trustworthiness itself is meaningless unless it serves as the basis for future action. Integrity is manifest in the recognition of a person, or organization, as worthy of trust so that at some time in the future you will interact with that person or an organization in the expectation that you will experience consistent, positive, responses (fair, equitable, professional interaction). There is no voluntary interaction where there is no trust. If a person or organization is untrustworthy, then your response is to avoid interaction (not calling the police after witnessing a crime, or not voting in an election, or not accepting an invitation to attend a meeting are simple examples).

Trustworthiness is a behavior that is observed as a cultural attribute of an organization. Organizational integrity, as a judgment about an organization, can be observed in the interactions of citizens with those agencies. Goodsell (2003) noted many years ago in his defense of bureaucracy that welfare clients, even when turned down for benefits, assessed their experience as "satisfactory" because the bureaucrat who was "just following the rules" was acting in a way that was consistent, fair, and honest; in other words they displayed professionalism.

Integrity is an organizational construct. In a sense integrity is an aspect of organizational culture and interpersonal relations. There is a human element in this. As Menzel (2012) suggests

> demonstrating personal integrity requires, (1) taking personal responsibility for errors one may commit, (2) recognizing and crediting others for their work and contributions to the organization's mission, (3) guarding against any conflict of interest or its appearance, and (4) being respectful of subordinates, colleagues, and the public.
>
> (p. 55)

Extending this to an organization-wide definition he offers the following:

> The guiding values and commitments make sense and are clearly communicated. Organizational leaders are personally committed, credible, and willing to take action on the values they espouse. The espoused values are integrated into the normal channels of management decision making and are reflected in the organization's critical activities. The organization's systems and structures support and reinforce its values. Managers throughout the organization have the decision making skills, knowledge, and competencies needed to make ethically sound decisions on a day-to-day basis.
>
> (Menzel, 2012, p. 78)

Six and Huberts (2008) emphasize the relational element of integrity. They note:

> Integrity is a concept similar to trustworthiness rather than trust. Both integrity and trustworthiness refer to attributes of a specific actor—in trust terminology, the trustee—that make that actor have higher or lower integrity or trustworthiness in the eyes of another actor—again in trust terminology, the trustor. In both cases, it is generally considered good to maximize the amount of each. The relationship between integrity and trust is such that the higher an actor's integrity, the more he will be trusted by another actor.
>
> Both concepts differ in important ways. Trustworthiness is restricted to the specific relationships: is the other actor interested in maintaining a relationship with me? Is the other actor benevolent to me? Are their norms acceptable to me? . . . *On the other hand, integrity, as shown above, is based on a "relevant set of moral values, norms and rules," not what I, personally, may hold as values and norms, not my personal interests.*
>
> (p. 70, emphasis added)

The validity of the organization is grounded in the integrity of organizational performance; i.e. in the trustworthiness of the actions of those in the organization. Stated another way, organizational effectiveness (success) is based upon presence of a culture of rule of law. Rules serve as guides to implementation, rather than as statements of barriers. Integrity and trustworthiness are core values and norms that form the basis for organizational behavior.

It is a simple fact of organizational life that bias and prejudice exist among the people in all organizations. Much like the discussion about ethics (Chapter 2) merely being an exemplar is insufficient. A culture of unethical behavior continues when it is tolerated by managers. Similarly, actions of bias and prejudice must be stopped. It must be clear to everyone in and out of the organization that such transgressions will have consequences. Cultural competence training should be integrated into employee training, but more importantly it needs to be embedded in the organizational culture. Bias and prejudice must be recognized for what it is: a threat to the effectiveness of the organization and the cause of harm to those the organization claims to serve.

To be culturally competent is to be as unbiased as humanly possible. It is to be a person of integrity in the work and roles assigned and to facilitate understanding.

DISCUSSION QUESTIONS

- Defend diversity of perspective as a critical valued in modern organizations. In such an explanation, identify both organizational and interpersonal components.
- What characteristics of healthcare might explain why culture competence was examined first in that setting?
- Can a cultural competence program be developed from the top?
- What are some of the attributes of the people in an organization if it is to be successful in developing a cultural competence agenda?
- Why is self-awareness important?

BIBLIOGRAPHY

Adler, N. J. *International Dimensions of Organizational Behavior*. Boston, MA: PSW-Kent, 1991. Cited in M. F. Rice. "Promoting Cultural Competence in Public Administration and Public Service Delivery: Utilizing Self-Assessment Tools", A paper prepared for presentation at the Annual Conference of National Association of Schools of Public Affairs and Administration, Minneapolis, MN. 2006.

Balcazar, F., Y. Suarez-Balcazar, and T. Taylor-Ritzler. Cultural Competence: *Development of a Conceptual Framework Disability and Rehabilitsion*, 31(14) pp. 1153–1160. 2009.

Betancourt, J. R., A. R. Green, J. E. Carrillo, and E. R. Park. "Cultural Competence and Health Care Disparities: Key Perspectives and Trends", *Health Affairs*, 24 (2), pp. 499–505. 2005.

Bhui, K., D. Bhugra, P. Edonya, K. McKenzie, and N. Warfa. "Cultural competence in mental health care: A review of model evaluations", *BMC Health Services Research*, 7 (15), pp. 1–10. 2007).

Campinha-Bacote, J. "The Process of Cultural Competence in the Delivery of Healthcare Services: A Model of Care", *Journal of Transcultural Nursing*, 13 (3), pp. 181–184. 2002.

Campinha-Bacote, J., and M. C. Narayan. "Culturally Competent Health Care in the Home", *Home Care Provider*, 5 (6), pp. 213–219. 2000.

Carrizales, T. "Exploring Cultural Competency Within the Public Affairs Curriculum," *Journal of Public Affairs Education*, 16(4) pp. 593–606. 2010.

Cox III, Raymond W., Gregory K. Plagens, and Keba Sylla. "The Leadership-followership Dynamic: Making the Choice to Follow", *International Journal of Interdisciplinary Social Sciences*, 5 (8), pp. 37–52. 2010.

Fiedler, Fred. *A Theory of Leadership Effectiveness*. New York: McGraw-Hill. 1967.

Fong, Elizabeth Hughes, Robyn M. Catagnus, Matthew T. Brodhead, Shawn Quigley, and Sean Field. "Developing the Cultural Awareness Skills of Behavior Analysts", *Behavior Analyst and Practice*, 9 (1), pp. 84–94. 2016.

French, John, and Bertram Raven. "The Bases of Social Power", in D. Cartwright (ed.) *Social Power*. Ann Arbor, MI: Institute for Social Research, pp. 150–167. 1959.

Frusti, D. K., K. M. Niesen, and, J. K. Campion. "Creating a Culturally Competent Organization: Use of the Diversity Competency Model", *Journal of Nursing Administration*, 33(1), pp. 31–38. 2003.

Gay, G. Culturally Responsive Teaching: Theory, *Research, and Practice*. New York: Teachers College Press. 2000.

Gaynor, T. S. "Through the Wire: Training Culturally Competent Leaders for a New Era", *Journal of Public Administration Education*, 20(3), pp. 369–392. 2014.

Goodsell, C. *The Case for Bureaucracy, 4th ed*. Washington, DC: CQ Press. 2003.

Gulick, L. "Notes on the Theory of Organization", in Luther Gulick and Lyndall Urwick (eds.) *Papers on the Science of Administration*. New York: Institute of Public Administration, pp. 3–46. 1937.

Landry, Lauren. "The Importance of Cultivating Cultural Awareness at Work", (Retrieved January 18, 2018, from www.northeastern.edu/graduate/blog/cultural-awareness-at-work/).

Menzel, Donald. *Ethics Management for Public Administrators: Leading and Building Organizations of Integrity, 2nd ed*. London: Routledge. 2012.

Rice, M. F. "Promoting cultural competency in public administration and public service delivery: Utilizing self-assessment tools and performance measures." Bush School Working Paper # 587.2006.

Rice, M. F. "Promoting Cultural Competency in Public Administration and Public Service Delivery: Utilizing Self-assessment Tools and Performance Measures", *Journal of Public Affairs Education*, 41–57. 2007.

Rice, M. F. *Diversity and Public Administration: Theory, Issues, and Perspectives*. New York, NY: Routledge. 2015.

Rubaii, N., and C, Calarusse. "Cultural Competency as a Standard for Accreditation", *Cultural Competency for Public Administrators*, Washington DC: NASPAA. 2012.

Roethlisberger, F. J. and W. J. Dickson. *Management and the Worker: An Account of a Research Program Conducted by the Western Electric Company*, Hawthorne Works, Chicago. Cambridge, MA: Harvard University Press. 1939.

Siegel, C., G. Haugland, and E. Davis Chambers. "Performance Measures and Their Benchmarks for Assessing Organizational Cultural Competency in Behavioral Health Care Service Delivery", *Administration and Policy in Mental Health and Mental Health Services Research*, 31 (2), pp 141–170. 2003.

Six, Frederique, and Leo Huberts. "Judging a Public Officials Integrity", in Huberts, L., M. Maesschalck, and C. Jurkiewicz (eds.) *Ethics and Integrity of Governance: Perspectives Across Frontiers*. Cheltenham, UK: Edward Elgar. 2008.

Seibert, P. S., P. Stridh-Igo, and C. G. Zimmerman. "A Checklist to Facilitate Cultural Awareness and Sensitivity", *Journal of Medical Ethics* (28), pp. 143–146. 2002.

Stork, E., S. Scholle, C. Greeno, V. Copeland, and C. Kelleher. "Monitoring and Enforcing Cultural Competence in Medicaid Managed Behavioral Health Care", *Mental Health Service Research*, 3(3), pp. 169–177. 2001

Sue, S. "In Search of Cultural Competence in Psychotherapy and Counseling", *American Psychologist*, 53(4), pp. 440–448. 1998.

Taylor, F. *The Principles of the Scientific Management*. New York. Harper Brothers. 1911.

Teel, K., and J. Obadiah. *Building Racial and Cultural Competence in the Classroom: Strategies From Urban Educators*. New York: Teachers College Press. 2008.

Van Wart, Montgomery *Leadership in Public Agencies: An Introduction*. New York: Taylor and Francis, 2017.

Wallace, Deborah. *The Perception of Cultural Competency in the Context of Cross—Cultural Mentoring Relationships: Mentoring as a Conduit to Teach Cultural Competency Attributes*. Dissertation, University of Akron, November 2018. 2018.

Weber, M. "Politics as Vocation", in H. Gerth and C. W. Mills (trans.) From Max Weber, New York: Oxford University Press. pp. 77–128. 1946.

CHAPTER

11

Citizen Engagement

The modern concept of democratic governance is associated with a set of relationships between the individual and the government. Weber defines a democracy as providing formal rights of equal opportunities. Popularly, democracy is linked to the idea of participation and the "right to vote." Yet to focus only on those concepts is too limiting. As Sheldon Wolin has commented:

> It is a way of constituting power. Democracy is committed to the claim that experience with, and access to, power is essential to the development of the capacities of ordinary persons because power is crucial to human dignity and realization. Power is not merely something to be "shared," but something to be used collaboratively in order to initiate, to invent, to bring about.
> (Wolin, 1987, p. 470)

The focus of this work is on initiating, inventing, and bringing about. Or, to put it more simply—deciding. The question to be explored is how the precepts or underlying assumptions of democracy relate to understanding public organizational decision-making. More specifically, the question to be examined is the nature of the structures or constructs that precede the practice of decision-making implied by democracy.

What is to be examined are not the practices that emerge from democratic government, but rather the more basic elements that inform practice. This is an endeavor somewhat akin to Weber's explorations of the ideal typical bureaucracy. Weber's goal was to achieve understanding of social actions, specifically the rationally developed action of the bureaucracy, although the methodology need not be confined to a study of bureaucracy. For example, Kirkhart (1971) used the methodology to develop and examine a non-hierarchical organization. This method also has been applied to another unique institution, the American-style legislature (Cox and King, 1985).

This chapter explores the first two aspects of Weberian methodology: (1) the control mechanisms used (structures and procedures) and (2) the purposes that are to be achieved (values). According to Weber, the interaction of structures and values creates the actions, or social consequences, that we identify as behavior or practice. Without knowledge of the structures and values, the behaviors and practices cannot be fully understood.

The first goal of this chapter is to examine the concept of democracy as an organizing structure. From there, it will be possible to comment on the problems of people in organizations that were briefly mentioned in the last chapter.

THE STRUCTURAL ELEMENTS IN DEMOCRACY

While it is common to think of democratic governance as a process or a set of actions, it is less common to step back from that process to examine the elements of structure that shape and give that process meaning. Three points are important to reiterate before specifying those structures. First, practice or action is shaped by the structure. Second, the values are related to the structures. While there is no simple one-to-one relationship between the structures and values, there must exist a structural element that supports or promotes all values. Third, the structural elements overlap and reinforce one another.

What then is the structure of democracy? There is no simple answer. One starting point would be to look at some of the concerns that government as an organization must address. Those would include

1. Who is to be involved?
2. How are "problems" to be approached?
3. What is the nature of society?
4. What is the character of decisions?
5. How public are decisions to be?

The democratic values that relate to these questions or concerns are equality, legitimacy, community, liberty, and citizen responsibility. Each of these values and the concerns they reflect relate to another concept: interdependence of people and of institutions.

The task of creating a structure to reflect these concerns is not easy. While Wilson may have been correct that by the 1880s it was already harder to run a constitution than to make one, the obligation to continue "making" the constitution remains. The question of structure is the core of the continuing necessity of making a constitution. After all, is a democratic process possible without a mechanism for ensuring equality, legitimacy, liberty, and responsibility? If organizational or structural independence (of, say, the bureaucracy) is permitted, can democracy based on interdependence exist? The structure is logically prior to the process, and, therefore, making a constitution is part of the act of running a constitution because it is prior to that act. But more importantly, both are continuous. Just as running a constitution is an everyday activity, making a constitution is an everyday event.

A democratic structure reflects the concerns above, both as abstract goals (such as liberty and equality) and as everyday practical realities (participation). The goals are not met fully, but rather the structures and processes become approximations of what can be achieved. The structure provides the context for the processes, which are judged by the standards of the abstract goals. Understanding the relationship of the structures to both the goals and the processes permits an analysis of what manner of democracy has been or can be achieved.

Five elements of structure are suggested here that relate to the values described and address the concerns of constitution making. These are the following:

1. Multiple review of policy
2. A generalist, broad-focus approach or perspective on problem definition
3. Limited, or constrained, time horizons
4. A duty of citizens to participate
5. Consensus decision-making

The next task of this review is to explore the structural aspects of each of these elements. The concern in this chapter is to put these structures into the context of the American governmental system, facilitating the subsequent examination of these elements within the framework of the democracy-efficiency and politic-bureaucracy controversies.

Multiple Reviews

Implicit in the idea of democracy in government is that some level of individuality exists in a society or an organization. People will see problems and, therefore, the solution to those problems differently. That we acknowledge individual differences is more critical than identifying the reasons for those differences. The key is to create a structure that preserves the opportunity to be heard (make others aware that you disagree). Further, the concept of being heard is one that begins at the point of defining problems not with the subsequent process of shaping solutions.

What kinds of structures are likely to promote the "right to be heard"? We need not look further than the original constitution-making efforts of the 1780s for answers. The structure of government is, after all, an attempt to structure participation and the opportunity to be heard. The lesson of this structure is that three elements are critical: (1) a meaningful process of public discussion (including tolerance and a disposition to be persuade), (2) a reliance on consensus building in decision-making, and (3) a recognition of the importance of community (Tinder, 1976). Democracy emerges from a sense of the collective responsibility for the creation of mutually acceptable goals and problems. The government that was intended was one that was organized to give the people the fullest opportunity to participate, directly or indirectly. We may disagree with the balance between direct and indirect participation chosen at the time, but the fundamental reasons for encouraging participation have not changed. Participation is not a mathematical process but a subjective, qualitative relationship between individuals and society. The institutions of government are built presumptively upon the continuing use of consensus. The goal is to define what is best for society, not for any individual or group. The "best for society" does not emerge from a simple vote, rather it emerges from a three-step process of open discussion, agreement on the scope of action, and then agreement on a temporary course of action. The focus is on collective social action, not on the implementation of the top choice among rationally analyzed alternatives.

This open, inquiring society would above all display the "virtue" of tolerance. But what kind of outlook on government is indicated by tolerance?

> The theory of tolerance . . . implies that it is not enough for tolerance to be widespread and enduring merely as an attitude on the part of individuals; it needs the support of institutions and social forms. If people are interdependent, if they are not very rational, and if they are not reliably cooperative, then it is vain to expect many individuals to be tolerant without encouragement from those around them and without support from conditions and structures in the surrounding society. . . .
>
> [In] reflecting on the nature of a tolerant society . . . gives rise to the idea that the viability of tolerance depends on politics. It is suggested that political artifice would be required for resolving conflicts ensuing from tolerance. But a politics of tolerance presumably would be concerned not just with settling immediate conflicts but also with more distant goals—with establishing enduring conditions that are conducive to tolerance and to communication.
>
> (Tinder, p. 150)

A government structured to make decisions through consensus is a government which prizes diversity of ideas and opinions. The deliberative process of the legislature (the government institution the founders understood best) reflects such a structure. The legislature relies on a series of structures by which to delay and obscure the decision process. This system of institutional checks and balances was a conscious design intended to prevent the legislature from acting precipitously. Ideally, this system allows every view to be examined and re-examined from several perspectives and by several distinct groups. Having established a process that obscures the boundaries of ideas to make them more permeable, the definition of mutual interest is made easier. In the blending and merging of ideas, what are otherwise opposite ideas come closer. Mutual interest becomes possible when a blending of several courses of action to a single course upon which all can agree does not violate anyone's norm of behavior. The knowledge seeking and deciding processes of the legislature cannot be understood as a single or continuous activity. They are multiphase processes involving a complex array of organizational elements which frequently take several years to complete. They are processes which are predicated on conflict. Without the clash of ideas and opinions the process shrinks into inactivity.

The structure of this process is founded in the concept of checks and balances. The purpose of this structure is not merely to delay action, although this is one result. Rather, a central purpose is to permit the many views that may exist on a policy issue to be heard and considered. The eighteenth-century advocacy of harmony (Zuckerman, 1970) seems at odds with that of the clash of interests, yet the reverse is true. The harmony sought emerges from frantic and chaotic public discourse. Harmony results from knowing and understanding the views of others, not from suppressing them. The notion of tolerance is necessary for this structure. Without a tolerance of views that may be contrary to one's own, the introduction

238 CHAPTER 11 Citizen Engagement

of additional views would appear to detract from rather than contribute to good decisions. Disagreement is expected but so also is a disposition to accept the possibility of being persuaded by opposing views.

A Generalist Perspective

Implicit in the use of mechanisms to promote consensus is support for the need for generalist rather than particularistic viewpoints. How such a need can be structured is more complex. Most often the structures are those just described—check and balances and open participation. The generalist perspective is presumed to reflect mutual and common interest. The seemingly archaic concept of commonwealth, that government is created to serve the common interest, sounds to many like a campaign slogan. We see government as the battleground of competing interests, not as the vehicle for promoting the common good. The founders sought haven from narrow interests in the search for common interests; that is the starting point for public debate. Like the modern-day advocates of pluralism, the founders were not troubled by narrow or particularistic interests. But what "structures" help convert the multiple particular interests into a common interest? The weakness of democracy may well be in that no such structures exist, except to the extent that politics, as a vehicle for decision-making, is generalist in character. The crux of the threat of bureaucracy to democracy is that it destroys politics and thus the generalist perspective.

Time

Except as we criticize government for its inability to act in a timely manner, we rarely see government, politics, or democracy as related to time. Yet a central tradition of democracy is the impermanence of decisions. The decision made today is based on what is known today. New knowledge or the simple fact of experience in implementing policy can suggest that a new or amended approach is called for.

The impermanence of decisions bears some resemblance to the concept of incrementalism. In both, decisions emerge slowly—caution is the watchword. There are further elements of overlap between the two processes, particularly in their orientation to the present rather than to strategic or long-range concerns. Charles Lindblom (1977) explains the emergence of incrementalism as a decision style in this way:

> Since people cannot intellectually master all their social problems they depend on various devices to simplify problem solving. Among them are trial and error and rules of thumb, as well as routinized and habitual responses to categories of problems. One commonplace strategy for a policy maker is to proceed incrementally and sequentially with close interplay between end and means. In such a strategy, a policy maker is less concerned with "correctly" solving his problem than making an advance. He is also less concerned with a predetermined set of goals than with remedying experienced dissatisfaction with past policy while goals and policies are both reconsidered.

(p. 314)

The sense of impermanence of decisions is likely to reinforce this orientation toward adjustment rather than solution. Nonetheless, the structure of these processes is different because of the different orientation to the problem itself. The process of consensus building is a process oriented first to problem definition and only then to problem resolution. The *obligation* to amend policy emerges from a redefinition of the problem, not simply the weight of the decision process as in incrementalism.

Democracy requires that society's problems be re-thought and re-examined. The process of adjustment implied by incrementalism is focused on the "solution" to problems and, as such, may obscure, or even hinder, the re-evaluation of problems. Put into public administration terms, impermanent decisions are a feature of policy implementation under any form of government.

The structure for impermanence requires that the policy development process dominate the policy implementation process. To be overly simplistic, this implies some variation of the much-discredited conveyor-belt theory of government. This need not be the case. Rather, the activities of government need to be structured to ensure adequate information for both policy development and policy implementation. This matter is explored in more detail in the second part of this chapter.

Responsibility

The idea of duty or responsibility seems somewhat misplaced in a discussion of democracy. Certainly, responsibility in an ethical sense is not directly linked to democracy (French, 1983). Nevertheless, the responsibility or duty to participate is central to democracy, particularly in the modern representative democracy.

While democracy does not require full or complete knowledge to participate, it does require that persons, as citizens or representatives, offer their views. Complete knowledge is not expected as it would be in other systems. Such knowledge would be believed impossible, and it is also believed unnecessary. Participation permits the accumulation of the incomplete knowledge of all participants to yield a common view. Such knowledge is not merely cumulative, it is synergistic (Hummel, 1986).

To deny participation is to threaten the entire decision-making scheme. It is for this reason that participation is not merely a "right" to be exercised at will, but rather a duty that undergirds the entire mechanism. The concern of the founders for "faction" can be viewed in this light. A faction is not simply a political party (though it is possible that an ideological party would be a faction) but any group that is so arrogant about its views and beliefs that it no longer needs to listen. A faction that even temporarily gains "majority" status threatens the very core of government because the mandate to "listen" and to be willing to be persuaded disappears. Not only would the government be held captive by views that could not be altered by subsequent experience but also the public would be the victim of "bad" policy because it was the product of less than complete knowledge.

Consensus

The popular concept of consensus decision-making is a process that presumes unanimity or near unanimity of decision. While there is an element of consensus decision-making that implies unanimous support, this definition is deceiving because it focuses on the wrong end of the process. Consensus decisions are not to be understood as the resultant of a vote. Rather, consensus decisions are a process for defining problems, the parameters of the decision, and only then possible solutions. The structure of consensus is in facilitating the act of defining and delimiting a problem rather than in the act of voting. The very finality of voting makes it suspect as part of the consensus process. The opportunity to learn and gain knowledge is what is implied by consensus building. Further, the consensus process suggests a joining or coming together. Voting, in contrast, is the ultimate in individual acts—there is no interaction, only a data point.

Knowledge in consensus structures flows from the bottom up, or more accurately, from each person to all others. In consensus operations the emphasis is not on control but on the debatability and the validity of the knowledge generated. The type of knowledge achieved in consensus formation is not simply additive, it is synergetic; it is more than the sum of its parts. The consensus process recognizes that many heads are better than one, not simply because there are more sources of knowledge and more perspectives on reality but because qualitatively *superior* problem definition can arise from such a structure. All parties gain from relationships in which assessment of the situation and the process of working out solutions are shared by all.

THE VALUES OF DEMOCRACY

The purposes that are to be achieved by democratic governance are the second element for understanding the actions and behaviors we associate with democracy. The key to understanding this second feature of the Weberian methodology is that for Weber the purposes or values of an organization become the criteria by which to evaluate the effectiveness of that organization. The evaluation process is one of comparing the values or purposes to be achieved to the actual purposes or values elicited in practice. Thus, it is a relative evaluation. The question is not whether this a democracy, but rather how much of a democracy this is. A final point is that this methodology is intended to yield archetypes—forms in the extreme. Thus, no type is ever pure or exact. The concern is in how close to any value "practice" can match "theory"; it is not ever a question of practice and theory overlapping completely.

To restate, the values of democratic government are as follows:

1. Equality
2. Legitimacy
3. Community
4. Liberty
5. Citizen responsibility

The question is how do these elements contribute to effectiveness? While it is beyond the scope of this chapter to explore this issue in much detail, much of the political theory literature of the last four hundred years, and to some extent since the emergence of classical Greek thought some 2,500 years ago, has been devoted to aspects of this question. This chapter is confined to affirming the linkages between the structures described above and these values.

Equality

Equality of opportunity and equality of treatment before the law are classic precepts. But why equality? After all, as John Adams noted in 1787, even in society with no classes to distinguish people, there exist the very obvious differences of wealth, skill, and competence. Stated simply, equality is the recognition that an individual's role in politics is presumed to be *unrelated* to economic status. The contribution to be made by the individual is that of perspective—one that is necessarily unique. It is precisely the differences and, therefore, the inequalities among persons that define an individual's contribution. If a society could exist in which equality were a physical and intellectual reality, then the artificial construct of legal equality would be unnecessary; but then the decision model based on consensus and discussion also would be unnecessary. In a perfectly homogeneous society, democracy would be meaningless—possibly even impossible.

Thus, we have the paradox that equality must be more "valued," and it may be more critical as the society becomes more unequal. The "heterogeneous" society needs democratic processes.

Legitimacy

It might be asked, "How is legitimacy a special concern of democracy?" In truth, it does not need to be a special concern, but most forms of government must establish a legitimacy in the mind of the public. The "effectiveness" question that might be asked is whether democracies may not be especially sensitive to questions of legitimacy. It is not the purpose of this chapter to address this very complex question. It is enough to ask this: How long can a form of government retain its legitimacy if it must rely on methods contrary to that form to maintain its legitimacy?

Community

The most complex relationship between a value and its antecedent construct is between the "ideal" of community and democracy. It is often presumed that community is not simply a value of democracy, but a necessary precondition for its very existence. Glenn Tinder's very thoughtful and provocative exploration of the concept of community at once suggests this link, and then, in denying the possibility of community, cuts that linkage (Tinder, 1980).

Yet we should not be too quick to reject the moral and ethical aspects of community. The moral force of democracy emerges from the concept of community (or Tinder's alternative "civility"). A government that cannot hope, that cannot respond to human need, is an uncivil government. And as Tinder points out, validation for an activity is not in successfully achieving a stated goal, but in the attempt (even where that attempt is futile). The common interest of consensus rests in just such "hopeless" projects.

The root of the complaint by rational economists about democratic government is its unforgivable tendency to overspend on "wasteful" social programs. To the extent that a link exists between community and democracy that endeavor should be less surprising but also more justifiable.

Liberty

No concept or value has undergone so radical a change during the last three centuries as has the ideal of liberty. This concept is at once a cornerstone of the dignity of the individual and the *raison d'être* for government regulation. The shift of "liberty from" to "liberty to" government in the latter part of the nineteenth century is a well-documented phenomenon.

There is a more fundamental aspect of liberty that undergirds democracy—freedom. Popularly we think in terms of four freedoms—speech, press, religion, and assembly. The fifth freedom of the Bill of Rights may represent the most important liberty: That liberty is the right to petition grievances. No freedom is more evocative of democratic government than the liberty to present public policy problems and proposals to the government. It is this last freedom that energizes and gives meaning to the other freedoms. The core value expressed is to reinforce not only the right to say what you think about political issues but also to be heard. There is no real dignity in a freedom of expression unless that freedom includes the responsibility of the government to listen.

Citizen Responsibility

It has been relatively rare since the time of the founding of the nation for political writers to talk of duty rather than rights. The idea that citizenship carries a responsibility to act seems quite foreign. Yet what could be more basic to democratic governance? This is most obvious in direct democracy where duty is assumed by practices such as appointment to office by lot. But a representative democracy is founded on the premise of citizen responsibility no less than in a direct democracy.

The focus on rights rather than responsibility poses a serious problem. This is a problem that extends beyond the issues of consensus and participation (although, as noted, to do so threatens the integrity and viability of decisions). The core concern is for the legitimacy of a regime in which citizen responsibility is denied (by government, or by the citizenry). The "effectiveness" of a democracy that cannot convince its citizens of their responsibilities is questionable. This is also true for the regime that denies the need for a responsible citizenry by taking policy influence and control out of their hands. It is not enough to evoke public opinion—citizens cannot be passive participants in decision-making.

The Structure of Democracy

Democracy like any "form" of government has an underlying structure that "shapes" the processes that emerge from that structure. The structure can also be thought of as the internal logic of democracy. Democracy is more than the sum of the processes that it invokes. The meaning of democracy is in its structure and the implications of that structure. By exploring that structure, we have a new way of looking at modern representative democracies. But also, we have a methodology for contrasting that structure with the way decisions are made in modern governments.

ENGAGING CITIZENS

This is a somewhat long way around to the central citizen engagement. Much like other aspects of the management toolkit, engaging citizens requires a mutual trust between citizens and those working for government. Public services must be both credible and effective. Citizen involvement in those decisions is at the core of representative democracy.

As suggested above, citizen input into the management of a public agency is somewhat problematic. Most civil servants have problems with the expectation of citizen participation in the policy and rulemaking roles of an agency. When the expectation is another level deeper—at the level of professional decision-making—there is even more pushback. Yet this is the expectation there is to be meaningful engagement. This is an important aspect of any public manager's toolkit precisely because it is difficult and goes against the very notion of professionalism. Yet those who object are clinging to outdated understandings of what it means to be a professional. Any manager who has thought to seek a second opinion about a doctor's diagnosis or has requested a meeting to seek answers to questions from a medical professional, or for that matter has written a letter to a legislator is doing exactly what is expected. Due diligence is not merely for the professional, but it is also for the person who is placing themselves into the care of another.

People have a right to ask questions (and, yes, we tell students to ask questions and encourage them by saying that there is no such thing as a stupid question). Understanding the question can be the difficult part for those in government. If we go back to Karl Weick's double interact of communications, we will realize that public questions often come because we didn't explain ourselves in such a way that the listener understands. No one is fully informed unless they have the opportunity to ask questions. The request for more information is not a challenge to the competence of the professionals in the agency, but it does suggest that the communication double loop is not yet complete.

If we remember that people outside the agency may well think differently (that does not mean incorrectly) about issues, therefore their understanding of the situation is different. Addressing that difference is the goal of the engagement. In an era when people are increasingly cynical and suspicious about the motivations of both politicians and bureaucrats, such questioning can easily be seen as pointless, but it is precisely why it must occur.

At two times in my public service career, ombudsman or citizen service activities were a part of my responsibility. In reflecting on that experience two things come to mind. First is that most of the time the decision of the public servant that was the source of the complaint was proven to have made the correct decision. But more importantly, in almost all cases, the person asking the question (even if a negative result) accepted the outcome of that re-examination of the issue. Further in those cases where no pathway to fixing a problem existed, the person seeking help was grateful that anyone would help. Again, the outcome was not the issue, it was that someone tried to help.

Citizen engagement is time-consuming. It takes patience. But once we get over the hang-up that our competence is being challenged and accept the responsibility

244 | **CHAPTER 11** Citizen Engagement

for a "failure to communicate," then the conflict that is inherent in the process somewhat dissipates.

To summarize:

- Be patient
- The communication loop is still open
- It comes with the territory of a democracy

DISCUSSION QUESTIONS

- Why is an engaged citizenry important?
- What is the difference between merely having a voice and having someone listen?
- What are some of the barrier to successful public interaction between the citizens and the government?
- What are the most important values that support democratic governance?
- Often government agencies focus on efforts to invite a range of people to attend meetings. However, this discussion suggests that focusing on the invitation is wrong. Why?

BIBLIOGRAPHY

Cox III, Raymond W. "American Political Theory and the Bureaucracy", *Dialogue*, 9 (2). Winter 1986–1987.

Cox III, Raymond W. "Going to War: A Commentary on Ethical Leadership and Politics", *Public Integrity*, 6 (4), pp. 319–331. Fall 2004.

Cox III, Raymond W., and Michael King. "American State Legislature: Models of Organization and Reform", Paper Presented at the Midwest Political Science Association. April 1985.

French, Peter. *Ethics in Government*. Englewood Cliffs, NJ: Prentice Hall. 1983.

Gruber, Judith E. *Controlling Bureaucracies*. Berkeley, CA: University of California Press. 1987.

Hummel, Ralph P. "Bureaucracy, Democracy, and Politics: Are They Compatible?" unpublished paper. 1986.

Kirkhart, Larry. "Toward a Theory of Public Administration", in Frank Marini (ed.) *Toward a New Public Administration*. Scranton, PA: Chandler. 1971.

Lindblom, Charles. *Politics and Markets*. New York: Basic Books, Inc. 1977.

Ruchelman, Leonard I. *A Workbook in Program Design for Public Manager*. Albany: State University of New York Press. 1985.

Tinder, Glenn. *Tolerance*. Amherst, MA: University of Massachusetts Press. 1976.

Tinder, Glenn. *Community: Reflections on a Tragic Ideal*. Baton Rouge: Louisiana State University Press. 1980.

Wolin, Sheldon. "Democracy and the Welfare State", *Political Theory*, 15 (4), p. 470. November 1987.

Yates, Douglas. *Bureaucratic Democracy*. Cambridge, MA: Harvard University Press. 1981.

Zuckerman, Michael. *Peaceable Kingdoms*. New York: W. W. Norton and Company. 1970.

CHAPTER
12

Strategic Management

For the better part of four decades, local, state, and federal government agencies have used strategic management for the planning and implementation of programs and policies. For the advocates of this technique, strategic management is regarded as the most effective tool for shaping, defining, and implementing change in the public sector. As this book was being written, it was unclear whether this chapter belonged in the support systems part or in the management toolkit part. Strategic thinking is imbedded in management and therefore is a perspective that fits the definition of a toolkit. On the other hand, even in relatively small government, a strategic assessment and strategic initiative begins with bringing a consultant into the organization. As such the details of the process and principles of strategic management can be left here.

Strategic management is composed of two core activities:

1. A systematic analysis of pivotal long-term trends and issues
2. A comprehensive analysis of the institution's capacity to respond to those trends

These two activities define the scope of strategic management; also, these activities reflect the central assumption of strategic management, which is that the future can to some degree be shaped to the benefit and advantage of the organization.

Strategic management implies the desire to consciously direct future events. In the context of the public sector, then, strategic management reflects the ambition to shape and guide governmental decision-making for the purpose of meeting the broad mandates of government.

To understand strategic management fully, it is necessary not only to outline the process but also to understand how the nature of the public sector shapes that process. Toward those ends, Chapter 12 focuses first on the public managerial environment that can inhibit the full exercise of this process, followed by a discussion of the advantages and disadvantages of public-sector strategic management. Following those analyses, a fuller description of the process is presented.

245

THE PUBLIC MANAGEMENT ENVIRONMENT

It is helpful in understanding strategic management practice to identify the characteristics of the public sector that make decision-making and, therefore, management particularly difficult and contentious. Susan Walter and Pat Choate (1983) who have written extensively on public-sector strategic management, suggest a number of factors that affect the ability to think, plan, and manage strategically. Those factors are the following:

1. Pressures created by the need of elected officials to perpetually campaign
2. Transient leadership in key appointed positions
3. Pressure from special interest groups to respond to the needs they articulate
4. The decline of political parties, which makes organizing for decisions more difficult
5. Intergovernmental responsibilities that require all levels of government to participate in service delivery
6. The "shared power," particularly between the executive and legislative branches
7. Media demands for action
8. The need to be sensitive to what may be a highly volatile public opinion

The sum of these pressures and counter-pressures is that public managers invariably focus on the near term. To think strategically, or in the long term, is regarded as a luxury. This lack of facility to think strategically has a number of consequences:

1. Fragmented and disorderly management practices permit no overall review of public needs and no overall specification of the roles of respective levels of government
2. In the absence of clearly documented needs and well-articulated priorities, pork-barrel politics often dominate public actions and public expenditures
3. The short-term payoff is invariably favored over long-term goals
4. Without coherent strategies that set investment needs and ways to meet them, specific public investment plans cannot be systematically formulated
5. Disordered management practices at one level of government are easily transferred to other levels
6. Disordered management practices in government limit, even inhibit, effective joint public-private-sector actions.

Even where strategic management is attempted, these pressures may severely limit the scope and quality of the strategic management effort. The result is a deficient process that invariably fails to yield the expected results from the effort. Those deficiencies often include the following:

1. Scant attention given to identifying and assessing the consequences of longer-term trends and events
2. Absence of clear goals
3. Poor or nonexistent strategic planning processes

4. Limited linkages between plans and actions
5. Absence of evaluation and feedback mechanisms

While Walter and Choate were speaking specifically about state government, their observations apply equally to other levels of government. In fact, the authors suggest that few organizations are successful in undertaking strategic management efforts.

The imagery of the organization suggested by Walter and Choate's analysis is that of an organization that *reacts* to events. There is no concerted effort to direct or guide the future because there is no clear understanding of the "place" of the organization in the present. The difficulty can be summed up with the question, "How can you change the future if you do not understand the present?"

ADVANTAGES AND DISADVANTAGES OF STRATEGIC MANAGEMENT

While clearly, many benefits would accrue to organizations undertaking a strategic management endeavor, we would like to clarify that we do not necessarily advocate strategic management implementation throughout government. There may be a number of obstacles to clear away before a strategic management effort could proceed in any particular agency. First and foremost, strategic management initiatives are time-consuming enterprises; these are not measures that can be put in place overnight. Planning and organizing alone may take weeks or even months. For many government agencies, particularly those closely linked to the political or policy processes, the time needed to get such a program off the ground may not be available (or, more importantly, participants may think it is not available).

Whether time is a "real" problem or only a perceptual barrier, it remains but one of the disadvantages to strategic management. A second, though closely related, disadvantage is that the public's demand for performance forces public managers to pay attention to the present rather than the future. Strategic management initiatives require managers to actively engage the future, even when that future is still relatively uncertain. The strength of the hierarchical model of organization is in controlling and reacting to the present. Despite the imagery of incompetent and ineffective bureaucracies, the truth is that many government agencies operate very well; in other words, they are successful in controlling and reacting to the present. Under such circumstances, an agency that is successfully reacting to its environment may regard efforts to look to the future as unnecessary and inappropriate. Techniques that help resolve (or seem to help resolve) the everyday problems of management would be attractive to managers in such circumstances. But to redirect agency energies toward the uncertain and unpredictable future would not make much sense.

For the manager who is unsuccessful in handling day-to-day affairs, strategic management similarly makes little sense. To quote the colloquialism frequently used by those in the federal government: "When you are hip deep in alligators, it is hard to remember that your main objective was to drain the swamp." Draining the swamp may be a good idea but dealing with the alligators is more critical. To many managers, strategic management sounds like a lecture on how to drain the swamp.

Whether they are successful or unsuccessful in current endeavors, to many managers, strategic management practices focus on secondarily important issues. At best, then, strategic management becomes an amusing technique to "play around with" if one has the slack resources and time to do so.

A third disadvantage of strategic management is that it invariably requires the cooperation and support of many individuals and possibly even many organizations. Such broad-based change is enormously difficult. Under the best of circumstances, the more persons who become involved, the more likely it is that implementation will not go as intended. Or as Murphy's Law notes, "If anything can go wrong, it will." Strategic management is a process premised on Murphy's Law being wrong (or more accurately, strategic management is a process premised on finding and correcting all those large and small problems as they happen). Put simply, strategic management is never an easy endeavor. Its purpose is to sort through and confront complex and seemingly intractable problems. Such efforts will not always succeed, because the complexity of the strategy for resolving such problems matches the complexity of the problems. Strategic management implies risk—the risk of failure, the risk of only partial success.

Given the difficult managerial environment facing public managers and the potential disadvantages of strategic management, it should not be surprising that it is not yet a broadly used management technique. Yet, as the work of Bryson (2004), Eadie (1983), and others have indicated, there has been strong interest since the late 1970s in the application of this technique to public management activities. The demands upon government continue to mount; and as they do, public officials are expected to respond. Traditional approaches are no longer adequate. Managers are expected to take risks to meet those demands (although the public is not forgiving of failure). The choice is seemingly simple; continue to follow long-standing practice and lose what is left of public confidence, or try new courses, even if failure in that effort may cost the manager's job. McClendon and Quay (1983) were speaking specifically to city planners, but their observations could apply to most public agencies.

Our research has revealed that successful planning agencies have, in fact, kept on moving and have been able to earn respect and influence by developing new entrepreneurial skills and practices in response to the needs of their clients. Conventional conservative wisdom holds that it is safer to stay with the tried and true, but these agencies have prospered by reviewing their basic premises, jettisoning outmoded programs, products, and services, and developing innovative, flexible, dynamic, and experimental risk-taking approaches to city planning. Functioning in an increasingly unstable, accelerative, and even revolutionary local government environment, these successful planning agencies are more than mere survivors; they are overachievers who have taken control of their destinies. Their successes have been founded on the development of aggressive management strategies and tactics and a commitment to excellence. They are truly masters of change.

One way to challenge old assumptions, to take risks, is to introduce strategic management into the decision process. Once strategic management has been incorporated into the basic management scheme of the organization, a number of advantages become apparent. Walter and Choate suggest nine such advantages.

1. Is indispensable to top management's effectively discharging basic responsibilities
2. Encourages and permits the manager to see, evaluate, and accept or discard more alternative courses of action
3. Reveals and clarifies future opportunities and threats
4. Provides an overall framework for decision-making—preventing piecemeal decisions
5. Provides a basis for other management functions, such as effective use of resources
6. Means communicating objectives, strategies, and detailed operating plans
7. Helps manager master change
8. Develops attitudes, perspectives, ways of thinking, decision-making habits, and a planning philosophy that will produce better decisions
9. Provides a basis for measuring qualitative performance—creativity, innovation, imagination, motivation, and knowledge can be assessed

(p. 51)

We want to review a few specific aspects of these advantages in more detail because they will reappear as we look at the steps in the strategic management process. Those elements are clarification of future *events*, emphasis on overall rather than piecemeal decision-making, and creation of a detailed implementation program. In addition, the first element above requires more detailed analysis because it is the most fundamental point of all—strategic management is the basis for any good management endeavor.

The Future

If a manager is to get beyond day-to-day problems, then some sense of what the future holds is critical. Strategic management is not about *predicting* the future; instead, it is about understanding the trends and future directions of events to take advantage of positive trends and avoid the worst aspects of negative trends. Strategic management involves anticipating the future and then directing events and activities so that the anticipated future does not happen. Another way to think about the future is to note the difference between the future you desire and the future based on what we expect to happen. Strategic management is a conscious effort to ensure that the future looks more like the one we desire as opposed to the one we expect. Again, the basic means for guiding the future is to promote positive trends and to ameliorate negative trends.

Broad Decision-Making

A second key element in understanding the advantages of strategic management is the emphasis on broad decision-making. Without the broad overview implicit in strategic management, decisions tend to be made in a piecemeal fashion. The problem is not in any individual decision but each individual decision may be made without regard to all other decisions. As advocates of strategic management note, few problems of modern government are that distinct and individual, whether they are the result of the link in the finite resources of the budget or because program decisions in one agency frequently require action by another agency. In either case, by stepping back from the level of piecemeal decisions, the full impact of such decisions can be seen. Anticipating the impact of individual decisions upon the ability to act in future circumstances is a critical aspect of strategic management.

Detailed Implementation

What separates strategic management from strategic planning is the intent to act. The elaborate process of analysis and planning is directed toward facilitating the implementation of whatever strategy is devised. Strategic management efforts are not judged by the elegance of its trend analysis or by the skill and precision employed in crafting a plan. Proof of success is in the accomplishment of the plan, not in its creation. When an agency pays scant attention to the implementation of a strategic management plan, it is, quite possibly, dooming the plan to failure. In insisting upon the inclusion of the implementation step in the process, strategic management becomes more than a way to think about the future—it becomes a way to act upon the future. The bias for action, the desire to master change is the product of this last phase of the process.

Strategic management's advantages and disadvantages suggest that it is a process which could potentially yield significant results for those managers who wish to apply it to process. It is not a foolproof system; on the other hand, it is an approach that can work if adequate time, energy, and resources are directed into it.

THE STRATEGIC MANAGEMENT PROCESS

The next step in the examination of strategic management is to look at the steps taken to complete the process. In the presentation that follows, the works of several researchers and consultants, including the authors of this book, are merged, producing a composite picture of strategic management practice. The type of organization, the specific policy or program involved, and the organization's prior experience with strategic management dictate how many of the steps need to be followed. The steps described here are most appropriate to an organization with little or no prior experience with strategic management and with broad operational concerns (rather than policy-specific concerns).

The basic framework for strategic management involves a nine-step process. Those steps are as follows:

1. Creating a *vision* for the organization
2. Outlining the missions and legal *mandates that* define the organization
3. Examining the factors that are *external to* the organization but which influence its performance

4. Examining the factors that are *internal to* the organization and that influence its performance
5. Examining the *trends* and potential futures of the organization
6. Setting *goals* for improving organizational performance over a specified period
7. Designing a strategic *plan* for reaching the goals set
8. *Implementing* and/or operationalizing the strategic plan
9. *Evaluating both* ongoing activities and the final outcome

VISION

The initiation of a successful strategic management effort begins with breaking out of the constraints of present circumstances. The essential point is to create a different future than the one anticipated. One useful technique for understanding and defining that future is to create a vision of the organization if it were performing at an optimal level. In some ways this is not unlike Max Weber's methodology in defining the "ideal typical" organization. Weber wished to critique the consequences of the structures and processes he defined. In this case, the vision of the ideal typical organization has the purpose of defining the limits of organizational achievement. The ideal organization envisioned is one that may be beyond our capability to achieve. Every "real" organization is a pale imitator of the ideal. That vision represents something to strive for, something by which to judge performance. McClendon and Quay (1983) describe vision in this way:

Vision is a mental journey from the known to the unknown, creating the future from a montage of current facts, hopes, dreams, dangers, and opportunities. True visionary leaders tend to see opportunities before they see threats. According to the research of Hickman and Silva, the visionary leader also:

- Searches for ideas, concepts, and ways of thinking until clear vision crystallizes
- Persuades employees to embrace the vision by setting an example of hard work
- Acts in a supportive, expressive way that says, "We are all in this together"
- Relates the vision to the cares and concerns of individuals
- Concentrates on those strengths within the organization that will ensure the success of the vision
- Remains at the center of the vision, as its prime shaper
- Looks for ways to develop further the corporate vision by taking note of changes inside and outside the organization
- Measures the success of the organization in terms of its ability to fulfill the vision
- Articulates the vision into an easy-to-grasp philosophy that integrates strategic direction and cultural values

(pp. 195–196)

The organizational vision becomes the starting point for strategic management. It provides the "direction" and "values" that bring people together. Thus, the vision has a two-fold purpose: It requires people to think beyond the known, and it provides a context for judging the future success of the organization.

Both of these purposes are of particular use in the development of the strategic management process, and, also, it helps get at the "everything is fine with the way we do things now" thinking that besets some organizations. It is the first step in breaking out of the psychological bonds some personnel feel in rapidly changing situations. Rather than perceiving themselves as victims of change, they take the first step toward thinking about change as an opportunity for improving their performance.

The objection to the idea of vision is that it seems so unrealistic. After all, the ideal organization does not exist. This objection misses a larger point. The vision created defines what the organization must strive toward. It gives those in the organization a point of reference by which to understand how to improve performance. In any particular strategic management effort, the goal is not to achieve the vision, because that is not possible. Rather, the goal is to reach certain levels of performance and service that more closely relate to the ideal and, therefore, presumably represent change from current performance.

Mandate

The context within which public organizations operate is critical to understanding what that organization can achieve. Operative mandates come in several forms; some may be the product of enabling legislation; many derive from internally defined mission statements. It must be presumed that neither the legal mandates nor the mission statements are so fixed that they cannot be altered, expanded, or changed. Nevertheless, if the strategic management process is to be grounded in practical realities of current roles and responsibilities, it is necessary to articulate those mandates and missions. It should be added that even the vision statement already prepared is grounded in the mission and mandate to the extent that those documents define the structure and general role of the organization. The vision of the ideal organization cannot escape these same constraints.

Two points need to be made when thinking about mandates and missions. First is that it is not unusual for very few persons within an organization to have a full knowledge of the legal constraints and responsibilities of the organization. Mandates are most frequently cast as statements of permitted activities and prohibited activities. As Bryson (1989, 2004) has noted, administrators in organizations often exaggerate the prohibitions and also take the statements of permitted activities as inclusive. In either instance, the range of programmatic and policy alternatives and operational activities are unnecessarily constrained. The simple process of reviewing and articulating mandates may free the organization to act differently.

The second point is that a key ingredient in understanding the mandate and mission of an organization is to define the "stakeholders." According to Bryson, a stakeholder "is any group or individual who is affected by or who can affect the future" of the organization and, thus, "place a claim on the organization's attention, resources, or output, or is affected by that output" (Bryson, 1989, pp. 33, 51). The stakeholders exercise considerable control over the organization because it is their presence that gives life to the organization. In defining the mission of an organization, it is necessary to define who the stakeholders are and what their relationship is to the work of the organization.

External Analysis

One assumption of strategic management is that facets both internal and external to the organization can affect performance (see Chart 12–1). The external analysis is particularly critical because it is the aspect most likely to be forgotten. The external analysis provides vital information with regard to present and future economic, political, technological, and social factors that will affect the organization. In assessing the influence of external factors, one is also defining the opportunities for improvement and threats to continued effectiveness that may face the organization in the future. For this reason, the internal and external analysis are often referred to as a SWOT Analysis (internal factors can be restated as the Strengths and Weaknesses of the organization; external factors can be restated as Opportunities and Threats, thus *SWOT*).

The three most critical factors involved in an external analysis involve economic circumstances, political circumstances, and assumptions about the influence of technological change on the organization. The economic assessment must address the overall economic forecast for the planning period and the likely funding stream that will be available to the organization through the budget or other sources. The interaction between revenues and economic growth is obvious, but funding is not a phenomenon tied exclusively to economic performance. Budget levels, and particularly the allocations within the budget, are primarily political not

---

CHART 12–1

Variables in External and Internal Analysis

External Analysis

> Economic Assessment Likely Funding Stream
> Future of Overall Economy
> Political Assessment
> Public Opinion
> Intergovernmental Cooperation
> Changes in Mandate
> Political Support (character, depth) Political Pitfalls
> Technology Assessment
> New Technology May Mean New Operations Obsolescence

Internal Analysis

> Organizational Assessment People (Values, Capabilities) Money (Now, Not in Future)
> Technology
> Information
> Political Assessment
> Legal Mandates
> Support Within Agency Discretion to Institute Change

economic decisions. Thus, the second critical factor in an external analysis is the political circumstances that will confront the organization. Elsewhere in this book, but most particularly in Chapter 4 on budgeting, the political character of the budget process was examined. It was noted that the past performance of an agency, perceptions of popular support, or the technical character of the organization's mission all play a role in the level of budgetary support achieved by an agency. But it must also be remembered that the broad incremental and decremental changes that occur at the department level mask more significant changes at the lower levels of the organization. Slow, modest growth at the department level obscures the reality of the abolition of some programs and the creation of other new programs within that department. The vagaries of the budget must be understood at the level of the strategic management analysis if it is to be of use.

A political assessment must be more than a budget review, though much useful information about public opinion, political support, and potential political pitfalls can emerge from that analysis. Two additional factors must be considered. First is the potential for changes in mandates or, as is more likely, a reordering of the relative emphasis on different mandates. A good example is the role and mission of the US Coast Guard. In the pre-Vietnam 1960s, serious consideration was given to the abolition of the agency. One tangible change was the removal of the Coast Guard from its traditional home in the Department of the Treasury and its transfer to the US Department of Transportation where its harbor police and harbor safety roles seemed to fit better. Beginning in the mid-1970s, the nearly forgotten Coast Guard found itself thrust into the midst of two of the biggest political issues of the day— water pollution and drugs. For many years the Coast Guard had been responsible for preventing the importation of illegal drugs by sea. Seemingly overnight, this agency, with its tiny fleet of ships and relatively little in the way of weapons, was being asked to stop multimillionaire drug lords with access to fast ships and planes and sophisticated weaponry much of which the Coast Guard had virtually never seen. If this were not enough, responsibility for the cleanup of hazardous waste sites that threatened navigable rivers was left to the Coast Guard, not the Environmental Protection Agency. The personnel of the Coast Guard not only found themselves fighting drug importers on the oceans but also found themselves in Kentucky hundreds of miles from any coast trying to stop the contamination of waterways by the illegal dumping of thousands of oil drums of hazardous and toxic chemicals! It was many years before the funding of the Coast Guard caught up with these newly elevated mandates. Needless to say, there is little discussion of the abolition of this agency any longer.

The final point in political analysis concerns the level of intergovernmental cooperation required to fulfill a mandate. Few government programs are the exclusive province of a single level of government. That simple reality means that coordination and cooperation among levels of government are necessary for a program to succeed.

The third element of external analysis concerns an assessment of the impact of technological change on the work of the organization. New technologies may mean new operations but also may change the timing of program efforts. For example, at one time the US Social Security Administration was a large labor-intensive agency, employing thousands to prepare, verify, and deliver many millions of benefit checks each month. The last three decades have seen a radical reduction in the number of employees; but now, aided by the computer, the agency prepares record numbers of benefit checks in less time. This is not merely a tale of the impact of computers on employment. It must be remembered that the skills and knowledge of the people who work in today's Social Security Administration are quite different than they were two or three decades ago.

Internal Analysis

The companion to the external analysis is the look inside the agency. Two factors must be examined in order to conduct a meaningful internal analysis: an organizational assessment and a political assessment. The internal assessment of the organization is a snapshot of the organization as it is today in terms of people, financial resources, technological capability, and information sources. In one sense this is a restatement of the qualities of the organization that supplements the analysis of mission and mandates. For most organizations the assessment of its people and its finances are the most important, precisely because it is these factors that define the organization qualitatively, as well as quantitatively. To stop this analysis after a quantitative assessment is complete, however, is to threaten the entire process. Simply knowing the sheer numbers of employees may not be enough when the key issues may become the skills they bring to the job or intangibles such as morale. Similarly, knowing the absolute size of the budget may be less important than knowing how flexibly that money can be spent. This type of analysis can be very painful. To know that thousands of loyal and competent employees are about to become redundant because of changes in technology (as with the computerization at the Social Security Administration) is never easy, but sometimes it is a reality that must be confronted. To know that the workforce is already overworked and showing signs of burnout is critical, if the ultimate goal of the strategic plan is massive (and, therefore, stressful) change. This qualitative look at the resources of the organization is the first indicator of the ability of the organization to succeed with the strategic change effort.

No less important is to look at the internal politics of the organization. Such a review begins with a re-examination of the legal mandates placed on the organization. This analysis is more overtly political than the missions and mandates analysis in that the purpose is, again, qualitative rather than quantitative. It is the extent to which a legal mandate is reflected in the day-to-day work of the organization that is important. With which mandates do employees most closely identify? Which work efforts reflect which mandates? It is important to know, for example, that the legal mandate that represents the core of future change is one that currently has a low priority among employees. Support for this change is likely to be very difficult; precisely because it implies a diminished emphasis on what is perceived to be more important by the employees. These political considerations become the foundation for understanding how complex and time-consuming the process of change will be.

Trend Analysis

One of strategic management's central assumptions is that in changing future activities, future outcomes will be different and that the future is composed of both good and bad outcomes. But to know this implies some knowledge of what the future may hold. The point is not to define an exact future. Trend analysis is not the prediction of the future. Rather, it is an activity whereby different assumptions about the future are constructed to define a possible future outcome. This process of scenario building is derived from extrapolating what we know today into the future. The scenarios thus created do not have to constitute an accurate prediction of the future for the simple reason that the purpose of the strategic management exercise is to create a different future. In one sense, it is not important if the scenario is very likely because it is simply serving as a guidepost as to what to pursue and what to avoid. What is most useful about a scenario is the process of building *back* from that scenario to see the kinds of events that must occur to get us from today to the future defined in it. The importance of a scenario is as much in recognizing the interim activities that must occur for it to happen as it is in the implications of the outcome itself.

Why do we care about the possible interim activities that are part of some future scenario? The key here is to remember that any future is composed of both good and bad outcomes. The ultimate purpose of the process is to increase the likelihood of good outcomes emerging and to diminish the occurrence of bad outcomes. The interim activities serve as indicators that specific outcomes are more likely. Thus, in building back from a scenario, we are identifying interim activities to pursue or avoid.

To recapitulate, the idea of trend analysis is not the prediction of the future. The primary benefit of such analysis is in the identification of interim activities that will be of concern in the implementation of the strategic plan.

Set Goals

Each of the steps in the process of strategic management to this point has focused on creating a comprehensive understanding of the organization. It is only now that a set of goals for changing the direction and quality of performance of the organization can be defined. Two points about these goals are important to note here. First is that the goals are set to be achieved over a specific period of time (logically, the same time frame used in scenario building). Second is that the goals must be derivative of the vision statement. The goals to be set move the organization closer to the vision in realistic ways because they are grounded in the comprehensive definition of the organization that has been the implicit purpose of the previous steps in the process.

It is rather easy to overlook this step in the process, not because goal-setting is not accepted as important but because there is a tendency to do it before the other steps in the process are complete. For many, goal-setting should represent the first step in the process. There does appear to be some logic to this argument. But a closer examination of the decision-making process indicates that goal-setting (where are we going?) is first only if a number of other steps are taken for granted, or at least taken as givens. Is not the ability to set a goal prefaced by the implicit analysis that the goal will be of benefit and further that there is some chance of achieving the goal? The steps prior to the goal-setting step are attempts to make explicit what otherwise would be implicit or unconscious steps.

A final point about strategic goal-setting is that the goals should define the benefits to be gained from the introduction of change in addition to a simple statement of desired outcomes. In defining the benefits of change, it permits a focus on the most important goals for the organization. This implicit prioritization permits the organization to concentrate on that which is important. Conversely, the definition of important goals reinforces the dire consequence of failure. The strategic process becomes quite "real" at this point.

A [further] consequence of the realization that strategic planning may be all too real in its consequences is that key decision makers may wish to terminate the effort at this point. They may be afraid of addressing the conflict embodied in the strategic issues. They may not wish to undergo the changes needed to resolve the issues. A crisis of trust or a test of courage may occur, and lead to a turning point in the organization's character. If at the completion of this step, the organization's key decision makers decide to push on, a final very important benefit therefore will have been gained: the organization's character will be strengthened. *Just* as an individual's character is formed in part by the way the individual faces serious difficulties, so too is organizational character formed by the way the organization faces difficulties. Strong characters emerge only from confronting serious difficulties squarely and courageously.

Strategic Plan

Having established a set of goals to be achieved, it is now necessary to arrange and order the activities and tasks that will be necessary to carry out the goals. The planning process must cover the full range of activities from defining and acquiring the necessary resources to establishing the timetable for the completion of tasks.

Bryson (1989) suggests a five-part approach for developing a strategic plan. This approach involves answering five questions:

1. What are the practical alternatives we might pursue to achieve this goal?
2. What are the barriers to the realization of these alternatives?
3. What major proposals might we pursue to achieve these alternatives or to overcome the barriers to their realization?
4. What major actions with existing staff must be taken within the next year to implement the major proposals?
5. What specific steps must be taken within the next six months to implement the major proposals and who is responsible?

(1989, p. 169)

In furthering the planning process, the six factors that will affect the ability to implement the plan are:

1. Scope (Where are the clients?)
2. Size (Who are the potential clients?)
3. Complexity (How specific are the objectives?)
4. Duration

258 | **CHAPTER 12** Strategic Management

5. Components (How many organizations? How many discrete activities?)
6. Innovativeness (How much of a break from the past?)

(Ruchelman, 1985, pp. 2–3)

Each of these factors contributes to making both the planning and the implementing processes more difficult.

Implementation

Many presentations on strategic management add an obligatory discussion of evaluation after the planning phase. This begs the question of the potential for failure at the implementation phase of the strategic management process. Randall Ripley and Grace Franklin after a review of the extant literature on implementation, drew eight conclusions.

1. No one, in the sense of a single institution or a small coordinated set of actors, is in charge of the implementation of domestic programs in the United States. In a very real sense there is no single government in the United States to promote, oversee, or conduct implementation. Rather, there are many governments and, in some cases, government is often indistinguishable from non-government. The contracting out of much public business has increased in recent years and further complicated an already complex situation.
2. Domestic programs virtually never achieve all that is expected of them in a straightforward and timely manner. This is the case in part because the expectations are numerous, diffuse, and often unrealistic.
3. The first two generalizations are true in part because of a series of complexities arising from the structure of American governments and the conflicting values, interests, and beliefs of key actors in the implementation process.
4. The most important set of actors in implementation processes are in various bureaucracies. They do not *control* implementation, but their influence is central.
5. Patterns of implementation vary, depending on the different major social purposes of policies being implemented.
6. The decentralized (federalist) nature of policy implementation has a series of critical effects on how that implementation occurs.
7. *Effective implementation* may have different meanings in different situations.
8. Even if implementation of a specific program is judged to be effective that does not guarantee that the program will necessarily achieve its desired impact.

(1986, p. 3)

Given the above, it is disappointing that the implementation process receives such scant attention in strategic management literature. The importance of the implementation phase of strategic management is in the opportunity to anticipate and, therefore, correct the problems cited above.

This is not the place for an extended discussion of the issue of implementation. Discussions of the complexity of implementation would (and do) fill volumes. Put most simply, implementation is a process of continuous problem-solving to permit an organization to achieve a particular goal. Another way to look at implementation is that it is the process of capitalizing on positive events and ameliorating negative events over time. It is a process of control and direction. In the narrowest sense of those terms, implementation involves the application of certain operational management techniques to ensure that planned tasks occur when and as designed. As such, concepts such as critical path and PERT (Performance, Evaluation, and Review Technique) are appropriate for use in program implementation.

Implementation can be thought of as an issue that goes beyond operational management. In this context it involves the entire gamut of political and interpersonal relations that must be attended to if any cooperative activity is to occur. Writers as diverse as Chester Barnard and Dwight Waldo have commented on these very critical management functions. It should be noted that the internal and external analyses conducted earlier are critical to implementing a program with any degree of success.

STRATEGIC MANAGEMENT IN PRACTICE

The emphasis in much of the literature on strategic management is as a way of guiding the long-term future. There is a tendency to regard strategic management as a very expensive and time-consuming practice. There is, however, another way to look at this process. The essential component of strategic management, process evaluation, is itself a sophisticated restatement of problem-solving. The time factor notwithstanding, strategic management represents a useful way to characterize the central concern of management—problem-solving. It would be a wise manager who approached the task of management as one of applying the practices and perspectives of strategic management to all facets of management. Next week's task, or assignment, no less than one of a decade from now, would benefit from the rigor of the strategic management process (and parenthetically, day-to-day management disintegrates into crisis management in the same way that strategic management is never quite completed). Use of this technique at this lower level of operation is well worth the time it would take to understand its application.

To summarize:

The purpose and benefits of strategic management are

1. Promotion of strategic *thinking, acting, and learning* through a strategic conversation among key actors
   a. Clarifies intentions
   b. Disciplined approach to goal attainment
2. Improvement of decision-making
3. Enhancement of organizational effectiveness, and
4. Enhancement of the effectiveness of broader societal systems

CONCLUSION

Strategic management is regarded by many researchers and practitioners as a key tool for instituting change. Further, it is a tool that can be useful both in introducing relatively broad-scale change; that is, at the program or policy level and in intro-

260   CHAPTER 12 Strategic Management

ducing change in the way organizations are managed. Strategic management can be thought of as a specialized type of organization development (OD) effort. The focus of both OD and strategic management are similar—both focus on planned change. The difference is that most OD efforts are inward or intra-organizational in focus. Strategic management can facilitate change either within an organization or at a much broader level. The attractiveness of strategic management is precisely in that it can serve both levels of concern. Whether one is a governor seeking to map out a bold policy perspective, or a mid-level manager trying to get a better handle on day-to-day operations, strategic management suggests a way of defining and understanding problems that can assist in either endeavor. Critically, strategic management is founded upon a way of thinking and understanding that is critical to management. The orientation to look outward or to the future is a central feature of current understandings of successful management practice. Managers who do not see the value will encounter problems in adjusting and responding to inevitable change. Strategic management is both a support system and a tool.

DISCUSSION QUESTIONS

- What is the purpose of the visioning process in strategic management?
- Much as with other analytic techniques, the implementation phase of strategic management is somewhat truncated. Why is there a tendency to simply assume that implementation is the easy part?
- What is a SWOT analysis?
- Under what circumstances would a strategic effort not be appropriate?
- What are the organizational conditions that are necessary before deciding to begin a strategic management process?
- How far into the future should a strategic plan go? Why that long?
- Can strategic management be developed into a way of thinking and acting rather than as a intermittent event?

BIBLIOGRAPHY

Bryson, John M. *Strategic Planning for Public and Non-Profit Organizations*. San Francisco: Jossey-Bass. 1989.

Bryson, John M. *Strategic Planning for Public and Non-Profit Organizations, 3rd ed.* San Francisco: Jossey-Bass. 2004.

Bryson, John M., and Farnum K. Alson. *Creating and Implementing Your Strategic Plan: A Workbook for Public and Nonprofit Organizations, 2nd ed.* San Francisco: Jossey-Bass. 2005.

Eadie, Douglas C. "Putting a Powerful Tool to Practical Use: The Application of Strategic Planning in the Public Sector", *Public Administration Review*, 43 (5), pp. 447–452. September-October 1983.

McClendon, Bruce W., and Ray Quay. *Mastering Change: Winning Strategies for Effective City Planning*. Washington, DC: American Planning Association. 1983.

Ripley, Randall B., and Grace A. Franklin. *Policy Implementation and Bureaucracy, 2nd ed.* Chicago: Dorsey Press. 1986.

Ruchelman, Leonard I. *Program Design*. Albany: State University of New York Press. 1985.

Sylvia, Ronald D., Kenneth J. Meier, and Elizabeth M. Gunn. *Program Planning and Evaluation for the Public Manager*. Monterey, CA: Brooks/Cole Publishing. 1985.

Walter, Susan, and Pat Choate. *Thinking Strategically*. Washington, DC: Council of State Planning Agencies. 1983.

CHAPTER
13

Leadership and Decision-Making

Leadership in organizations is essential to the change process, whether it is in fostering "instability" or in envisioning the future as a starting point for cultural transformation. Helping an organization follow an unknown path of change and innovation is not an easy task. It takes a manager of insight and courage. Few managers are prepared for such a career.

One overlooked element of leadership is the relationship between leaders and followers. Much of the academic analysis of change has focused on the change agent/leader. Before we close this discussion, we offer a few words about the "partner" of the leader—the follower.

The key to change is often less about what the leader does and more about what the followers do. But who are "followers"? We tend to define the follower in hierarchical terms—the leader is the "boss" and the follower is a subordinate. This imagery is misleading. Leadership is an action based upon judgment and understanding. The exercise of leadership in successful organizations is the result of the mutual cooperation and interaction among those in the organization. It *transcends* concepts such as power and authority. Burns (1978) asserts that the act of leadership is to engage followers; it affirms and blends needs, aspirations, and goals in a common enterprise.

The above suggests a different way of conceptualizing the leader-follower relationship. The act of leadership occurs across all aspects of successful organizations. It has little to do with titles and expertise. We can argue that leadership is often the opposite of traditional organizational trappings such as titles and position. Organizations are creative and successful to the extent that position, hierarchy, and authority are subordinated to problem-solving and goal accomplishment. What is required is the ability to know when to exercise leadership and when to exercise *followership*. Followership is not the same as following: Following is impelled (consciously or unconsciously influenced) by the attributes and actions of a leader. The follower has no choice. But the act of followership is an a priori choice (self-conscious) of the organizational participant. Leadership and followership are mutual and complementary. Problem-solving may require both leadership

---

CHART 12–1

Organizational Leadership

- Leadership is less about hierarchy and more about *goal accomplishment*
- Leadership is less about authority and more about *knowledge*
- Leadership is less about management and more about *policy*
- Leadership is less about how and more about *why*

---

and followership; leadership in the choice to solve the problem and followership in the choice to accept the advice and counsel of others. The leadership-followership interactive process is one in which an individual chooses to seek out another who is thought to have expertise (leadership); asks for help (followership); expert chooses to provide (or not provide) the help (leadership); initiator accepts proffered help (followership). The action closes with the response of the initiator (the "original" leader), in other words by an act of followership. It is critical to understand that *both leader and follower have a choice.* There are three key points:

- Informal process; continuous search and interaction
- "Leader" is the reactor to request
- Leaders look for opportunities to follow

Since the introduction of the idea of transformational leadership (Burns, 1978), the nexus between ethics and leadership has been apparent. In earlier works (Cox, 2014; Cox, Hill, and Pyakuryal, 2008) the foci were on first the capture of the idea of transformational leadership by academics who ignored the leadership-ethics link (see for example Bass, 1990) and, second the tendency to focus leadership research on the putative "leader" (Cox, Plagens, and Sylla, 2010) and ignore the place of the follower in the relationship. This work will add a third perspective by examining the complex relationship between professionalism and expertise.

"PROFESSIONAL" PUBLIC ADMINISTRATION

The evolution of public administration from un-scrutinized practice to an academic field of study has been marked by a changing understanding of professionalism. In the early years the goal was to first define and then recruit based upon rudimentary notions of competence. Over time the definition of "professional" would shift to that of a class or group of individuals with shared, interests, language, and knowledge (Cox, Buck, and Morgan, 2011). In each period over the last century and a half, views about public administration *practice* have been influenced by our understanding of professionalism.

For those involved in the development of American public administration as an academic pursuit, the progressive era connotes an unprecedented time in American history. In this period improved performance of programs and of employees was paramount. Woodrow Wilson (1887) cryptically observed that it was, by then, harder to run a constitution than to make one. While not rejecting politics per se, the public administration reformers of this era sought better government by expanding administrative functions (planning, analyzing), keeping them distinct from political functions (deciding). The politics/administration dichotomy emerged as a conceptual orientation whereby the world of government was to be divided into two functional areas–one administrative, one political. Civil service reform, which borrowed heavily from developments in the UK in the middle of the nineteenth century, replacing patronage appointment with appointment on the basis of merit, was but one example of how to better "manage" government. Furthermore, the use of independent regulatory agencies, such as the Interstate Commerce Commission, was to bring to bear the expertise and knowledge of civil servants to quickly, factually, and knowledgeably (neutrally) make decisions that would be beyond the ken of political bosses (legislatures and city councils). Government would be transformed by changing not only who came into government employ, but also the locus of many decisions, from elected officials to appointed officials.

The work of Frederick Taylor (1911) and the concept of scientific management were to have a profound effect on public administration for decades. The specific tenets of scientific management were quite similar to the already familiar views of the progressive era reforms of the 1870s. In fact, scientific management's priorities often did little more than reinforce tendencies, attitudes, and expectations generated by the progressive period. Thus, Taylor's emphasis on division of labor, an idealized "one best way of practice," and empirical analysis were essentially no different from the views of the municipal research bureau reformers. However, the managerial focus of scientific management directed the attention of public administration *inward*. The scope of public administration was narrowed to that of managing and organizing. Any evaluative judgments on policy and program output were left to the political realm, while those in public administration focused on structuring the workplace to ensure the most *efficient* output.

The Friedrich-Finer debate would briefly refocus attention on the values that must underlie the actions and decisions of individual bureaucrats if government is to achieve its goal of a better society. Finer (1941), following the fifty-year-old precepts of the progressive era and its emphasis on science and neutral competence, argued that the professionalization of the bureaucracy was the vehicle for "better" government. Left to follow the path defined as best by the "profession," Finer felt that government decision-making would be improved. Friedrich (1940), following a still older constitutional governmental tradition, argued that only by immersing themselves in constitutional values and political traditions could bureaucrats make correct decisions. In Friedrich's view, the role of the bureaucracy was more active and less deferential to the constitutionally mandated institutions.

Waldo (1948) raised the level of this debate by challenging, if only indirectly, both views. According to Waldo, the trust in professionalism and expertise of the Finer perspective was misplaced. Often there is no "one best way"; and further, to leave the public out of any decision-making equation was to destroy the very governmental traditions the process was designed to uphold. However, in Waldo's view, the Friedrich formulation was similarly flawed. The reality of government decision-making experienced by Waldo and later by others during World War II was one in which most decisions were made implicitly, or explicitly, by bureaucrats. Day-to-day operations require a degree of discretion and even independent thinking that would be unacceptable under the deference model proposed by Friedrich. The point that Waldo was making was that the fundamental values of the bureaucrat must be those of American political thought and constitutionalism, but the choice of actions must also be grounded in a knowledge of management practice and organizational theory to ensure that those fundamental values were effectively achieved.

In the postwar era there emerges a movement in the academy toward a new social *science* perspective. Much as scientific management understood its role as finding the "one best way," the new policy analyst trained in the latest techniques of quantitative analysis could "optimize" policy decisions. The most significant change during this period is the emergence of a new understanding of professionalism (Stillman, 1991). The language of the earlier reform eras used the concept of professionalization to connote competence and dedication. These were first and foremost *work* attributes. The emerging definition of a professional was linked to specific educational experience, certifications, and shared language. To be a professional was to be admitted to a "club" of like-minded and similarly educated persons. "Professional" credentials were the entry requirement, rather than a designation based upon performance. Competence and performance were judged by those credentials and by "peers," not by workplace rules and practices (Stillman).

The later 1960s was a period in which many long-held academic notions were criticized and often rejected. This period is best symbolized by a conference held at the Minnowbrook Conference Center at Syracuse University in 1968. The purpose of the conference was to explore emerging theories of public administration, with particular emphasis on views that were anti-hierarchical and also "people-oriented" (Marini, 1971). An important point in understanding this perspective was that the goal was not only to alter the theory of public administration, but also to alter its practice. Thus, this analysis emphasized the need not only to reject hierarchy, because it was failing, but also to consciously and specifically give more influence to those in government closest to the problems of society—the working public servant or so-called street-level bureaucrat. Ostensibly, government could be made to work by permitting those with the most intimate knowledge of the problems—legally, politically, and organizationally—to resolve the problems.

In the 1990s academics in Public Administration began to incorporate ideas from public choice economics and the political movement to privatize various parts of the government. Beginning in Europe in the early 1980s, the perspective was stimulated most visibly by the book *Reinventing Government* (Osborne and Gaebler, 1992). The New Public Management has served as the basis for the transformation of the governments of Eastern Europe (where there was a need for privatization after the fall of the communist governments) and of African and Asian nations, but most particularly New Zealand, Australia, and Korea.

Both the public choice and "reinventing government" perspectives share a suspicion about the capacity and capability of government organizations and a faith in "market-driven" perspectives as the path to organizational effectiveness. Both also share the use of a set of techniques and practices (program evaluation, cost-benefit analysis, etc.) that begin from an economic perspective (both academic and practical). In this sense they represent an extension of the generic management movement and the emergence of the *science* of social existence. These perspectives also yield the same result. Public decisions are to be left to the expert (Ott, Boonyarak, and Dicke, 2001). Decisions cannot be allowed to be left to amateurs. *The criteria for "right decisions" is in who decides, not in the quality of the process.* The answer often was that the private sector should decide. The private sector would serve the public better not only because it would be more efficient, and, therefore, less costly, but also because it would be immune to political dealings that caused corruption and waste.

Public management as a distinct perspective deserving of academic analysis has a spotty history. The "enemy" for the progressives was *politics*. Well into the 1950s it was assumed that the practice of management was a socio-psychological endeavor, not a sector-specific practice. One of the significant changes over the last century has been a shift from a sense that public managers have the capability to address problems of policy implementation to one in which public managers are viewed as incapable. The conflict for decades was who should control operations (first politicians vs. administrators, then managers vs. functionaries). However, three plus decades ago the issue became one of what sector is best able to manage government activities. This shift from an essentially internal discussion about best practices to one in which the capability of the public sector was challenged came during times of fiscal distress (Thatcher's reforms and those in the Commonwealth countries of the Pacific were based upon policy choices emphasizing budget control and, secondarily personnel control [Fry, 1988; Coombs, 1977]; Reagan sought primarily personnel control, but also control over state and local budgets [Rector and Sanera, 1987]; more recently the New Public Management was touted as the solution to the world-wide economic decline [McCann, 2013, see also Cox and Ostertag, 2014]).

Since the era of cut-back management some three decades ago, the language of public management has become precipitous, invoking stress, crises, and emergency. The essence of these terms is that of a problem that occurs in a moment in time that *requires immediate attention*; nevertheless, they are addressed based upon the same principles of governance as decision-making in non-crisis situations.

The contentious nature of American intergovernmental relations and the ongoing search for budget control in the developed countries of Europe and Asia affirm the sense that government is in a perpetual state of crisis. Whether it is the substantial and persistent federal deficits, aggressive political rhetoric about how wasteful governments are, or the constant battle over funding of services, the impression is that of failed policies and incompetent employees. With no margin for error and fewer employees, governments will likely remain in a crisis state for years to come. They face a future of growing demand for services but less funding for those services.

ON KNOWING AND UNDERSTANDING

Arendt (2003), following Kant, asserts that thinking and judging are interrelated but separate. Thinking is the result of forming abstractions. Judging is the first step toward deciding (deciding to decide as it were). It is the product of understanding the situation in its fullest sense. She goes on to posit that some individuals are better at one activity than the other. Therefore, one could do well at abstract thinking and another could be better at judging. Judging follows thinking and knowing and emerges from understanding. It is the capacity to understand that is the key aspect of judging.

Successful organizational decision-making is predicated upon what Arendt describes as the capacity to think *to* conclusions. As Arendt (2003) would explain it, we must think about our work, before we can do our work. But also, without a particular focus, abstract thinking cannot become tangible work. The obvious dilemma for organizations is in recognizing these different capacities and assigning persons roles that fit those capabilities. The "problem" of the exercise of discretion is embedded in this dilemma—we need those with the capacity for judging, not those with the capacity for thinking, to exercise discretion. It is a problem precisely because the need for discretion is when the situation is not-routine, i.e. when the situation and circumstances, not the abstractions such as SOPs, dictate. Those with the capacity to think can (and will) develop appropriate standards of performance and behavior, those with the capacity to judge will understand when it is time to step outside the routine.

Usually, decision-making is controlled by formal rules and regulations and is guided by organization preferences and practices. However, when a unique situation arises in an organization, it brings along new uncertainties as well as new alternatives; decision-making then selects courses of action that are expected to perform well given the understanding of goals and the conditions of uncertainty (Choo, 2002). This then results in the capacity to develop new knowledge by a process of complex interplay between existing knowledge and sense making.

The capacity to judge, and, therefore, to understand and then act is intertwined with tacit knowledge. While explicit knowledge can yield *decisions* (as an individual act or as an organizational mandate) it is more closely aligned with Arendt's notion of thinking. Rules and regulations, hierarchical relationships, in fact the entire range of structural-functional understandings of modern organizations emerge from *thinking* about organizational design and process. The decision is the result of the process of thinking. The classic model of policy analysis in which the *optimal alternative* is uncovered is an example of this form of decision-making. There can only be one decision; therefore, the analysis yields the answer. *Working* in contrast emerges from understanding of the circumstances and events that result in actions, which is close to the application of tacit knowledge. In this context, understanding informs us when the process (analysis) has not produced the right decision.

Understanding and Valuing

A variety of authors from Selznick (1957) to Burns (1978) have emphasized the importance of organizational learning that reinforces the values and mission of the organization. These are to them the key ingredients in organizational leadership. The importance of value statements (Day, 1999) such as missions, goals, and code of ethics are part of the mantra of "best practice" modern management. However, unless attitudes, values, and behaviors of the individual support and reinforce the decision-making process, the process is bound to fail. Day (1999) argues that value statements can be used by organizational leaders to begin the process of defining an organizational ethic. True to the notion of the conversion of explicit knowledge into tacit knowledge (internalization), she also warns that "to guarantee compliance with new policies, values should also be supported by coherent and congruent regulatory practices within the framework of the existing culture" (p. 164). In other words, the value system of the organization (or of the government) must be reconciled with that of the organization members. But this need not be a reduction to the lowest common denominator of behavior. Rather, it can be a significant exercise in "cultural" renewal and the foundation for a collectively defined organizational ethic that can guide practice and thus the exercise of discretion.

One of the basic tenets of representative democracy is that public policy is subject to continual and multiple reviews. Time and expertise do not drive the decision process. It is the outcome (what is decided), not the process that is valued. The essential fact with relation to the construction of popular government is that decisions are non-expert driven. Stated another way, breadth of knowledge is more highly valued than depth of knowledge. This is not to imply that depth of knowledge is ignored, but it is viewed as less relevant to the decision than breadth of knowledge. This attitude is linked to the view on time. A depth of knowledge is the most ephemeral of all knowledge. The expert with a deep knowledge of a subject is adjudged so only within the context of the present. The future represents a diminution of that knowledge. What is sought to uncover are precisely those issues that the expert finds extraneous. Knowing that the problem will be defined in conjunction with others deprives the "expert" of any overriding justification for exclusive decision-making. The very narrowness of the expert's knowledge makes the expert ineligible to decide. The only appropriate way to approach a problem is to subject it to frequent review and analysis to *negate* the narrowness of the "expert."

A broader perspective provides the opportunity to appreciate the complexity of problems and, therefore, a better sense of the many different courses the future may represent. It is the expert's certainty of today that makes an understanding of the future questionable. This need to think broadly has the advantage of making the decision process more complicated. The straight line, linear thinking of the expert fails because it is too simple. The decision maker with broad knowledge may not know as much about part of the problem as an expert, but that decision maker knows more about the entire problem than any individual expert.

Sensitivity to the very things that the expert must ignore (opinion, feelings, values, bias, and ideology, along with a range of emotions) is necessary for a generalist perspective. This is the unrecognized element of politics, particularly representative democratic politics—the ability to tap the conscious and unconscious values and senses that are part of all of us. A simpler description of this element in decision-making is to label it "politics." Hummel aptly summarizes the views of Habermas and Weber on the problem inherent in the contest between expert judgment and political judgment when he comments:

in the face of the overwhelming force of bureaucratization, it is no longer possible to have politics because political questions are translated before they are even phrased and put on any agenda into administrative and technical ones. Both Weber and Habermas attribute such transformations to the power of the

CHAPTER 13 Leadership and Decision-Making

over-all rationalization/technicalization process. It is left to a philosopher to explain how people's minds become so turned around that they can think of (political) ends only in terms of (technical and administrative) means.

(Hummel, 1986, p. 5)

The allure of expert judgment certainly facilitates that turn of events. In the failure to recognize that the tool is controlling the decision-process, "politics" disappears.

The second element in consideration of time is its relation to the ability to understand a given problem. "Time" permits a more careful and detailed examination of a problem and the possible solutions to that problem. The difficulty is that at some point a decision must be made. The formula that has been developed is to accept decisions as temporary. This is closely akin to the admonition of those who have examined chaos theory and management (Kiel, 1994) that the best stance for the manager is that of experimentation. Each decision is made on the best currently available information. When new information (experience) suggests that a problem exists with the current approach, then the decision process is reopened.

To build a consensus for a decision before attempting to implement a program is little more than a truism. To attempt to introduce change in the face of active opposition is to invite failure. Ruchelman notes, "Open organizations that invite different points of view are more likely to promote new ideas; but those ideas may never be implemented if a consensus and a pulling together doesn't take place after the idea has been adopted." This is especially critical in more highly formalized organizations where it is likely that there will be "some rule that gets in the way" (Ruchelman, 1985, p. 24).

Consensus building makes sense as a technique of management, but it also makes sense as a tool for effective decision-making. The problem confronting government is understanding or defining the problem, as often as it is determining the solutions. Consensus building is first and foremost a process for defining and understanding problems (public policy). Often solutions are more apparent, and easier to understand, when there is agreement on the nature of the problem. Consensus permits a focus on that earlier (and more critical) stage of analysis—problem definition. The most serious weakness of the rational comprehensive model of decision-making is not satisficing (Simon, 1976), instead of maximizing behavior, nor even the possibility of a normative component to incrementalism (Lindblom, 1959), but rather it is the failure to focus on the extreme difficulty in defining and understanding problems (performance measures).

The use of time and the valuing of generalist knowledge in the consensus process play critical roles in the application of this structure as a means of problem defining. To the extent that this activity is dismissed as incidental, the entire process of "solving" a problem is diminished. The "effectiveness" of consensus is in helping understand problems more than in the determination of "solutions." The oft-cited example of citizen participation (Yates, 1982, 1988; Gruber, 1987; Cox, 1997) illustrates this problem. In introducing a requirement for citizen participation into bureaucratic decision-making it was assumed that bureaucrats would become more "sensitive" to public opinion and public concern. The effort has invariably failed, but why? This analysis would suggest two reasons. First, is that the value the bureaucrat exhibits in problem-solving is that of regard for expert opinion. The process of selecting the best solution is a complex task that requires specific expert knowledge. No amount of citizen input can aid that analysis, because such input cannot increase expert knowledge. The bureaucrat "knows" the right way to find the solution to the problem. Citizen participation is little more than interference—a delay in the decision process, which is tolerated (probably with ill humor) precisely because there is no "value" to such an exercise. Second is that democratic practice values highly, and is most effective at, problem definition and knowledge seeking (Cox and Hummel, 1988). The time to seek new knowledge is not when an alternative is to be selected, but earlier, when the problem is being defined. Citizen participation, defined as holding a public hearing before rendering a final decision, cannot work. The bureaucrat is correct that such a practice can contribute little. But citizen participation before the problem has been defined would be efficacious. The concept of citizen participation is a critical value in democratic governance, but it also must contribute to the decision process. Bureaucrats are correct to reject citizen participation, as currently practiced, though they do so for the wrong reason.

Ethics and Professionalism

Professions evolve as a specific set of practices and shared norms that are first taught and then emerge as "proper" or accepted behavior (practice). Shared credentials and ultimately a shared "language" separate those who are capable of "understanding" from those who cannot understand. According to Mosher (1968), professions have their

> own particularized view of the world and of the agency's role and mission in it. The perspective and motivation of each professional are shaped at least to some extent by the lens provided him by his professional education, his prior professional experience, and by his professional colleagues.
>
> (p. 106)

Ethics must be judged by the consequences for others, over the long haul (Cox, 2004; French, 1983; Weber, 1946). Ethical decision-making is anything but naïve or unworldly. It takes considerable courage and strength of will to do what one thinks is right, regardless of the personal consequences. But that is the essence of ethical decision-making because the concerns are directed to the consequences for others, not for oneself. These are individuals who must be firm in their convictions that the decisions they make are right and necessary, even if the personal price is quite high.

French (1983) would argue that the very purpose of an ethical framework is to make those hard choices. If the decision is simple or straightforward, it is unlikely to rise to the level of an ethical problem. Hard choices imply not only a complicated situation, but also a desire to act ethically, a focus on the outcome, and a willingness to accept public scrutiny both during the decision and after (Cox, 2000a, 2004). Such a framework is not for the faint of heart. It requires both a commitment of purpose and the strength to endure failure. That is the essence of ethical decision-making, because the concerns are directed to the consequences *for others*, not for oneself (see Weber's "Politics as Vocation"). But it is also more than a lack of concern for person or career. Public decisions have consequences beyond person and "political" interests. Not all actions produce only "benefits." An examination of consequences is an articulation of "what is next." Hiding from consequences does not make them go away, but rather it means we will be caught unaware when they inevitably occur. Hiding from consequences is a way of pretending that actions do not have consequences. There are no rosy scenarios in this examination. In all likelihood, every action has "negative" consequences (this fact is the real "dirty hands" of politics). The hard choice is to acknowledge that no alternative is going to "solve" the problem. The hard choice is to acknowledge the consequences of every alternative.

Only the ethical public servant will act despite the "bad" that will happen along with the good. And, only the ethical public servant will accept responsibility (and, possible negative personal consequences) for the decisions made. That is the essence of ethical decision-making. It is not easy, nor simple, but it is needed. Very often, the difficult or hard choice that a public servant makes is not whether to help someone but to define the limits of that help, or to determine ethically when to end assistance. This is a situation for which neither bureaucratic routines, nor policies, nor court rulings can provide professional guidance. It is the individual and organizational tacit knowledge that leads to good, consistent decision-making and it is informed by the understanding that emerges from the application of specific individual and organizational tacit knowledge (Cox, Pyakuryal, and Hill, 2008; Cox and Pyakuryal, 2013).

Discretionary Judgment

Much like ethics, discretion represents a judgment as to what activities in an agency are to receive priority. Exercising discretion presumes that both the need for judgment and the capacity to exercise it are not just about implementing "routine" activities (Cox, Hill, and Pyakuryal, 2008). Situations and circumstances drive the decision to exercise discretion. Judging events and circumstances at a moment in time and then acting on that judgment ensures proper discretionary decision-making. Those a priori judgments are largely informed by an understanding that emerges from the application of specific individual and organizational tacit knowledge. The capacity to make sense of the situation and judge, and therefore to understand and then act, is intertwined with tacit knowledge (Cox, Hill, and Pyakuryal, 2008).

The "professional" knowledge and understanding about responsibility for executing policy directives are replaced by the need for skills based upon juggling *competing* demands. Today, public managers are less the technical *administrator* of the early twentieth century and more a *manager* of diverse interests and perspectives. Many public servants are much more deeply engaged in *policy making*, rather than mere *policy implementation*, than has been acknowledged. Success depends upon skills and relationships unlike those envisioned decades ago. Having moved from technical-professional "administrator" to professional manager, the "new" manager needs the skills of leadership to be successful; needing more than ever the capacity and capability for ethical decision-making.

Decisions are directed toward the outcomes for a wider public, but a follower may have a quite different understanding of the consequences for whom.

Professional training and job roles push the follower toward another-directedness that is much narrower than the public *at large*. Professionally defined responsibilities and practices establish the constituency for the work output. "Doing it right" may become more of an assessment of the application of methods, rather than a statement of ethics. The complaint often expressed in the classroom, *we* did it right but the politicians (or the higher ups in the department) changed it, is at its core an argument about relevant constituencies.

As noted in an earlier discussion (Chapter 6) Arendt (2003) asserts that thinking and judging are interrelated, but separate. Usually, decision-making is controlled by formal rules and regulations and is guided by organization preferences and practices. However, when a unique situation arises in an organization, it brings along new uncertainties as well as new alternatives; decision-making then selects courses of action that are expected to perform well given the understanding of goals and the conditions of uncertainty (Choo, 2002). Rules and regulations, hierarchical relationships, in fact the entire range of structural-functional understandings of modern organizations emerge from thinking about organizational design and process. The decision is the result of the process of thinking.

In a public-sector context, what is being decided relates, not to a single policy or problem, but to the relationship of that problem to all other public policy concerns. The issue is how first to define the problem (which necessarily involves

---

CHART 13–1

The dynamics of the leader-follower relationship (place for both in organizations)

Followership NOT the same as following
- Following is impelled (consciously or unconsciously influenced) by actions of leader; follower has no choice
- Followership is an a priori choice (self-conscious) of the nominal leader

Leader-Follower: reactive
- Success is predicated on the "proper" reaction of the follower to the initiative of the leader
- Action closes with response of the follower
- Commander as leader
- Formal (rule-bound) relationships critical to process (both have to know role).
- Leader looks for followers

Leadership-Followership: interactive
- Similar to Weick's double interact
- Talent search
- Individual chooses to seek out another who is thought to have expertise; asks for help; expert chooses to provide (or not provide) the help; initiator accepts proffered help
- Both leader and follower have a choice
- Action closes with the response of the initiator
- Informal process; continuous search and interaction
- "Leader" is the reactor to request
- Leaders look for opportunities to follow

the relational question of the importance of this problem to all others). No public policy problem should be examined as though no other problems or concerns exist. Yet, the dictates of instrumental decision-making permit expert judgment to be rendered under exactly those circumstances.

This brings us back to Arendt and the importance of understanding. Ethical decisions will emerge as the leadership-followership relationship is played out (Cox, Plagens, and Sylla, 2010), The danger is not a lack of rigor in applying the techniques of analysis, but in the hubris to believe that a perfectly neutral instrument exists. Still more problematic is that those without knowledge of the limitations of the techniques are led to believe that these techniques generate "true" answers. When the "answer" of the supposedly neutral analyst and the decision of policy makers are compared, rarely is the policy decision cast in a favorable light. The biases of the policy maker are presumed; the biases of the analyst are ignored. Both methods of decision-making are biased.

IMPLICATIONS FOR MANAGING

Many of the studies of public-sector leadership affirm the importance of ethics (Burns, 1978; Carnevale, 1995; Ciulla, 2004). More recent works (Baker 2007; Cox, Plagens, and Sylla, 2010) introduce the centrality of followership in organization decision-making. Followership is the more complex, and potentially important, side of the leader-follower relationship. Public service ethics is applicable to all those in the public sector. Unethical behaviors are just as debilitating when initiated by those lower in the organization as by those in higher levels. Because it is the "street-level" bureaucrat who interacts directly and most frequently with the public, a person's experience of government and judgment of whether it is corrupted or not is based upon those encounters with those at the street-level. Similarly, the policy analyst who refuses to correct errors and falls into the trap of adherence to dogma distorts policy analysis and cannot "speak truth to power" (Wildavsky, 1979, 2007).

It is in the focus on analysis that followership ethics becomes clear. As Burns (1978) asserted we are engaged in a common enterprise, and in the process to make better citizens of both leaders and followers. Wildavsky spoke about the need for the analyst to have "values." In this context values mean an adherence to the principles of democratic governance and public ethics. As Wildavsky noted, analysis is both a technical activity and an art (1979, 2007). As an art the analyst must admit to the limits of technique and be cognizant of how those techniques narrow the range of options to be studied (see also House, 1982). The analyst must avoid the hubris of the elegant solution in favor of the "popular" choice. If we want to continue to lay claim to democratic governance, then the analyst must accede to the choices of the public. The analyst has a leadership role in crafting and shaping the analysis, but the analyst is also the follower who offers truth to those who decide. Unless the analyst trusts democratic governance, and unless both the analyst and the citizen accept the "common enterprise," then such leader-follower dynamics will fail.

In the emphasis on leadership responsibility we give the follower something of a free ride. Responsibility rests with the person with the authority and capacity to decide. However, as the discussion of discretion has demonstrated, ethical decisions require an understanding of time and circumstance that is beyond that of the management level of the organization. Discretion is most critical at the level of interaction and citizen engagement. There is a conflict inherent in the position of the individual who must exercise discretion and the training of that person. These are not persons who are routinely exposed to "politics" or decisions not within their professional knowledge. It is not necessarily apparent how stepping outside the rules and standard operating procedures helps in decision-making. Emphasizing the technical seemingly is the safe path, but, of course, that is the road to a choice devoid of ethical content. The decision is technically accurate, but it does not consider the context and situation. The public servant falls back on content-less training, becoming the theoretician (Kant, 1983) who, "lacking judgment, can never be practical in their lives."

Having suggested that leadership ethics and followership ethics are different still leaves us with the conundrum of how these differences can be addressed in the context of organizational dynamics. How, for example, does one reconcile the duty of responsibility to the public that rests upon all public servants with the responsibility to *decide* what rests with those in positions of authority? What do both the leader and follower share? More critically, how do we address the nuanced understanding of who is a leader and who is a follower—when we all enact both roles?

The more important question comes in the formal interactions between leaders and followers. Again, Burns captures the key characteristics of such interactions as essentially transformational and ethical. But hidden within this description is an interesting question about the motivation to be ethical and particularly concerned about consequences. Decisions are directed toward the outcomes for a wider public, but a follower may have a quite different understanding of the consequences for whom. Professional training and job roles push the follower toward another-directedness that is much narrower than the public *at large*. "Doing it right" may become more of an assessment of the application of methods rather than a statement of ethics. As suggested earlier, this has the potential of creating a conflict pitting methodological correctness against ethical practice. The consequence of the choice of methods is in the judgment of and assessment by peer professionals, not the consequences for a constituency. The oft heard complaint, we did it right but the politicians (or the higher ups in the department) changed it, is at its core an argument about relevant constituencies. If the analyst refuses to consider that which cannot be quantified, then the exercise will yield partial and incomplete results. Those who receive the analysis may be no further along in understanding the situation (a qualitative as well as quantitative judgment) if only that which can be quantified are analyzed. The analyst is responsible for providing the best available analysis, but what is to be analyzed is not a "professional" judgment, but rather a public decision that is about politics and policy, not rigor of methods.

What happens when we reintroduce the notion that, under certain circumstances, individuals take on and adopt both leader and follower roles in pursuit of organizational goals? To gather information (seeking implicit and tacit knowledge) prior to judging/deciding may require a person with the authority to act to seek help (ask questions) of persons who are otherwise viewed as subordinates. In that exchange, the person asking the question is the follower (you don't ask questions

CHAPTER 13 Leadership and Decision-Making

of those you do not find creditable; therefore, you expect to *follow* the answer provided) and the responder to the question is the one exercising leadership. The above discussion does help explicate this issue. When the analyst is asked a question, the analyst should not reshape the question into a professionally acceptable form. The codicil to this is that the analyst must appreciate that he/she is not the only person to whom the decision maker will turn with questions.

DISCUSSION QUESTIONS

- Explain the inter-relationship between leaders and followers.
- Importance of consensus building.
- How does Arendt distinguish between thinking and understanding? How do those distinctions influence decision-making?
- Must good leaders be ethical in their inter-personal relations? In their organization relation?
- What is the difference between leading and leadership?
- Can a person be both a leader and a follower?
- Is leader a job title or a set of behaviors?

BIBLIOGRAPHY

Arendt, Hannah. *Responsibility and Judgment*. New York: Schocken Press. 2003.

Argyris, Chris. *Knowledge for Action: A Guide to Overcoming Barriers to Organizational Change*. San Francisco: Jossey-Bass. 1993.

Argyris, Chris. *Organizational Learning, 2nd ed*. Malden, MA: Blackwell. 1999.

Avolio, Bruce, and Bernard Bass. "Re-examining the Components of Transformational and Transactional Leadership Using the Multifactor Leadership Questionnaire", *Journal of Occupational and Organizational Psychology*, 72 (4), pp. 441–462. 1999.

Baker, Susan. "Followship: The Theoretical Foundation of a Contemporary Construct", *Journal of Leadership & Organizational Studies*, 14 (1), pp. 50–60. 2007.

Bass, Bernard M. *Leadership and performance beyond expectation*. New York: Free Press. 1985.

Bass, Bernard M. "From Transactional to Transformational Leadership: Learning to Share Vision", *Organizational Dynamics*, pp. 19–31. 1990.

Bass, Bernard M. *Bass &Stogdill's Handbook of Leadership, 3rd ed*. New York Press. 1990.

Baumard, Phillipe. *Tacit Knowledge in Organizations*. Thousand Oaks, CA: Sage. 1999.

Bissau, Min. "Leading Others to Think Innovatively Together: Creative Leadership", *The Leadership Quarterly*, 15 (1), pp. 103–121. 2004.

Bok, Sissela. *Lying: Moral Choice in Public and Private Life*. New York: Vintage Books. 1978.

Browne, Stephen H. *Edmund Burke and the Discourse of Virtue*. 1993.

Bryman, A. "Leadership in Organization", in S. Clegg, C. Hardy, and W. Nord (eds.) *Handbook of Organization Studies*. London: Sage, pp. 276–292. 1996.

Burns, James MacGregor. *Leadership*. New York: Harper Collins. 1978.

Carnevale, David. *Trustworthy Government: Leadership and Management Strategies for Building Trust and High Performance*. San Francisco: Jossey-Bass. 1995.

Choo, Chun Wei. "Sense-Making, Knowledge Creation and Decision Making: Organizational Knowing as Emergent Strategy", in C. W. Choo and N. Bontis (eds.) *The Strategic Management of Intellectual Capital and Organizational Knowledge*. New York: Oxford University Press. 2002.

Choo, Chun Wei. "Sense-Making, Knowledge Creation and Decision Making: Organizational Knowing as Emergent Strategy", in C. W. Choo and N. Bontis (eds.) *The Strategic Management of Intellectual Capital and Organizational Knowledge*. New York: Oxford University Press. 2002.Chulwoo, Kim. "Developing Effective Leadership Skills", *Public Administration Review*, 63 (3), pp. 547–549. 2009.

Ciulla, Joanne B. "Leadership and the Problem of Bogus Empowerment", in Joanne Ciulla (ed.) *Ethics, the Heart of Leadership*. Westport, CT: Praeger, pp. 59–82. 2004.

Cox III, Raymond W. "Administrative Discretion," in J. Shafritz (ed). *The International Encyclopedia of Public Policy and Administration*. Boulder, CO: Westview Press. 1997.

Cox III, Raymond. W. "Administrative Discretion: The Conundrum Wrapped in an Enigma", in van Baallen, Schwella, and Burger (eds.) *Public Management and Governance: The Seventh Winelands Conference*. Stellenbosch, SA: University of Stellenbosch, pp. 249–263. 2000a.

Cox III, Raymond W. "Creating a Decision Architecture", *Global Virtue Ethics Review*, 2 (1), pp. 1–31. 2000b.

Cox III, Raymond W. "Performance Measurement: Cultural and Socio-psychological Factors", in van der Molen, van Rooyen, and van Wyk (eds.) *Outcomes-based Governance: Assessing the Results*. Johannesburg, South Africa: Heinemann, pp. 160–191. 2002.

Cox III, Raymond W. and Ralph Hummel. "A Congressional Declaration of Independence: Why Legislative Politics Cannot and Should Not Be Managed," Paper Presented at American Political Science Association 1988.

Cox III, Raymond W. "Going to War: A Commentary on Ethical Leadership and Politics", *Public Integrity*, 6 (4), pp. 319–331. 2004.

Cox III, Raymond W. "Accountability and Responsibility in Organizations: The Ethics of Discretion", *Public Policy and Administration* (Lithuania), 13 (November), pp. 39–51. 2005.

Cox III, Raymond W., Susan J. Buck, and Betty Morgan. *Public Administration in Theory and Practice, 2nd edition*. New York: Longman. 2011.

Cox III, Raymond W., Michael L. Hill, and Sucheta Pyakuryal. "Tacit Knowledge and Discretionary Judgment", *Public Integrity*, 10 (2), pp. 153–166. 2008.

Cox III, Raymond W., Michael L. Hill, and Sucheta Pyakuryal. "Tacit Knowledge and Discretionary Judgment", *Public Integrity*, 10 (2), pp. 153–166. 2008.

Cox III, Raymond W., and Tricia Ostertag. "Doing Less with Less: The Decline of American Governments", *International Journal of Organization Theory and Practice*, 17 (4), pp. 437–458. 2014.

Cox III, Raymond W., Gregory K. Plagens, and Keba Sylla. "The Leadership-followership Dynamic: Making the Choice to Follow", *International Journal of Interdisciplinary Social Sciences*, 5 (8), pp. 37–52. 2010.

Cox III, Raymond W., and Sucheta Pyakuryal. "Tacit Knowledge: The Foundation of Information Management", in Frederickson and Ghere (eds.) *Ethics and Public Management, 2nd ed*. Armonk, NY: M.E. Sharpe, pp. 216–239. 2013.

Cox, Jr., Taylor. *Cultural Diversity in Organizations: Theory Research and Practice*. San Francisco, CA: Berret-Koehler Publishers, Inc. 1993.

Day, Carla. "Balancing Organizational Priorities: A Two-Factor Values Model of Integrity and Conformity", *Public Integrity*, 1 (2), pp. 149–166. 1999.

Dror, Yehezkel. *Public Policymaking Re-examined*. San Francisco: Chandler. 1968.

Dror, Yehezkel. *The Capacity to Govern: A Report to the Club of Rome*. Portland, OR: Frank Cass Publishers. 2001.

Erchul, William, and Bertram Raven. "Social Power in School Consultation: A Contemporary View of French and Raven's Bases of Power Model", *Journal of School Psychology*, 35 (2), pp. 137–171. 1997.

Fiedler, Fred. *A Theory of Leadership Effectiveness*. New York: McGraw-Hill. 1967.

Fiedler, Fred, and Joseph Garcia. *New Approaches to Effective Leadership: Cognitive Resources and Organizational Performance*. New York: John Wiley & Sons. 1987.

Finer, Herman. "Administrative Responsibility in Democratic Government", *Public Administration Review*, 1. Summer 1941.

French, Peter. *Ethics in Government*. Englewood Cliffs, NJ: Prentice Hall. 1983.

Friedrich, Carl J. "Public Policy and the Nature of Administrative Responsibility", in Carl J. Friedrich and Edward S. Mason (eds.) *Public Policy*. Cambridge, MA: Harvard University Press. 1940.

Fry, G. K. "The Thatcher Government: The Financial Management Initiative, and the 'New Civil Service," *Public Administration*, 66 (1), pp. 1–20. 1998.

Follett, M. P. "The Essentials of Leadership", in P. Graham (ed.) *Mary Parker Follett: Prophet of Management*. Boston: Harvard Business School Publishing, pp. 163–177. 1996.

Gulick, Luther. "Notes on the Theory of Organization", in Luther Gulick and Lyndall Urwick (eds.) *Papers on the Science of Administration*. New York: Institute of Public Administration, pp. 3–46. 1937a.

Gulick, Luther. *Papers on the Science of Administration*. New York: Institute of Public Administration. 1937b.

Haugen, Brenda. *Douglas MacArthur: America's General*. Minneapolis, MN: Compass Point Books. 2006.

Hollander, E. P. "Leadership, Followership, Self and Others", *The Leadership Quarterly*, 3, pp. 43–54. 1992.

Hollander, E. P. "How and Why Active Followers Matter in Leadership", In Adams and Webster (eds.) *Kellogg Leadership Studies Project Working Papers: The Balance of Leadership and Followership*. College Park, MD: Academy of Leadership Press, pp. 11–30. 1997.

Hollander, E. P. "Ethical Challenges in the Leader-Follower Relationship", in Joanne B. Ciulla (ed.) *Ethics, the heart of leadership*. Westport, CT: Praeger, pp. 47–58. 2004.

Hollander, E. P., and W. B. Webb. "Leadership, Followership, and Friendship: An Analysis of Peer Nominations", *Journal of Abnormal and Social Psychology*, 50, pp. 163–167. 1955.

House, Peter W. *The Art of Policy Analysis*. Beverly Hills, CA: Sage. 1982.

Hummel, Ralph P. "Bureaucracy, Democracy, and Politics: Are They Compatible?" unpublished paper. 1986.

Jung, Dong, and Bruce Avolio. "Opening the Black Box: An Experimental Investigation of the Mediating Effects of Trust and Value Congruence on Transformational and Transactional Leadership", *Journal of Organizational Behavior*, 21 (8), pp. 949–964. 2000.

Kant, Immanuel. *Perpetual Peace and Other Essays on Politics, History and Moral Practice*. Indianapolis: Hackett Publishing. 1983.

Kouzes, James M., and Barry Z. Posner. *The Leadership Challenge, 4th ed*. San Francisco: Josey-Bass. 2007.

Lindblom, Charles E. "The Science of Muddling Through", *Public Administration Review*, 19, pp. 79–88. 1959.

Locke, Chiok-Foong. "Leadership Behaviours: Effects on Job Satisfaction, Productivity and Organizational Commitment", *Journal of Nursing Management*, 9, pp. 191–204. 2001.

Marini, Frank, ed. *Toward the New Public Administration*. Scranton: Chandler Publishing Co. 1971.

McCann, L. "Reforming Public Services after the Crash: The Roles of Framing and Hoping", *Public Administration*, 91 (1), pp. 5–16. 2013.

Morgan, Gareth. 1986. *Images of Organization*. Newbury Park, CA: Sage.

Mosher, Frederick C. *Democracy and the Public Service*. New York: Oxford University Press. 1968.

Nitin, Nohria, and R. G. Eccles. *Networks and Organizations: Structure, Form and Action*. Boston: Harvard Business School Publishing. 1992.

Ott, J. Steven, Pitima Boonyarak, and Lisa Dicke. "New Public Management: Public Policymaking Dilemmas: Balancing between Administrative Capacity, Control and Democratic Governance", *Public Organization Review*, 1 (4), pp 487–492. 2001.

Raven, Bertram. "The Bases of Power and The Power/Interaction Model of Interpersonal Influence", *Analyses of Social Issues and Public Policy*, 8 (1), pp. 1–22. 2008.

Rector, R. and Sanera, M. *Steering the Elephant: How Washington Works*. Washington, DC: Universe Publishing. 1987.

Ruchelman, Leonard I. *A Workbook in Program Design for Public Manager*. Albany: State University of New York Press. 1985.

Taylor, Frederick. *The Principles of the Scientific Management*. New York: Harper Brothers. 1911.

Stillman II, Richard J. *Preface to Public Administration*. New York: St. Martin's Press. 1991.

Urwick, Lyndall. "Organization as a Technical Problem", in Luther Gulick and Lyndall Urwick (eds.) *Papers on the Science of Administration*. New York: Institute of Public Administration, pp. 47–88. 1937a.

Urwick, Lyndall. "The Function of Administration: With Special Reference to the Work of Henri Fayol", in Luther Gulick and Lyndall Urwick (eds.) *Papers on the Science of Administration*. New York: Institute of Public Administration, pp. 115–130. 1937b.

Waldo, Dwight. *The Administrative State*. New York: Holmes and Meier. 1948.

Weber, Max. *From Max Weber*. (Gerth and Mills, Trans.). New York: Oxford University Press. 1946.

Weick, Karl. *Social Psychology of Organization, 2nd ed*. Reading, MA: Addison-Wesley Publishing. 1979.

Weick, Karl. *Making Sense of the Organization*. Malden, MA: Blackwell. 2001.

Wildavsky, Aaron. "The Self Evaluating Organization", *Public Administration Review*, 32 (September-October), pp. 509–520. 1972.

Wildavsky, Aaron. *Speaking Truth to Power: The Art and Craft of Policy Analysis*. Boston: Little, Brown and Co. 1979.

Wildavsky, Aaron. *Speaking Truth to Power, 2nd ed*. New Brunswick, NJ: Transaction Publishers. 2007.

Wilson, Woodrow. "The Study of Administration", *Political Science Quarterly*, 2 (June), pp. 197–222. 1887.

Yao, Dennis A., Douglas Yates, and Herbert Kaufman. "The Politics of Management", *Journal of Policy Analysis and Management*, 6(3), pp. 487–500. 1988.

PART

IV

Outside Looking In

Until now the focus of our discussions has been on the inter- and intra-organization issues associated with American-style executive organizations. While American Public Administration does not exclude the legislative and judicial branches from its purview, the choice to focus on the executive branch goes back nearly a century. We also note that the early development of public administration as both a practice and an academic field was predicated upon the idea of the politics-administration dichotomy. The confluence of these events has meant that public administration as presented to those in the United States often fails to discuss two topics—non-American administration, particularly in countries in parliamentary systems, and the relationship between representative democracy and bureaucracy. It is these issues that will be addressed in this final part of the text.

Public Administration as taught by schools in the United States has the tendency to be ethnocentric. We easily lose sight of the fact that the process of governing is universal. Further, while the political and theoretical foundations of governments play a key role in understanding the bureaucratic activities that we associate with public administration, the act of governing suggests a set of common processes that must be understood in a social and cultural setting no less than in a political setting. On one hand public administration is quite similar throughout the world; certainly, the use of hierarchies and rule-enforcing mechanisms is found all over the world. The management activities that support and maintain public organizations also are similar. On the other hand, the social and cultural environments that undergird government operations suggest differences of style and practice that radically alter the nature of governmental decision-making. The differences among British, French, American, or Chinese public administration systems are as likely to be cultural as political.

The chapter on comparative administration provided a glimpse at how the fundamental questions of organization, operation, and politics are approached by other nations. The benefit of a comparative approach to public administration is not to see how the "other half" governs. The benefit is in the cultural sensitivity, not only about how others operate but also about the social and cultural influences that shape American public administration. Our governments work as they do not because of American democracy but because of the social, political, and cultural constraints that we as Americans place on those activities. Once we understand this simple notion, we have made considerable progress in understanding our government as surely as such understanding leads to an awareness of practice in other nations. That is the task of Chapter 14.

Implicit in many of the discussions in this text has been the underlying tension between the precepts of how to organize and operate a government agency and how to run a government. The conflicts that arise from attempts to ensure ethical decision-making graphically illustrate the conflict between organizational loyalty and the need to "blow the whistle" on inappropriate, as well as illegal, activities within an organization. Pressures for affirmative action, which emphasize social responsibility in hiring, at times conflict with our ideals of hiring persons based on the objective results of the merit process. These issues only begin to illustrate the differences between organizations that are based on hierarchical and expert-based perspectives and governments that are premised on the concepts of equity and representation. In preceding chapters this tension has been examined through the filter of two perspectives that are not always examined in public administration texts. In looking at the administrative patterns and practices of other nations, we have suggested that the structures and practices of executive agencies in this country are neither the only way to structure government organizations nor the only way to integrate the political and bureaucratic elements of a government. Chapter 15 has a distinct viewpoint. It is not a viewpoint to which everyone need agree. Like the prior chapter, it simply suggests that other ways and means of miming governments exist and are deserving of consideration. Just because we have developed a "habit" of structuring organizations along hierarchical lines does not mean that such structures have a permanent place in government organizing. More importantly, in recognizing that such structures may adversely affect our ability to govern democratically, we are obligated to try to alter those adverse effects. To do anything less would be to leave the impression that democratic representative governance is less important than hierarchical organizational structures.

This closes in a sense where it began by looking at public administration as an integral part of our collective daily lives and how it helps shape our experiences of government and the act of governance.

Learning Outcomes

At the conclusion of Part IV a student should be able to:

1. Appreciate the influences of political culture on public administration across the globe.
2. Effectively assert the role of bureaucracy in supporting democratic processes.
3. Anticipate how current theory has evolved up to the present and anticipate how it may change in the future.
4. Be an advocate for the importance of administration and management in governance.

CHAPTER

14

Bureaucracy, the Rule of Law, and Representative Democracy

REPRESENTATIVE GOVERNMENT AND BUREAUCRACY

For nearly a century, the relationship between democracy and the bureaucracy has been a major topic of debate among academics and politicians alike. That debate has been sharpened in the last three decades by the emergence of two dichotomous views: first, that of the advocates of the view that bureaucracy is the single greatest threat to political institutions, and second, that of the advocates of bureaucracy as a key representative institution. There does not appear to be a ready synthesis between these views because little, if any, common ground supports the two views. The first perspective has advocates among both economists and in political science who hold neo-liberal views about government in general. The second perspective has fewer academic adherents; nevertheless, it will be the one presented in some detail here. To wit, this chapter is written in two parts. The first part examines the assumptions about democratic government and about bureaucracy that exist today. There are two components to the first perspective, first is the concern most often expressed by some in political science that bureaucracy and democracy are incompatible. Reducing the influence of bureaucracies is seen as freeing the public to exercise the rights and privileges of democratic governance. The second component of this perspective is that governments per se are too large and that government regulations stifle the market and parenthetically the market better serves democracy because democratic governance is little more than a specialized market. Stated most succinctly, the central theme of the second perspective is that effective bureaucracy is critical to the exercise of democratic governance. The bureaucracy, as the embodiment of the rule of law, is the agent by which governance is manifest.[1]

FRAMEWORK AND ANALYSIS

Today we recognize democracy only as a method of selecting elected officials. We no longer see its potential (and purpose) as a process of governmental decision-making that guides and dominates all other governmental processes.

Representative government, either as a democracy or as its elitist antecedent republicanism, is a form of government that is focused on how decisions are to be made, not merely the end product of a decision. Ultimately, the quality of decisions is judged to be the result of the nature of the decision process as much as the nature of the decision. A century-long process of bureaucratization of government transferred the primary responsibility for the decision process to the hands of bureaucratic experts, and ultimately, even judgments as to the nature of decision results were turned over to the bureaucrats in deference to the notion of the preeminence of technical expertise. Democracy was reduced to the affirmation (or disaffirmation) through the ballot of policy selected by technical experts. Thus, in this scenario, democracy is little more than the means for replacing one elite with another and has no real relationship to governmental decision-making. Policy can, in theory, be redirected, but that is hardly the process envisioned two centuries ago when every aspect and determinant of policy was subject to critique and review. Representative government was intended to dictate the form and processes of government, not merely to define the relative scope of suffrage.

In treating democracy as merely a process of government, rather than as both a process and a form of government, any understanding of that key element in a full definition of democracy is lost. The public seems unable to understand, and thus successfully implement, such concepts as a representative bureaucracy, or even industrial democracy. This failure is not one of merely an imperfect government. It is also our failure to understand what can be done to change the situation. It would seem that we are so bound up in our misunderstandings that the courses we choose to correct past practice have made matters worse rather than better. With the progressive-era emphasis on efficiency of management also came a belief in the importance of unity of command.

Aspects of modernity such as liberal democracy, legal rational bureaucracy and socio-economic and political development usually go hand in hand. The development of liberal democracy is contingent upon the existence of a legal rational, merit-based bureaucracy. Although Max Weber was wary about the possible aberration that could result in bureaucracy taking over democratic institutions, he did concede that the two phenomena of mass democracy and modern bureaucracy' develop in parallel. The concepts of individual liberty, delegated sovereignty, political legitimacy and equality are results of modern man's ability to rationalize. To act upon the will of the majority in a modern mass-democracy, legal rational bureaucracy emerged as its necessary administrative tool.

This important facet of political modernity, however, has largely been ignored by democracy and development experts. The profound "reassessment" of the role of bureaucracy in the hope of curtailing fiscal crisis has resulted in extensive cutback programs that have destroyed the core segments of bureaucracy. Despite billions of dollars pouring into regions of Africa and Asia, new democratic states have not been able to deliver "good governance." Technically liberal democracy should facilitate modern bureaucracy but that has not been the case as shown by so many studies in public administration. Instead, there has been a conscious effort to stifle bureaucratic development in the belief that bureaucracy acts as a hindrance to democratic development.

(Pyakuryal, 2010, pp. iii–iv)

The primacy of efficiency over traditional views of democracy meant that a democracy existed if the bureaucracy was efficient, but ceased to exist if government became inefficient (even if the cause of the inefficiency was public action). The progressives in the United States sought to reform politics and administration by isolating them from "politics." Politics was reformed by electoral changes that sought to break the power of the ward bosses. The initiative and referendum, the short ballot, citywide elections, and weak major governments are four examples of such reforms. All but the short ballot has long since been recognized as of dubious value in "democratizing" politics.

Reinhold Niebuhr echoing Weber is one of the first to note that our notion of liberty depends more upon administrative competence than upon constitutional structures (Niebuhr, 1932). The passage of seven decades seems to have left this observation on the scrapheap, yet when looked at more closely we are struck by the clarity and accuracy of that observation. This leaves us to ponder: Does bureaucracy help liberal democracy or does bureaucracy hinder liberal democracy? Weber (1946) would argue that the development of democracy and bureaucracy are parallel phenomenon, the process of this development in the third world democracies has been sidetracked by the insistence upon strong markets as a better basis for democracy. Yet in the name of development administration during the 1960s and the 1970s and New Public Management during the 1990s, the natural progression of modern bureaucracy as an offshoot of modernity and democracy was thwarted.

The result was the rise of inept public institutions. Left to evolve, administrative institutions started taking the form of a hybrid state and administrative institutions were subsequently termed "prismatic" by Riggs (1964). These bureaucratic structures function very differently from Weber's modern legal-rational bureaucracy. Under the façade of modern bureaucracy, non-merit bureaucrats belonging to traditional class and caste elites retained their bureaucratic status. They then formed a self-protecting network to safeguard their special interests, especially their right to stay in office, which subsequently resulted in increasing inefficiency (Riggs, 1964). Under such conditions, bureaucracy is incapable of serving as an instrument of positive political change.

BUREAUCRACY AND DEMOCRACY

According to Riggs, if one is concerned with effective administration in the transitional societies, building political foundations for public administration is a prerequisite to erecting administrative superstructures with formally elaborated machinery for planning, staffing, budgeting, coordinating, and all the other administrative refinements (Riggs, 1964, p. 262). By political foundations he means a broad modern, legal-rational political base on which the administrative apparatus should be built. Unfortunately, as he indicates, the bureaucracies in transitional societies are prismatic in nature, i.e., not fully developed nor modernized and are therefore incapable of performing as effectively or as equitably as their counterparts in modernized societies. It is these prismatic bureaucracies that pose a danger to democratic institutions by acting as impediments to the democratic vitality of nascent liberal democratic states. But, why is bureaucracy seen as a threat to democratic development universally? To answer this question, one may first look at the historical development of the theories of modern bureaucracy and liberal democracy.

Modern Bureaucracy

Modern bureaucracy is a component of political modernity. Weber's (1946) analysis of bureaucracy remains the theoretical framework within which most empirical research on this subject is pursued. To understand Weber's idea about bureaucracy, it is necessary to begin with the framework of his political sociology in which the concept of bureaucracy finds its place. Weber's analysis begins with the assumption that all authority requires a belief in its legitimacy if it is to become stabilized. Accordingly, Weber set up his typology of the grounds on which a claim to legitimacy may be based.

Legitimacy rests first and foremost upon the belief in legality of normative rules and the right to issue commands on the part of those elevated to authority under those rules. In other words, obedience is owed to the legally established impersonal order. The second possible basis for legitimacy is traditional authority where legitimacy rests in the established beliefs on traditions and the legitimacy of the status of those exercising authority under them. The third basis for a belief in legitimacy is the expectation that an order will be obeyed is charismatic. Here legitimacy rests on the devotion to the specific and exceptional sanctity or heroism of an individual person and of the normative patterns or order revealed or ordained by him or her (Weber, 1946).

According to Weber (1946) legal authority rests on the acceptance of the validity of mutually interdependent ideas such as any given legal norm may be established by agreement or by imposition, on grounds of value rationality; every body of law is constructed from a consistent system of abstract rules which have normally been intentionally established. A person in authority is subject to an impersonal order and orients actions to it in his or her own dispositions and comments. The person who obeys authority does so only in the capacity as a "member" of the organization and what he or she obeys is only "the law" of an association, of a community, of a church, or a citizen of a state. Weber stresses the fact that while members of the organization obey a person in authority, they do not owe this obedience to the person in authority as an individual, but to the impersonal order (Weber, 1946).

The typical interpretation of Weber is that he is arguing that legal-rational bureaucracy and democracy are at once inextricably linked and antagonistic and, therefore, must be in constant and inescapable tension and conflict. Yet, Weber also saw legal-rational bureaucracy as an alternative to the (undemocratic) rule of the dilettantes (aristocrats). The paradox here is that as a system brought about by a modern democratic egalitarianism and universalism which promoted professional, expert impartial bureaucrats comes in constant clash with democracy, i.e., the "norms and desires of the masses."

Peters (1984) observes that a significant public bureaucracy is the distinguishing feature of a contemporary government. The massive increases in the number and complexity of government functions since the end of World War II or even the mid-1960s have generated demands for governance that could only be met through an increased capacity of public bureaucracy. Despite political pressure to minimize the policy-making role of the bureaucracy he believes that public bureaucracy remains in a powerful policy-making position. That power according to him may be the prerequisite of effective government in contemporary society. Goodsell (2003 p. 157), too, has argued that a good bureaucracy is indispensable to a free society and to democratic polity. According to him, the ability to vote a government out of office without disruption requires a reliable administrative apparatus.

Liberal Democracy

Today any critical examination of the term "democracy" immediately discovers its ambiguity and the multiplicity of meanings which it carries. Etymologically democracy translates to the rule of the people. In contrast with the two other primary forms of government, "aristocracy" and "monarchy," the Greek attitude towards democracy was simply one of weighing the advantages and the disadvantages inherent in this type as compared with those inherent in the other two primary forms. They did not conceive of democracy as a final end and goal of human existence. To this original meaning, however, there have been added extensions such as social and legal equality, individual liberty, economic opportunity, and equal rights of all (Rohr, 1978).

The roots of modern, liberal, representative democracy can be traced to the era of Enlightenment in Europe (eighteenth century). Despite many differences the writers and theorists of the era shared a conviction that human rationality could discover universal principles, whether of nature, morality, or aesthetics—the belief in universal human rights arose during and as a consequence of the Enlightenment. Reason became the core component of liberal democracy. Kant had argued that rational agents must agree to enter a social contract establishing a civil constitution—for only under a civil constitution can freedom be exercised. He concluded that to do otherwise would lead to the recourse to force, i.e. a state of war (Kant, 1983).

Barry (2000) inferred that at the center of liberal philosophy is the idea of a general good, which is capable of being shared by everyone, and which provides a standard for legislation. Accordingly, it is impossible that a government should be liberal merely by standing aside and refraining from legislation, or that a liberal society should come into being merely, so to speak, by political inadvertence. The function of a liberal government is to support the existence of a free society.

Thus modern liberal democracy belongs to the sphere of the political in the broadest sense, defined as collectively binding decision-making, whatever the group may be, from the family to the state. Its basic principles are that such decision-making should be controlled by all members of the group considered as equals—the principles in other words, of popular control and political equality. Bentham (1996) writes, "A system of collectively binding decision-making can be judged democratic to the extent that it embodies these principles, and specific institutions or practices to the extent that they help realize them" (p. 159). The role of the modern bureaucracy was set. The democratic process of collective decision-making thus gets transformed into rational action via modern bureaucracy—it helps the state to administer its policies and to govern according to its wills (Weber, 1946).

The Problem of New Democracies

The struggle to consolidate new democracies in the continents of Asia, South America, and Africa led to intensive study comparing polities, restructuring economic and political institutions as well as economic and social conditions. The success of democratic consolidation in Germany, Italy, and Japan after the Second World War had convinced policy makers that consolidating democracies in the developing nation-states would bear similar results (Pyakuryal). The optimism was further fueled by the second and third wave of democracy that came in during the 1970s and the 1980s respectively (Huntington, 1991). However most of those third-wave democracies, especially in Asia and Africa have either relapsed into authoritarianism or have teetered towards a state of anarchy.

Diamond (2006) stresses that these countries lack the more basic conditions of a viable political order. Consequently, before a country can have a democratic state, it must first have a state, i.e., a set of political and administrative institutions that exercise authority over a territory, make and execute policies, extract and distribute revenue, produce public goods, and maintain order by wielding an effective monopoly over the means of violence. As Weber suggested more than a century ago, for a state to exercise authority, it has to first have legitimacy. The end of the twentieth century was accompanied by various challenges to legitimacy (Morlino, 2002). These challenges prompted scholars to speak of the "crisis of democracy" with particular references to distancing of citizens from political parties, the emergence of anti-party attitudes, and a general dissatisfaction and anti-establishment attitude. Overall, scholars saw a general decline of confidence in public institutions. Absence of the rule of law results not only in disorder, it also erodes institutional strengths. Without a strong democratic system of the rule of law in place, institutions as well as citizens are vulnerable to arbitrary actions of the leaders, political players, as well as individuals (Pyakuryal).

Unlike in the past when democratic regimes fell due to coups or revolutions, the third-wave democracies according to Huntington (1991) are facing erosion, or the gradual weakening of democracies by those elected to lead them. A second potential threat comes from electoral victories of parties or movements apparently committed to anti-democratic ideologies. A third more serious threat to democracy is executive arrogation, which occurs when an elected chief executive concentrates power in his own hands, subordinates, or even suspends the legislature and rules largely by decree (Huntington, 1991, pp. 8–9).

MAKING SENSE OF IT ALL

As mentioned above there is an overlap of concepts between liberal democracy and legal-rational bureaucracy theories. Both are offshoots of modernity. As democracy seeks to achieve equality and freedom, bureaucracy acts as a tool to achieve that end by exercising neutrality, order, and predictability. Democracy and modern bureaucracy appear as two distinct yet complimentary concepts.

Weber (1946) observes that the progress of bureaucratization within the state administration is a phenomenon paralleling the development of democracy. However, there is also a general agreement that in many developing nations bureaucracy has gained ascendency over other political institutions and that the number of such cases has increased, at least until recently, with a resulting current imbalance in bureaucratic and political development (Heady, 2005).

One argument of this "institutional imbalance thesis" is that the existence of a strong modern bureaucracy in a polity with political institutions that are generally weak presents itself as a major obstacle to political development. The counter-argument is that a high level of bureaucratic development can be expected to enhance rather than hinder prospects of overall political development (Heady, 2005). According to Riggs (1964), the form of government usually found in nations generally regarded as modern is balanced whereas many developing nations have unbalanced polities. Riggs called the latter polities bureaucratic polities with the tendency to inhibit political development which he argued results from "premature or rapid expansion of bureaucracy when the political system lags behind." Lucian Pye (1963) also argued that the greatest problem in nation-building is how to relate the administrative and authoritative structures of government to political forces within the transitional societies in the face of the usual imbalance between administrative tradition and a confusing political process.

The question seemingly is does the risk of jeopardizing a more balanced political equilibrium in the future justify a deliberate policy of stifling further bureaucratic development whenever current imbalance exists favoring the bureaucracy. Pyakuryal (2010) argues that a relatively modern national administrative system is a necessary precondition of, not a hindrance to, societal modernization, including political development. Although Weber was wary of hyper-bureaucratization and of the influences of advancing bureaucracy on individual freedom, he himself conceded that as democracy levels the traditional power centers, modern bureaucracy helps dismantle the traditional administrative structures (Weber, 1946).

After six decades and number of predictive models, democratic consolidation is still as uphill a task. Hostility towards bureaucracy has also been a durable feature, especially among political conservatives and economic liberals. They regard bureaucracy as a manifestation of big government and an instrument for governmental interference in the operations of the private sector (Pyakuryal). All who share this distaste believe that they are faced with some formidable problems through internal contradictions in the democratic political structure itself; especially created by the role of bureaucracy in it (Etzioni-Halevy, 2000).

Weber himself was concerned about the ultimate effects of growing bureaucratization on democracy and freedom. More often than not, academics and development experts see bureaucracy as a mechanism that acts against the spirit of democracy, a system that impedes the very process of democracy. Consolidation of democracy has been attributed to everything from urbanization to industrialization, from economy to education, from religion to culture. However, one phenomenon that is the cornerstone of these occurrences—i.e., the development of modern bureaucracy and its potential influence on democracy consolidation has been sidelined. The study of public bureaucracy languishes in the backwaters of democracy projects (Pyakuryal, 2010).

The society that was intended to emerge from the new United States was one which cherished harmony and consensus but not at the expense of the beliefs and values of citizens. Disagreement was expected. But disagreement introduced through public forums (either the town meeting or the somewhat more restricted forum of the legislature) was the starting point for uncovering and then resolving problems. This may not have been the most agreeable way of going about solving public problems, but it was regarded as the only appropriate way in a republic or commonwealth. To withhold oneself from public debate is an act of irresponsibility.

Tinder's (1980) discussion of community is quite helpful in seeing the society that the founders strove to achieve.

> community is entered through communication and communication depends on certain kinds of social unity, such as common language and similar values. But community is not equivalent to, is not assured by, and may conflict with, social unity. Man is shaped and confined by society, but not wholly. To a degree, he transcends society; he can use it, question it, change it, destroy it. Community brings together persons in their essential being and therefore cannot consist of the social unity that persons partially transcend.
>
> (p. 32)

Society as an inheritance comes into our hands in the form of tradition. The communal idea is that tradition is wholly integral in inquiry, but that means it is to be examined rationally and be accepted, revised, or repudiated in complete clarity of mind. In other words, community entails an effort to master society as the collective past and relate it, if only by consciously accepting it, to the living present (Tinder, pp. 32–33).

There was also a moralistic, and even religious, overtone to the belief in the process developed in eighteenth-century America. On the one hand, the fallibility of man was accepted and understood. But in the turning to society and thus following social norms, man could achieve a better life and a better society. There was a consciousness of the importance of society as an arbiter of man's actions. Thus, public discussion was a means of "creating" society. But more importantly, the norm of that society, not a segment of that society, was being defined or refined.

BUREAUCRATIZING DEMOCRACY

The emergence of democratic thought in American politics in the mid-nineteenth century and ultimately across the globe is associated with an emphasis on universal suffrage, laissez-faire economics, and the opening of government employment to a wider segment of society through the patronage personnel system. The new democratic governments have been simultaneously larger and more restricted than the governments of the earlier era. Government has been growing very rapidly, yet the purpose of the growth has been to foster private development, not the growth of government enterprises.

The alignment of a bureaucratic government with the ideal of democracy was a crucial development in our history, precisely because the factor that made the parallelism possible—equality—was soon rejected as a bureaucratic norm. The norms that came to characterize the bureaucracy—rationalism, legalism, elitism, command government, and conflict suppression (Weber, 1946)—ultimately became norms for all of government. Very quickly the ideal of equality disappeared as a relevant factor in the bureaucracy. As the civil service reforms of the 1870s and 1880s point out, government became too complicated to be left to uneducated, inexperienced, political hacks. Rather, an educated elite with the knowledge gained from higher education and long government experience was considered to be a far more suitable personnel foundation upon which to achieve "good government." Democracy is preserved by the assumption of the political neutrality and pliability of the bureaucrat. The "people" vote for political leaders who then set policy that is to be efficiently implemented by the bureaucrat. The application of democracy to government is limited to the electoral process. After all, to have the people (or even the equally amateurish Congress) shape policy, rather than the bureaucratic expert would be inefficient. As Wilson notes, running a government is a very difficult task. In fact, it is a task too precious and complex to be left to the people. They could provide the broad policy parameters, but the running of government, the specifics of policy development and implementation, are to be given over to the executive agencies. The concept of democracy as an aspect of governmental policy making is thus lost. Democracy is being defined as only a mechanism for selecting officials of government. Democracy is a mythical version of majority rule, where the concept of majority means only the intermittent results of an election. In all other respects, democracy is nonexistent.

In saying that the political institutions of government had failed, it was determined that the process of defining the policies of government had failed or at the least were inefficient. The accepted solution was to simplify policy determination. Elections became plebiscites on bureaucratically generated policy (or on the policy implementation strategy of the bureaucracy).

One of the most persistent critics of the modern bureaucracy was Hummel (1987). He introduces a chapter by quoting Max Weber: "In a modern state the actual ruler is necessarily and unavoidably the bureaucracy" (p 213). Hummel's central thesis is that, in today's government, bureaucratic values have displaced political values and the new politician is a bureaucrat, not an elected official. In our faith in expertise and distrust of politicians, he argues that it is virtually impossible for a politician to change policy if faced by bureaucratic opposition. This is not merely a test of wills or of political power. Rather, this is a product of public support for bureaucratic rather than political decision-making. Yet the basis of bureaucratic decision is a technically based expertise that has no room for those who do not share that expertise.

> The solution of technical problems is not dependent on public discussion. Rather, public discussions could render problematic the framework within which the tasks of government action present themselves as technical ones.
> (Hummel, 1987, quoting Habermas, p. 231)

In the denigration of the political process, the public, no less than the politician, is left without power or influence. The practices and activities associated with representative government serve less purpose as people realize that they do not have any relationship to what is going on in government. The responsibility to select government officials to set policy is rather hollow when those selected do not set policy.

Toward a Democratic Government

A qualitative understanding of government requires that democracy mean more than the mechanistic process of voting. The ideal of a government as a commonwealth provides a model by which to understand a more broadly defined democracy. The perspective of the founding period emphasized consensus, harmony, social values, and problem resolution. To achieve those goals, participation had to be encouraged. But more importantly, the qualitative nature of participation requires that such participation have a direct relationship to the possibility of change. Further, that participation must be founded upon the desire to create a sense of community. As Glenn Tinder has suggested, this ideal of community is much broader than social unity. It transcends the minimalistic style of government suggested by the town meeting. The day when the town meeting could be the dominant vehicle for decision-making in government is over, yet surrogate processes are available. The representative institutions of government must be responsive to the public and must reflect the norms of behavior required for decision-making in a commonwealth. Only in this way can a quality democracy, and thus a quality government, be created.

Three key elements must characterize a democratic government: a meaningful process of public discussion (including tolerance), a reliance on consensus building in decision-making, and recognition of the importance of community. Democracy emerges from a sense of the collective responsibility for the creation of mutually acceptable goals and policies. The linkage of democracy to a libertarian equality is as much a dead end as its linkage to bureaucracy. This does not mean that equality is not an explicit goal of a democratic government, but, rather, that a society founded on an atomistic and individualistic structure cannot achieve democracy precisely because there is never any common ground on which people can join together. We achieve only that which we have already achieved: Small groups (the factions of *Federalist 10*) compete to achieve sufficient numeric superiority so that their views can be imposed upon all others.

Without the rejection of liberty as a wholly individualistic concept, there can be no movement toward democracy. Democracy is not a simple problem in mathematics. It is more than liberty. While the founders clearly were not attempting to create a democracy, the regime values that underlay the US Constitution represent an appropriate beginning in understanding democracy. But it is not merely in the listing of values such as equality, fairness, and equity that democracy emerges. It is the interaction of these goals, or how a people balance these values, that suggest the nature of government. As implied, today we seem content to pick among these values to find the one that benefits us as individuals in order to avoid the much harder choice of blending and balancing these values. The problem again is that in taking the easy way all links to democracy are lost. Just as Rousseau's majoritarianism could easily become tyranny, the reliance on a single value as the sole definition of action leads to tyranny. The regime values of this nation are not separable; they can exist only in conjunction with the other values.

The government that was intended for this country was organized to give the people the fullest opportunity to participate, directly or indirectly. We may disagree with the balance between direct and indirect participation chosen at the time, but the fundamental reason for desiring participation has not altered. Participation was not a mathematical process but a subjective, qualitative relationship between individuals and society. The institutions of government were built upon the use of consensus because the information supplied to government officials was part of a larger consensus-building effort. The goal was to define what was best for society, not for any individual or group. The "best for society" did not emerge from a simple vote; rather it emerged from a three-step process of open discussion, agreement on the scope of action, and then agreement on a temporary course of action. The focus was on collective social action not on the implementation of the top choice among rationally analyzed alternatives.

This open, inquiring society would above all display the "virtue" of tolerance. But what kind of outlook on government is indicated by tolerance?

> The theory of tolerance implies that it is not enough for tolerance to be widespread and enduring merely as an attitude on the part of individuals; it needs to [sic] the support of institutions and social forms. If people are interdependent, if they are not very rational, and if they are not reliably co-operative, then it is vain to expect many individuals to be tolerant without encouragement from those around them and without support from conditions and structures in the surrounding society. . . .
>
> The nature of a tolerant society gives rise to the idea that the viability of tolerance depends on politics. It is suggested that political artifice would be required for resolving conflicts ensuing from tolerance. But a politics of tolerance presumably would be concerned not just with settling immediate conflicts but also with more distant goals—with establishing enduring conditions that are conducive to tolerance and to communication.
>
> (Tinder, 1976, p. 150)

Can these understandings of the way governments develop policy be used to examine the relationship among and within the institutions of government in decision-making?

GOVERNMENTAL DEMOCRACY

Every schoolchild is taught that two key ideas underpin the relationship of the three branches of American government: separation of powers and checks and balances. Unfortunately, these are not closely linked ideas, and, in fact, many political thinkers of the founding period thought that the task of shaping government was in picking one or the other of these approaches (Fisher, 1982). The choice was that of checks and balances, because it better reflected the principle of interdependence. It is this latter point that is central to understanding the concept of checks and balances; it was a procedural and structural means of promoting the interdependence of the elements of government. Separation of powers was an historic artifact of English thought where the concern was for the independence of the parliament from political domination by the king and his ministers. The historic division of governmental functions from the earliest colonial times made this a moot issue.

The more critical problem was in determining how the separate institutions would work together. Checks and balances implied a procedural and functional interdependence. To the extent that political domination of one branch over another was possible, the reality of organizational separation would protect that branch.

The interdependence of the branches of government served to promote a broad perspective in decision-making. Each branch's duty and responsibility was to use its resources and energies to determine what was best for society. The likelihood of that collective good being defined was enhanced by the interaction with the other branches, which applied quite different resources and energies to the same problem.

But what of the bureaucracy, the fourth branch of government? Does the concept of interdependence suggest how interaction with bureaucracy might take place? Most who look at this problem find it necessary to remake the bureaucracies into non-hierarchic organizations. Yet, this would not necessarily alter the elitist orientation of the organization. In fact, the major thrust of the new public administration has been that the more traditional government institutions have failed and that bureaucracies, of necessity, have taken up political tasks to compensate for this failure. Adherents to the idea of a "representative bureaucracy" do not wish to alter the elitist technocratic character of the bureaucracy, but rather, argue that bureaucrats would understand the problems of society better if, demographically, they matched society. This is playing the same kind of quantitative numbers game that has caused so much confusion in defining democracy.

Attempts to "open" the bureaucracy have generally met with failure. The focus has been on creating rules by which clients can communicate with bureaucrats. But the problem is in a belief that is as fundamental to bureaucracy as to science, that the application of expertise and knowledge can produce permanent and final answers. The rule-bound administrator is still a captive of the linear thinking of turn-of-the-century scientific management. Under those circumstances, any action that diminishes the ability of the manager (bureaucrat) to plan and apply technology reduces the likelihood of an effective and efficient job being done. Thus, allowing public input is to diminish the appropriateness of the outcome because it implies that non-experts ought to rule experts.

The solution to this problem rests in an approach to the work of the bureaucracy that recognizes that its authority is derived from the public and the other institutions of government, not from autonomy. The concept of checks and balances that was created to regulate the competing authorities of the three branches of government must similarly apply to the bureaucracy. Rather than claiming special privilege, either because of the claim of being apolitical or because of the claim of expertise, the bureaucracy must be placed within the same decision-community within which the other institutions of government are placed. The bureaucracy must be subjected to the same competing claims of the public as other branches into its domain, not to stop action but because it is the only way that "right" action is possible. The bureaucratic expert still plays a critical role. The expert perspective cannot be ignored. However, the role is constrained by a larger decision process.

The bureaucracy must accept a hostile environment in which every decision is criticized, critiqued, and subject to amendment (see Dahl, 1966). Only then may a bureaucracy that can earn the title of representative bureaucracy be created. Such a bureaucracy would be representative in the Burkean sense of representation; the purpose of representation is in creating the opportunity for national goals and national beliefs to be defined and clarified. The action of government would be but the final result of this pursuit of common interest, an interest that could result only from the collective interaction of all elements of society and government. This common interest as emerging from the public development of national goals may be a reasonable definition of "public interest."

How can a rule-bound, technocratic bureaucracy be made democratic? Focusing only on the external interaction of governmental institutions is not sufficient. The internal operations of bureaucracy must be changed. But in this latter change a shift to "industrial democracy" is not enough. The internal processes of the bureaucracy must be democratized in the sense of reducing emphasis on technological and managerial expertise in favor of a process that emphasizes consensus, harmony, and interdependence. The concepts of open discussion and even checks and balances can be introduced. New definitions would have to be accepted. Duplication and overlapping jurisdictions may not be proof of ineffectiveness. In being as concerned about how we set policy as we are of the policy itself, traditional concepts of inefficiency and ineffectiveness become meaningless. A return to Weber's ethic of means, rather than reliance on an ethic of ultimate ends, produces a very different set of judgments about how decisions are made. In "Politics as Vocation," Weber (1946) espouses an ethic of means that treasures the process of decision-making, not merely the final result. But more importantly, this ethic is tempered by a set of principles upon which to base social interaction. It could be argued that for those in the federal government the US Constitution ought to serve as that set of principles. Another analogy is in Wildavsky's *Speaking Truth to Power* (1978), which contrasts the art of policy analysis with the science of policy analysis. Truth comes not from science but from art. Effectiveness of government is not merely in the execution of policy but begins with the process by which public issues are defined through the oft-amended act of executing policy.

CONCLUSION

For seven decades academicians have sought to create and/or explain links between the bureaucracy and democracy. The focus of much of the last decade has been a Weberian attack on the structural and organizational roadblocks to democracy created by the hierarchical nature of bureaucracy. Such critiques have been a necessary starting point. Recognizing the failure of the hierarchic model must precede any change in the basic organization of bureaucracy.

The weakness of these critiques is that they presume that a more open, participative management is the key to the advent of bureaucratic or industrial democracy. While participative management represents an appropriate style of operation, the understanding of democracy implied by this process is as restrictive as in the governmental context.

This chapter has suggested that a broader definition of democracy that accounts for both qualitative and quantitative decision styles must be accepted before governmental democracy is possible. This concept implies a greater concern about the process of problem definition, particularly as the process relates to uncovering the political, social, economic, and moral values that underlay an understanding of the issue as a "problem." Opening the bureaucracy to input from the public is not sufficient. A sense of interdependence with the public at large and particularly the other institutions of government is necessary for anything as otherwise cursory as public comment to have meaning. Only in a belief that the appropriateness of the action is dependent on that communication is a change in bureaucratic decision-making possible. Further, the recognition of the temporary character of such decisions becomes the next link to the new definition of democracy.

In this way the bureaucracy earns the title of representative bureaucracy, being required to act in conjunction with, and on behalf of, the public and other institutions. In seeking this objective, the bureaucracy will very quickly become "unbureaucratic," because the pursuit of such a goal of national common interest is beyond the capacity of traditional bureaucratic processes.

Governmental democracy constitutes a very different concept of governmental (and particularly bureaucratic) decision-making. It is necessary if we are ever to achieve any kind of democracy in this nation. Introduced in conjunction with the changes in management style implicit in the anti-hierarchical viewpoint, governmental democracy will change both the way decisions are made and the very nature of the bureaucratic experience.

DISCUSSION QUESTIONS

- Do you think that democracy and bureaucracy are incompatible?
- To what extent are the issues of bureaucratic governance universal?
- What are the possible solutions to the failure of bureaucracies in emerging democracies?
- In what specific ways can bureaucracy support democratic processes?

NOTE

1. The work of Dr. Sucheta Pyakuryal is central to much of this analysis. Her earlier work on bureaucracy and the work that we are doing together are imbedded in much of what is presented in this chapter.

BIBLIOGRAPHY

Barry, N. *An Introduction to Modern Political Theory,* 4th ed. Basingstoke, UK: Palgrave. 2000.

Bentham, Jeremy. *An Introduction to the Principles of Morals and Legislation.* New York: Oxford University Press. 1996.

Crenson, Matthew A. *The Federal Machine: Beginnings of Bureaucracy in Jacksonian America.* Baltimore, MD: Johns Hopkins University Press. 1975.

Dahl, Robert. *Political Opposition in Western Democracies.* New Haven: Yale University Press. 1966.

Etzioni-Halevy, Eva. *Bureaucracy and Democracy.* London: Routledge. 2000.

Fisher, Louis. *The Politics of Shared Power.* Washington, DC: Congressional Quarterly Press. 1982.

Habermas, Jurgen. *Toward a Rational Society.* Boston: Beacon Press. 1971.

Hallowell, John. *The Moral Foundation of Democracy.* Chicago: University of Chicago Press. 1954.

Hummel, Ralph P. *The Bureaucratic Experience, 3rd ed.* New York: St. Martin's Press. 1987.

Hummel, Ralph P., and Robert Isaak. *The Real American Politics*. Englewood Cliffs, NJ: Prentice Hall. 1986.

Huntington, Samuel. *The Third Wave: Democratization in the Late Twentieth Century*. Norman: University of Oklahoma Press. 1991.

Lindblom, Charles. *Politics and Markets*. New York: Harper Collins. 1977.

Morlino, Leonardo. "Democratic Anchoring: How to Analyze Consolidation and Crisis", *Central European Political Science Review*, 3 (10), pp. 6–19. 2002.

Pyakuryal, Sucheta. *Weberian Bureaucracy: A Requisite for the Consolidation of Liberal Democracy. Dissertation*. Akron, OH: University of Akron 2010.

Pye, Lucian. *Communications and Political Development*. Princeton: Princeton University Press. 1963.

Riggs, Fred W. *Administration in Developing Countries: The Theory of Prismatic Society*. Boston: Houghton Mifflin. 1964.

Sabine, George. *A History of Political Theory*. New York: Holt, Rinehart and Winston. 1961

Tinder, Glenn. *Tolerance*. Amherst, MA: University of Massachusetts Press. 1976.

Tinder, Glenn. *Community: Reflections on a Tragic Ideal*. Baton Rouge: Louisiana State University Press. 1980.

Weber, Max. "On Bureaucracy", in From Max Weber (eds.) and H. H. Gerth and C. Wright Mills (trans.). New York: Oxford University Press. 1946.

Wildavsky, Aaron. *Speaking Truth to Power*. Boston: Little, Brown and Co. 1979.

CHAPTER 15

Administration in a Global Perspective

FRAMEWORK FOR STUDY

The field of comparative administration emerged in the late 1950s. At that time, it was a sub-field driven by American scholars who applied the then known tools of public administration and political science to the new post-colonial governments of the world. While the perspective was not ethno-centric, it did begin from an assumption that American-style government and *governing* practices were the appropriate starting point for studying other governments. As the sub-field grew, a more "global" perspective developed. Academics in the United States became less "judgmental" and began to search for common themes and common understandings across nations. Gone was the simplistic assumption that "we" knew how to do it right. Lessons and innovations in administrative practice were documented in Europe and Asia. Topics such as ethics and governance were seen as "problems" that all governments shared rather than as defects in the operations of "transitional" governments. We came to realize that we *all* had much to learn. We also have become more aware of how political culture, social history, and prior experience shape administration. There is no one "model" of government or governance that fits the world.

One important feature of comparative administration is the opportunity to explore how we can learn from each other—despite, or maybe because of—our differences. We will examine administration as both a technical and political phenomenon. We will also explore the central issues of governance today—democratization and public integrity.

Comparative administration requires acceptance of the notion that public administration is an integral part of a nation's political system. This implies more than accepting the reality of the role of bureaucracy in policy implementation (or, to use the words of the US Constitution, the "faithful execution of the laws"). This viewpoint suggests three points of interaction between the political system and public administration. The first is in decision-making. The process of decision-making is shaped by the nature of political-bureaucratic linkages. Second, the impact of decisions (or policy implications) is shaped by the relationship between political and administrative institutions. Third, cultural and environmental factors can generate different policies despite the apparent similarities in the structures of government.

POLITICAL CULTURE AND PUBLIC ADMINISTRATION

Central to the existence of wide varieties of governments is the influence of culture on government. The most obvious influence is in the way people are socialized to accept certain forms of government as good or bad. Political socialization, which is simply a part of the more general socialization and enculturation processes, permits persons in a society to make judgments about what constitutes "good government." But it must also be noted that political norms cannot be wholly separated from economic and social norms. The interaction of these three norms in effect defines a culture. Also, by defining what is good or bad in government, the culture creates a framework for defining permissible government action. This understanding of the "right kind of government" goes beyond acceptance of the institutions of government to the very character of the government activity. The easiest way of visualizing this is to recognize that the labeling of a regime as conservative or liberal often has more to do with policy and action than the type of government institutions employed. It is this fact that is relevant to understanding the impact of culture on public administration.

The influence of culture can be understood to influence public administration at three levels: the societal level, the political level, and the administrative level. The interrelationship of culture at all three of these levels defines public administration in any cultural setting.

Impact of General Cultural Norms

Cultural anthropologists and sociologists have assisted public administration theorists greatly in understanding the impact on how government decisions are made through the influence of societal or cultural norms. Bendix (1956) conducted a series of studies in the 1940s and 1950s that led him to distinguish between entrepreneurial and bureaucratic societies. The entrepreneurial society is dominated by an informal, personalized style of decision-making. The bureaucratic society favors an impersonal, rule-bound authority structure and decision style. Not surprisingly, where hierarchical bureaucratic structures of government decision-making are overlaid on an informal decision process, considerable tension and stress results. (As a point of reference, the United States is more entrepreneurial than bureaucratic. Our desire to seek exception to all rules is a manifestation of the stress resulting from the conflict of decision norms.)

In 1964 Fred Riggs offered a new tool for analyzing and classifying governments (see Chart 15–1). He presented a framework for comparative analysis and in particular for conceptualizing transitional societies. His framework gave us new tools for:

- Understanding the forces that lead to administrative transformation
- Understanding the process of changes from traditional, status-oriented bureaucracies to "modern" organizations in which efficiency and effectiveness are basic operating principles

296 | **CHAPTER 15** Administration in a Global Perspective

Riggs argues that there are three "types" of administration organization based upon the relationship between structure of the organization and the function of the organization. He classified the organizational types as:

- Fused
- Diffracted
- Prismatic

Importantly, he sees these types as both *societal* and *governmental* characteristics. Therefore, all societies have elements of all three operating within them. The "dominant" type emerges as a result of factors such as the power distribution in society (Riggs uses two classifications—traditions and legalisms—that mimic Weber's three classes of authority), the "manifest and latent" functions of organizations, the level of commitment or social acceptance of legal mandates, and finally the scale of organization/nation-state. Riggs foresees a battle for social control between the central authority (government) and "local" elites. Change occurs when the "interest" configuration of the competing social networks change. Thus, "nations" emerge when local elites find interests compatible with those of central elites and the central elites willingly "decentralize."

Sartori (1969) offers an extension of this notion found in the distinction between rationalist and pragmatic societies. The rationalistic culture, epitomized by continental Europe, emphasizes a deductive style of decision-making. This style when applied to government suggests three norms:

CHART 15–1

Riggs' Typology

- Fused Administration (traditional societies)
  - Social status as source of influence
  - Non-specific functional assignment of duties
  - Organizations perform multiple tasks and activities
    - Generalist administration
    - Central control/direction
    - Limited level of complexity in tasks/assignments
- Diffracted organizations ("developed" societies)
  - Multiple agencies with narrow functional responsibilities
    - Specialization
    - Expert-driven
    - Decentralized control
    - Hierarchical organizations and relationships among organizations
- Prismatic organizations
  - Transitional phase or a distinct form?
    - Era of creation
    - Complexity of task assignment
      - Some organizations are non-specific, others are functionally specific
      - Both generalist and expert-driven decisions

1. Universality and impersonality of rules
2. Specifics defined by reference from the general
3. Limited discretion

In contrast, the pragmatic cultures, which include Great Britain, the United States, and much of Africa and Asia, apply an empirical or inductive style of decision-making. Such cultures produce government decisions that are characterized as follows:

1. Common law style practice of generalities defined by specifics
2. Personal concern—rules never fit circumstances
3. Discretion key for bureaucrats
4. Emphasis on individual rights

In many societies, decision rules are not so straightforward because of the dominance of the hierarchical structure of governments and therefore the attempt to superimpose the rationalistic style on pragmatic cultures. Katz and Eisenstadt (1960) thus have noted that often bureaucrats shift norms of rule compliance to accommodate the norms of a pragmatic society. Again, while the assumption is that the societies in which such shifts in rule compliance occur are strictly "third-world" nations, it is factually no less a factor in the United States and English-culture nations.

Political Norms and Public Administration

While it is easy to speak in terms of a Western political culture, considerable diversity of policy emerges from that common heritage. What is essential is the specific orientation and belief system of individuals toward the role of politics and government as one type of social action and societal decision-making. The limits of bureaucratic action are culturally defined. Also, the relative esteem of the public servant is culturally defined. Goodsell (2003) very forcefully and effectively argues that the popularly perceived shortcomings of the American bureaucrat are exacerbated by the inability of the bureaucrat to achieve cultural acceptance. Particularly in the United States, the culture praises the private sector and mistrusts the public sector. Government attempts to solve economic and social problems are met with more cynicism in the United States than in other nations with an English political heritage and with far more doubt than in nations with a more continental European political heritage. As a people, Americans are far less willing to endorse government action to solve social and economic problems. Further, this viewpoint is cultural rather than ideological as evidenced by the campaigns of successive presidents (Carter, Reagan, Clinton, and George W. Bush), which were based on a formula of "running against (the bureaucrats in) Washington." Even the so-called conservative governments of Europe, most particularly that of Prime Minister Thatcher, operate from an assumption of the role of government that would be branded as "socialistic" if endorsed by an American politician. Thus, while a national system of health insurance is regarded as too liberal in the United States today, such plans were first endorsed in England in the 1920s and the nationalization of health care was instituted in 1946. The relationship between the public and private sector is quite different in these two countries that are normally quite close politically.

Pye (1965) offers insight in his elaboration of four dimensions of political culture. A particular political culture can be defined by placing it along the continuum of each of the four dimensions. Those dimensions are the following:

1. Hierarchy and equality
2. Liberty and coercion
3. Loyalty and commitment
4. Trust and distrust

While we have implicitly discussed some of these issues already, they deserve reiteration. The dimension of hierarchy and equality is closely related to concepts such as the pragmatic versus rationalistic societies or the entrepreneurial versus bureaucratic societies. Pye's insight is in recognizing that these distinctions represent the extremes of a continuum of styles, not a more simplistic dichotomy. The point remains, made by Bendix a half century ago, that there is considerable tension introduced into the political system where the norm is equality; but the nominal structure of the style of government reflects norms of hierarchy. This tension produces many different responses in government. In Belgium, for example, many agencies operate as dual bureaucracies—one Flemish, the other French—because the hierarchy could not accommodate the equality of language and culture that the country thought was appropriate. The use of hiring quotas based on ethnicity or religion in many European nations reflects this same tension.

The political dimension of liberty and coercion seems on the surface to be the least well related to public administration. However, if this dimension is not treated as a question of the theoretical relationship of the individual to government but rather is cast in terms of authority to act, then the relationship to public administration is more explicit. The question becomes one of the expectation of compliance with government rules and, therefore, the nature of the force required to achieve compliance. In other words, what level of government intervention into individual or corporate decision-making is appropriate and what level of non-compliance with the law is to be tolerated. For example, the level of underpayment of taxes in Italy is notorious, yet the continuation of a process of collection that is basically voluntary is more important than forced compliance. The political norm of the myth of the voluntary tax system is more important than increasing revenue collection by admitting the level of corruption in the system. A lesser problem exists in the United States, but it is a growing concern. However, few would dare publicly suggest that under-reporting of income is so serious that alternative (and in fact simpler) methods of collection and enforcement should be tried. The myth of the "voluntary" tax system is too powerful. There are numerous other examples of nations tolerating cumbersome or outmoded methods of operation because a change would challenge a mythical norm of social behavior.

The third dimension, loyalty and commitment, at first strikes one as not a continuum at all. As applied by Pye, this dimension was intended to examine the level of social cohesion in society. Loyalty meant association with a subgroup, whereas commitment suggested a concern that was national in scope or focus. How government accommodates loyalties to achieve some degree of national commitment is a problem of public administration. As noted previously, it is not uncommon in Europe for ethnic or religious loyalties to be accommodated by establishing hiring quotas in national government agencies. Many African governments try to achieve commitment to a national government by accommodating the leaders of the various tribes that live within the national boundaries. Decisions, whether by political leaders or by bureaucrats, are of necessity the result of coalition building and compromise. The character of such decisions may also be affected by the fact that mere majority vote may be insufficient. Where loyalty to a subgroup is stronger than commitment to the nation, a minority in strong opposition can stop all government action.

The final dimension concerns the level of trust or distrust in government institutions. This dimension is more related to what people allow government to be involved in rather than trust or distrust in the legitimacy of the government. The issues raised by Goodsell concerning what policies and programs government is deemed competent to undertake reflect this dimension; the greater the level of distrust, the less likely the support for an expansion of authority for government action. Also, even where the general public has endorsed a government initiative, the scope of action may be constrained by public distrust. Thus, this dimension has both a normative and a practical facet. From a normative perspective, certain activities can be undertaken in somewhat tangential ways. For example, the choice of private or self-regulation or government regulation in lieu of government operations reflect the greater distrust of government in the United States than in Europe.

Political Culture and Management

The final impact of political culture is in the manner and style of management. This perspective suggests that norms of political culture shape the way government programs are managed. The acceptance of authority, the requirement of rule compliance, and the proper role of bureaucrats as policy makers are political and theoretical concerns that shape administration.

Max Weber's analysis of the sources of authority are important for an understanding of the influence of political culture on administration. According to Weber those sources are tradition, charisma, and legal-rational authority (1946). Management practice, as understood by Western cultures, is founded on principles of legal-rational authority. This authority is created by the application of hierarchical organizational structures. Thus, even as Western nations have moved toward more open, participative styles of government, the internal operations of those governments have remained bound by authoritarian and autocratic notions of management. This has created a considerable tension as theorists and practitioners attempt to reconcile political notions of democracy and participation with management views that do not support participation.

The conflict of authority and management is similarly present in many third-world nations. Here the power base of leaders has been in acceptance of traditional authority. The introduction of hierarchy and, therefore, a legal-rational authority structure destroys that traditional power base. This problem runs deeper than who is "in" and who is "out" of power. Weber's concept of authority incorporates the legitimacy of that authority. Thus, a full picture of this conflict is the challenge to the value and legitimacy of traditional authority when confronted by the legal authority of the hierarchy. This conflict is both political and social-psychological. "Giving orders" may be as difficult as "taking orders." Except where the traditional authorities can be accommodated through the informal organization (the existence of which is in itself an anathema to the hierarchical concept), the decision-making of such an organization is likely to be halting and slow at best.

In Western democracies, the electorate expects their democratically chosen representatives to make policy decisions. This political norm is inherently in conflict with the hierarchical management expectation that decisions will be made by experts with special competence in the policy area. The old saying "On tap, not on top" reflects a considerable naïvety. Simply recognizing this does not provide a theoretical perspective that preserves the concept of representative democracy and at the same time does not subject society to decision-making by the unprepared. The perplexing question becomes "How can a hierarchical management style be maintained if it undermines the decision-making institutions it is designed to assist?"

The second area in which political norms and administration conflict is in theories of motivation and productivity. How are political theory and norms of the political culture related to motivation? Motivation is traditionally thought to be stimulated by coercion, psychological or ideological intervention, monetary reward, or participation. Each of these concepts may be predicated on a set of political beliefs or norms. Thus, for example, to coerce an employee physically is not acceptable behavior. But is it acceptable to fire, demote, or transfer employees who are presumed to oppose the policy initiatives of a particular leader? The infamous "spoils system" of mid-nineteenth-century America endorsed just such a system. It must also be pointed out that to this day in the United States and in many developing nations, the idea of removal for political reasons and the need for partisan loyalty from senior civil service officials are considered necessary ingredients of successful government. This stance goes beyond the British concept of "neutral competence." Europeans are seemingly quite comfortable with a civil service operating under a norm of neutral competence with civil servants holding even sub-cabinet positions. Americans and officials in many third-world countries favor a patronage hiring system that extends down into the bureaucracy and an expectation of personal loyalty to a particular political figure that has no equivalent in Europe. Having rejected neutral competence, political control through coercive personnel policies is the only way to ensure an effective and "loyal" government.

The type of coercion implied by the threat of transfer and demotion is different from the psychological or ideological pressures placed on government employees. Yet both seek to achieve the same result—an efficient and effective workforce. One means of achieving this goal is to indoctrinate employees so that they internalize a certain political doctrine or philosophy. This practice, which Lindblom calls preceptoral education (1977), seeks to overcome technical or education competence with a belief in the political culture so that effective work is achieved.

The notion that monetary rewards are the key to motivating workers is widely held, despite the numerous studies that suggest that intrinsic rewards are more effective. Interestingly, monetary rewards are a strong indicator of the culture's regard for and status of public employees. In the United States low salaries clearly reflect the low status of most public employment. Yet, the concept of work as intrinsically rewarding is also used to justify low salaries. Employees are told that they did not go to work in government to get rich, so they should be content to accept low salaries. At the other extreme, in a number of third-world countries the only effective means of career and personal development is through government. Therefore, those with a high degree of entrepreneurial spirit enter government service. Not only are such positions well paying, but it may also be regarded as appropriate to seek additional monetary reward from these public-private ventures.

The question of monetary reward has both a practical and a normative dimension. For those political cultures that distrust government, both practical and normative considerations dictate lower salaries. In communities that exhibit strong support for government higher salaries, it may be only a normative concern (as in England). In a few countries that support this, it is manifested by high salaries.

The last concept that contributes to the motivation of public employees is that of participation in organizational decision-making. The political culture of most Western nations would suggest that participation is a strongly held value. In northern Europe this is true, but in the United States the concept of participative management receives academic support but is rarely practiced. The top-down chain-of-command notions of hierarchy, still strongly endorsed by the business community, leave the implicit impression that most forms of participation are somewhat suspect. This disapproval is exacerbated by the popular myth of governmental/bureaucratic incompetence. A participative style of management evokes images of chaos and indecisiveness. In this view, only the hardheaded businessperson who knows how to give orders can straighten out such a mess! The influence of the political culture ultimately results in the turning away from norms that culture otherwise would endorse.

PERSONNEL PRACTICE IN COMPARATIVE PERSPECTIVE

The influence of cultural norms is no less apparent on personnel practice than on management style. Specifically, we will explore the approaches to common personnel activities such as recruitment, affirmative action/minority rights initiatives, pay, and retention. The goal of this section is to facilitate your understanding of how the interplay of culture and management theory yield quite varied governmental activities and, therefore, understanding of what is appropriate practice.

RECRUITMENT IN THE PUBLIC SECTOR

How is it determined that a person is qualified for a particular public office? This is, in fact, one of the most basic of all questions faced in public administration. Sociologist Talcott Parsons (1951) addressed this question in distinguishing between "ascriptive" societies and "achievement" societies. Advancement in an achievement society is presumed to be based on what the individual can do, not by who that person is. In ascriptive societies, persons are recruited into the bureaucracy (government) on the basis of ascriptive criteria—class, status, race, language, caste. In other words, an individual's position is determined largely by immutable personal characteristics.

No nation fully exhibits the characteristics of either an ascriptive- or achievement-oriented society. Further, while we often associate modern precepts of management with a preference for achievement-oriented origin, the pattern of recruitment and hiring in most "modern" nations may be more ascriptive than presumed. Part of the reason for this is an increasing sensitivity to minority rights (which will be discussed in more detail later), but also preference for hiring based on partisan political viewpoints, class, race, religion is common. The concern of many governments is to balance ascriptive and achievement-based hiring—thus, for example, the deep-rooted American preference for the recruitment of the small cadre of senior managers from the political ranks rather than from the career bureaucracy. In other instances, ascriptive hiring is masked by the need for nominally achievement-based credentials, such as education. Although the attractiveness of government employment is on the wane for those from Oxford and Cambridge, the bias toward a liberal arts education in England yields a bureaucracy that is dominated at the senior levels by persons of a distinctly upper-class background. Peters points out that even into the 1980s "studies of the British civil service . . . show over two thirds of the senior civil service having gone to Oxford or Cambridge" and the education bias in Japan is even more pronounced than in the UK (Peters, 2010, p. 113). The same seems to be true in India, France, and elsewhere. As Peters concludes, "The importance of not only attending college but also the right college is indeed unmistakable" (Peters, p. 113). Given the elite nature of the "right colleges," one is hard-pressed to claim that educational attainment is exclusively achievement-based criteria.

The most common form of ascriptive recruitment is that of patronage hiring. Virtually every political system has some level at which appointments are quite clearly political, although they also have jobs for which appointment is made on a relatively routine basis and on some sort of merit system. As desirable as the idea of employing the "best" person for each job in the public service may be, from the point of view of enforcing the "achievement" norms of a modern society (and perhaps of achieving new goals of social equality in a developing society), some important complications may result from merit recruitment. These may be especially noticeable when contrasted to the alternative: patronage appointment. Merit recruitment implies a more mechanistic conception of the administrator or bureaucrat as a value-free administrator of programs who administers public policies regardless of their intentions or impacts on society. This conception of the administrator often fails to conform to the reality. Individuals may be more disposed toward the programs of the political party in power than the supposedly neutral appointees of a merit system, or they may in fact be hostile to the program. This requires that political appointees be selected for some combination of political disposition and administrative talent. The search for new public employees then is never as simple as matching party affiliation, or as simple as applying a set of technical criteria for judging ability.

This situation is complicated by efforts to make bureaucracy more representative. While cast as an attack on the ascriptive hiring practices of those in the "majority," programs to facilitate the hiring of minorities often conflict with both the goal of merit hiring and the goal of political hiring. Nations go to rather surprising lengths to accommodate minorities. Many "merit systems" are retained only by creating parallel systems that operate side by side but are not co-mingled. Thus, as noted earlier, the Belgians operate two bureaucracies in many departments (such as in education). In other countries, one's religion will determine which agencies of government one may work in.

The most common means of accommodation is through some variety of quota system. Such systems, while politically unpopular in the United States, have become the only means by which ethnically, racially, or religiously divided nations can keep the various factions of their societies together. Government employment is a very common route to the middle class for persons throughout the world. Merit systems often display a tendency to reinforce middle-class (in the United States) or upper-middle class (in the United Kingdom) hiring because those are the groups that define merit and thus the qualifications for jobs.

While the developments in South Africa since apartheid may be the except that proves the rule, the distinction between ascriptive hiring, merit hiring, and "affirmative action" style hiring often stems from concern about government policy, not government management. Objections to merit grow whenever those in newly in government believe that certain people in government will be less than neutral, and possible even hostile, to the policy plans of political leaders. Whether the concern is (1) to put your "own person" in charge to be vigilant against the "wrong" policies being implemented, (2) to create administrative coalitions that parallel the political coalitions to ensure that any policy that emerges has been agreed to by all, or (3) to accept differences and allow groups to do it "their way," the core idea is an assumption that the political forces and the administrative forces have different concerns and therefore different policy perspectives. The more heterogeneous the political society the more likely that non-meriting hiring will be government policy.

Pay, Social Status, and Public Employment

It would probably come as something of a surprise to Americans who are often bombarded in the press and by politicians that bureaucrats are lazy, ineffective, and incompetent that public employment is viewed with respect in much of the world and even that to seek a public service career in the early years of our own nation was quite commendable. Variations in status, pay, and motivation to seek the public service all blend to shape public service careers. These variations yield differing definitions of career. Civil service systems differ in the extent to which their members have experience outside government; or in other words, who choose government as a lifelong vocation. For example, in a study of the British civil service careerists, only 7 percent had worked in the private sector and an equally small 12 percent had experience in teaching (Peters, 1984, p. 83). In contrast, the pattern in the United States is for senior people (as political appointees) to leave the private sector to work for brief periods (two to four years) in government. This pattern has created what Hugh Heclo (1977) calls the "government of strangers." Another pattern is one in which persons leave government at a certain stage in their careers to work in the private sector. In the United States this career shift is most common among retired military officers who go to work in defense industries. This pattern is also common in Japan and France. While this pattern does not invoke much concern in Japan, there is wider concern in France. The French object because a great deal of skilled senior personnel, educated at public expense, suddenly are lost to government and are devoting the skills sharpened in government for narrower, private-sector concerns (Wright, 1978). The problem of the "golden parachute" continues to this day.

Another way of looking at the public service career is to ask why a person seeks such a career. Clark and Wilson (1961) developed a classification scheme by which to analyze the incentives that an organization can offer an employee. The three incentives related to material, purpose, and social status are called "solidary." Material incentives include pay, benefits, and other direct financial rewards. Purposive incentives relate to the ability of the individual within the organization to have some influence over the shape of public policy, or simply to get something done in the job. Incentives related to social status include the prestige of group membership in a respected organization or simply in joining an organization of peers.

In examining surveys in a number of countries, two features of the analysis must be noted (Table 15.1). First is the relative low importance of purposive incentives. Second is the higher importance of solidary or status incentives. Two reinforcing aspects of status incentives are that where hiring is through masked ascription (such as in the use of education standards in the United Kingdom), status is affirmed by the method of hiring ("come join your peers"), simultaneously creating an elite, which in itself serves as an incentive to join.

The importance of material concerns in recruitment and retention leads directly to the question of pay. The comparability of public-sector pay with that of the private sector is an important consideration in determining the satisfaction of government workers with their jobs and for determining the satisfaction of citizens with their public servants.

Studies of pay comparability between the public and private sectors show that government employees at the lower echelons are often better paid than their private-sector counterparts. This is especially true of workers in unskilled or semiskilled positions, for example, sanitation workers or bus drivers. This relative advantage of public-sector workers derives at least in part from the ability of these workers through their unions to exert pressure on political leaders by real or threatened strikes. However, as responsibilities increase, government employees become less well paid than workers in the private sector. Those working at the very top of public organizations frequently earn a mere fraction of what they would be earning with similar responsibilities in the private sector.

There are some exceptions to these generalizations, however. In societies with traditions of strong and prestigious government, such as the United Kingdom, senior civil servants are often well paid. There, the very top officials of the civil service (the "open structure") are well paid in comparison to the majority of like executives in the economy, although their pay has been falling behind since the late 1970s. Nevertheless, these civil servants lack some of the perquisites of private-sector employees (company cars, for example) but do have an index-linked pension to look forward to after retirement. Also, in societies dominated by government, for instance, the former Soviet Union and many third-world countries, government is by far the most rewarding place to be employed.

Despite the differences, several generalities can be made about government pay. First, a balance must be struck between budgetary constraints and the need to attract qualified personnel. This is obviously a greater problem at the upper levels of government but may become a problem for skilled trades-people as well as executives. Secondly, in times of economic slowdown, public-sector pay makes a convenient target for those who want to control the costs of government. Third, public-sector employees, by virtue of their central positions in the economy and society (public transportation workers, firefighters, defense) and their increasing levels of unionization, are in powerful positions to influence their pay. Finally, "take-home" pay is only a part of the total compensation package; to understand fully the benefits of public employment, factors such as index-linked pensions must also be considered.

The picture presented above would suggest a pattern. Where material concerns are relatively important, lower pay for senior people in the public sector will encourage the early abandonment of public careers (as in France, Japan, and the United States). Where status concerns are reinforced by adequate pay, a lifelong career (as in the United Kingdom) becomes more attractive.

BUDGET PRACTICE IN COMPARATIVE PERSPECTIVE

Three features of the budgetary process provide a comparative framework within which to understand budgeting. The first concerns the allocation perspective—how much and on what should government spend. The second concerns the structural mechanisms chosen to create a budget. The third concerns the decision-making or, as it is most often presented, the use of incrementalism in budgeting.

The Allocation System

The decisions to tax, how much, and for what programs are the fundamental questions for government. Governments must decide how much they are willing and able to tax citizens in order to provide public benefits through subsequent expenditures. While it remains true that the Western industrialized nations extract more from their citizenry, revenues have grown considerably in all nations.

In addition to the importance of these decisions for overall economic management and for the general nature of programs in a nation, several factors limit the ability of governments to make definitive decisions about the overall scope and size of government, and these must be understood when analyzing how governments decide to spend money. Four such constraints exist: the level of "uncontrollable" items in the budget; economic fluctuations that alter revenues and expenditures; the role of multiple levels of government in budget decisions; and, finally, the internal battle among agencies for a share of the expenditures. Critics of government expenditure, however, rarely acknowledge the intricacies of this complex and often frustrating process.

By 1992, up to 81 percent of public expenditure at the federal level in the United States could be classified as uncontrollable in any one budget year. In the nearly two decades since, that percentage has waived little. Four-fifths of the budget is simply outside of the capacity of either of the political branches to effectively control. The programs that composed the nearly $1,500-billion total were entitlement programs such as social security, unemployment compensation, and Medicare, which depend on demographics and economic conditions to determine levels of expenditure more than on explicit political decisions. While the majority of other industrialized countries have even higher proportions of uncontrollable expenditures than the United States (given their larger-scale social programs and smaller defense budgets), the apparent recalcitrance of entitlement budgets as percentages of overall budgets in recent years has exposed the decision-making process to political opportunism.

A second set of factors further exacerbating the decision-making process are uncontrollable, unpredictable fluctuations in government revenues. Governments have taken upon themselves the control of the economy as a crucial function since at least the end of World War II, but despite the successes in the 1960s, 1970s, and at the close of the last century, governments are not always capable of producing the sustained economic growth they desire. The best-made budgetary allocations and calculations can be overturned by fluctuations in economic circumstances. Governments invest a good deal of time and effort in forecasting the future state of their economies, often to no avail. These forecasting failures result in part from the time span over which the estimates must be made—sometimes the budgetary process is initiated eighteen months or more prior to the implementation of the budget—and results also from the still inadequate knowledge of economic dynamics in industrialized economies. Further, governments themselves have an interest in presenting overly optimistic forecasts to their citizens. Even in socialist economies, where greater control is assumed over the major elements of the economy, difficulties still exist in forecasting the state of the economy for more than a few months in advance.

The third factor limiting the efficiency allocations is the simple fact that there is almost invariably more than one level of government involved in deciding how much the public sector will spend. This is especially true of federal political systems in which sub-national governments have fiscal autonomy. Provincial governments in the Canada, for example, make their revenue and expenditure decisions almost entirely independently from the federal government. Some central governments in federal systems have found this degree of fiscal autonomy unacceptable and have sought mechanisms to coordinate spending better at all levels of government.

Finally, for the majority of actors involved in the budgetary process, the ratio of public expenditure to available economic resources is not always the primary consideration in their budgetary behavior. For spending agencies (whether they are managing "uncontrollable" programs or not), the primary consideration is how much they can extract from the central pool of resources. This means that the spending agencies tend to coalesce to oppose attempts at controlling expenditures by finance ministers and/or the principal executive. This parochial perspective holds that if their collective success in extracting resources means that the ratio of expenditures to GNP would increase, that is someone else's problem. Likewise, it is always some other agency's programs that should be reduced or terminated.

The last point concerning allocation brings us to the stage of budgetary process in which decisions must be made among the huge number of competing programs in government, each one considering itself especially worthy and each one competing with all other programs for limited funding. The separation of these decisions from broader budgetary decisions may be artificial, since the constraints imposed upon the funding of any particular agency are at least in part a function of the desire of those controlling the economic management functions of government to bring the total budget in at a particular total. Not surprisingly, when that level of expenditure is low, compared to previous levels of expenditure and levels of inflation, then those programs with the fewest uncontrollable costs will be the targets for disproportionate cuts.

It is at this level of allocation that most of the politics of budgeting occurs. It is at this level that the priorities of individual political leaders interact to produce allocations within government. Despite the enormity of the task of assembling the public budget in any modem society, the budgeting decision process eventually produces an allocation of resources ostensibly matching the policy preferences of the public or at least those of their elective officials. But a number of barriers prevent the process from reaching such an optimal allocation.

One of the principal factors affecting the rationality of the allocation is the disaggregation of the budgetary process. Separate committees or sections of budgetary review organizations perform the major analyses and make the major decisions about budgets. In Sweden, with the allocation of resources among the boards under a ministry, there is a process that allocates predetermined blocks of expenditures rather than attempting to compare the marginal value of expenditure across a range of functions. Only in a cabinet setting where the entire budget is (at least in theory) open to determination is any real detailed consideration of competing priorities made. And even in those settings, the outcome may be determined by the deliberations of staffs or by the personality of a few dominant members of the cabinet, so that the confrontation of all the alternative utilizations of public expenditures does not occur.

A second factor affecting the range of consideration of budgetary alternatives is the status quo. The magnitude of the budget in a modern government makes it difficult for a legislature to make any extensive analysis of the possible patterns of expenditures. There is a tendency to accept the previous year's allocation as a given and to examine primarily marginal changes in that allocation. There is a tendency to regard not only the existing distribution of expenditures as acceptable but also the rate at which the budget has been increasing. Agencies tend to retain the same rates of increase in their budgetary allocations from year to year. This rate of increase would not be the same across agencies—in some instances there might be significant differences—but for each agency there is an accepted rate of increase on top of the accepted base, which allows the budget to increase from year to year. Many of the innovations in the budgetary process have been introduced for the explicit purpose of rectifying the "problem" of incrementalism (see later discussion).

The Structure of Budget Decision-Making

The budget process is often characterized by inter-bureaucratic battles, battles that may be as intense and as important as the executive-legislative conflict with which those in the United States are more accustomed. The most common form of such conflict is that between central budget offices—such as H. M. Treasury in the United Kingdom—and the various line agencies. Such central agencies have the responsibility for preparing the overall budget, a process that invariably brings them into conflict with other agencies, each of whom believes they should have a higher allocation.

The relative success of the competing bureaucratic organizations depends upon situational factors such as those that are economic as well as the relative powers of each one in the political process. Times of economic insecurity aid the central managers, especially when they are backed by external agents such as the International Monetary Fund or foreign banks threatening to call in loans. On the other hand, the perception of specific needs for expenditures, for example, a perceived need to increase defense spending, tends to favor the spending agency. Few spending ministers would be willing to sacrifice their own expenditures in order to finance another minister's expansion, and consequently the entire level of spending increases to accommodate every agency. Finally, the introduction of budgeting innovations may provide financial agencies with a variety of weapons—one of them being the complexity and obscurity of the method itself—that can be used to exercise control of spending ministries. The power of these instruments frequently is overstated, and further, such techniques are a complement to politics, not a substitute for it.

The Budgetary Decision Process

Two of the most important factors in determining budgetary decision styles are wealth and predictability (Wildavsky, 1975). While the concept of wealth as related to the budget is self-explanatory, the concept of predictability is not. The variability and instability of the overall economy of a nation means that predictions of both revenues and expenditures will similarly vary. Without some degree of predictability, decision makers are only guessing what they will receive as revenues and what they will spend and must, therefore, develop strategies for coping with that uncertainty. Four strategies have been postulated by Caiden and Wildavsky (1974). The four strategies plot the interrelationships among revenue predictability, wealth, and relative political stability.

According to Wildavsky, affluent nations with predictable revenues and expenditures tend to have incremental budgeting styles. This is indicative of a stable political process in which government can fund its commitments while minimizing the number of difficult choices made among competing expenditure priorities. At the other end of the spectrum, poor countries with uncertain revenues engage in repetitive budgeting and will, of necessity, construct a succession of budgets during a fiscal year in order to adjust to changing conditions. Political systems that are relatively poor but that can predict their revenues engage in "revenue budgeting." They spend what they know they can collect—no more and no less—but lack the type of predictable, incremental patterns of change that would characterize more affluent political systems. Lastly, wealthy nations with uncertain budgetary systems alternate between incremental and repetitive budgeting as a reflection of political instability, or their administrative incapacities lead them to supplemental budgeting. In this form, the basic budget document remains in force, but supplements are added throughout the fiscal year as the revenue and expenditure figures become clarified. This pattern was common in the state governments of the United States in the 1970s as recessions and inflation made most revenue and expenditure predictions questionable.

One of the budgetary strategies just described, incrementalism, has long been associated with budgeting, both as practiced in legislatures and as an internal agency strategy (independent of perspectives on legislative decision-making). As such it is worth exploring this oft-noted but also often criticized process. Borrowing heavily from Peters (2010), we will examine incrementalism as an aid to budget allocations and also as a problem for "effective" allocations. Finally, we will explore some of the strategies employed by central budget offices to avoid the "problem" of incrementalism.

Incrementalism

Incrementalism in budgeting is both a descriptive and prescriptive concept. Descriptively, it is the observable pattern of change in budgets. Numerous studies over decades have chronicled the tendency of both agencies and legislatures to follow relatively simple and stable decision rules on the budget—the starting point for analysis of this year's expenditures is last year's expenditures. Prescriptively, it is argued that such stability and predictability lay the foundation for the best possible decision process. Peters (2010) explains the viewpoint of advocates as follows:

> It makes planning simpler for the agencies and reduces the decision-making load on the legislative body. More importantly, it is argued that a more comprehensive (synoptic) approach to decision making would not of necessity produce better decisions, because of the absence of information about the future and about the social and economic processes being addressed through the budget. In addition, major departures from the status quo may be irreversible without extreme expense. Therefore, the incrementalists would argue, the most rational approach to budgeting of other types of decision-making is to make relatively minor departures from the status quo, monitor the effects of those new policies, and then adjust the policies in future decision making.
>
> (p. 239)

Two factors in the budgetary process work in favor of incremental outcomes. First is the magnitude of the process itself. A typical public budget in an industrialized country involves making decisions that allocate nearly one half of the total goods and services in the economy. In addition, the decisions to spend these sums must be made in a very brief period under considerable political pressure and scrutiny. The tendency is to accept the existing programmatic distribution of funds as a given and, therefore, to concentrate time and attention on the relatively few exceptions to that pattern. In France two types of budget items are presented: *measures novelles*, which receive considerable scrutiny, and *services votes*, which receive little scrutiny. The common practice in the United States is to present annual budgets in two columns, the current budget and the proposed budget. In this way deviations from incremental funding are immediately noticed and can be targeted for additional review.

The second feature that helps to produce incremental solutions is the sequential and repetitive nature of budgeting. New budgets must be created each year or even more often. Both the administrators and the legislators involved in the process tend to assume that errors made in one year can be corrected in subsequent years. Further, those involved in making the budget—bureaucrats, legislators, and analysts—tend to retain their positions for long periods. This is especially true where, unlike the United States, a change in government involves very few changes in those responsible for constructing the budget, or where a central agency with a permanent and expert staff tends to dominate the budgetary process, as is true at the Treasury in the United Kingdom. The tenure in office of the principal actors in budgeting results in their having the opportunity to develop means of cooperating among themselves and to shape the budget in the manner they find acceptable; all they must do on an annual basis is to make marginal adjustments from the accepted pattern. Further, those wishing to make any departures from existing patterns have several strong incentives to adopt cautious strategies. Since they are involved in a long-term "game" where slow adjustments are far more probable than sudden shifts, all actors play the "confidence game" and gain the trust and respect of others involved in the budgetary process to be effective in getting what they want. Obviously, this cautious and conservative behavior in budgeting produces considerable frustration for those who come into political office with new ideas and priorities, expecting to generate change overnight.

Alternative to Incrementalism

It has been argued that an incremental approach to budgetary decision-making tends to institutionalize the status quo and to curtail creative thinking about alternative uses of funds. The solution is often cast as a need to create a more comprehensive and rational approach to budgeting. The simple and seemingly "irrational" decision rules of incrementalism have led to the pursuit over the last four decades of several alternatives that presumably can better optimize the use of government funds. Two features of these alternatives that must be noted are (1) all call for a greater level of centralization of the budget decision process than is possible (or necessary) under incrementalism, and (2) most of these decision processes break down because of opposition from legislators (who lose most of their control over the budget process under such centralizing mechanisms).

The most common budget model is that of program budget or as it was called in the United States, PPBS (Planning, Programming, Budgeting System). At various times France, Canada, and the United Nations all have used this process or some version of it. Two features of this model are (1) as a program-based system the concept of organization or agency is downplayed in favor of an understanding of programs as interconnected and (2) such systems presume a very sophisticated capacity to create and subsequently analyze data about programs and alternatives to those programs.

In the United Kingdom, the financial crises of the 1960s and 1970s led to the development of a Public Expenditures Survey Committee (PESC), whose responsibilities focused on the planning and execution of the budget. Thus, for example, the PESC examined the long-term financial implications of all current programs. Further, the committee could recommend program allocations where requests exceeded resources. Lastly, the committee reviewed the cost effectiveness of ongoing programs and could recommend alternatives. While the governments of the United Kingdom have not fully followed through on the use of this committee, it has the potential to introduce a stronger element of "rationality" into the budget process.

Two other ideas or experiments that may not be fully removed from incrementalism but are nonetheless worth noting are bulk budgeting and envelope budgeting. Under bulk budgeting the organization managers are given lump sums rather than line-item specified allocations. Each manager then becomes responsible for allocations by program and function within that lump sum. Under envelope budgeting, the primary policy areas and responsibilities (in Canada they operate with eleven) each are allocated a set amount. The cabinet ministers and department heads then negotiate budget allocations within the context of the amount in the envelope.

POLICY MAKING IN COMPARATIVE PERSPECTIVE

The third feature of government activity to be explored is that of policy making. Our concern is to explore policy making from the perspective of the interactions between bureaucrats and the public. While this choice does not give full breadth to the concept of policy making, it does provide a useful comparative perspective.

Policy making is not an easy process to readily define, covering as it does, processes as varied as policy analysis and program implementation. Randall Ripley suggests that public policy can most easily be understood as a set of six stages or activities, each of which create some form of governmental response (Figure 15.1). Those six activities are:

1. Agenda setting
2. Goal-setting
3. Alternative development and selection
4. Implementation of the selected alternative
5. Evaluation of implementation
6. Evaluation of results (impact)

From the brief explanation of these activities presented in Figure 15.1, it is obvious that the public is involved and can influence policy at any of these stages. Thus, even though we associate public input with the agenda-setting stage, public influence is felt throughout. As Goodsell has pointed out, the evaluation of and political perspectives on programs can be influenced by what he calls the "public encounter." But beyond this, the very way that the public, particularly as an organized group, is involved in a program can shape the operations of the program

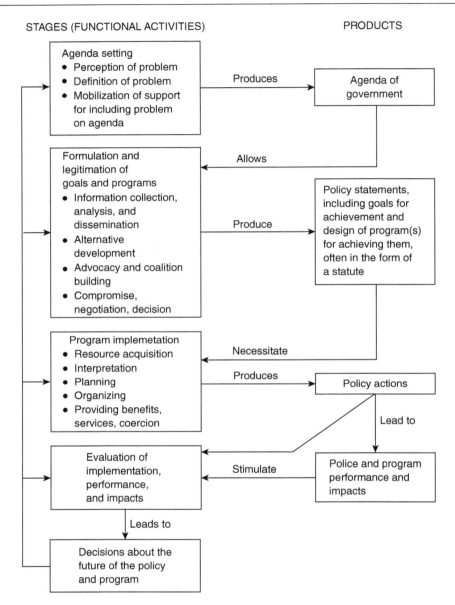

FIGURE 15.1
The Flow of Policy Stages, Functional Activities, and Products

and even the type of programs that are designed and implemented. Guy Peters has developed a classification scheme which contrasts the interactions between bureaucrats and different types of interest groups for the purpose of examining the scope, influence, style, and impact of those interactions. The central feature of Peters's analysis is that the type of interest group is the dominant factor in determining the bureaucrat-pressure group relationship and, therefore, the level of cooperation

Policy Making in Comparative Perspective | **313**

achieved in shaping and implementing policy. The following presentation is drawn from that work.

The different types of interest groups can be classified as follows: legitimate, clientela, parantela, and illegitimate (Table 15.1). While all four types exist in all nations, there are forms that dominate in certain countries and therefore give the bureaucratic policy-making process a rather distinct flavor.

Legitimate Interactions

Legitimate interactions are classified as such not merely because the role of such interest groups is an accepted fact of political life but also because such groups are legally and officially involved in the process of making and administering public policy. This pattern of interaction is quite common in northern Europe.

Three variations on the style interaction can be observed. First is corporatism, in which a single interest group is given full access to the bureaucracy to offer "advice" on how to proceed. A less extreme version of this pattern is "liberal corporatism," in which several interest groups bargain among themselves and with the bureaucracy over the shape of policy. Such relationships carry both benefits of the bureaucracy and disadvantages for the government. The presence of a corporatist interest group greatly aids in the legitimation of bureaucratic actions and implementation decisions. On the other hand, since such groups relate to specific agencies, conflict across governmental policy areas is heightened as each agency, reinforced by its supporting interest group, lays claim to public resources.

A more common process, which resolves some of the inherent conflict across policy areas that emerges from corporatism, is that of required consultation. Interest group involvement is channeled through a variety of rules that require government agencies preparing new regulations to consult with "relevant" interest groups for their opinions and to solicit advice and information from them. In addition to mandating that agencies seek written information from groups, such consultation can be achieved through advisory committees that designate interest groups as members of the committees. The central feature of these processes is that the interest group is not an outsider but is accepted as an integral part of the decision process with a status equal to other "official" participants.

TABLE 15.1

Types of Interaction Between Pressure Groups and Bureaucracy

Types	Scope	Influence	Style	Impact
Legitimate	Broad	Great	Bargaining	Redistribution/Self-regulation
Clientela	Narrow	Moderate	Symbiosis	Self-regulation/Distribution
Parentela	Narrow	Moderate	Kinship	Regulation/Distribution
Illegitimate	Variable	None/great	Confrontation	None/Redistribution

Source: B. Guy Peters, *The Politics of Bureaucracy*, 6th ed. (London: Routledge 2010, p. 171)

The third form of legitimate interaction is the use of interest groups as the "agents of implementation." The interest groups serve virtually as quasi-official agents of the political system, implementing such programs for which they are presumed to have the requisite expert knowledge and skill. In the Scandinavian countries such arrangements are quite common in agriculture. In many ways such groups become much like clientela groups. The scope of interaction between pressure groups and administration in "legitimate" situations tends to be quite broad. A single interest group may be consulted on a variety of policies, and virtually all policy areas may be the subject of inputs from interested parties. Further, the influence of the groups on policy may be expected to be great relative to other types of interaction patterns. The legitimacy of the groups, their frequency of interaction with administrators and their official or quasi-official status make it possible for these groups to have an impact that they would not have elsewhere. In part this is a result of not having to expend organizational resources simply to gain access and in part a result of the roles adopted by the interest group participants in the process. Such perceived roles contribute to the bargaining style of their interactions. The dominant-role type in these negotiations is the expert who supplies information and opinion but who does not serve merely as an advocate of his or her particularistic viewpoint.

Clientela Relations

Clientela relations exist when an interest group succeeds in becoming the natural expression and representative of the social sector that is the natural "constituency" of the government agency. This type of interaction is the result of a "perceived" legitimacy by administrators of one or more groups rather than a formal designation of legitimacy by administrators (as occurs in legitimate interactions). The scope of interactions between clientela groups and the bureaucracy is severely constrained. While influence on a specific range of policies may be virtually exclusive, influence outside that policy set is nonexistent. Further, the result of the establishment of clientela relationships generally reduced the overall influence of interest groups, since only those with special clientela status have any influence. All other groups are helpless to influence policy.

The interactions between interest groups and administration in clientela politics lead to the characterization as symbiotic. As in biological symbiosis, this implies a mutual dependence of the two participants. The administrative agency depends upon the interest group for information, advice, prior clearance of policy decisions, and most importantly, for political support in its competition with other agencies for the scarce resources within government. The interest groups depend upon the agency for access to decision-making and ultimately for favorable decisions on certain policy choices. For both sides the clientela relationship serves to regularize the political environment and to develop friendships in what might otherwise be a hostile political world. This form of pressure group relationship with administration has been used by several authors as a means of describing much of the politics of policy in the United States. It also would seem to be prevalent in a number of other political systems that have strong interest groups but where the interactions of these groups and the government is at the margin of acceptability. Others have argued that this "clientelist" pattern is now less descriptive of the United States than it once was, and a much broader array of interests has come to be represented in Washington. On the other hand, the standard lament concerning the impact of "single issue politics" on American government may lead one to continue to accept the clientelist description.

Parentela Relationships

A parantela relationship is somewhat less direct than with clientela relationships. Such relations are often described as kinship relations and are most closely associated with the relationship between a pressure group and the government or a dominant political party. The interest group obtains access to administrative decision-making through the ability of the political party to intercede in its behalf with the bureaucracy. The success of this relationship is based on the political control of the party, and, therefore, it is most common in single-party political systems. Another point is that the prime mover in the relationship is neither the bureaucracy nor the interest group. The focus is in the political party, and the means of control is by co-opting interest groups which then influence the bureaucracy.

The influences of parantela relations can be quite broad and pervasive, simply because such influence is in the interest of the party. Policies are often distributive in character as the party seeks to distribute various goods and services among the "faithful" and also to develop programs that provide services to the representatives of social sectors (i.e., the parantela interest group).

Illegitimate Group Processes

A number of circumstances exist in which interaction between an interest group and bureaucracy is regarded as inappropriate. Influence from such groups is not part of the normal pattern of decision-making, the point being that the interest group feels that only by going outside the bounds of normal behavior and interaction can its cause be heard. The range of interactions can be from rather staid petitioning of bureaucrats to protests, demonstrations, and even violence. Such interactions between such groups and bureaucrats often result in considerable frustration and alienation. An illegitimate group playing by the bureaucrat's rules does not result in influence and change. On the other hand, to "escalate" to other forms of interaction merely confirms their status as illegitimate groups. It must be remembered, however, that while rarely so, illegitimate groups can be successful, but only if and when political opinion shifts in their favor.

INTEREST GROUPS AND BUREAUCRATS

The conflict between the demands of interest groups and the role of the bureaucracy in decision-making is, in most societies, one of the most basic in governance. On the one hand, there are the institutions of government representing the authority of the state. On the other side of the conflict are groups that by their nature represent only specialized narrow interests seeking some preferential treatment from government. This type of division of the role of the state and the role of interests is perceived differently in different cultures. The conflict may not be as intense in Norway as in France, for instance, but interestingly, this conflict has been sufficiently ameliorated in most societies so that the two sets of organizations are able not only to co-exist but even to cooperate effectively. Further, those societies that tend to have the most positive conception of the public bureaucracy—Germany, the Netherlands, and the Scandinavian countries—have been more successful in accommodating the roles of interest groups in policy making than have political systems that have a less exalted conception of their civil servants. In fact, a positive evaluation of the civil service may be required to allow civil servants latitude in dealing with the pressure groups and in making accommodations to their demands.

Given the apparent conflict in the roles of these two sets of political actors and institutions, their ability to cooperate so well and so often is central to understanding policy making. The stereotypical descriptions of the policy roles of these two sets of actors obscure some of the reality of their interactions. For example, the civil service rarely speaks or acts as a unified entity; it is divided into organizations with narrow interests that correspond to the interests of certain pressure groups. Furthermore, interest groups in most Western countries have found that acting in a less blatantly self-interested manner may produce more benefits for them in the long run.

Second, both groups need each other to be successful. Bureaucrats need the political support and influence of pressure groups in their external relationships with other political institutions, and they also need the information supplied by pressure groups for making and defending policies. Similarly, the interest groups need access to the political process and influence over the decisions that are made. This mutual need, given the fragmentation of decision-making in modern governments, is the dynamic explaining the cooperation between public bureaucracies and pressure groups.

MODELS OF GOVERNANCE

In 2000 B. Guy Peters developed a taxonomy of forms of government operations to better classify governments in a comparative sense. The models represent the spectrum of models that can be labeled as either within the traditional (New Public Administration) perspective and those that follow approaches rooted in economics rather than public administration. Because this is ground covered in earlier chapters, the focus here will be on the influence of the "market" and "deregulated" governments on governance.

As already noted, the New Public Management has been the dominant framework guiding administrative reform in the industrial democracies and to some extent across the world.

One of the most consistent recommendations coming from the New Public Management has been that governments would work better if large, multi-purpose organizations were broken up into smaller, more autonomous offices that would in turn function in a semi-independent mode. Managers in these new operations would be given greater managerial and decision-making autonomy. The assumption is

TABLE 15.2

The New Public Management

Types of Concerns	Market Government	Participative Government	Flexible Government	Deregulated Government
Principal Diagnosis	*Monopoly*	*Hierarchy*	*Permanence*	*Internal regulation*
Structure	*Decentralization*	*Flatter organizations*	*"Virtual organizations"*	*No particular recommendation*
Management	*Pay for performance; other private-sector techniques*	*TQM; teams*	*Managing temporary personnel*	*Greater managerial freedom*
Policy Making	*Internal markets; market incentives*	*Consultation; negotiation*	*Experimentation*	*Entrepreneurial government*
Public Interest	*Low cost*	*Involvement; consultation*	*Low cost; coordination*	*Creativity; activism*

Source: B. Guy Peters, *The Future of Governing*, 2nd revised ed. (Lawrence: University of Kansas Press, 2001)

that this change in the public sector will produce greater efficiency and also greater accountability. That greater efficiency would result from reducing involvement of politicians in the affairs of the organization derived from the greater decision-making authority granted to managers. Enhanced accountability would occur because each organization would be responsible for a single, or at least a limited number of, functions. The presumption is that large multi-purpose organizations made financial accountability more difficult, and that breaking them up into many smaller organizations would make them more efficient. One variation on this model is to devolve program responsibility to state and provincial governments.

DEMOCRACY AND BUREAUCRACY

One of the continuing debates among both academics and practitioners is the relationship between democracy and bureaucracy. It is often assumed that bureaucracy is antithetical to democracy. Organizations as varied as the World Bank and the United Nations rank the strength of a nation's democratic institutions by the weakness of the bureaucracy. Rather than see bureaucracy as a force for the rule of law, bureaucracies are seen as tools for repression. Partly out of zeal for "market-driven" government, outside organizations often seek democracy by stripping bureaucracy of the capacity to implement and enforce the rules.

As political scientists and then those in public administration begin to explore this issue in more depth, the simple assumption of a conflict between bureaucracy and democracy is being questioned. Recent work has suggested that the relationship between democracy and bureaucracy is more complementary and synergistic. Countries, especially new countries that have emerged from colonialism, are suc-

CHART 15–3

Consolidation to Democracy

- A free and lively civil society "where self-organizing groups, movements, and individuals, relatively autonomous from the state, attempt to articulate values, create associations and solidarities, and advance their interests."
- A relatively autonomous and valued political society. This is an arena within which the polity organizes itself to exercise control over public power and the state apparatus.
- The rule of law "to ensure legal guarantees for citizens' freedoms and independent associational life."
- A state bureaucracy which can be used by the democratic government; this is important for making the government effective and thereby generating a support base.
- Institutionalized economic society, meaning a set of norms, institutions, and regulations that mediate between state and market. A legal and regulatory framework instituted by the government is the most common form this takes.

Source: Graeme Gill, *The Dynamics of Democratization: Elites, Civil Society and the Transition Process* (New York: St. Martin's Press, 2000, p. 72)

cessful as democracies in part to the extent that equity and equality are achieved because of the adherence to the notion of the rule of law by bureaucrats. For example, many young nations holding relatively scandal-free elections are a benchmark of emerging democracy. Yet it is less the outside observers and more the will and capacity of the bureaucracy to implement the elections free of corrupt practices that determines the extent to which those elections are "free." It is the extent to which bureaucrats implement policies with which they, personally, might disagree that fosters faith that a democratic regime can survive and thrive. It is the bureaucracy that is the bulwark of the rule of law. A "corrupt" bureaucracy is one that will bend to the will of elected and appointed leaders, rather than follow the law. This is a bureaucracy that not only adheres to notions of fairness and equality of treatment but stands up to political forces that do not want the rules that foster equity and equality enforced. Whether the bias is born of tribalism, corruption, or ideology, only a capable and effective bureaucracy stands between the citizens and political leaders who wish to diminish democracy.

It will be interesting to see how this seemingly incongruous symbiotic relationship between a healthy and effective bureaucracy and a healthy and effective democracy play out in the future.

Conclusion

While this chapter has certainly covered a wide variety of perspectives and concepts, the primary emphasis is to assist the reader in envisioning how cultural norms shape government activities and management. Three essential lessons can be derived from this perspective. First, while administration is an activity that is common throughout the world, it is an activity that is often circumscribed and controlled by the cultural heritage and norms of a given society. Second, the pattern of administration and management in a given country must be judged by the norms of that particular culture, not by the norms of administrative behavior that emerge from academic texts. The third and most important lesson is to see ourselves and administrative practice in the United States as if we were looking at a foreign country, not just the differences in practices around the world. The success of a comparative perspective is in seeing ourselves, not as the nation that has the right answers, but merely as one of many nations searching to find the unique style that fits our own political culture. The challenge is not so much what we can learn from others about how they run their governments but to give ourselves the opportunity to critique ourselves in the same way we critique their systems of administration.

DISCUSSION QUESTIONS

- How are administrative activities circumscribed and controlled by the cultural heritage and norms of a given society?
- Link the concept of culture competence with more effective and accurate analysis of the norms of a particular culture.
- Discuss the implications for a country other than the US by applying the Peters governance model.
- Apply the Peters governance model to the United States.
- How has political socialization influenced US Public Administration (then pick another country and do the same)?

BIBLIOGRAPHY

Aberbach, Joel D., Robert D. Putnam, and Bert A. Rockman. *Bureaucrats and Politicians in Western Democracies*. Cambridge, MA: Harvard University Press, p. 55. 1981.

Bendix, Reinhard. *Work and Authority in Industry*. New York: John Wiley & Sons. 1956.

Caiden, Naomi, and Aaron Wildavsky. *Planning and Budgeting in Poor Countries*. New York: John Wiley & Sons. 1974.

Clark, Peter B., and James Q. Wilson. "Incentive Systems: A Theory of Organizations", *Administrative Science Quarterly*, 6, pp. 129–166. 1961.

Gill, Graeme. *The Dynamics of Democratization: Elites, Civil Society and the Transition Process*. New York: St. Martin's Press. 2000.

Goodsell, Charles, ed. *The Public Encounter: Where State and Citizen Meet*. Bloomington: Indiana University Press. 1981.

Goodsell, Charles. *The Case for Bureaucracy, 2nd ed.* Chatham, NJ: Chatham House. 1985.

Goodsell, Charles. *The Case for Bureaucracy, 4th ed.* Washington, DC: CQ Press. 2003.

Heady, Ferrel. *Public Administration: A Comparative Perspective, 6th ed.* New York: Marcel Dekker. 2005.

Heclo, Hugh. *A Government of Strangers*. Washington, DC: Brookings Institution Press. 1977.

Katz, Elihu, and S. N. Eisenstadt. "Some Sociological Observations on the Response of Israeli Organizations to New Immigrants", *Administrative Science Quarterly*, 5 (1), pp. 113–133. 1960.

Lindblom, Charles. *Politics and Markets*. New York: Basic Books, Inc. 1977.

Parsons Talcott, and Edward Shels. *Toward a General Theory of Action*. Cambridge, MA: Harvard University Press. 1951.

Peters, B. Guy. *The Politics of Bureaucracy, 2nd ed.* New York: Longman, p. 95. 1984.

Peters, B. Guy. *The Future of Governing, 2nd rev. ed.* Lawrence, KS: University of Kansas Press. 2001.

Peters, B. Guy. *The Politics of Bureaucracy, 6th ed.* London: Routledge. 2010.

Pye, Lucian W. "Introduction: Political Culture and Political Development", in Lucian Pye and Sidney Verba (eds.) *Political Culture and Political Development*. Princeton, NJ: Princeton University Press. 1965.

Sartori, Giovanni. "Politics, Ideology and Belief Systems", *American Political Science Review*, 63, pp. 398–411. June 1969.

Weber, Max, H. H. Gerth, and C. Wright Mills, ed. and trans. *From Max Weber: Essays on Sociology*. New York: Oxford University Press. 1946.

Wildavsky, Aaron. *Budgeting: A Comparative Theory of the Budgetary Process*. Boston: Little, Brown and Co. 1975.

Wright, Vincent. *The Government and Politics of France*. New York: Holmes and Meier. 1978.

CHAPTER
16

Concluding Thoughts

REDEFINING PA THEORY AS GOVERNANCE

Seemingly the suspicion and lack of trust in the professional civil service is growing. How can public administration, or government itself, survive such cynicism? At one level it probably cannot. It will be a long time before the public will tolerate the aggressive, service-oriented, and progressive governments that typified the 1960s in the US and Europe and spurred independence movements across the globe. The public (and therefore, many politicians) agrees with Ronald Reagan's notable one-liner from the 1980s: government is the problem. But the more critical question is whether the damage is the result of self-inflicted wounds, rather than the barbs and rhetoric of politicians. Can we come down from the mountain of professionalism to serve the public, even as they continue to criticize? Can we establish a theory of public administration practice that makes democracy more, rather than less viable? Can we be responsive to the public and effective in the delivery of services by listening, rather than deciding?

If we are to create a public administration theory of governance we must seek to achieve three goals:

- Public Administration as embodiment/extension of governance
- Politics and democracy as core methods and means of acting
- Ethics as the basis for decision-making (Cox, Buck, and Morgan, 2011)

As Philip Selznick (1957) noted more than five decades ago, successful organizations require more than management, they require leadership.

> The limits of organization engineering become apparent when we must create a structure *uniquely adapted to the mission and role of the enterprise*. This adaptation goes beyond a tailored combination of uniform elements; it is an adaptation in depth, affecting the nature of the parts themselves. This is really a very familiar process, brought home to us most clearly when we recognize that certain firms or agencies are stamped by distinctive ways of making decisions

or by peculiar commitments to aims, methods, or clienteles. In this way the organization as a technical instrument takes on values. As a vehicle of group integrity it becomes in some degree an end in itself. This process of becoming infused with value is part of what we mean by institutionalization. As this occurs, *organization management* becomes *institutional leadership*. The latter's main responsibility is not so much technical administrative management as the maintenance of institutional integrity.

(Selznick, p. 138)

Although Selznick limited his discussion to performance measurement, that admonition to acknowledge the distinct characteristics of organizations is important to a meaningful theory of practice in a public setting. Only with an understanding of how decisions are made can theories of practice be understood.

The advent of public choice theory, reinventing government and then the New Public Management, (re)introduced theories of operational practice and management that are in some cases more than a century old. The core all three of these management perspectives are predicated on two premises: first, management practice is essentially about command and control, and second, rational analysis is basic to right decision-making. For a variety of reasons, it is important to challenge these notions, if only to better understand governance and policy making as those processes are conducted by those who accept those premises.

Essentially, public administration has traveled two distinct paths for more than four decades. This divide is partially played out as the split between the MPA and the MPP.

The divide is also played out in the fundamental conflict between an emphasis on efficiency and an emphasis on effectiveness. The first path, informed by policy analysis and economics, focuses on the logic of managerial decision-making with an emphasis on technical analytics and rational decision models. There is also a bias for business (private sector) management approaches because of the emphasis on efficiency. Scientific management is the older, distant cousin of these views. For simplicity's sake, this version will be labeled as the New Public Management (NPM), though intellectually it is more closely related to public choice theory. The second path, informed by socio-psychological understandings and organizational dynamics, focuses on interpersonal and inter-organizational relations as the frame or lens for decision-making. Collaborative practices and leader-follower relations are the near cousins of this path. For simplicity, this version will be labeled as Collaborative Management.

PATH ONE

As Lindblom notes in his analysis of two models of government, the first model is based on instrumental decision-making that is the product of elite interpretation. This system is presumed to work because the elite has access to, or has already acquired, more complete knowledge (Lindblom, p. 249). Path one shares a suspicion about the capacity and capability of government organizations and a faith in "market-driven" perspectives as the path to organizational effectiveness.

They also share the use of a set of techniques and practices (program evaluation, cost-benefit analysis, etc.) that begin from an economic perspective (both academic and practical). These perspectives also yield the same result.

- Public decisions are to be left to the expert. Decisions cannot be allowed to be left to amateurs.
- The criteria for "right decisions" is in who decides, not in the quality of the process. The answer often was that the private sector should decide. The private sector would serve the public better not only because it would be more efficient, and, therefore, less costly, but also because it would be immune to political dealings that caused corruption and waste.

Rules and regulations, hierarchical relationships, in fact the entire range of structural-functional understandings of modern organizations emerge from *thinking* about organizational design and process. The decision is the result of the process of thinking. The classic model of policy analysis in which the *optimal alternative* is uncovered is an example of this form of decision-making. There can only be one decision; therefore, the analysis yields answers. *Working* (Hummel, 1987) in contrast emerges from understanding of the circumstances and events that result in actions. In this context, understanding informs us when the process (analysis) has not produced the right decision.

The conflict for decades was who should control operations (first politicians vs. administrators, then managers vs. functionaries). However, three plus decades ago the issue became one of what sector is best able to manage government activities.

This shift from an internal discussion about best practices to one in which the capability of the public sector was challenged came during times of fiscal distress. Tools and practices that would ultimately become lumped together as the New Public Management arose in the UK in response to fiscal setbacks in the 1970s. Thatcher's reforms and those in the Commonwealth countries of the Pacific were based upon policy choices emphasizing budget control and, secondarily personnel control; Reagan sought primarily personnel control, but also control over state and local budgets; more recently the NPM was touted as the solution to the world-wide economic decline (Cox and Ostertag, 2014).

How Competition Fails Government (And Maybe Even Business)

Adam Smith (1776) introduced the world to the hidden hand that guided economic transactions. Lost in time is the simplicity of Smith's relationships. Three conditions are essential. First, and most critically, is that both parties to the transaction have an equal capacity to judge quality. Second is that both understand that the possibility of alternative choices exist (competitors close at hand). Third is that the final price in the transaction is a negotiation whereby the purchaser balances quality and price. The successful negotiation is one in which the purchase is made at the ideal price given the quality of the item.

The conditions described by Smith capture a moment in time and space. It requires an urban setting to ensure ready access to competitors and also a knowledge by the purchaser that permits that purchaser to correctly judge the quality of a range of goods.

The industrial revolution would soon make the second condition impossible. New urban dwellers just from the farm might understand the proper value of much of what they need, but within a generation or two fewer and fewer would have that capability. Not long after, shop owners making their own products on the city streets were replaced with manufactured goods sold by store employees. The dynamic of a negotiation between equals is now a transaction in which the negotiation is replaced by a price tag. By the late 1800s the commercial and retail world was one in which ignorant buyers paid for a product about which the sales clerk was equally ignorant. Corporations replaced shop owners. Financial success came not by efficiency, but by buying up the competition. The era of government regulation in Europe and in the US began by efforts to reign in the greed of owners and to demand that they protect workers who were little more than appendages of the machines. Industrial productivity (efficiency) was the result of finding workers who would accept lower and lower wages (women and children) to bolster profits. Monopolies ruled.

The calculus of transaction was quite simple: you bought what was available and what you could afford, regardless of quality. Where there was competition the transaction did not revert to the Smith ideal because those conditions no longer existed. People did not know how to judge quality, so the question was simply affordability. Marketing and branding began in the 1920s because you needed to find ways to attract otherwise ignorant customers, who often were convinced to mistake price for quality. Competition temporarily lowered prices (at least until the competition disappeared), but without a point of reference with regard to quality, prices stabilized around norms even without collusion. Productivity was only secondary and customer needs tertiary. Despite this dismal record, by the 1970s these same core values of the myth of competition found a new home in government. Despite little evidence of real productivity gains and even less evidence of product quality (TQM after all doesn't get much traction in US businesses), Smith's vision of the benefits of competition is introduced in government. The NPM collective models begin from the simple logic that competition means lower cost and higher quality. The "other side of the coin" would be that monopolies were bad, but also that only governments were monopolies. Reducing government would free businesses to be more productive, and privatization would produce the miracle of higher quality at a lower cost.

PATH TWO

Collaborative Leadership and Management

The interplay of theory and practice of leadership has followed a somewhat dialectic path. Even as each theory is presented, there seems to emerge a counter-argument or opposing perspective expressed by those in the academy. New ideas and theories emerge, followed by a critique and counter proposal. This synthesis-antithesis byplay is the basis for this discussion of collaboration. In this instance the emphasis shifts from a primarily organizational perspective to an individual and/ or interpersonal perspective. This shift to a more interpersonal basis created an opportunity for a closer examination of followership. Fundamentally, current leadership theories exist on the parallel planes of the organization and the individual (Cox, Plagens, and Sylla, 2010).

The concept of leadership emerged in the early twentieth century along with theories of management. The "Scientific Management" theory introduced by Frederick Taylor (1911), the charismatic and authoritarian leader evoked by Max Weber (1946), and the command approach in business organizations, and in government (Gulick, 1937) all point to control and power from the top down, leaving subordinates in these organizations under the submission of the leader.

From the beginning there were those who doubted and challenged this approach. Exemplars of these critiques of the accepted views on leadership were Follett (1996) and Barnard (1968). The vision of the leaders expressed here is that of a conciliator and facilitator. Follett's view on the giving of orders presages future works of much later scholarship. It is in her work on orders that the emphasis on individualism and the dignity of the work come through most clearly. Follett firmly believed that orders, like control, involved a reciprocal, integrative activity. Compliance with orders was not simply the product of the authority of the issuer of the orders (Follett, 1996). Barnard (1938) influenced generations of organization theorists. His emphasis on cooperation, leadership, and the informal group represents a major departure from the structural and authoritarian assumptions characteristic of classical organization theory.

During the middle and later decades of the twentieth century (and into this first part of the twenty-first century), concern for the worker both as an individual and as part of a group becomes paramount. This is a time when the human element in organizations becomes defined as the most important factor in an organization's success. Concerns as varied as individual motivation to managerial capability to lead are facets of human relations in the organization. The basic premise of this "group-based" style of leadership is that leaders must work with followers who are heterogeneous and respond to quite different internal and external "stimuli."

A dissatisfied or unmotivated worker will make little use of a well-structured facility, and a motivated employee will be able to do better under adverse physical conditions.

The Hawthorne experiments were the emotional and intellectual wellspring of the organizational behavior perspective and modern theories of motivation. The Hawthorne experiments showed that complex, interactional variables make the difference in motivating people—things like attention paid to workers as individuals, workers' control over their own work, differences between individuals' needs, management willingness to listen, group norms, and direct feedback.

(Roethlisberger, 1989, pp. 28–29)

Criticism of the group dynamics perspective came from both those who were unwilling to relinquish the traditional views of leadership and from those (primarily psychologists) who found the focus on group dynamics did not leave sufficient room to explore individual relationships. Maslow first presented his views on human motivation in 1943. In that work he presented his now famous hierarchy of needs: physiological, safety, love, esteem, and self-actualization. First, it is important to understand the interrelationships among these needs. Second, satisfaction need not be complete before the needs of a higher level are addressed. Third, and probably most important, is that these needs are generally unconscious. While higher-level needs can be brought out in each of us and therefore become conscious, this is not often the case. Fourth is that all behavior is motivated; some behavior is an expression of personality and experience rather than needs. All this suggests that goals are the central principle within the concept of motivation. Gratification through the attainment of goals is the basic process for determining a shift to other needs (and therefore goals). The point is that the work setting must be taken into account if the manager is to create a work environment where achievement of higher needs is possible (Fiedler, 1967). For Fiedler, the differences are likely to be found in the flexibility and adaptability of management style of the respective manager.

Van Wart (2017) summarized these perspectives as follows:

> Leadership in organizations has become more difficult since the 1980s for a variety of reasons. . . . First, the rate of change in organizations increased substantially almost universally and has actually accelerated again with the advent of the Great Recession in 2008. Public and non-profit organizations are still adjusting to the movement from a traditional bureaucratic paradigm to a post-bureaucratic paradigm that integrates much higher levels of customer service, devolution, coproduction, and competition. This makes the job of leadership more interesting, but also more confusing and risky. . . . Second, the range of leadership activities required of leaders is simply greater. . . . This is hard work. Third, in a more cynical age it is more difficult to be a leader. Followers are not only more cynical about institutions. . . , but also more likely to be cynical about individuals who lead them.
>
> (p. 313)

Collaboration and Networks

Agranoff and McGuire (2003) described the American government as being in an "Age of Collaboration" (p. 20). Policy making has always been a shared responsibility whether between councils and managers in a city or across levels and types of governments. Shared governance is not a conveyor belt; it is an iterative and self-reinforcing process of feedback and response. If organizations are to be successful, both the formal and the informal aspects of the organization must be predicated on the following understandings of trust:

- Trust should affirm the organizational-interpersonal link
- Trust should promote cultural values such as respect, vision, diversity, and empowerment
- Trust should be built through the application of the skills of: talent searching, communicating, deciding, self-assessing, enabling, culture creating, and culture affirming

Miller and Cox (2014) posit that the boundaries of a network emerge as individuals or government recognize shared interests, shared problems, and shared history. This in itself is enough to bring people "to the table," but it is not sufficient to get them to agree to act. The barrier is that the emphasis on markets seemingly provides justification to not act. The arrangement becomes a network whose purpose is to obfuscate and delay.

Through the Glass Darkly: When Things Go Wrong

Corruption in all its forms, from straightforward bribery to influence pedaling to distorting the justice system to protecting criminal behavior and money-laundering, sadly, are common across the globe. There is also the problem that is endemic in certain parts of the world in which governments seem to fall into a dispiriting cycle of corruption, revolution, and back to corruption (Hope, 1999). Hope assessed the pattern in Africa of revolutionary leaders who promise abolition of corruption, but instead mimic the very same corrupt practices once in office. These are systems helpless against strong authority figures. This puzzle of corruption in former colonies seems to be a persistent problem. One partial explanation is that the political zeal which supported the revolution will wane in the face of the slow pace of reform. While there are many explanations for the slow change, frustrations with the idea of a rule of law have the appearance of barriers. After more than twenty years of slow and erratic movement toward democracy, unrest in El Salvador and distrust of the government are rampant (Renderos and Cox, 2013). When both elected and appointed public officials are viewed as corrupted, then government itself becomes untrustworthy.

This may be the key issue in understanding the breakdown of integrity. Episodes of corruption by those in government may occur, but as long as the public continues to see the bureaucracy as fundamentally trustworthy then governance continues. It is when the expectation that no one in authority (political or administrative) is trustworthy that the governance process collapses. This also means that the collapse of trustworthiness puts the entire system of governance in jeopardy. It is not the random actions of corrupt persons or even revolutions (actions which the governance system will survive), but rather it is the collapse of the internal systems which are the problem. The danger is in changing the system when the corruption is individual, rather than address actors. Regime change may result in a corrupt government when the foundational trustworthiness of the administration too is compromised (such as in the return to chaos after the Arab Spring or the collapse of government at all levels in Iraq). In contrast, regime change, even change impelled by corrupt political officials, can survive when the trustworthiness of the administrative systems is maintained.

As noted earlier, when we observe an organization in action, we tend to see what we want to see. In other words, we see organizations operating as they "should." If we think of an organization as a machine, we see a machine. But also, we will want it to operate as a machine (i.e. workers are parts, not people). We will define an effective organization based upon how closely it mimics our preferred metaphor. We will measure those aspects of organizational activity that can confirm or deny our expectations.

Ethics and integrity address issues of organizational behavior from different perspectives. And because of those differing perspectives, the assumptions about what can go wrong and, especially the causes of corruption, are viewed from quite different perspectives. A caveat is important here. Even in the discussion of individual choice as a frame for ethics, there is an obvious organizational construct involved. Public servants after all work in organizations. Similarly, the framework of integrity does not reject the possibility of individual ethical transgressions and illegal behavior. However, we tend to comprehend organizational behavior with the aid of metaphors (Morgan, 1989). An individual's dominant metaphor will affirm the "correctness" of behaviors that fit the metaphor. The dominant metaphor of integrity is linked to consistent collective, organizational behaviors. Macaulay (2009) would see this as overly legal-rational inclination. The dominant metaphor of ethics is the isolated individual trying to make things right. Just as right behavior is defined here, the opposite, corrupt behavior, will emerge from a failure of the same metaphor. Integrity failure is the classic failure of bureaucratic structures. The ethics failure is the bad apple problem. More importantly the solutions to the problem of corruption are based upon conformance to the dominant metaphor. Organizational failures inevitably lead to wider systemic adjustments in either or both the political and administrative spheres. Bad apple failures lead to calls for better training, better hiring practices and more professional development. At a certain level these are not bad starting points, but they are limited to the perspectives acknowledged through the metaphor. Unethical behavior, particularly at senior levels, may bring down a government. The solution is not necessarily a major reorganization or even a reconceptualization of governance. We are only slowly realizing in the US, as we confront the racism that exists in many police departments, the sub-culture reinforces those beliefs; bringing new officers into the department will not change that. Tellingly, the problem of policing in the US is a lack of integrity in the organization itself. The bad apple is a reflection of the organization, not the exception.

Blind Spots

Another way of thinking about Morgan's metaphors is to examine what the metaphor prevents one from seeing. When we envision ethics as the expression of the values and norms of an individual we will tend to see corruption as the "behavior on the part of officials . . . in which they unlawfully enrich themselves" (Fijnaut and Huberts, 2002, p. 4). Fijnaut and Huberts define public ethics:

> as the collection of values and norms in the public sector, functioning as standards or yardsticks for assessing the integrity of one's conduct. The moral nature of these principles refer to what is judged as right, or good conduct. Values are principles or standards of behavior that should have a weight in choice of action (what is good to do, or bad to refrain from doing). Norms state what is morally correct behavior in a certain situation. Values and norms guide the choice of action and provide a moral basis for justifying or evaluation what we do.
>
> (p. 5)

While the context is international rather than organizational, Fijnaut and Huberts's elaboration about the definitions of corruption and integrity are informative. They note that "[A]lthough organizations like Transparency International argue that cultural relativism concerning corruption should be out of the question, it is undeniable that culture, religions and ideologies differ in their appreciation of values and norms" (p. 5). The blind spot is that an organizational sub-culture may define "correct behavior in a certain situation" differently than the broader society. If the broader society sees ethics as the manifestation of individual choice, then violations of those norms and values would be the result of misjudgment or bad choices. This is the bad apple problem. Corruption is rooted out by finding the bad apple and removing it. The solutions to the problem of corruption are in changing the behavior of individuals through counseling and training, among others.

If we flip this around and see ethics as broadly reflecting social norms, we are likely to see corruption as systemic. The solutions are to change the processes and procedures of governance. Political and administrative reforms become the solution to the problem of corruption. What happens when the loci of norms are wrong? For example, what happens if the bad apple is simply the one who got caught and the sub-culture supports and protects corrupt behavior? Or, what happens if there is a bad apple (particularly a politically powerful bad apple), not the system, that is the problem. In both of these cases our metaphors lead us to reforms and corrections of corruption that are at best incomplete and may even be counterproductive. The reality is that the sources of corruption are wider and possibly deeper than we assume. The problem of corruption is both cultural and individual. It manifests itself because it is tolerated and it thrives because it is accepted as the norm for that organization. Edmund Burke famously argued that bad things happen when men of good character do nothing. The stable state of most organizations (especially in the US model) is one of good people doing nothing.

For organizational integrity to thrive, it is not enough to have good people making good decisions that reflect norms and values. It is not enough for there to be a "transformational leader." As Six and Huberts (2008) suggested a decade ago, trust is critical. But trustworthiness is one aspect of social relationship that bonds persons, and those bonds may as easily affirm a corrupt sub-culture as an ethical one. Ethics and integrity are social constructs that are manifest in the actions of people. It cannot be merely the product of individual choice or individual capacity to reason to an ethical choice. In the public service the norms and values that support organizational integrity are essentially social and cultural in nature.

Pulling Things Together: Concluding Thoughts

Metaphors express or define how we think an organization should operate. Each of us has preferred metaphors. The mind-trick of metaphors dominates our thinking about organizations. As different people apply different metaphors to comprehend what we see, we see things differently. We will define an effective organization based upon how closely it mimics our preferred metaphor. Rarely is the metaphor one of an open, engaged, and collaborative discourse.

Attempts to "open" the bureaucracy generally have met with failure in part because we have conflicting, and even faulty, "vision." The focus has been on creating rules by which clients can communicate with bureaucrats. But the problem is the rule-bound administrator is still a captive of the linear thinking of turn-of-the-century scientific management. Under those circumstances, any action that diminishes the ability of the manager (bureaucrat) to plan and apply technology reduces the likelihood of an effective job being done.

To be successful, organizational actions must serve the institution, not the organization. In doing this it elevates the sights of the field away from organizational "results" to the mission and goals of the institution. It is worth remembering Selznick's (1957) words.

> Organizations are technical instruments, designed as means to definite goals. They are judged on engineering premises; they are expendable. Institutions, whether conceived as groups or practices, may be partly engineered, but they have also a "natural" dimension. They are products of interaction and adaptation; they become the receptacles of group idealism; they are less readily expendable.
>
> (pp. 21–22)

Organizations look inward, while institutions look outward. Institutional performance should be an outward looking process, i.e. one that is focused on mission. The goal is to reject current practice and to seek new goals.

How can public administration, or government itself, survive such cynicism? At one level it probably cannot. It will be a long time before the public will tolerate the aggressive, service-oriented, and progressive governments that typified the 1960s. But the more critical question is whether or not the damage is the result of self-inflicted wounds, rather than the barbs and rhetoric of politicians. Can we come down from the mountain of professionalism to serve the public, even as they continue to criticize? Can we establish a theory of public administration practice that makes democracy more, rather than less viable? Can we be responsive to the public and effective in the delivery of services by listening, rather than deciding (Cox and Ostertag, 2014)?

The solution to this problem rests in an approach to the work of the bureaucracy that recognizes that its authority is derived from the public and the other institutions of government, not from autonomy. The concept of checks and balances that was created to regulate the competing authorities of the three branches of government must similarly apply to the bureaucracy. Rather than claiming special privilege, either because of the claim of being apolitical or because of the claim of expertise, the bureaucracy must be placed within the same decision-community within which the other institutions of government are placed. The bureaucracy must be subjected to the same competing claims of the public as other branches into its domain, not to stop action but because it is the only way that "right" action is possible. The bureaucratic expert still plays a critical role. The expert perspective cannot be ignored. However, the role is constrained by a larger decision process.

The bureaucracy must accept a hostile environment in which every decision is criticized, critiqued, and subject to amendment. Only then may a bureaucracy that can earn the title of representative bureaucracy be created. Such a bureaucracy would be representative in the Burkean sense of representation; the purpose of representation is in creating the opportunity for national goals and national beliefs to be defined and clarified. The action of government would be the final result of this pursuit of common interest, an interest that could result only from the collective interaction of all elements of society and government. This common interest as emerging from the public development of national goals may be a reasonable definition of "public interest."

How can a rule-bound, technocratic bureaucracy be made democratic? Focusing only on the external interaction of governmental institutions is not sufficient. The internal operations of bureaucracy must be changed. But in this latter change a shift to "industrial democracy" is not enough. The internal processes of the bureaucracy must be democratized in the sense of reducing emphasis on technological and managerial expertise in favor of a process that emphasizes consensus, harmony, and interdependence. The concepts of open discussion and even checks and balances can be introduced. New definitions would have to be accepted. Duplication and overlapping jurisdictions may not be proof of ineffectiveness. In being as concerned about how we set policy as we are of the policy itself, traditional concepts of inefficiency and ineffectiveness become meaningless. In "Politics as Vocation," Weber (1946) espouses an ethic of means that treasures the process of decision-making, not merely the final result. But more importantly, this ethic is tempered by a set of principles upon which to base social interaction. It could be argued that for those in the federal government the US Constitution ought to serve as that set of principles. Wildavsky (1978), contrasts the art of policy analysis with the science of policy analysis. Truth comes not from science but from art. Effectiveness of government is not merely in the execution of policy but begins with the process by which public issues are defined through the oft-amended act of executing policy.

There are obvious organizational implications of the changed decision-making processes. Most importantly are those that bring the bureaucracy within the constitutional framework by subjecting it to the same constraints that the other three branches operate within. In this way the bureaucracy earns the title of representative bureaucracy, being required to act in conjunction with, and on behalf of, the public and other institutions. In seeking this objective, the bureaucracy will very quickly become "unbureaucratic," because the pursuit of such a goal of national common interest is beyond the capacity of traditional bureaucratic processes.

The importance of bureaucracy cannot be underestimated in a modern representative democracy. Such democracies are founded on certain distinct postulates such as: every human individual is regarded as an "inexhaustible well of energy" and an active being dominated by mundane interests and by ascendancy of the rational element in human nature (Lindblom, 1959). It is this faith in rationality that modern democracy has in common with modern legal-rational bureaucracy. Both are products of modernity and work best in conjunction with the other.

Bureaucracies in developing nations are usually looked upon with certain mistrust. As noted in Chapter 15, comparative theorists have rigorously argued that "stronger" bureaucracies in developing nation-states overwhelm and take control of weak, partially developed democratic institutions pushing democratic development of those states into quandary. This gives an impression that these bureaucracies are well developed. Riggs (1964) termed these seemingly modern organizations "formalistic" or "prismatic" which according to him are common among transitional societies. These organizations do not facilitate modernity; neither do they encourage democratic development. Bureaucracy therefore should be studied in the context of governance. The rules that determine procedures in the bureaucracy, formal and informal, are especially important for public perceptions of how the state operates (Hyden et al., 2004).

A modern bureaucracy is a tool for dispensing efficient and effective as well as equitable administration. It can be the means for achieving the minimal equity and order that developing states lack but at the same time should not be allowed to transform itself as an end by itself (Hummel, 2008; Weber, 1946). The importance of the presence of modern, Weberian bureaucracy in the process of democracy consolidation among new democracies is a study that is, as yet, incomplete. If we are to understand the proper role of bureaucracy in representative democracies, then this work must be vigorously pursued.

DISCUSSION QUESTIONS

- Is pursuing a strong bureaucracy in support of a strong democracy an impossibility?
- Where would one begin to undertake such a task (impossible or not)?
- What is the appropriate role of bureaucracy in governance?
- Is a "hostile environment" inevitable, or is that a reflection of American political norms?
- Can a theory of public administration practice that makes democracy more, rather than less viable be established?
- Can bureaucrats be responsive to the public and effective in the delivery of services by listening, rather than deciding?

BIBLIOGRAPHY

Adam Smith. *Wealth of Nations*. Chicago: University of Chicago Press (1977) 1776.

Agranoff, Robert, and M. McGuire. *Collaborative Public Management: New Strategies for Local Government*. Washington DC: Georgetown University Press. 2003.

Barnard, Chester. *The Functions of the Executive*. Cambridge, MA: Harvard University Press. 1968.

Burns, James McGregor. *Leadership*. New York: Harper Collins. 1978.

Cox III, Raymond W., Susan J. Buck, and Betty Morgan. *Public Administration in Theory and Practice, 2nd ed.* New York: Longman. 2011.

Cox III, Raymond W., and Tricia Ostertag. "Doing Less with Less: The Decline of American Governments", *International Journal of Organization Theory and Practice*, 17 (4), pp. 437–458. 2014.

Cox III, Raymond W., Gregory K. Plagens, and Keba Sylla. "The Leadership-followership Dynamic: Making the Choice to Follow", *International Journal of Interdisciplinary Social Sciences*, 5 (8), pp. 37–52. 2010.

Cox III, Raymond W., and Sucheta Pyakuryal. "Tacit Knowledge: The Foundation of Information Management", in Frederickson and Ghere (eds.) *Ethics and Public Management, 2nd ed.* Armonk, NY: M.E. Sharpe, pp. 216–239. 2013.

Dunn, William. *Public Policy Analysis: An Introduction*. Englewood Cliffs, NJ: Prentice Hall. 1981.

Fiedler, Fred. *A Theory of Leadership Effectiveness*. New York: McGraw-Hill. 1967.

Follett, M. P. "The Essentials of Leadership", in P. Graham (ed.) *Mary Parker Follett: Prophet of Management*. Boston: Harvard Business School Publishing, pp. 163–177. 1996.

Gulick, L. "Notes on the Theory of Organization", in L. Gulick and L. Urwick (eds.) *Papers on the Science of Administration*. New York: Institute of Public Administration, pp. 3–46. 1937a.

Gulick, L., and L. Urwick, eds. *Papers on the Science of Administration*. New York: Institute of Public Administration. 1937b.

Habermas, Jurgen. *Toward a Rational Society* Boston: Beacon Press. 1971.

Hope, Kempe Ronald. "Corruption in Africa: A Crisis in Ethical Leadership", *Public Integrity*, 1(3), pp. 289–308. 1999.

Hummel, Ralph P. *The Bureaucratic Experience, 3rd ed*. New York: St. Martin's Press. 1987.

Hummel, Ralph P. *The Bureaucratic Experience, 5th ed*. New York: St. Martin's Press. 2008.

Hyden, G., C. Julius, and K. Mease. *Making sense of governance*. Colorado: Lynne Reinner Publishers. 2004.

Lindblom, Charles E. "The Science of Muddling Through", *Public Administration Review*, 19, pp. 79–88. 1959.

Lindblom, Charles E. *Politics and Markets*. New York: Harper Collins. 1977.

Macaualy, Michael. "The I that is We" in Cox III, Raymond W. (ed). *Ethics and Integrity in Public Administration: Concepts and Cases*. Armonk, NY: ME Sharpe. 2009.

Miller, D. Y., and Raymond W. Cox III. *The Metropolitan Region: Governing America's New Frontier*. Armonk, NY: M.E. Sharpe. 2014.

Morgan, Gareth. *Creative Organization Theory*. New York: Sage. 1989.

Morgan, Gareth. *Images of Organization*. Newbury Park, CA: Sage. 1986.

Renderos, Hugo and Raymond W. Cox III. "Achieving Peace: An Organizational Analysis of the Implementation of the 1992 Salvadorean Peace Accords", *International Journal of Social Sciences*, 2 (8), pp. 60–68. 2013.

Roethlisberger, Fritz .J. and W. J. Dickson. *Management and the Worker: An Account of a Research Program Conducted by the Western Electric Company*, Hawthorne Works, Chicago. Cambridge, MA: Harvard University Press. 1939.

Selznick, Philip. *Leadership in Administration*. Berkeley, CA: University of California Press. 1957.

Taylor, F. *The Principles of the Scientific Management*. New York. Harper Brothers. 1911.

Van Wart, Montgomery *Leadership in Public Agencies: An Introduction*. New York: Taylor and Francis, 2017.

Weber, Max. *From Max Weber*. (Gerth and Mills, Trans.). New York: Oxford University Press. 1946.

Wildavsky, A. *Speaking Truth to Power*. Boston: Little, Brown and Co. 1978.

SUGGESTED READINGS

CHAPTER 1.
Normative Foundations of Public Administration

Appleby, Paul H. *Morality and Administration in Democratic Government*. Baton Rouge: Louisiana State University Press. 1952.

Appleby, Paul. *Citizens as Sovereigns*. Birmingham: University of Alabama Press. 1975.

Finer, Herman. "Administrative Responsibility in Democratic Government", *Public Administration Review*, 1. Summer 1941.

Friedrich, Carl J. "Public Policy and the Nature of Administrative Responsibility", in Carl J. Friedrich and Edward S. Mason (eds.) *Public Policy*. Cambridge, MA: Harvard University Press. 1940.

Marini, Frank, ed. *Toward the New Public Administration*. Scranton: Chandler Publishing Co. 1971.

Osborne, D, & T. Gaebler. *Reinventing Government: How the Entrepreneurial Spirit Is Transforming the Public Sector*. Reading, MA: Addison-Wesley. 1992.

Osborne, D., and Hutchinson, P. *The Price of Government: Getting the Results We Need in an Age of Permanent Fiscal Crisis*. New York: Basic Books. 2004.

Rawls, John A. *Theory of Justice*. Cambridge, MA: Harvard University Press. 1971.

Rohr, John A. *Ethics for Bureaucrats*. New York: Marcel Dekker. 1978.

Rohr, John A. *To Run a Constitution*. Lawrence, KS: University Press of Kansas. 1986.

Simon, Herbert. *Administrative Behavior, 3rd ed*. New York: Free Press. 1976.

Waldo, Dwight. *The Enterprise of Public Administration*. Novato, CA: Chandler and Sharp Publishers, Inc. 1981.

Waldo, Dwight. *The Administrative State, 2nd ed*. New York: Holmes and Meier. 1984.

Wamsley, Gary L. *Refounding Public Administration*. Newberry Park, CA: Sage. 1990.

Wamsley, Gary L., and James Wolf. *Refounding Democratic Public Administration: Modern Paradoxes, Postmodern Challenges*. Newberry Park, CA: Sage. 1996

CHAPTER 2.
Ethical Foundations

Appleby, Paul H. *Morality and Administration in Democratic Government*. New York: Greenwood Press. 1979.

Audi, Robert. *The Good in the Right* Princeton, NJ: Princeton University Press. 2004.

Barnard, Chester. "The Nature of Executive Responsibility", in *The Functions of the Executive*. Cambridge, MA: Harvard University Press. 1938.

Bentham, Jeremy. *An Introduction to the Principles of Morals and Legislation*. New York: Oxford University Press. 1996.

Bok, Sissela. *Lying: Moral Choice in Public and Private Life*. New York: Vintage Books. 1999.

Browne, Stephen H. *Edmund Burke and the Discourse of Virtue*. Tuscaloosa: University of Alabama Press. 1993.

Cooper, Terry L. *An Ethic of Citizenship for Public Administration, 5th ed*. San Francisco: Jossey-Bass. 2006.

Cox III, Raymond W., ed. *Ethics and Integrity in Public Administration: Concepts and Cases*. Armonk, NY: M.E. Sharpe. 2009.

Donner, Wendy. *The Liberal Self; John Stuart Mill's Moral and Political Philosophy*. Ithaca: Cornell University Press. 1991.

Fijnaut, Cyrille, and Leo Huberts (Ed.) *Corruption, Integrity and Law Enforcement* The Hague: Kluwer Law International. 2002.

Frederickson, George H. *Ethics and Public Administration*. Armonk, NY: M.E. Sharpe. 1993.

French, Peter A. *Ethics in Government*. Englewood Cliffs, NJ: Prentice Hall. 1983.

Gawthrop, Louis C. *Bureaucracy in the Spirit of Democracy: The Ethical-Moral Imperatives of Public Service*. New York: Chatham House. 1998.

Geuras, Dean, and Charles Garofalo. *Practical Ethics, 3rd ed.* Vienna, VA: Management Concepts. 2011.

Kant, Immanuel. *Perpetual Peace and Other Essays on Politics, History and Moral Practice*. Indianapolis: Hackett Publishing. 1983.

Kernaghan, Kenneth, and John Langford. *The Responsible Public Servant*. Toronto: Institute for Research on Public Policy and IPAC. 1990.

Kolthoff, Emile. *Ethics and New Public Management*. Amsterdam: BJu Legal Publishers. 2007.

Lasthuizen, Karin. *Leading to Integrity*. Amsterdam, VU University. 2008.

Machiavelli, Niccolo. *The Prince*. (George Bull, Trans.). New York: Penguin Books. 2003.

MacIntyre, Alasdair. *Dependent Rational Animals: Why Human Beings Need the Virtues: The Paul Carus Lectures*. Chicago: Open Court. 1999.

MacKinnon, Barbara. *Ethics: Theory and Contemporary Issues, 6th ed.* Belmont, CA: Wadsworth. 2007.

Menzel, Donald. *Ethics Moments in Government* Boca Raton, FL: CRC Press. 2010

Menzel, Donald. *Ethics Management for Public Administrators: Leading and Building Organizations of Integrity, 2nd edition*. London: Routledge. 2012.

Moore, Mark H. *Creating Public Value*. Cambridge, MA: Harvard University Press. 1995.

O'Leary, Rosemary. *The Ethics of Dissent: Managing Guerilla Government*. Washington, DC: CQ Press. 2005.

Rohr, John A. *Ethics for Bureaucrats*. New York: Marcel Dekker. 1978.

Rohr, John A. *Public Service: Ethics and Constitutional Practice*. Lawrence, KS: University of Kansas Press. 1998.

Taylor, Charles. *A Secular Age*. Cambridge, MA: Harvard University Press. 2007.

Tessitore, Aristide. *Reading Aristotle's Ethics: Virtue, Rhetoric and Political Philosophy*. Albany: State University of New York Press. 1996.

Wood, Allen W. *Hegel's Ethical Thought*. Cambridge, MA: Cambridge University Press. 1990.

CHAPTER 3.
Personnel Practices

Berman, Evan, J. Bowman, J. West, and M. Van Wart. *Human resources Management in Public Service*. Thousand Oaks, CA: Sage, 2015.

Bureau of Intergovernmental Personnel Programs. *Job Analysis: Developing and Documenting Data*. Washington, DC: US Government Printing Office. 1973.

Cayer, Joseph. *Public Personnel Administration 6th rd*. Birkdale Publishing 2016.

Denhardt, Robert. *Managing Human Behavior in Public and Nonprofit Organizations 4th ed.* Thousand Oaks, CA: Sage 2016.

Dresang, Dennis. *Personnel Management in Government Agencies and Nonprofit Organizations 6th ed*. New York: Taylor and Francis. 2017.

Fish, Carl. *The Civil Service and the Patronage*. New York: Russell and Russell. 1963.

Hoogenboom, Ari. *Outlawing the Spoils*. Chicago: University of Illinois Press. 1968.

Dye, Thomas R. *The Politics of Equality*. Indianapolis: Bobbs-Merrill. 1971.

Hall, Francine, and Maryann H. Albrecht. *The Management of Affirmative Action*. Santa Monica, CA: Goodyear Publishing Co. 1979.

Krislov, Samuel. *Representative Bureaucracy*. Englewood Cliffs, NJ: Prentice Hall. 1974.

Merriam, Lewis. *Personnel Administration in the Federal Government*. Washington, DC: Brookings Institution Press. 1937.

Pynes, Joan. *Human Resources Management for Public and Nonprofit Organizations, San Francisco: Jossey-Bass*. 2013.

Reeves, T. Zane. *Cases in Public Resources Management, 2nd ed*. Wadsworth. 2006.

Sayre, Wallace. "The Triumph of Technique Over Purpose", *Public Administration Review*, 8 (Spring), pp. 134–147. 1948.

336 | Suggested Readings

Shafritz, Jay, Albert Hyde, and David Rosenbloom. *Personnel Management in Government, 3rd ed.* New York: Marcel Dekker, Inc. 1986.

Nigro, Lloyd G., Felix A. Nigro, and Edward Kellough. *The New Public Personnel Administration, 6th ed.* Belmont, CA: Thomson/Wadsworth. 2007.

US Civil Service Commission. *History of the Federal Civil Service 1789 to the Present.* Washington, DC: US General Printing Office. 1941.

US Office of Personnel Management. *Position Classification: A Guide for City and County Managers.* Washington, DC: US Government Printing Office. 1979.

Van Riper, Paul. *History of the United States Civil Service.* Evanston, IL: Row, Peterson and Co. 1958.

Waldo, Dwight. *The Enterprise of Public Administration.* Novato, CA: Chandler and Sharp Publishers, Inc. 1981.

CHAPTER 4.
Budgeting Practices

Alt, J. E., and R. C. Lowery. "Divided Government, Fiscal Institutions, and Budget Deficits: Evidence from the States", *American Political Science Review*, 88 (4), pp. 811–828. December 1994.

Bland, Robert L. *A Revenue Guide for Local Government, 2nd ed.* Washington DC: ICMA. 2007.

Bland, Robert L., and Irene S. Rubin. *Budgeting: A Guide for Local Governments.* Washington, DC: ICMA, 1997.

Coe, Charles K. *Public Financial Management.* Englewood Cliffs, NJ: Prentice Hall. 1989.

Covaleski, M. A., and M. W. Dirsmith. "The Management of Legitimacy and Politics in Public Sector Administration," *Journal of Accounting and Public Policy*, 10 (2), pp. 135–156. 1991.

Cox III, Raymond W. "Seeding the Clouds for the Perfect Storm: A Commentary on the Current Fiscal Crisis" *State and Local Government Review.* 41 (3) 216–22. 2009.

Grizzle, G. A. "Does Budget Format Really Govern the Actions of Budgetmakers?" *Public Budgeting & Finance*, pp. 60–70. Spring 1986.

Levine, Charles H. *Managing Fiscal Stress* Chatham, NJ: Chatham House. 1980.

Lynch, Thomas. *Public Budgeting in America, 2nd ed.* Englewood Cliffs, NJ: Prentice Hall. 1985.

Meyers, Roy T. *Handbook of Government Budgeting.* San Francisco: Jossey-Bass. 1999.

Mikesell, John L. "Government Decisions in Budgeting and Taxing: The Economic Logic", *Public Administrative Review*, 38 (6), pp. 511–513. November-December 1978.

Mikesell, John L. *Fiscal Administration, 2nd ed.* Chicago: Dorsey Press. 1986.

Reed, B. J., and J. W. Swain. *Public Finance Administration.* Englewood Cliffs, NJ: Prentice Hall. 1990.

Rubin, Irene S. *Public Budgeting.* Armonk, NY: M.E. Sharpe. 2008.

Rubin, Irene S. *The Politics of Public Budgeting, 6th ed.* Washington, DC: CQ Press. 2010.

Ryu, Jay R. *The Public Budgeting Primer.* New York: Routledge 2015.

Schick, A. "The Road from ZZB", *Public Administration Review*, (38), pp. 177–180. 1978.

Wildavsky, Aaron. 1984. *The Politics of the Budgetary Process, 4th ed.* Boston: Little, Brown and Co. 1984.

Wildavsky, Aaron, and Naomi Caiden. *The New Politics of the Budgeting Process, 4th ed.* New York: Longman. 2001.

Public Budgeting and Finance (Wiley) journal

CHAPTER 5.
Administrative Law

Barry, Donald D., and Howard R. Whitcomb. *The Legal Foundations of Public Administration, 2nd ed.* St. Paul: West Publishing Co. 1987.

Bozeman, Barry, and Mary Feeney. *Bureaucracy and Red Tape.* New York: Taylor and Francis 2011.

Breyer, Stephen C., Richard B. Stewart, Cass Sunstein, Adrian Vermeule and Michael Herz. *Administrative Law and Regulatory Policy: Problems, Texts, and Cases, 8th ed.* Wolters-Kluwer Publishing 2017.

Cooper, Phillip. *Public Law and Public Administration, 4th ed.* Belmont, CA: Thomson/Wadsworth. 2007.

Cooper, Phillip, and Chester A. Newland. *Handbook of Public Law and Administration.* San Francisco: Jossey-Bass. 1997.

Federal courts: www.uscourts.gov

Federal Register: www.gpoaccess.gov/fr.

Goodnow, Frank. *The Principles of Administrative Law in the United States.* New York: Putnam. 1905.

Hall, Daniel. *Administrative Law in a Democracy, 7th ed.* Pearson, 2019.

Landis, James M. *The Administrative Process*. New Haven: Yale University Press. 1938.

Rosenbloom, David H. *Administrative Law for Public Managers 2nd ed*. New York: Taylor and Francis, 2014.

Scheb, John E., and John E. Scheb II. *Law and the Administrative Process*. Belmont, CA Thompson/Wadsworth. 2014.

Wilson, James Q. *The Politics of Regulation*. New York: Basic Books, Inc. 1981.

Woll, Peter. *Administrative Law: The Informal Process*. Berkeley, CA: University of California Press. 1963.

CHAPTER 6.
Policy Analysis

Allison, Graham, and Philip Zelikow. *Essence of Decision, 2nd ed*. New York: Longman. 1999.

Anderson, James E. *Public Policy Making: An Introduction, 6th ed*. Boston: Houghton Mifflin. 2006.

Argyris, Chris. *Knowledge for Action: A Guide to Overcoming Barriers to Organizational Change*. San Francisco: Jossey-Bass. 1993.

Argyris, Chris. *Organizational Learning, 2nd ed. Malden, MA: Blackwell. 1999*.

Bardach, Eugene. *Practical Guide for Policy Analysis, 4th ed*. Washingto, DC: CQ Press, 2012.

Birkland, Thomas A. *An Introduction to the Policy Process: Theories, Concepts, and Models of Public Policy Making, 2nd ed*. Armonk, NY: M.E. Sharpe. 2005.

Cohen, M. D., and J. G. March. "A Garbage Can Model of Organizational Choice", *Administrative Science Quarterly*, 17 (1), pp. 1–25. 1972.

Dunn, William. *Public Policy Analysis, 5th ed*. New York: Taylor and Francis, 2016.

Fischer, Frank. *Democracy and Expertise*. Oxford: Oxford University Press. 2009.

Fischer, Frank, and John Forester, eds. *Confronting Values in Policy Analysis: The Politics of Criteria*. Newbury Park, CA: Sage, 1987.

Fischer, Frank, and John Forester. *The Argumentative Turn in Policy Analysis and Planning*. Durham, NC: Duke University Press. 1993.

House, Peter W. *The Art of Public Policy Analysis*. Beverly Hills, CA: Sage. 1982.

Kingdon, John W. *Agendas, Alternatives, and Public Policies*. New York: Longman. 2003.

Lindblom, Charles E., and David K. Cohen. *Usable Knowledge: Social Science and Social Problem Solving*. New Haven: Yale University Press. 1979.

Lynn, Laurence E., Jr. *Managing Public Policy*. Boston: Little, Brown and Co. 1987.

Mazmanian, Daniel, and Paul A. Sabatier, eds. *Effective Policy Implementation*. Lexington, MA: Lexington Books. 1981.

Mohr, L. B. *Impact Analysis for Program Evaluation*. Sage. 1995.

Quade, Edward S. *Analysis for Public Decisions, 3rd ed*. New York: North Holland. 1989.

Radin. Beryl A. *Beyond Machiavelli: Policy Analysis Comes of Age*. Washington, DC: Georgetown University Press. 2000.

Schneider, Anne L., and Helen M. Ingram. *Deserving and Entitled Social Constructions and Public Policy*. Albany: State University of New York Press. 2005.

Weimer, David L., and Aidan R. Vining. *Policy Analysis: Concepts & Practice, 4th ed*. Upper Saddle River, NJ: Pearson- Prentice Hall. 2005.

Wildavsky, Aaron. *Speaking Truth to Tower*. Boston: Little, Brown and Co. 1978.

CHAPTER 7.
Program Evaluation

Birkland, Thomas A. *An Introduction to the Policy Process: Theories, Concepts, and Models of Public Policy Making, 2nd ed*. Armonk, NY: M.E. Sharpe. 2005.

House, Peter W. *The Art of Public Policy Analysis*. Beverly Hills, CA: Sage. 1982.

Kingdon, John W. *Agendas, Alternatives, and Public Policies*. New York: Longman. 2003.

Lindblom, Charles E., and David K. Cohen. *Usable Knowledge: Social Science and Social Problem Solving*. New Haven: Yale University Press. 1979.

Lynn, Laurence E., Jr. *Managing Public Policy*. Boston: Little, Brown and Co. 1987.

Mazmanian, Daniel, and Paul A. Sabatier, eds. *Effective Policy Implementation*. Lexington, MA: Lexington Books. 1981.

Mohr, L. B. *Impact Analysis for Program Evaluation*. Sage. 1995.

Newcomer, Kathryn E., Harry P. Hatry, Joseph S. Wholey. *Handbook of Practical Program Evaluation 4th ed*. New York: Wilry. 2015.

338 Suggested Readings

Rossi, Peter H., Mark W. Lipsey, and Howard E. Freeman. *Evaluation: A Systematic Approach, 7th ed.* Newberry Park, CA: Sage. 2005.

Royse, David, Bruce Thyer, and Deborah Padgett. *Program Evaluation 6th ed.* Cengage. 2016.

Stone, Sharon. *The Policy Paradox: The Art of Decision Making, 3rd ed.* New York: W. W. Norton and Company. 2011.

Wholey, J. S. *Handbook of Practical Program Evaluation.* San Francisco: Jossey-Bass. 1994.

Yanow, D. "The Communication of Policy Meanings: Implementation as Interpretation and Text", *Policy Sciences*, 26 (1), pp. 41–61. 1993.

CHAPTER 8.
Organization Dynamics and Change

Bennis, Warren, and Bert Nanus. *Leaders: The Strategies for Taking Charge.* New York: Harper & Row. 1985.

Carnevale, David. *Organizational Development in the Public Sector.* Boulder, CO: Westview Press. 2003.

Cawsey, Thomas, Gene Deszca, and Cynthia Ingols. *Organizational Change: Action-Oriented Toolkit, 3rd ed. Thousand Oaks*, CA: Sage, 2016.

Cummings, Thomas and Christopher Worley. *Organization Development and Change, 10th ed.* Cengage Learning, 2015

Drucker, Peter. *Innovation and Entrepreneurship.* New York: Harper & Row. 1983.

Faber, Nancy, *Community Action and Organizational Change: Images, Narrative, Identity, 2nd ed. Southern Illinois University Press. 2002.*

Golembiewski, Robert T. *Humanizing Public Organizations.* Mt. Airy, MD: Lomond. 1985.

Golembiewski, Robert T., and William H. Eddy, eds. *Organizational Development in Public Administration.* New York: Marcel Dekker. 1978.

Golembiewski, Robert, and Glenn Varney. *Cases in Organization Development. New York: F,E. Peacock.* 2000.

Goodman, Paul S. *Change in Organizations.* San Francisco: Jossey-Bass. 1982.

Kanter, Rosabeth M. *The Change Masters.* New York: Simon & Schuster. 1983.

Lipsky, Michael. *Street-level Bureaucracy.* New York: Russell Sage Foundation. 1980.

McClendon, Bruce, and Ray Quay. *Mastering Change.* Planners Press. 1988.

Palmer, Ian. *Managing Organizational Change: A Multiple Perspective Approach, 3rd ed.* New York: McGraw-Hill. 2017.

Peters, Thomas, and Robert Waterman. *In Search of Excellence.* New York: Harper & Row. 1982.

Steiner, George. *Strategic Planning.* New York: Free Press. 1979.

Zaltman, Gerald, and Robert Duncan. *Strategies for Planned Change.* New York: Harper & Row. 1977.

Margulies, Newton, and Anthony P. Rara. *Conceptual Foundations of Organizational Development.* New York: McGraw-Hill. 1978.

Meyer, Marshall W. *Change in Public Bureaucracies.* Cambridge, MA: Cambridge University Press. 1979.

Tichy, Noel M. *Managing Strategic Change.* New York: John Wiley & Sons. 1983.

Weiner, Bryan J., Megan A. Lewis, and Laura A. Linnan. *Using Organization Theory to Understand the Determinants of Effective Implementation of Worksite Health Promotion Programs.* London: Oxford University Press. 2008.

CHAPTER 9.
Transboundary Interactions

Agranoff, Robert. "Managing Federalism Through Metropolitan Human Services Bodies", *Publius*, 20 (1), pp. 1–22. 1990.

Agranoff, Robert. *Crossing Boundaries for Intergovernmental Management.* Washington, DC: Georgetown University Press. 2017.

Agranoff, Robert, and M. McGuire. "Big Questions in Public Network Management", *Journal of Public Administration Research and Theory*, 11 (3), pp. 295–326. 1999.

Cox III, Raymond W. "Seeding the Clouds for the Perfect Storm: A Commentary on the Current Fiscal Crisis", *State and Local Government Review*, 41 (3), pp. 216–222. 2009.

Miller, David Y., and Raymond W. Cox III. *The Metropolitan Region: Governing America's New Frontier.* Armonk, NY: M.E. Sharpe. 2014.

Downs, A. *New Visions for Metropolitan America.* Washington, DC: The Brookings Institution. 1994.

Feiock, Richard, ed. *Metropolitan Governance: Conflict, Competition and Cooperation.* Washington, DC: Georgetown University Press. 2004.

National Research Council. *Governance and Opportunity in Metropolitan America.* Washington, DC: National Academy Press. 1999.

O'Toole, Laurence, Jr., and Robert Christensen. *American Intergovernmental Relations.* Washington, DC: CQ Press. 2012.

Zuckerman, Michael. *Peaceable Kingdoms.* New York: W. W. Norton and Company. 1970.

CHAPTER 10.
Cultural Competence

Bernstein, Richard J. *The Restructuring of Social and Political Theory.* New York: Harcourt Brace Jovanovich. 1976.

Burrell, G., and Gareth Morgan. *Sociological Paradigms and Organizational Analysis.* London: Heinemann Brooks. 1977.

Cady, Elizabeth. *Citizens as Partners: Information, Consultation and Public Participation in Policy-making.* Paris: OECD. 2001.

Chin, Jean L., and Joseph Trimble. *Diversity and Leadership.* Thousand Oaks, CA: Sage. 2014.

Ellison, Ralph. *Invisible Man.* New York: Vintage Books. 1952.

Lipsky, Michael. *Street-level Bureaucracy.* New York: Russell Sage Foundation. 1980.

Marini, Frank. *Toward the New Public Administration.* Scranton: Chandler Publishing Co. 1971.

Morgan, Gareth. *Creative Organization Theory.* New York: Sage. 1989.

Parvis, Leo. *Understanding Cultural Diversity in Today's Complex World, 6th ed.* Embrace Publishing, 2018.

Pateman, Carole. *Participation and Democratic Theory.* Cambridge, MA: University Press. 1970.

Riccucci, Norma. *Unsung Heros.* Washington, DC: Georgetown University Press. 1995.

Rice, M. F. *Diversity and public administration: Theory, issues, and perspectives.* New York, NY: Routledge. 2015.

Tinder, Glenn E. *The Tragic Ideal: Reflections on Community.* Baton Rouge: Louisiana State University Press. 1980.

Tinder, Glenn E. *Tolerance and Community.* Columbia: University of Missouri Press. 1995.

Verkuyten, Maykel. *Identity and Cultural Diversity.* London: Routlrdge. 2014. Wildavsky, Aaron. *Speaking Truth to Power.* New Brunswick, NJ: Transaction Publishers. 1987.

Yates, Douglas. *Bureaucratic Democracy.* Cambridge, MA: Harvard University Press. 1982.

CHAPTER 11.
Citizen Engagement

Appleby, Paul. *Citizens as Sovereigns.* Birmingham: University of Alabama Press. 1975.

Arendt, Hannah. *Responsibility and Judgment.* New York: Schocken Press. 2003.

Argyris, Chris. *Knowledge for Action: A Guide to Overcoming Barriers to Organizational Change.* San Francisco: Jossey-Bass. 1993.

Argyris, Chris. *Organizational Learning, 2nd ed.* Malden, MA: Blackwell. 1999.

Behn, Robert D. *Rethinking Democratic Accountability.* Washington, DC: Brookings Institution Press. 2001.

Bernstein, Richard J. *The Restructuring of Social and Political Theory.* New York: Harcourt Brace Jovanovich. 1976.

Baumard, Phillipe. *Tacit Knowledge in Organizations.* Thousand Oaks, CA: Sage. 1999.

Bozeman, Barry. *Public Values and Public Interest.* Washington DC: Georgetown University Press. 2007.

Bozeman, Barry, and Mary Feeney. *Bureaucracy and Red Tape.* New York: Taylor and Francis 2011.

Burrell, G., and Gareth Morgan. *Sociological Paradigms and Organizational Analysis.* London: Heinemann Brooks. 1977.

Faber, Nancy. *Community Action and Organizational Change: Images, Narrative, Identity, 2nd ed.* Southern Illinois University Press. 2002.

Fischer, Frank. *Democracy and Expertise.* Oxford: Oxford University Press. 2009.

Gormley Jr., William T., and Steven J. Balla. *Bureaucracy and Democracy, 2nd ed.* Washington, DC: CQ Press. 2008.

Gruber, Judith E. *Controlling Bureaucracies.* Berkeley, CA: University of California Press. 1987.

Habermas, Jurgen. *Knowledge and Human Interests.* Boston: Beacon Press. 1972.

Hummel, Ralph P. *The Bureaucratic Experience, 5th ed.* Armonk, NY: M.E. Sharpe. 2007.

Lindblom, Charles E. *Politics and Markets.* New York: Basic Books, Inc. 1977.

Morgan, Gareth. *Creative Organization Theory.* New York: Sage. 1989.

Nicolini, Davide, Silvia Gherardi, and Dvora Yanow, ed. *Knowing in Organizations*. Armonk, NY: M.E. Sharpe. 2003.

Osborne, David, and Ted Gaebler. *Reinventing Government*. Boston: Addison-Wesley. 1992.

Pateman, Carole. *Participation and Democratic Theory*. Cambridge, MA: University Press. 1970.

Simon, Herbert. *Administrative Behavior, 3rd ed.* New York: Free Press. 1976.

Thompson, Frank J., ed. "The Winter Commission Report Revisited", *Public Administration Review*, 68. supplement 2008.

Waldo, Dwight. *The Administrative State, 2nd ed.* New York: Holmes and Meier. 1984.

Weber, Max. *From Max Weber.* (Gerth and Mills, Trans.). New York: Oxford University Press. 1946.

Weick, Karl. *Social Psychology of Organization, 2nd ed.* Reading, MA: Addison-Wesley Publishing. 1979.

Weick, Karl. *Making Sense of the Organization.* Malden, MA: Blackwell. 2001.

Wolin, Sheldon S. "Democracy and the Welfare State", *Political Theory*, 15 (4) November, pp. 467–500. 1987.

Yates, Douglas. *Bureaucratic Democracy.* Cambridge, MA: Harvard University Press. 1982.

CHAPTER 12.
Strategic Management

Baker, David. *Strategic Change Management in Public Sector Organizations.* Oxford: Chandros. 2007.

Bryson, John M. *Strategic Planning for Public and Non-Profit Organizations, 3rd.* San Francisco: Jossey-Bass. 2004.

Bryson, John M., Barbara C. Crosby and Laura Bloomberg. *Public Values and Public Administration.* Washington DC: Georgetown University Press. 2015.

Bryson, John M., and Robert C. Einsweiler, eds. *Strategic Planning—Threats and Opportunities for Planners.* Chicago: The Planners Press of the American Planning Association. 1988.

Burns, J. M. *Leadership.* New York: Harper & Row. 1978.

Choo, Chun Wei, and N. Bontis, eds. *The Strategic Management of Intellectual Capital and Organizational Knowledge.* New York: Oxford University Press. 2002.

Freeman, R. Edward. *Strategic Management: A Stakeholder Approach.* Boston: Pitman. 1984.

Gardner, James R., Robert Rachlin, and H. W. Allen Sweeny, eds. *Handbook of Strategic Planning.* New York: John Wiley & Sons. 1986.

Hill, Charles, and Gareth Jobes. Essentials of Strategic Management, 2nd ed. Boston: Houghton-Mifflin. 2009.

Lamb, R., and P. Srivastava. *Latest Advances in Strategic Management.* Greenwich, CT: JAI Press. 1985.

Pearce, John. *Strategic Management, 14th ed. Callas: Richard D. Itwin, Inc. 2015. OECD. Benchmarking, Evaluation and Strategic Management in the Public Sector.* Paris: OECD. 1997.

Olsen, John B., and Douglas C. Eadie. *The Game Plan: Governance with Foresight.* Washington, DC: Council of State Planning Agencies. 1982.

Steiss, Alan W. *Strategic Management for Public and Nonprofit Organizations.* New York: Marcel Dekker. 2003.

Walstein, Steven L., *Strategic Healthcare Management, 14th ed.* Health Administration Press, 2014.

CHAPTER 13.
Leadership and Decision-Making

Argyris, Chris. *Knowledge for Action: A Guide to Overcoming Barriers to Organizational Change.* San Francisco: Jossey-Bass. 1993.

Argyris, Chris. *Organizational Learning, 2nd ed.* Malden, MA: Blackwell. 1999.

Behn, Robert. *Leadership Counts.* Cambridge, MA: Harvard University Press. 1991.

Bennis, Warren, and B. Nanus. *Leaders: The Strategy for Taking Charge.* New York: Harper Collins. 1985.

Bernstein, Richard J. *The Restructuring of Social and Political Theory.* New York: Harcourt Brace Jovanovich. 1978.

Burrell, G., and Gareth Morgan. *Sociological Paradigms and Organizational Analysis.* London: Heinemann Brooks. 1977.

Burns, James McGregor. *Leadership.* New York: Harper Collins. 1978.

Carnevale, David. *Trustworthy Government.* San Francisco: Jossey-Bass. 1995.

Cleveland, Harlan. *The Future Executive.* New York: Harper & Row. 1972.

DePree, Max. *Leadership is an Art.* New York: Dell Publishing. 1989.

DePree, Max. *Leadership Jazz*. New York: Dell Publishing. 1992.

Fiedler, Fred, and Joseph Garcia. *New Approaches to Effective Leadership*. New York: John Wiley & Sons. 1987.

Fisher, Frank, and Carmen Shirianni, eds. *Organization and Bureaucracy*. Philadelphia: Temple University Press. 1984.

Forester, John. *The Deliberative Practitioner*. Cambridge, MA: MIT Press. 1999.

Kiel, Douglas. *Managing Chaos in Government*. San Francisco: Jossey-Bass. 1994.

Marini, Frank, ed. *Toward the New Public Administration*. Scranton: Chandler Publishing Co. 1971.

Selden, Sally C. *The Promise of Representative Bureaucracy: Diversity and Responsiveness in a Government Agency*. Armonk, NY: M.E. Sharpe. 1997.

Van Wart, Montgomery. *Leadership in Public Agencies: An Introduction*. New York: Taylor and Francis, 2017.

Waldo, Dwight. *The Administrative State, 2nd ed*. New York: Holmes and Meier. 1984.

Warnsley, Gary L., and Mayer N. Zald. *The Political Economy of Public Organization*. Lexington, MA: Lexington Books. 1976.

Wilson, James Q. *Bureaucracy*. New York: Basic Books. 2000.

CHAPTER 14.
Bureaucracy, the Rule of Law, and Representative Democracy

Cox III, Raymond W. "Politics, Administration and Legislatures", *American Review of Public Administration*, 18 (1). March 1988.

Dodd, Lawrence C., and Bruce I. Oppenheimer, eds. *Congress Reconsidered, 4th ed*. Washington, DC: Congressional Quarterly. 1989.

Dodd, Lawrence C., and Richard L. Schott. *Congress and the Administrative State*. New York: John Wiley & Sons. 1979.

Fiorina, Morris P. *Congress: Keystone of the Washington Establishment, 2nd ed*. New Haven: Yale University Press. 1989.

Hutson, James. *To Make All Laws: The Congress of the United States, 1789–1989*. Washington, DC: US Government Printing Office. 1989.

Richardson, William D. *Democracy, Bureaucracy, and Character: Founding Thought*. Lawrence, KS: University Press of Kansas. 1997.

Selden, Sally C. *The Promise of Representative Bureaucracy: Diversity and Responsiveness in a Government Agency*. Armonk, NY: M.E. Sharpe. 1997.

Stivers, Camilla, ed. *Democracy, Bureaucracy, and the Study of Administration*. Boulder, CO: Westview Press. 2001.

CHAPTER 15.
Administration in a Global Perspective

Anton, Thomas J. *Administered Politics: Elite Political Culture in Sweden*. Boston: Martinus Nijhoff. 1980.

Bell, David S. *Democratic Politics in Spain*. London: Pinter. 1983.

Berman, Evan, and E. Prajojo. (ed.). *Leadership and Public sector Reform in Asian Countries*. Bingley:UK: Emerald Publishers. 2018

Cox III, Raymond W., ed. *Ethics and Integrity in Public Administration: Concepts and Cases*. Armonk, NY: M.E. Sharpe. 2009.

Dror, Yehezkel. *The Capacity to Govern*. Portland, OR: Frank Cass Publishers. 1994.

Farazmand, Ali, ed. *Modern Systems of Government*. Thousand Oaks, CA: Sage. 1997.

Farazmand, Ali, ed. *Bureaucracy and Administration*. Boca Raton, FL: CRC Press. 2009.

Gill, Graeme. *The Dynamics of Democratization: Elites, Civil Society and the Transition Process*. New York: St. Martin's Press. 2000.

Heady, Ferrel. *Public Administration: A Comparative Perspective, 6th ed*. New York: Marcel Dekker. 2005.

Hogwood, Brian W., and Michael Keating. *Regional Government in England*. London: Oxford University Press. 1982.

Holzer, Mark, and Menhzhong Zhang, eds. "Special Issue on Comparative Chinese/American Public Administration", *Public Administration Review*, 69 (Supplement 1). December 2009.

Kettl, Donald F. *The Global Public Management Revolution, 2nd ed*. Washington, DC: Brookings Institution Press. 2005.

Kellas, James. *Nationalist Politics in Europe: The Constitutional and Electoral Dimensions*. Basingstoke, UK: Macmillan. 2004.

Lane, Jan-Erik, ed. *Public Sector Reform: Rationale, Trends and Problems*. Thousand Oaks, CA: Sage. 1997.

Machin, Howard. *The Prefect in French Public Administration*. London: Croomhelm. 1977.

342 | Suggested Readings

McKevitt, David. *Managing Core Public Services.* Malden, MA: Blackwell. 1998.

Peters, B. Guy. *The Future of Governing, 2nd rev. ed.* Lawrence, KS: University of Kansas Press. 2001.

Peters, B. Guy. *The Politics of Bureaucracy, 6th ed.* London: Routledge. 2010.

Peters, B. Guy, Patrick von Maravic, and Tero Erkkila. *Public Administration: Concepts and Theories.* London: Routledge. 2015.

Peters, B. Guy. *Governance and Comparative Politics Cambridge: Cambridge University Press. 2016.*

Pollitt, C. "Managerialism Revisited" in B.G. Peters and D. Savoie (Eds.). *Taking Stock: Assessing Public Service Reforms.* Montreal: McGill–Queens University Press, 45–77. 1998.

Pollitt, C., and Bouckaert, G. *Public Management Reform: A Comparative Analysis – New Public Management, Governance, and the Neo-Weberian State* (3rd ed.). Oxford, UK: Oxford University Press. 2011.

Stone, Diane, and Kim Moloney. *Oxford Handbook of Global Policy and Transnational Administration.* Oxford, UK: Oxford University Press. 2019.

Riggs, Fred W. *Administration in Developing Countries: The Theory of Prismatic Society.* Boston: Houghton Mifflin. 1964.

Wessels, J. S., and J. C. Paw, eds. *Reflective Public Administration: Views from the South.* Oxford: Oxford University Press. 1999.

CHAPTER 16.
Concluding Thoughts

Arendt, Hannah. *Responsibility and Judgment.* New York: Schocken Press. 2003.

Argyris, Chris. *Knowledge for Action: A Guide to Overcoming Barriers to Organizational Change.* San Francisco: Jossey-Bass. 1993.

Argyris, Chris. *Organizational Learning, 2nd ed.* Malden, MA: Blackwell. 1999.

Barnard, Chester. *The Functions of the Executive.* Cambridge, MA: Harvard University Press. 1968.

Baumard, Phillipe. *Tacit Knowledge in Organizations.* Thousand Oaks, CA: Sage. 1999.

Bozeman, Barry. *Bureaucracy and Red Tape.* Upper Saddle River, NJ: Prentice Hall. 2000.

Bernstein, Richard J. *The Restructuring of Social and Political Theory.* New York: Harcourt Brace Jovanovich. 1978.

Burrell, G., and Gareth Morgan. *Sociological Paradigms and Organizational Analysis.* London: Heinemann Books. 1977.

Fischer, Frank. *Democracy and Expertise.* Oxford: Oxford University Press. 2009.

Gawthrop, Louis C. *Administrative Politics and Social Change.* Boston: Houghton Mifflin. 1971.

Gormley Jr., William T., and Steven J. Balla. *Bureaucracy and Democracy, 2nd ed.* Washington, DC: CQ Press. 2008.

Gruber, Judith E. *Controlling Bureaucracies.* Berkeley, CA: University of California Press. 1987.

Habermas, Jurgen. *Knowledge and Human Interests.* Boston: Beacon Press. 1972.

Hummel, Ralph P. *The Bureaucratic Experience, 5th ed.* Armonk, NY: M.E. Sharpe. 2007.

Lindblom, Charles E. *Politics and Markets.* New York: Basic Books, Inc. 1977.

Morgan, Gareth. *Creative Organization Theory.* New York: Sage. 1989.

Nicolini, Davide, Silvia Gherardi, and Dvora Yanow, ed. *Knowing in Organizations.* Armonk, NY: M.E. Sharpe. 2003.

Osborne, David, and Ted Gaebler. *Reinventing Government.* Boston: Addison-Wesley. 1992.

Ostrom, Vincent. *The Intellectual Crisis in Public Administration.* Tuscaloosa: University of Alabama Press. 1971.

Selden, Sally C. *The Promise of Representative Bureaucracy: Diversity and Responsiveness in a Government Agency.* Armonk, NY: M.E. Sharpe. 1997.

Shafritz, Jay M., and Albert C. Hyde, eds. *The Classics of Public Administration, 2nd ed.* Chicago: Dorsey Press. 1987.

Simon, Herbert. *Administrative Behavior, 3rd ed.* New York: Free Press. 1976.

Stivers, Camilla, ed. *Democracy, Bureaucracy, and the Study of Administration.* Boulder, CO: Westview Press. 2001.

Waldo, Dwight. *The Administrative State, 2nd ed.* New York: Holmes and Meier. 1984.

Weber, Max. *From Max Weber.* (Gerth and Mills, Trans.). New York: Oxford University Press. 1946.

Weick, Karl. *Social Psychology of Organization, 2nd ed.* Reading, MA: Addison-Wesley Publishing. 1979.

Weick, Karl. *Making Sense of the Organization.* Malden, MA: Blackwell. 2001.

INDEX

Note: Page numbers for charts are in *italic* type, and page numbers for tables are in **bold** type.

ABA (American Bar Association) 129–130
abortion policies 35
absolute ends, ethic of 18–20, 291
absolutism 151
academic approaches 216–217
accountability 16, 225–226
accounting procedures 100
achievement societies 301–303
activism 141
Adams, H.: *The Study of History in American Colleges and Universities* 141
Adams, J. 241
adjudication 130, 134
administration, defined 11
administrative law 50, 124–138; defining 126–136; evolution of 124–126; management support system 136–137
Administrative Procedure Act (APA) 129–136
administrative responsibility 7–8, 13, 21–23
administrative state, size and role of 11–14
administrative theory 28–30
adopters 177–178
affirmative action 54, 81–84, 278
affordability 324
Africa: commitment to government in 299; corruption in 327; good governance and 280; new democracies in 284; New Public Management (NPM) in 264; as pragmatic 297
AFT (analysis-from-the-top) change agents 179
age, pay and 82
Agranoff, R. 211, 225–226, 326
Agricultural Experiment Stations 141
Albert (Prince) 140
Albuquerque, New Mexico 165–166
Alexander of Macedonia 139
Allison, G.: *Essence of Decision* 152
allocations 101–102, 305–307
American Bar Association (ABA) 129–130

American Federation of State, County, and Municipal Employees (AFSCME) v. Washington State (1981) 78–79
American Political Science Association (APSA) 141
American Society for Public Administration (ASPA) 32
analysis-from-the-top (AFT) change agents 179
ancient Greece 283
ancient history 9–10
anti-democratic ideologies 284
anti-hierarchical views 264
APA (Administrative Procedure Act) 129–136
Appleby, P. 149
appropriation 102, 113
a priori judgments 37
APSA (American Political Science Association) 141
aptitude tests 145
arbitrary and capricious standard 135
Arendt, H. 148–149, 265–266, 271–272
Aristotle 38, 44, 139
Arizona 76
Arkansas 99
Army Corps of Engineers 138n5
"Art and Method of Process Evaluation, The" (Sylvia, Meier, and Gunn) 156–157
Arthur (King) 10
Arthur, C. 58–61
ascriptive societies 301–303
Asia: budgeting in 265; comparative administration and 294; good governance and 280; new democracies in 284; New Public Management (NPM) in 264; as pragmatic 297
ASPA (American Society for Public Administration) 32
attitude-based cultural competency 221
auditing 100, 112–113
Australia 264

authority: impersonal order and 282; leadership and 224–225; sources of 299–300

bad apple problem 328–329
Balanced Budget and Emergency Deficit Control Act (Gramm-Rudman-Hollings; 1985) 108
Balcazar, F. 218
Barnard, C. 223–224, 259, 325; *The Functions of the Executive* 224
Barnes, H.: *A History of Political Theories: Recent Times* 143–144
Barry, N. 283
BBC 12
Beard, C. 141–142
behavioralism 142, 145–147
behavior change 192
Behn, R. 88
Belgium 228, 298, 303
Bendix, R. 295, 298
benefit-cost analysis 134, 161
Benne, K. 181
Bennis, W. 181
Bentham, J. 283
Berger, P. 17
Bernalillo Chamber of Commerce 166
best practices 159, 266, 323
Betancourt, J. 220
Bhugra, D. 218
Bhui, K. 218
bias: affirmative action and 81–84; comparable worth and 79; cultural awareness and 228–232; education and 302; policy analysis and 151; program evaluation and 157, 161; selection process and 73; social class and 302; in standardized examinations 163
Bigelow, J. 58
Bill of Rights 11, 14, 242
BIRU (brain injury rehabilitation unit; Liverpool Hospital) 229–230
Blair, T. 114
Board of Regents v. Roth 36
Boateng, J. 88
BOB (Bureau of the Budget) 99
Bok, S. 45

343

344 Index

Bold State model 15
Bollens, S. 209–210
Booth, C.: *Life and Labour of the People of London* 140
Bork, R. 138n3
brain injury rehabilitation unit (BIRU; Liverpool Hospital) *229–230*
Brennan, W. *36*
Brewer, G. 152
Britain. *see* United Kingdom
Broad, C. 45
Brookings Institution 143
Broward County, Florida 161–163
Brownlow Commission (1937) (President's Committee on Administrative Management) 63–65, 99
Bryson, J. 248, 252, 257
Buchanan, J. 57
Buck, S.: *Understanding Environmental Administration and Law* 137n1
Budget and Accounting Act of 1921 99
Budget and Impoundment Control Act of 1974 108
budgetary theory 33–34
budgeting practices 49–50, 97–123; global fiscal crisis and 113–121; in global perspective 305–311; in historic perspective 98–100; macro-budget perspectives 100–111; management support system and 121; micro-budget perspectives 111–113
bulk budgeting 311
bureaucracy: criticisms of 11–12; cynicism and 330–331; democracy and 317–318; federal *vs.* state 13–14; founding period and 10–11; as fourth branch of government 80; global perspective of 315–319; increase in 11–13; interest groups and 315–316; legal-rational 282; modern 282–285, 331–332; prismatic 281–282; representative 290–291; role of 3; rule of law and 279–293; strength of 247; values of 25–26; Weberian 12, 32, 194
bureaucratic societies 295
bureaucratization 204, 284–289
Bureau of the Budget (BOB) 99
Bureau of the Census 141
Burger, W. *36*
Burke, E. 329
Burkean model 55, 291, 330–331
Burns, J. 261, 272; *Leadership* 26
Bush, G.H. 163–164
Bush, G.W. 39, 83, 134–136, 138n5
Bush, J. 39–40
Bush-Cheney administration 136
business taxes 118–119

cabinet agencies, establishment of 11
Caiden, N. 308
Califano, J. 35

California 39–40, 65, 118
Campinha-Bacote, J. 85
Canada 114, 228, 306, 310
capitalism, democracy and 34
capital outlay 98
career development 76–77, 192
Carrizales, T. 220
Carter, J. 109, 134–136
Case for Bureaucracy, The (Goodsell) 12
Catch-22 (Heller) 34
causality, defined 16
censuses 140–141
Central Intelligence Agency 145
centralization 201, 205, 310
certainty 166–167
Chancellery of Latvia 86
change: agents of 177–181; in behavior 192; implementing 179–181; participation and 288; strategic 189, 248; technical and structural 189–190
Charlottesville workshop 89
checks and balances 237–238, 289–291, 330–331
Chevron U.S.A. Inc. v. Natural Resources Defense Council (1984) 135
Child, R. 25
Chin, R. 181
China 139, 277
Choate, P. 246–249
citizen engagement 234–244; structural elements in democracy and 235–240; values of democracy and 240–242
citizenship 141, 230–231
city, defined 208–209
city management 21–23
City of Lauderhill (Florida) 161–163
Civil Rights Act of 1964 78, 81–82, 219
civil rights movement 222
civil service: decline of centralized control in 63–64; English 10, 59; pay, social status, and 303–305; performance appraisals under 86–87, 164–165; politicians and 88–91; reform of 263, 287; role of 7; Scientific Management Movement and 61–63; twentieth century 61
Civil Service Commission 61–65
civil service examinations 59
Civil Service Reform Act (1883) (Pendleton Act) 59–61, 64, 142
Civil Service Reform Act (CSRA) of 1978 41, 64–66, 66, 78, 86–87, 164
civil service reform movement 58–59
Clark, P. 304
Clean Air Act 134–135, 150–151
Cleveland, G. 60–61
clientela groups *313*, 314–315
Clinton, B. 134–136
CODE 2000 (Ohio) 206

Code of Fair Competition 125
Code of Hammurabi 9, 139
codes of conduct 31, *32*, 139
coercion 298–300
cohesion 225–226
Cold War 145
collaboration 225–226, 322–332
collective good 101
collective vision 166–168
Columbus, Ohio 206
command and control approach 216, 223, 226, 325
commitment 298–299
commonwealth 238, 288
Commonwealth countries 323
communication: approaches to 89; citizen engagement and 243–244; cultural awareness and *229–230*; innovation and 176
communism 114
community 241, 286
community-based cultural competency 221
comparable worth 79
comparative administration: of budget practice 305–311; of personnel practice 301; of policy making 311–315; *see also* global perspective
competition 323–324
complexity 45
compliance-based approaches 41–46
compromise 34
Comte, A. 140
conflicts of Interest 31
Confucian system 139
Congress: agency actions and 134–136; budgeting and 99, 111; civil service system and 64; delegation of powers and 124–127; Federal Register Act (1935) and 129; regulatory process and 134; spoils system and 57
Congressional Budget Office 160
Connecticut 40–43
Connecticut Compromise 13
Connor, P. 189
consensus 236–240, 268–269
conservatism 151
consilience, defined 115
Constitution. *see* United States Constitution
constitutional law 126
continental law 8
continuous process improvement concept 155
Cook County, Illinois 35, *36*
COPS program 162
corporatism 313
corruption 114, 327
Corwin, E. 142
cost-benefit analyses 150
counter-culture movement 147

county government 209
court packing 125–126
Cox, A. 138n3
Cox, R. 46, 226, 326–327
Crenson, M. 204
crime 162–168
criminal law 126
critical path concept 259
Cross 219
cross branch relationships 212–213
CSRA (Civil Service Reform Act) of 1978 41, 64–66, 66, 78, 86–87, 164
CSST (culturally specific support team) 229
Cuban missile crisis 152
cultural analysis 184
cultural competence 216–233; decision making and 223–226; defined 217; diversity and 222–232; interpreting cultural values and 222; managing and 226–232; models for 218–219; personnel practices and 84–85; public administration and 219–222
culturally specific support team (CSST) 229
cultural norms 295–297
cultural relativism 329
cultural self-awareness 227–232
Cultural Sensitivity and Awareness Checklist 229–230
culture, defined 227
Cummings, T. 179–180, 183
Cuomo, M. 35
Curtis, G. 58–59
cut-back management 114, 265
cybernetics 146

data collection and analysis 140–143, 186–187
Day 266–267
decentralization 201, 204–205, 258
decision making: consensus and 236–240; democracy and 234, 280; discretionary judgment and 37–39; in diverse settings 223–226; impermanence and 238–239; innovation and 177–178; knowing, understanding, and 265–272; leadership and 261–276; managing and 272–274; models for 46; motivation of employees and 301; motives and 45; participation and 288–289, 301; policy analysis and 149; politics and 267–268; process of 177–178, 294–295; professional public administration and 262–265; responsibility and 239; strategic management and 249–250
deficits 108–110, 119–121
delegation of powers 124–127
deLeon, P. 152
deliberative process 237

democracy: bureaucracy and 284–289, 317–318; capitalism, free markets, and 34; consolidation to 318; defined 234; global perspective of 317–319; government and 279–293; idea of 142; industrial 280, 291; liberal 283; new 284; structural elements in 235–240; values of 240–242
Democratic party 57–61
democratic responsibility 33
Department of Commerce 145
Department of Education 83
Department of Health and Human service (HRSA) 219
Department of Homeland Security 138n5
Department of Justice 165
Department of Justice Community Policing program 161–163
Department of Labor and Agriculture 141
Department of Transportation 254
Depression: administrative law and 128; policy analysis and 144; tax policy and 121; trust in government and 118
deregulated governments 316–317, 317
development administration 281
Dewey, J. 142
diagnostic models 183–186
Diamond 284
Dickson, W. 56
diffracted organizations 296
direct participation 236
Disability Act (1990) 219
discretion 37–39, 266–267, 270–273
diversity 84–85, 222–232. see also cultural competence
Diversity Competency Model 218–219
documentation, budget 100
double-loop communication approaches 89
Douglas, W. 35–36
Dragnet (television show) 146
Dror, Y. 146–149
drug culture 147
dual bureaucracies, in Belgium 298
due process 50
Dunn, W. 149

Eadie, D. 248
Earth Day 147
Eastern-bloc nations 211
Eastern Europe 114, 264
Eaton, D. 58–59
Edonya, P. 218
education bias 302
EEOC (Equal Employment Opportunity Commission) 81–82
effectiveness 156–157, 242, 322
efficiency 156–158, 281, 322
efficiency and economy perspective 114

egalitarianism 282
Egypt 9
Eichmann, A. 29
Eisenhower, D. 28
Eisenstadt, S. 297
elasticity 117
elections 287–288, 318
elitism 12, 290
Elliott, W. 142
Elrod v. Burns 36
El Salvador 327
empowerment 166–168
Endangered Species Act of 1973 131
enforcement 39–44
England: civil government in 8–10; common law in 10; independence of parliament 289; industrial revolution in 139–140; nationalization of health care in 297; political culture of 29, 300
Enlightenment 283
entitlement programs 306
entrepreneurial societies 295
entrepreneurship culture 88
envelope budgeting 311
environmental law 147
Environmental Politics and Policy (Rosenbaum) 138n4
Environmental Protection Agency (EPA) 131, 135, 137n2, 150–152, 254
Equal Employment Opportunity Commission (EEOC) 81–82
equality 35, 241, 286–288
Equal Pay Act of 1963 78
equal protection clauses 78
equity 77–79, 118
Essence of Decision (Allison) 152
ethical foundations of public administration 7–8, 28–48; administrative theory and 28–30; consequences of 45–46; constitutional values and 34–37; discretionary judgment and 37–39; enforcement of 39–44; public policy and 44–46; types of public morality 30–34
ethics 23, 269–270, 328–329
Ethics Commission (Miami-Dade County, Florida) 42
ethics commissions 39–44
Ethics for Bureaucrats (Rohr) 34–36
ethnocentricity 277, 294
etiquette, cultural 228
Europe: budgeting in 114, 265; comparative administration and 294; conservative governments of 297; Enlightenment era in 283; hiring quotas in 298–299; political culture in 200–201, 300; regional governance and 211; trust of government in 299
European Union (EU) 211

Index

evaluation 150, 156, 170, 240–242
executive branch 14; administrative law and 129; arrogation of power by 284; budgeting and 99, 107–113; legislative branch and 204
Executive Branch Plan 99
executive-legislative relations 212–213, 307–308
Executive Order 12291 134
Executive Order 12866 134
executive privilege 138n3
expenditures 98–102, 110–111, 119, 305–307
experimentation 268
expertise 148–150, 267–268, 278
explicit knowledge 38–39, 267
Extension Service 141
external analysis 253, 253–255
external constraints 16–17
external equity 77

face diversity 220
factions 239
failure, accommodation of 88–90
Fair Employment Practices Act 81
fair employment practices laws 82–83
Fair Political Practices Commission (California) 39
fair share payments 88
federal bureaucracy 13–14
Federal Emergency Management Agency (FEMA) 138n5
federal employees, 1790s characteristics of 55
Federal Executive Institute 76
federal government: intergovernmental relations and 180–181; program evaluation mandated by 163–164; public support for 118; rulemaking and 130–136; taxes and 117–120
federal grant programs 163–164
Federalist 10 (Madison) 12
Federalist 68 (Hamilton) 7
Federalist 72 (Hamilton) 11
Federal Labor Relations Council 65
Federal Register Act (1935) 129–134
federal stimulus package of 2010 120–121
FEMA (Federal Emergency Management Agency) 138n5
Ferguson's Community Curriculum Model 218
Fertile Crescent 9
feudal system (Britain) 10
Fiedler, F. 224, 326
field office-central office relations 204–207
field reports 206
Fifth Amendment 78
Fijnaut, C. 328–329
Fillmore, M. 57
Final Report of the Attorney General's Committee on Administrative Procedure 129–130

financial disclosure regulations 31
Finer, H. 16, 263
Firefighters Local Union No. 11783 v. Stotts 82
fiscal crises of 2008 and 2009 28
fiscal crisis, global 113–121
fiscal orientations 107
Flagstaff, Arizona Oath of Office *35*
flat rate income tax 118
flexible government **317**
Florida: civil service performance measures in 87, 164; coordination and cooperation in 212; ethics commissions in 39, 42; performance measurement in 161–163
Follett, M. 223, 325
follower-centric approaches 223
followership 261–262, 272–274, 324–325
formal rulemaking 132–133
formative evaluation 150, 156
founding period 10–11, 54–55
Fourteenth Amendment 14, 78
Four-Year Tenure of Office Act (1820) 57
France: budgeting in 114, 309–310; civil service in 303–304; interest groups in 316; public administration system in 277; Roman codified law in 9
Frankfurter, F. 126–127
Franklin, G. 258
Frederickson, H. 210
freedom 35, 242
Freedom of Information Act 130, 136
free market 34
French, J. 225
French, P. 45, 269–270
Freund, E. 126–128, 141, 144
Friedrich, C. 7, 16, 263–264
Friedrich-Finer debate 263
Frug, G 209–211
Frusti, D. 218–219
functionalism 141
Functions of the Executive, The (Barnard) 224
fused administration organization 296
future orientation 166

Gabris, G. 158–159
Gaebler, T.: *Reinventing Government* 264
Gale, S. 17
game, budgeting as 101–108
gangs 164–168
Garfield, J. 58–59
Gay 221
gender, pay and 77–79, 82
general good, idea of 283
generalists 23, 238, 268–269
geography, perceived relevance of 211–212
George I (King) 10
George II (King) 10

Georgia 76
Germany 284, 316
global fiscal crisis 113–121
global perspective 294–320; budgeting practices in 305–311; democracy, bureaucracy and 317–319; framework for study of 294–295; interest groups and 313, 314–316; models of governance in 316–317; personnel practice in 301; policy making in 311–315; political culture and 295–301; recruitment in the public sector and 301–305
goal displacement 164, 167
goals 169, 224, 256–257
golden parachutes 304
Golembiewski, R. 193–196
good governance 280, 287, 295
Goodman, P. 227
Goodnow, F. 126–127, 141
Goodsell, C. 231, 283, 297–299, 311–312; *The Case for Bureaucracy* 12
Gosnell, H.: *Negro Politicians* 143
governance 208, 316–317, 321–332
government: branches of 3, 14; bureaucracy and 7; change and 158, 174–175; decision making of 2; democracy 279–293; establishment of departments of 11; governance and 208; growth of 286; personnel practices and 53; planned change and 174–175, 183; program evaluation mandated by 163–164; role of 174; size of 305; trust in 28; two-tiered 210
Government in the Sunshine Act 130, 136
graduated income taxes 117
Gramm-Rudman-Hollings (Balanced Budget and Emergency Deficit Control Act; 1985) 108
Grant, U. 58–59
Great Recession (2008) 225, 326
Great Society 147
Griswold v. Connecticut 35–36
Grizzle, G. 167–171
Gross National Product 145
group behavior 190
group dynamics perspective 224, 325–326
group-level intervention 188
Guiteau, C. 59
Gunn, E.: "The Art and Method of Process Evaluation" 156–157

Habermas, J. 267–268
habitual behavior 193–196
Haitian immigrants 161–162
Hamilton, A.: *Federalist 68* 7; *Federalist 72* 11
Hanoverian kings 10
harmony, advocacy of 237
Harrison, B. 61

Harrison, W. *57*
Harvard Law School 127
Hawley, J. *59*
Hawthorne experiments 168, 190, 224, 325
Hayes, R. *58*
Head Start program 163–164, 183
Health, Education, and Welfare (HEW) 147
Heclo, H. 303
Hegel, G. 17
Heller, J.: *Catch-22* 34
Heritage Foundation 80–81
Hickman, C. 251
hierarchical practices *102*, 278
hierarchy of needs 224, *325–326*
History of Political Theories: Recent Times (Merriam and Barnes) 143–144
honesty, public morality and 31
Hoover, H. 143
Hoover Commission (1947) 99, 109
Hope, K. 327
horizontal relationships 208–209
House, P. 149, 160–161
House of Representatives 13
HRSA (Department of Health and Human service) 219
Huberts, L. 232, 328–329
human process interventions 190–192
human rights 283
Hummel, R. 17, 87, 287
Huntington, S. 284
Huse, E. 179–180, 183–187
Huse Matrix **185**, 185–187
Hutchinson, P. 116, 120
hybrid rulemaking 132–135
Hyde, A. 74
hyper-bureaucratization 285

ICMA (International City Management Association) *32*
ideal typical organizations 251
illegitimate groups *313*, 314–315
immigrants 161–162
Immigration and Naturalization Service 136
imperialism 10
impermanence 238–239
implementation, strategic management and 250, 258–259
incentives 304–305
incrementalism 110–113, 238–239, 307–311
independent regulatory commissions 41, 263
India 139, 302
indirect participation 236
individual change 175
individuality, democracy and 236
individual-level intervention 188–189
industrial democracy 280, 291, 331

industrial revolution 139–140, 200–201, 324
inelasticity 117
informal organizations 38
informal rulemaking 132–133
innovation 170–171, 175–178
instability 261
Institute for Government Research 143
Institute of Economics 143
institutional constraints, public sector 193–194
institutional imbalance thesis 285
institutionalization 322
integrity 41–43, 231–232, 328–329
intelligence tests 145
interactions, legitimate 313–314
interactive relationships *271*
inter-departmental agreements 210–211
interest groups *313*, 314–316
intergovernmental relations 180–181, 209–212, 211
Interior Department 11
internal analysis *253*, 255
internal checks 16–17
internal equity 77
International City Management Association (ICMA) *32*
International Monetary Fund 308
inter-organizational relations 322
interpersonal relations 322
interpretive rules 131
Interstate Commerce Commission 263
intervention 179–192, 192
Investments Committee (New Mexico) 39
Iran-Contra 28
Iraq, war in 28, 44
Italy 284, 298

Jackson, A. *55–57*, 204–206
Japan 114, 284, 302–303
Jefferson, T. *55–57*
Jenckes, T. *58*
job analysis 66–72
job description sample *62–63*
Johnson, L. 147
Joyce, P. 109–110, 160
judicial branch 14, 129
judicialization 128–129
judicial review 134–136
judiciary: Constitution and 13
Justice Department 11, 83, 162
justifiability 45

Kant, I. 17, 20, 265, 283
Katz, E. 297
Kaufman, H. 80
Kennedy, J., assassination of 147
Kennedy School at Harvard 152
Kentucky 254
Key, V. 33
Kirkhart, L. 234

knowing 265–272
knowledge: consensus and 240; decision process and 177–178; explicit 37–39, 267; responsibility and 239; tacit 37–39, 148, 267
knowledge-based cultural competency 221
Korea 264

labor unions 87–88
Labour Government (UK) 114
laggards 178
Lake, L. 189
landowners, titled 10
Landry, L. 226–227
Langseth, P. 183–187
language barriers 228–231
Las Cruces, New Mexico 165–166
Laswell, H.: *The Policy Sciences* 146–147
Latvian School of Public Administration 86
Lauderhill (Florida) Police Department 161–163
Lauer, R. 175–178
law: administrative 50, 124–138; conformity to 31; fair employment practices and 82–83; marriage 82; role of bureaucrats and 80–81; rule of 279–293
leader-follower relationship *271*, 272–274, 322
leadership: concept of 325; decision-making and 261–276; knowing, understanding, and 265–272; managing and 272–274, 321–322; power and 224–225; professional public administration and 262–265; theories of 223–225; transformational 26, 262; vision and 251–252
Leadership (Burns) 26
leadership-followership relationships *271*, 272–274
legal-rational bureaucracy 282, 299, 328
legislative branch 14; budgeting and 107–112; deliberative process 237; executive branch and 204
legitimacy 13–16, 241, 282–284, 299
legitimate interactions *313*, 313–314
Le Play, F.: *Les Ouvriers Europeens* 140
Lerner, D. 140; *The Policy Sciences* 146–147
Les Ouvriers Europeens (Le Play) 140
Lewin, K. 181
LGBTQ community 82–84
liberal corporatism 313
liberal democracy 283
liberty 242, 281, 288, 298
Life and Labour of the People of London (Booth) 140
Lincoln, A. 57–58
Lindblom, C. 110–111, 238, 300, 322

line-item budgets 100, 108–112
Lippitt, G. 183–187
local government: intergovernmental relationships and 209–212; peer-to-peer relationships and 208–209; public support for 118
Lorentzen, P. 89
Los Angeles 165
Los Angeles Police Department 162
Lowell, A. 141
loyalty 298–299
loyalty oaths 34–35
Lynch, T. 109
Lynn, L. 182

Macaulay, C. 328
Machiavelli, N. 44, 139
Mackenzie, G. 43
macro-budget perspectives 100–111
Madison, J. 57; *Federalist 10* 12
Maesschalck, J. 41–42
majoritarianism 288
Maleck Manual 136
management support system 49–51; administrative law and 136–137; budgeting practices and 121; organizational dynamics, change, and 197; personnel practices and 91; policy analysis 152; program evaluation 168–171
managerial constraints, public sector 194–195
managerial toolkit 200–276; citizen engagement and 234–244; cultural competence and 216–233; leadership, decision-making, and 261–276; strategic management and 245–260; transboundary Interactions and 203–215
managing at the margin 213
mandates 252
manorial courts 10
Marcy, W. 57, 92n2
marginality 180–181
market-driven perspectives 264–265, 279, 316–317, **317**, 322–324
marriage laws 82
Marx, K. 140
Maslow, A. 224, 325–326
Massachusetts 59–60, 117–118
Masters of Public Administration (MPA) 322
Masters of Public Policy (MPP) 322
material incentives 304–305
mathematics 139–140
mature man, ethic of 19–20
May, R.: *Thinking in Time* 152
Mayhew, H. 140
McCarthy era 34
McClendon, B. 248, 251
McCulloch v. Maryland 13–14
McGuire, M. 211, 225–226, 326

McKenzie, K. 218
means, ethic of 291
measures novelles 309
Mediterranean civilizations 9
Meier, K. 211; "The Art and Method of Process Evaluation" 156–157
mentoring 38
Menzel, D. 231
merit systems: pay and 77; personnel practices 10, 59–66, 278, 302–303; pros and cons 59
Merit Systems Protection Board 41, 65
Merriam, C.: *A History of Political Theories: Recent Times* 143–144
metropolitanization 209–211
metropolitan regions, defined 208–209
Miami-Dade County, Florida 42
Michael, B. 40
micro-budget perspectives 111–113
Miller, D. 226, 326–327
Minnesota 79
Minnowbrook Conference Center 264
minorities: employment and 73, 76, 82–84; rights of 30, 302
modern bureaucracy 282–285, 331–332
monarchies 200
monetary rewards 300–301
monopolies 324
Montesquieu 16
moral relativism 30
Morgan, G. 168, 328
Mosher, F. 269
Mossop, J. 183–187
motivation 224, 300–301
motives 45–46
MPA (Masters of Public Administration) 322
MPP (Masters of Public Policy) 322
multiple budgets, utilization of 98
Murphy's Law 248
mutual aid agreements 210–211

National Bureau of Economic Research 143
National Cancer Institute 64
National Civil Service Reform League 58
national defense 101
National Environmental Policy Act (NEPA) 131
National Institutes of Health 64
National Labor Relations Board 65
National Recovery Administration (NRA) 125
National Resources Planning Board 144
National Science Foundation (NSF) 64, 145
nation building 285
necessary and proper clause 14
negotiated rulemaking 133–134
Negotiated Rulemaking Act of 1990 134–136
Negro Politicians (Gosnell) 143

neoliberalism 279
NEPA (National Environmental Policy Act) 131
Netherlands 140, 316
networks 326–327
Neustadt, R.: *Thinking in Time* 152
neutral administration 142
neutral competence 29, 80–81, 300
neutrality 29, 151, 161
neutrality/equality principles 220
New Deal 11, 125–129, 144
new democracies 284
New Mexico 39, 165–166
New Public Administration 80, 205
New Public Management (NPM) 90, 114–115, 201, 205, 264–265, 281, 316–317, **317**, 322–324
New York Civil Service Reform Association 58–59
New Zealand 114, 264
Niebuhr, R. 281
Nixon, R. 117, 138n3, 163
Noe, T. 39
non-merit bureaucracies 281
nonprofit organizations 208
nonverbal communication 229
normative foundations of public administration 1–3, 7–27; administrative responsibility and 16–20; ancient history 9–10; bureaucratic values and 25–26; founding period and 10–11; informal constitutional amendment and 11–13; legitimating administration and 13–16; profession of public management and 21–25
normative-re-educative strategy of change 181–182
norms: bureaucratic 286–287; cultural 295–297; legitimacy and 282; political 297–299; social system and 177
Northcote-Trevelyn Report of 1854 10
Norway 316
No State model 15
Notice and Comment Rulemaking 132–133
NPM (New Public Management) 90, 114–115, 201, 205, 264–265, 281, 316–317, **317**, 322–324
NRA (National Recovery Administration) 125
NSF (National Science Foundation) 64, 145
Nyhan, R. 88

oaths 34–35
Obadiah, J. 221
Obama, B. 83
objectivity 73, 161
obligation, defined 16

Index 349

occupations 21–23
OD. *see* organization development (OD)
Office of Personnel Management
(OPM) 41, 64–65
Ogburn, W.: *Recent Social Trends* 143
Ohio 39, 205–207, 212
Ohio Ethics Commission 39
operating budget 98
opinion leaders 177
optimal alternative model 149, 266, 323
organizational dynamics and change
174–199; change agents and
179–181; diffusion of innovation and
175–178; implementing change and
179–181; management support
system and 197; planned change,
government action, and 174–175,
183; public sector and 193–197
organizational functions and
competencies 49–199;
administrative law 50, 124–138;
budgeting practices 49–50, 97–123;
organizational dynamics and change
174–199; personnel practices
53–96; policy analysis 50, 139–153;
program evaluation 50, 154–173
organizational learning 154–155, 160
organization development (OD):
change agents 179; intervention and
187–192; organizational dynamics,
change, and 183–192; public sector
and 193–197; strategic management
and 260
organization theory 29, 224
Osborne, D. 116, 120; *Reinventing
Government* 264
O'Toole, L. 211
Ott, J. 184
outcomes 110–111, 156–157, 167
output analyses 184

parentela relationships *313*, 314–315
parliamentary democracy 12
Parsons, T. 301
participation 236–239, 269,
288–289, 301, *317. see also* citizen
engagement; decision making
passion, politics and 18–19
patronage 10, *35, 36*, 56–59, 302. *see
also* merit systems; spoils system
pay-for-performance system 65
pay/salaries: civil service 65; fair
share 88; as motivation 300–301;
personnel practices 77–79; social
status and 303–305
peer evaluation 38
peer-to-peer relationships 207–209
Pendleton, G. 59
Pendleton Act (1883) (Civil Service
Reform Act) 59–61, 64, 142
people-change-technology (PCT)
change agents 179

Performance, Evaluation, and Review
Technique (PERT) 259
performance appraisals 74–76, 87,
164–165
performance-based budgeting 108–110
performance measures 86–87,
159–161, 171
Perry v. Sinderman 36
personnel practices 53–96; in
comparative perspective 301;
founding period 54–55; issues
and concerns regarding 80–85;
job analysis 66–72; management
support system 91; merit systems
59–66, 302–303; pay 77–79;
performance appraisal 74–76, 87;
professional development 85–91;
recruitment, selection, and 72–74,
301–305; spoils system 56–59;
training 76–77
persuasion 177–178
PERT (Performance, Evaluation, and
Review Technique) 259
PESC (Public Expenditures Survey
Committee) 311
Peters, B. 282–283, 302, 309,
312–313, 316
Pharaohs 9
Pierce, F. 57
place, defined 211–212
planned change 174–175, 183
Planning, Programming, Budgeting
System (PPBS) 310
planning agencies 248
plans, strategic 257–258
Plato 149–151
Plunkett, G. 59
Plunkitt, G. *32*
pluralism 238
Poister, T. 196
policing 161–163, 164
policy, defined 139
policy analysis 50, 139–153;
management support system 152;
New Deal 142–148; origins of
139–140; progressive era 141–142;
role of 148–152
policy making, in global perspective
311–315
policy sciences 143–149
Policy Sciences, The (Lerner and
Laswell) 146–147
policy stages, flow of *312*
political culture 295–301, 298–299,
299–301
political neutrality 80–81
political norms 297–299
political socialization 295
politicians 19, 24–25, 88–91
politico-legal cities 208
politics: budgeting and 102, 107–113;
bureaucracy and 281; city managers

and 23–25; cross branch relationships
and 212–213; cultural competence and
226; decision making and 267–268;
defined 18; government organization
and 200–201; progressives and 265;
public administration and 2; scientism
and 144–147
politics/administration dichotomy 263,
277
"Politics as Vocation" (Weber) 17–20,
291, 331
Polk, J. 57
position classifications 62, 77
poverty 140
Powell, L. *36*
power, leadership and 224–225
PPBS (Planning, Programming,
Budgeting System) 310
practical ethics 17
practitioner approaches 216–217
pragmatic cultures 297
pragmatism 142
praxis 3
prejudice 228–232. *see also* bias
presidency: budgeting and 99,
107–113; Connecticut Compromise
and 13; executive leadership and
80–81; regulatory process and 134;
spoils system and 56–59
President's Commission on Budget
Concepts (1967) 99
President's Committee on
Administrative Management (1937)
(Brownlow Commission) 63–65, 99
President's Committee on Social
Trends 143
Pre-State model 15
prismatic organizations 281–282, 296,
331–332
privacy 35–36
Privacy Act of 1974 130, 136
private foundations 208
private sector: governmental programs
and 208; organization development
(OD) in 195; organization theory
and 29; taxes and 118
privatization 114–116, 136, 264–265
procedural fairness 32–33, 50
procedural rules 131
procedure, defined 128
process 156–157, 250–259
process consultation 190
productivity 324
professional development 85–91, 208
professionalism 21, 262–265,
269–270, 330
professions, defined 21
program budgeting 109–111
program evaluation 50, 149–150,
154–173; efficiency and
effectiveness 156–157; government
mandated 163–164; management

350 Index

support system 168–171;
measurement 157–168
programmatic orientations 107
progressive era: budgeting and 99,
116; bureaucracy and 280–281;
policy analysis and 141–142; public
administration and 262–264
property, as regime value 35
Proposition 2.5 (Massachusetts) 118
Proposition 13 (California) 118
Pro-State model 15
Protestant work ethic 142
Pruitt, S. 150–151
Prussia 200
public administration: administrative
law 50, 124–138; branches of
government and 14; budgeting
practices and 49–50, 97–123;
bureaucracy, rule of law,
representative democracy, and
279–293; change and 174;
citizen engagement and 234–244;
cultural competence and 216–233;
ethical foundations of 7–8,
28–48; in global perspective
294–320; historical/political/legal
framework for 1–3; leadership,
decision-making, and 261–276;
normative foundations of 1–3,
7–27; organizational dynamics and
change 174–199; organizational
functions and competencies 49–199;
personnel practices 53–96; pillars of
114; policy analysis 50, 139–153;
political culture and 295–301;
practice of 1–4; professional
262–265; program evaluation 50,
154–173; redefining theory of
321–332; strategic management and
245–260; theoretical foundations of
3, 7–48; transboundary Interactions
and 203–215
Public Administration Quarterly 193
Public Administration Review 64
public choice theory 30, 264, 322
public employee labor unions 87–88
Public Expenditures Survey Committee
(PESC) 311
public interest 331
public law 124–126. *see also*
administrative law
public management 21–25, 24, 246–247
public morality 30–34
public policy 30, 33–34, 44–46
public sector 193–197, 301–305
public service 44–46, 303–305
Pyakuryal, S. 285, 292n1
Pye, L. 285, 298–299
Pygmalion (Shaw) 32

quality of work life *191*
Quay, R. 248, 251

Quetelet, A. 140
quota systems 82–83, 298–299, 303

RARG (Regulatory Analysis and
Review Group) 134
rational analytic perspective 166–167
rational comprehensive model 268
rational-empirical strategy of change
181–182
rationalist societies 296–298
Raven, B. 225
reactive relationships *271*
Reagan, R. 134–136, 163–164, 265,
321–323
Realpolitik 44
reason 283
Recent Social Trends (Ogburn) 143
recruitment 72–74, 301–305
redistribution 101, 117–118
red tape 204
*Regents of the University of California
v. Bakke* 83
regime change 327
regime values 35–37, 288
Regional Governing Organization
(RGO) 209
regional government 208–213
regionalization 210–211
Regulatory Analysis and Review
Group (RARG) 134
Rehnquist, W. *36*
Reinventing Government (Osborne
and Gaebler) 264
reinvention, budgetary 114
re-invention movement 205, 322
relativism 3, 30, 329
religious/spiritual beliefs 229
Rell, M. 40, 43
Reorganization Act of 1939 99
repetitive budgeting 308–309
representation: Burkean model of 55,
291, 330–331; hiring practices and
302–303
representative bureaucracy 290–291
representative democracy 279–293
representativeness 80–81
republicanism 15, 280
Republican party 58–61
responsibility: of citizens 242;
democracy and 239; ethics and
18–20, 45
retrenchment 114
revenues 98, 115–119, 305, 308
reverse discrimination 82–84
Revolutionary War 54–55
revolutions, corruption and 327
RGO (Regional Governing
Organization) 209
Rice, M. 220
Richardson, E. 138n3
Riggs, F. 281–282, 285, 295–296, 331
Riggs' typology *296*

rights 236, 239, 283
Ripley, R. 258, 311
risk aversion 90
Rogers, E. 175–178, 181
Rohr, J. 13–14, 40, 44; *Ethics for
Bureaucrats* 34–36
Rome 8–10
Roosevelt, F. 64, 125–129, 144
Roosevelt, T. 60
Rosenbaum, W.: *Environmental
Politics and Policy* 138n4
Rosenbloom, D. 12, 74
rotation in office theory 56–57
Rourke, F. 5
Rousseau, J-J. 288
Rowland, W. 40
Royal Statistical Society 140
Ruchelman, L. 268
rulemaking 124, 130–136
rule of law 279–293

salaries. *see* pay/salaries
Santa Fe, New Mexico 165
Sartori, G. 296
Sayre, W.: "The Triumph of Technique
over Purpose" 64
Scandinavia 314–316
*Schechter Poultry Company v. United
States* (Sick Chicken Case) 125–126
school segregation 30
scientific management 21, 29, 223,
263, 322, 325
Scientific Management Movement 61–63
scientism 141–146
secondary legislation, defined 14
Second Hoover Commission (1955)
64–65, 99
Seibert, P. 216, 223
self-awareness 45, 227–232
self-reporting 42–43
Selznick, P. 158–159, 171, 321–322, 330
Senate 13
Senior Executive Service (SES) 65, 136
sensitivity 228, 267–268
sensitivity training (T-Groups) 190
separation of powers 13–14, 289–291
service delivery 208
service orientation 32–33
services votes 309
seven-level analysis 184–185
Shafritz, J. 74
Shang dynasty (China) 9
Shaw, G.: *Pygmalion* 32
Sheppach, R. 120
SHRM (Society for Human Resource
Management) 226–227
Sick Chicken Case (*Schechter Poultry
Company v. United States*) 125–126
Siegel's cultural competency model 218
Silva, M. 251
Sinclair, J.: *Statistical Account of
Scotland* 139–140

Singapore 114
single-loop communication approaches 89
Six, F. 232, 329
skepticism 44
skill-based cultural competency 221
Smith, A. 200, 323–324
Snow, C. 149
social class and status 302–305
social indicator 146–147
social integration 34
socialism 297
socialization, political 295
social processes of innovation 176–177
social resources 101
Social Science Research Council 144
social sciences 143–148, 264–265
Social Security Administration 254–255
Society for Human Resource Management (SHRM) 226–227
solidary 304
South Africa 303
South America 284
sovereign power 10
space program 147
Spain 9
Speaking Truth to Power (Wildavsky) 148–149, 152, 291
Special Committee on Administrative Law 129
specialization 23, 143
Special Prosecutors 138n3
spending 108
Spiro, H. 16–17
spoils system 56–59, 300
Sputnik 145
stakeholders, defined 252
standardized examinations, bias in 163
Stanley, D. 159
state bureaucracy 13–14
State Department 11
state government: budgeting and 111–112, 116–121; employment practices in 82–83; merit system and 60; public support for 118; vertical relationships and 208
stateless government 15
statesmen 45
Statistical Account of Scotland (Sinclair) 139–140
Statistical Society 140
statistics 139–143
Steffens, L. 140
Stewart, P. 36
Stewart, R. 128
Stillman, R. 14–15
Stork 218–219
strategic change 189
strategic management 155–157, 168, 171, 184, 245–260; advantages and disadvantages of 247–250;

in practice 259; process 250–259; public management and 246–247
strategic plans 257–258
Strengths-Weaknesses-Opportunities-Threats (SWOT) analysis 184, 253
stress management 192
Stridh-Igo, P. 216, 223
structural change 189–190
structure of democracy 235–240
Study of History in American Colleges and Universities, The (Adams) 141
Suarez-Balcazar, Y. 218
substantial evidence criterion 132
substantive rules 131
success, criteria for 155
summative evaluation 150, 156
Sumner, C. 58
Supreme Court: administrative state and 13–14; affirmative action and 81–83; agency actions and 134–136; *Board of Regents v. Roth* 36; *Chevron U.S.A. Inc. v. Natural Resources Defense Council (1984)* 135; civil service reform and 66; *Elrod v. Burns* 36; on fair share requirements 88; *Firefighters Local Union No. 11783 v. Stotts* 82; *Griswold v. Connecticut* 35–36; *McCulloch v. Maryland* 13–14; oaths and 35; *Perry v. Sinderman* 36; *Regents of the University of California v. Bakke* 83; *Schechter Poultry Company v. United States* (Sick Chicken Case) 125–126
Swartwout, S. 57
Sweden 114, 226–227, 307
SWOT (Strengths-Weaknesses-Opportunities-Threats) analysis 184, 253
Sylvia, R.: "The Art and Method of Process Evaluation" 156–157
Syracuse University 264
systemic change 175

tacit knowledge 37–39, 148, 267
Taft, B. 39, 99
tax policy: allocation system and 305–307; equity 117; expenditures 101; incentives 118–119; legislative appropriations process and 108; progressivity in 117–119; redistribution and 117–118; states and 116–119
tax system, as voluntary 298
Taylor, F. 29, 223, 263, 325
Taylor, Z. 57
Tayloresque management 204
Taylor-Ritzler, T. 218
team building 190–192
technical change 189–190
technically based budgets 108–110
technological guidance approach 149

Teel, K. 221
Tenure of Office Act of 1867 61
Texas 99
T-Groups (sensitivity training) 190
Thatcher, M. 114, 297, 323
theoretical foundations of public administration 3, 7–48; ethical foundations 7–8, 28–48; normative foundations 7–27
Theory X and Theory Y 216
Thinking in Time (Neustadt and May) 152
third-party interventions 190–192
third-wave democracies 284
third world 281, 297–301
time: democracy and 238–239; innovation and 177–178; leadership, decision making, and 267–269
Tinder, G. 241, 286–288
tolerance 237–238, 289
top-down communication approaches 89
Total Quality Management (TQM) 155, 168–169, 205
Toxic Substance Control Act of 1976 133–135
training: for employees 76–77; in ethical conduct 41–42
transboundary interactions 203–215; cross branch relationships and 212–213; field office-central office relations and 204–207; intergovernmental relationships and 209–212; managing at the margin and 213; peer-to-peer relationships and 207–209
transcendental formula of public right 20
transcendent ethics 17
transformational leadership 26, 262
transmission belt theory 128
Transparency International 329
Treasury Department 11, 99, 254
trend analysis 255–256
"Triumph of Technique over Purpose, The" (Sayre) 64
Truman, H. 64, 109
Trump, D. 83, 150
trust: building of 89–91; in civil service 321; collaboration and 326; cultural awareness and 228–232; decline of 284; in government 299, 321, 329
trusteeships 55
trustworthiness 231–232, 327, 329
Turkey 211
two-tiered government 210
Tyler, J. 57

ultimate ends, ethic of 18–20, 291
uncertainty 166–167, 266
understanding 265–272
Understanding Environmental Administration and Law (Buck) 137n1

UNESCO 227
unfunded mandates 116–118
United Kingdom: budgeting in
310–311, 323; census in 140;
civil service in 80, 263, 303–305;
education bias in 302; executive-
legislative conflict in 307–308;
political culture of 300; as pragmatic
297; public administration system
in 277
United Nations 310, 317
United States: ancient influences
on 9–10; bureaucracy in 11–13,
286–289; census in 140; civil
service in 303–305; comparative
administration and 294;
conception of government in
14–15; constitutional principles
of 37; disagreement in 285–286;
distrust of government in 299;
diversity in 216, 222; ethics
commissions in 39–44; fiscal crisis
and 114–121; founding period
of 10–11; industrial revolution in
140; language in 229; management
in 227; metropolitanizing of 209;
political culture of 29, 200–201;
politics-administration dichotomy
and 277; as pragmatic 297; program
implementation in 258; progressive
era of 141–142, 262–264; public
expenditure in 305–307; realigning
fiscal system of 116–117; salaries
and status in 300–301; spoils
system in 56–59, 300
United States Constitution: balanced
budget amendment and 108; census
and 140; Connecticut Compromise
and 13; equal protection clauses of
78; ethics and 34–37, 331; Fifth
Amendment 78; founding period

and 10–11; Fourteenth Amendment
14, 78; informal changes to 11–13;
institutional arrangements and
54; making of 235–238; necessary
and proper clause of 14; regime
values and 35–37, 288; on role
of government 174; separation of
powers and 125; tradition and 14
unity of command 280
universal human rights 283
universalism 282
University of Akron 86
University of Chicago Law School 127
University of Latvia 86
urban reform movement 21
US Civil Service System 41
US Coast Guard 254
US Government Accountability Office
112

values: Constitution and 35–37; of
democracy 240–242; democratic
235; leadership, decision making, and
266–270; policy analysis and 148
value statements 266–267
Van Buren, M. 92n2
Van Wart, M. 326
vertical relationships 208
Vietnam War 28, 147
Vigil, R. 39
Virginia Tech 1
vision, strategic management and
251–259
volatility 111
voting 287–288, 318

Waldo, D. 1–2, 149, 200, 259,
263–264
Walter, S. 246–249
Wanat, J. 101–102
War Department 11

Warfa, N. 218
War on Poverty 147
Washington (state) 78–79
Watergate scandal 28, 65, 138n3
Weber, M. 9, 12, 15, 29, 32, 44–45,
167, 223, 234–235, 240, 251,
267–268, 280–287, 299–300, 325;
"Politics as Vocation" 17–20, 291,
331
Weberian bureaucracy 12, 32, 194,
234–235, 240, 332
Weick, K. 243, *271*
welfare state 11
Western Europe 114
whistleblowers 65
Wiener, N. 146–147
Wilbern, Y. 30–33
Wildavsky, A. 110–111, 154–155,
160, 170–171, *272*, 308–309;
Speaking Truth to Power 148–149,
152, 291
Wilson, J. 204, 287, 304
Wilson, W. 141, 235, 262
Wisconsin 41–43
Wolin, S. 234
women, pay and 77–79, 82
workers 224, 325
work life, quality of *191*
World Bank 317
World Trade Center attack 136, 138n5
World War I 99
World War II 144–145, 263–264,
282–283
Worley, C. 179–180

Yes, Minister (television program) 12
Yin, R. 170
youth gangs 164–168

zero-based budgeting 109
Zimmerman, C. 216, 223